Teaching Elementary
School Science

Teaching Elementary School Science: A Competency-Based Approach

Clifford H. Edwards
and Robert L. Fisher
Illinois State University

Praeger Publishers • New York

Published in the United States of America in 1977
by Praeger Publishers,
200 Park Avenue, New York, N. Y. 10017

Library of Congress Cataloging in Publication Data

Edwards, Clifford H
  Teaching elementary school science

  Includes index.
  1. Science—Study and teaching (Elementary)
I. Fisher, Robert L., joint author. II. Title.
LB1585.E33   372.3'5'044   75-47
ISBN 0-275-22510-0

Printed in the United States of America

789 074 987654321

Preface

When a teacher thinks about teaching science to elementary school children, two concerns come to mind. First, he or she must decide what the student should be taught. Topics such as magnetism, insects, and clouds are usually included in the content. Second, the teacher must decide how these topics will be presented. Techniques such as a reading assignment or a demonstration of an experiment are useful approaches. But eventually, the question arises: "What should students know as a result of this instruction?"

As authors of this text, we had to ask ourselves a similar question: "What must a teacher know how to do in order to teach elementary school science?" We could not merely present you with a variety *about* teaching science, because knowing how to plan science instruction is different from knowing how to plan a lesson. Similarly, it is more important for you to be able to specify what goals you expect students to attain as an outcome of instruction than it is for you to know the advantages and disadvantages of writing precise instructional objectives. This text is designed to help you develop the skills or competencies by which you will be able to provide for specified learning outcomes for your students.

In a competency-based approach to teacher education, the focus is on teaching the prospective science teacher how to develop instructional skills. With this point in mind, we have designed exercises that require the student to demonstrate his or her teaching skills. A list of these exercises follows this preface. Reading through the titles will provide you with an idea of the skills being developed.

To further provide you with a focus for learning, the precisely stated objectives included in most chapters describe the desired behavior you should be able to exhibit as a result of your learning from the text and from your instructor. The exercises have been chosen to assist you in developing the skills described by the objectives. It is only through practice of the desired skills that you will develop the necessary ability to provide students with a quality science experience.

To make use of every chapter of this book, you will most likely read them in sequence. However, it is possible to use only a portion of the chapters when the situation warrants it.

The most effective way of learning to teach elementary school science is to become directly involved in an actual classroom situation. If this is not possible, perhaps you can view videotapes or movies of actual classroom instruction. At various points in the text, we suggest that you observe or participate in a classroom activity.

Most classroom teachers will derive their actual classroom science program from a commercial science program. Therefore, it is important that representative elementary school science programs are available to you. Chapter 12 provides an orientation to some curriculum materials for teaching elementary school science. The chapter provides descriptions of the various approaches used in organizing the materials, and specific examples are reprinted from several of the programs. The chapter is also designed so that it can be read independently, without relying on the content of previous chapters. In fact, many of the other chapters refer to Chapter 12 for examples of the curriculum materials to be used in completing the exercises included throughout the text. Again, it is important that you learn to make use of these materials, since this is what is involved in actually teaching science to children.

When scanning the table of contents and the list of exercises, you will notice that this text seeks to develop competencies in teaching science, not learning it. To gain an understanding of science as a discipline, you will need to pursue another course and use another text. However, there are elementary school science resource books that are designed to help the teacher identify particular strategies for teaching specific content areas. You may find one of these very useful as an adjunct to this text. This will, of course, depend upon your prior training in science.

Teaching elementary school science may not seem to be one of the courses you would most enjoy teaching to elementary school children. We have watched many elementary school teachers overcome their fear or reluctance for this kind of teaching. In most cases, they have learned the course content right along with their children, and have enjoyed it as much. We hope that you too will develop this point of view toward science instruction. Give yourself the opportunity by using this text with an open mind.

The development of a book such as this reflects the thoughts and works of many individuals; however, acknowledging everyone is not possible. The individual most responsible for the photographs used throughout is Dr. Orrin Mizer, a science teacher who enjoys making a pictorial record of the activities and accomplishments of his pupils. We are especially grateful to him for allowing us to use some of his pictures.

C.H.E.

R.L.F.

Contents

Exercises

1

A Model for
Professional Development

In our scientific age, a critical goal of the teacher is to achieve competence in teaching science to elementary school children. Competency implies that the elementary teacher is able to help students learn and understand the fundamentals of a science education program both efficiently and effectively. The teacher must know how to determine worthwhile objectives for students, formulate strategies that will enable them to achieve these objectives, implement these strategies, and then determine their effectiveness in accomplishing the desired ends. Traditionally, teachers have not taught using a specific, well-articulated set of objectives, nor have they thought of schooling as being a series of contrived experiences that will help children attain prespecified goals. Rather, education has consisted essentially of planning experiences for children which served as ends in and of themselves. In addition, teaching skills have not been operationally defined and directly related to student achievement. In other words, there is no clear definition of what students should know or be able to do specifically as a result of schooling, nor what teacher behaviors are most likely to help bring about meaningful instruction. This along with public criticism of schools and other related factors has led to the present emphasis on competency in the schools. In recent years, schools have been criticized for their ineffectiveness in teaching certain basic skills and for creating a stultifying environment in which students are expected to learn (Silberman, 1970). Schools have been accused of permitting students to move along and eventually graduate without having learned what the schools claim they teach. In at least one case, a suit has been brought against a school for certifying that a student had successfully completed the requirements of the school, when in fact he could not read.

This chapter will provide the elements of a competency-based program and show how these contribute toward your professional development. The present controversy over competency-based programs

1

and their ability to produce professional teachers will also be explored, along with the directions necessary to produce truly professional school personnel.

Specifying Teacher Competencies

In order to be qualified to teach science to children, it is essential that the teacher master certain basic teaching skills. The nature of these skills is directly related to the effect the teacher wishes to have on students. The purpose of emphasizing competencies in the first place is to insure valid accomplishment of our goals. However, there may not be complete agreement as to what the goals should be. Thus our efforts to achieve the necessary competency may be limited. In addition, it sounds like a rather simple process to indicate what teacher competencies are necessary for students to acquire the knowledge and skills we believe they should have but the implications of this procedure are actually quite complex.

As stated earlier, the competencies a teacher must have are dependent upon the kind of goals he has for students. Even when considering this, there are a number of bases upon which to generate statements of teacher competency. These include philosophical, empirical, and subject matter (Cooper, Jones, and Weber, 1973), as well as role analysis, needs assessment, course translation, and theoretical model analysis (Dodl, 1973).

The Philosophical Base

When using a philosophical base to determine teacher competencies, it is necessary to clarify what is meant by such terms as the nature of man, the purpose of education, and the nature of learning and instruction. Of course, these considerations cannot be demonstrated empirically; they are primarily related to one's belief system. One difficulty with the philosophical approach is in coming to an agreement about man's nature and other related questions. Once consensus is reached and the basic assumptions are delineated, it is relatively easy to generate desired pupil outcomes, and the role of the teacher can then be conceptualized. From this conceptualized role of the teacher it is possible to elicit statements of teacher competency. In order to determine whether or not the competencies are valid, we must demonstrate consistency between the assumptions about man, the desired pupil outcomes, the conceptualized role of the teacher, and the competencies.

The following is an example of assumptions, pupil outcomes, teacher role, and competencies that are consistent with one another:

Assumptions
1. Children should engage in investigations.
2. Children should apply the modern scientific point of view.
3. Children should have direct experiences with natural phenomena.
4. Children should engage in discussions of their ideas and observations.
5. Children should extend their investigations when these lead in interesting directions.
6. Children should become aware of the tentative nature of scientific truth. (SCIS, 1974)

Desired Pupil Outcomes
1. Students who approach natural phenomena and problems in life using valid investigative procedures.
2. Students who are able to explain the nature of their investigations and the ideas and conclusions they have reached.
3. Students who pursue lines of investigation into various areas of interest.
4. Students who show by the nature of their study in science that they hold scientific knowledge tentative.

Role of the Teacher
1. To provide situations where students can investigate natural phenomena.
2. To create an environment where investigation can proceed based upon student interest.
3. To provide materials and equipment which children need to investigate.
4. To provide feedback as needed to help students pursue investigations while at the same time not giving students direct answers.

Teacher Competencies
1. Ability to be flexible in allowing students to investigate problems in which they are interested.
2. Ability to be supportive to students when they may be confused or discouraged.
3. Ability to provide feedback on a variety of different projects which encourages continued investigation.
4. Knowledge about science and its investigative principles.

The above listed competencies are not exhaustive. They are intended to illustrate the kind of competencies teachers must have when the philosophical base is essentially behavioristic. Notice how competencies are related to the statements regarding the teacher's role, desired pupil outcomes, and assumptions.

The Empirical Base

If competencies are derived from an empirical base, they are essentially linked to experimental evidence. This means that knowledge from the various behavioral and social sciences can be used as a basis

for determining the teacher's role. For example, much has been learned about self-concept, socialization processes, reinforcement, learning, development, and the like. Teacher competencies may be generated which encompass the ability to apply the knowledge from the behavioral and social sciences. Some research has also been done regarding the teaching process itself and certain teaching skills have been shown to enhance learning in specified ways. Examples of such teaching skills include stimulus variation, set induction, recognizing attending behavior, cuing, repetition, and behavior modification techniques.

One empirically based procedure that has received varying support is that of defining competency in terms of pupil outcomes rather than in terms of the knowledge or behavior of the teacher. The explicit assumption is that the quality of teaching must be judged exclusively from the performance of the students. Advocates of this approach argue that, in the final analysis, the critical issue in the educational process centers on what the student learns. What a teacher does is not as important as the results he achieves in terms of student learning. One of the basic problems with this conclusion is that in order to train teachers it is necessary to specify exactly which teacher behaviors are directly associated with increased student learning. Here the knowledge base is extremely meager. Empirically, we know very little about what teaching skills enhance student learning. In addition, the effect the teacher has on the students depends to some extent on the students themselves. Certainly students come to the learning situation with a wide variety of competencies, skills, and experiences which interact in a very complex way with the teacher's behavior during the instructional process.

There are very few empirically derived competencies that are associated with desired cognitive skills and attitudes of students. There is no evidence to support one teaching performance as being more successful than any other. As Elam (1972) states: "No one can provide an all-purpose answer to the evidence question, partly because answers are situation specific, but more fundamentally because our knowledge base is too thin."

Another problem is that teaching skills are not amenable to paper and pencil types of evaluation. It is difficult to measure the relationship between teacher competencies and student achievement. Nor can the quality of teaching performance be validly inferred from simple quantitative measures. It is precisely because the quality aspect of teaching is so elusive that some have been led to consider pupil achievement as a viable indicator of teaching skill. However, focusing upon the product of learning as an indicator of quality teacher performance is self-defeating. For evaluation to be an essential corrective tool in helping teachers adjust their behavior, educators must look beyond the product of learn-

ing to the process of learning and beyond the product of teaching to the process of teaching. It is most likely that any number of teaching styles will produce equal results in terms of student achievement. but it is highly unlikely that the other more intangible benefits of the teaching-learning process will be similarly manifest.

When using empirically derived teacher competencies as indicators of good teaching performance, a danger exists that somehow good teaching will become merely a sequence of discrete performances rather than a total act. According to Broudy (1972), drilling on separate parts of complex acts has generally yielded disappointing results. It is not until after a pattern has been sensed or understood that subcomponents can be perfected separately. Consequently, it is a good idea in teacher training to help students gain a sense of the complete teaching act before practicing subcomponent skills.

In the midst of the controversy over empirically based competency determination is the accountability movement. Accountability refers to judging the competency of a teacher in terms of student performance and making his salary or achievement in his position depend upon his students' academic achievement. The problem with this is that we have no valid or reliable means at the present time of demonstrating that the students' behavior is directly related to the behavior of the teacher (Popham, 1974). The Coleman report (Coleman, 1969) provides evidence that many factors outside the teacher's control may exert as much or even greater influence over the achievement levels of children. In addition, a good deal of difficulty has been experienced in demonstrating that tests of student achievement are a valid or reliable measure of related teacher performances. Basing the measurement of competency exclusively on the ends of instruction flatly ignores a multitude of uncontrolled variables. Smith (1971) has identified some of the more cogent ones. First, he states that pupils enter the instructional process already in possession of varying levels of knowledge, skills, and attitudes. Consequently, attributing any gains made to teacher intervention is very precarious. Some may argue that a program of careful pre–post testing will help solve this problem, but this assumes that the influencing factors become neutral during the educational process, which, of course, is entirely erroneous.

Secondly, Smith claims that the classroom is not a closed system which excludes outside influences. There is no viable means of assessing the magnitude of these influences, nor how they affect the instructional process. No complex formulas can take all of the variability into account.

Finally, Smith says that judging performance on the basis of end-product criteria requires more evidence than can readily be provided and more than that demanded of any other profession. For example, physicians are not licensed because they are able to cure a given percentage of their patients, nor do lawyers receive a license to practice when they can guarantee a successful defense to a certain proportion of their clients. By the same token, teachers cannot be expected to be certified competent only when their pupils achieve certain standards. However, this does not mean that teachers should *not* be certified on the basis of their competency; it means that at the present time we must defer to competencies which have little or no empirical base, but which can be defended at least on some philosophical grounds. Perhaps one day better relationships will be established between teacher competencies and student achievement. Even then, it will probably be unfair to judge the teacher in terms of accountability in a system where he has such limited control over a rather diverse set of inputs.

The Subject Matter Base

Teaching competencies may also be derived from the various disciplines and subject matter areas which are taught in the schools. These competencies focus primarily upon cognitive activities. In science, for example, the elementary teacher might be expected to demonstrate knowledge competencies in such things as photosynthesis, ecology, states of matter, and how a dry cell battery works. Not understanding the basic concepts and processes of science would be an indication of the teacher's incompetence. In addition to basic knowledge, the teacher may also be expected to demonstrate performance competencies. For example, the teacher should probably know how to focus a microscope or streak a petri plate with a bacteria culture.

Some serious questions come up in trying to specify what subject matter competencies a teacher should be expected to have. Among these are the following: What knowledge and skills should be the minimum necessary requirements? Given the fact that knowledge in science is always changing, what subject matter competencies are most likely to stand the test of time? These questions are not easy to answer. It would be desirable for the elementary teacher to have as much science sophistication as possible, but the elementary teacher must be able to teach numerous other subjects as well. Therefore, it is important that the competencies for teaching elementary science be selectively chosen and efficiently learned, and that they be those competencies which will have the greatest utility for the longest time.

The Role Analysis Base

Another base for determining competencies for elementary teachers is role analysis. Role analysis implies that competencies be determined from studying what effective practioners do in their teaching. This data may be obtained by observing teachers, by self-reporting of job tasks, or by conceptualizing new roles for the future. The competencies one selects vary with the situation. Many elementary teachers are generalists. There are, however, teachers who act as science specialists in the elementary school. In addition, there are various configurations of staffing in the schools which influence what specific skills are needed to teach science. For example, in some schools science instruction takes place within the confines of a single classroom, while in other schools special rooms are provided for it. Instruction in science may involve groups of children or it may be individualized. With the increase in differentiated staffing where teachers become more specialized, the role of the elementary science teacher is significantly altered. The specialist may be expected to deal with large groups of children or prepare lessons for videotaping. He may be expected to move his learning and demonstration materials from room to room, or to establish and operate a science learning center.

There are specific teacher roles which are likely to be crucial to the teaching of science in most any situation. These generic skills include such things as organizing logical sequences for learning, conducting demonstrations, asking questions, giving directions, leading discussions, selecting and organizing science materials, and formulating appropriate science goals. Every elementary teacher who teaches science should be competent in the generic skills. Other chapters in this book will help the reader achieve these minimum levels of competency.

The Needs Assessment Base

In the future, teacher preparation will probably take place to a greater extent in field-based situations. This means that the traditional practice of training teachers at the university campus and then giving them a student teaching experience will be replaced by programs where training is based upon close articulation of practical experience in the field and the theoretical concerns of teaching. Entire teacher training programs conceivably would be housed and operated in the field with a good deal of cooperation and articulation being achieved between university and public school personnel. Thus teacher competencies will be evolved out of needs determined by practitioners, students, and the community. University-based teacher educators will cooperate with the practitioners in delineating specific competencies and in providing the experiences which will help the trainee achieve them.

The Course Translations Base

When practical considerations such as courses currently on the books, certification blockages, current practices of generating credit hours, and record-keeping systems limit other means of deriving competencies, a course translation approach may have to be used. This involves the rather simple process of converting present course content into behaviorally stated outcomes. This usually results in a program that is weighted heavily in terms of knowledge about teaching, with little demonstration of actual teaching skills. Many consider this to be the first step toward a full-fledged competency-based teacher education program. It may gradually lead to a destructuring and reclustering of outcome expectancies and instructional strategies to attain the goals of a competency-based program. Although the competencies referred to in this book were not derived from courses, they may well be taught in a traditional classroom with a few minor adaptations.

The Theoretical Models Analysis Base

Finally, competencies may be derived from theoretical models of instruction. On this basis, the competencies will be logically selected from the behaviors and actions which are indicated by a particular model for instruction. The model for instruction that is used must be decided upon through a searching philosophical study. The model of instruction must properly articulate the basic assumptions regarding the nature of man, the purpose of education, and other similar philosophical considerations. Although this book will not strictly adhere to any one particular model of instruction, a good deal of emphasis will be placed on an efficiency learning model which we call the Basic Instructional Model (BIM). This model makes strategic use of the concept of precise instructional objectives. Essentially, the goal of instruc-

Figure 1–1   Basic Instructional Model

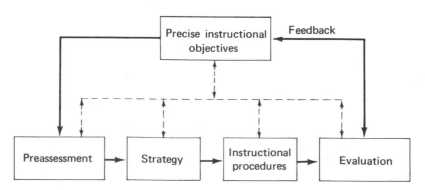

tion from this point of view is to maximize the efficiency with which students are able to achieve prespecified objectives. The Basic Instructional Model is illustrated in Figure 1–1. Notice that the Precise Instructional Objectives component is diagrammed so as to show its strategic function in the total model. The objective constitutes the basis upon which all other components are formulated and implemented. There is a necessary interaction between the objective and each of the other components as well as a line of direct action beginning with the objective and going successively to preassessment, strategy, instructional procedures, evaluation, and feedback. This means that even though there is a line of action in the instructional process from objectives on through to the evaluation process, there is still feedback between the objectives component and each of the other components as well as among the other components.

As previously indicated, the precise instructional objective is the central component of the BIM. Its function is to provide the focus for the whole instructional process. Each of the other components of instruction is formulated with a clear view of the objective in mind. This is why it is essential that the objective be stated in behavioral terms, so that each of the instructional components can be precisely delineated. When there is a direct correspondence between the objective and the other components of instruction, greater learning efficiency is possible. The most efficient way to achieve prespecified objectives is emphasized. The assumption, of course, is that the objectives represent what children should learn in school. If the objectives are indeed sufficiently adequate and inclusive, using the most efficient means of accomplishing them seems defensible.

Once the precise instructional objectives have been formulated, it is possible to prepare and administer preassessment instruments to determine the present capabilities or limitations which students have in achieving the objective. Preassessment is obviously designed with efficiency in mind. It should be both diagnostic as well as prescriptive. It should provide a means of determining what students do and do not know in terms of achieving the goals of education and indicate what specific means of instruction may be useful in making up any deficiencies. If students lack certain prerequisite skills, preassessment can be used to identify these. Students can then be given the opportunity to master these skills prior to engaging in instructional activities for which they are unprepared. Preassessment can also pinpoint the extent to which students already possess certain subcomponent knowledge and skills. If certain subcomponent skills and abilities are already mastered, the student can receive better direction in his learning and avoid the boredom associated with pursuing previously mastered material. If the student is already competent in performing the terminal behavior called for in the objective, the preassessment can be used as a means of determining that competency and the student can be directed to focus his attention on other goals.

With the objectives precisely stated and the present skill levels of students determined, the next step is to formulate strategies for helping students achieve the objectives, given the constraints identified by the preassessment. Strategy is simply a plan formulated to provide students with the most efficient and effective means of accomplishing the objectives after careful consideration of present skills. Strategies should be planned using all available input about how students learn, ability levels of the students involved, skills already mastered, as well as the nature of the skill which is involved in achieving the goals of instruction.

Selecting the proper instructional procedures is the next step in the model. Efficiency is also of prime importance in this step. Emphasis is given here on providing students with appropriate practice. This means that students should have the benefit of instruction designed to help them achieve the objectives with no interference from engaging in extraneous learning activities. All instruction should contribute directly to helping the students achieve the objectives. This is done, of course, by careful examination of learning activities to insure that they do not lead to unrelated goals or that learning activities do not become ends in and of themselves. Appropriate practice is usually divided into two components, analogous practice and equivalent practice. Analogous practice refers to learning activities which are simulations of the terminal behavior. Ordinarily, analogous practice precedes equivalent practice and involves such things as discussions about the skills which will later be developed in equivalent practice situations or various kinds of simulations which lack some of the qualities of practice in an equivalent sense. For example, children may be asked to write down and later discuss the steps they would go through in encouraging the "city fathers" to clean up the city's pollution problems in advance of actually approaching the city officials with their proposal. Writing down steps and discussing them is analogous practice. Equivalent practice may be presenting formal positions to the class which are precisely like the ones they plan to use in actuality. In both analogous and equivalent practice, a liberal amount of feedback needs to be given so that the students can correct their performances appropriately.

Equivalent practice refers to activities which are exactly like the behaviors called for in the objective. This provides the teacher with the opportunity to have students demonstrate the terminal behavior in a practice setting where appropriate corrections can be made prior to evaluation. In the traditional classroom, this trial and feedback session often does not take place. Information is simply transmitted and students are expected to formulate their related responses without benefit of feedback. When the final evaluation is made, it is no wonder that so many students fail to achieve the desired performance levels. From what we know about communication and the lack of it, failure is predictable without feedback. The teacher must know in advance of the final evaluation whether he has succeeded in his teaching goals. Students need to know in advance if they are likely to be successful in demonstrating the expected behaviors in a testing situation. Equivalent practice with appropriate feedback activities provides both with this information. Without proper communication, the teacher does not know when to use more examples, give further explanations, relate new information to previous student experiences, or when to say he is satisfied that students are able to fulfill the requirements of the objective in an evaluation situation. Without accurate feedback on equivalent performances, students are unable to determine when they need more practice and approach the examination situation without knowing whether or not they are well prepared.

The evaluation component of the BIM is designed not only to obtain knowledge about the extent to which students can achieve the objectives, but also to gain relevant information necessary to adjust objective, preassessment, strategy, instructional procedures, and/or the evaluation itself. The first requirement of the evaluation is that it must indeed measure the student's ability to achieve the objective. This is indicated by the arrow which leads directly from the evaluation component to the precise instructional objectives component. The other lines of relationship are indicated by broken arrows. Many times in the traditional science lesson, for example, tests lack the capability of measuring the extent to which students achieve predetermined goals. This may be because the objectives are ambiguous or because the instructional procedures are unrelated to the evaluation in some respects. One of the major purposes of the BIM is to bring a closer correspondence between these elements of instruction so that objectives are defensible, learning is efficient and adequate, and evaluations are valid.

The heavy unbroken arrows in the BIM represent the basic fundamental flow of the instructional process. The broken line arrows represent internal relationships between the components of the model. The most important relationship, as has already been explained, is between the objectives and the other components of the model. However, other important relationships also exist in the system. Going backward, a relationship between strategy and preassessment exists, for example. If preassessment is not providing sufficient information to formulate successful strategies, adjustments have to be made.

There is also an important relationship between strategy and instructional procedures. In instructional settings the strategy which is developed often proves to be inadequate, and unanticipated contingencies require changes in the strategy. This is called tactics; new plans must be made which take into account the unforeseen developments in the normal learning situation.

Knowledge obtained from the evaluation process can be useful in adjusting any part of the system. It can help pinpoint problems, for example, in the instructional procedures and indicate that a change in strategy may be necessary before students can adequately meet the expectations outlined in the objective. Evaluation may also aid in determining poor preassessment diagnosis or prescription. If goal attainment is not possible, given the time and other instructional constraints, evaluation information will help determine this.

In using the BIM as a model, it appears obvious that teachers must have: the ability to formulate valid objectives which are attainable for the specific students for which they are intended; the ability to determine the present readiness of students through preassessment procedures; the ability to formulate strategies which take into account the differences in learners and the complexity of the learning environment; the ability to design learning sequences which are logical and which economize on student time, while, at the same time, they ensure that, the student is able to achieve the prespecified goals; the ability to formulate means of evaluation which validly measure the extent to which students are able to achieve the objective; and the ability to make any necessary adjustments in the system as a result of implementing it with children in the learning situation. The development of such compentecies is the primary goal of this book.

A Competency-Based Program

The competencies outlined in the chapters of this book have been derived from a number of the bases previously described. These competencies are reflected in the objectives stated at the beginning of each chapter. You should let these objectives be your guide as you read and practice the skills called for. In traditional programs, a student has been expected only to read and recall information in order to demonstrate his competency. As you read through the materials presented in this book you will be expected to react to ideas, develop materials, as well as demonstrate specific teaching skills. In essence you will be asked to perform the skills of teaching rather than just know them.

The competencies you will master have been determined primarily from an explicit conception of a teacher's role and constitute minimum skills in planning, teaching, and evaluating science lessons. You should practice the skills included in each chapter until you are able to demonstrate the required level of mastery. Even though you will be expected to recall information, the primary emphasis will be upon using information about science teaching in a practical demonstration of teaching behaviors. Some individuals may take longer than others to demonstrate competency. This is to be expected. Not everyone can demonstrate competency with the same amount of practice. You will find it necessary to adjust your schedule of practice to permit you to reach the desired levels of competency within the time available to you in your training program. You may find that you are unsuccessful in your first attempts. Do not let this discourage you. In traditional, norm-based programs trainees are forced to accept scores taken in a "one shot" type examination as a final evaluation. With a competency-based program it is expected that you continue to work developing your skills until you have reached an appropriate level. It may require more of your time, but in the end it is possible for you to have reached a much higher level of mastery than you would otherwise achieve. You should not look upon this "recycling" procedure as failure on your part. Remember that the levels of mastery expected are likely to exceed those ordinarily expected in traditional programs. Remember too that your persistence will pay off in the long run when you have your own class and begin teaching science lessons to them.

As you work through these chapters, you may find it to your advantage to consult frequently with your instructor in order to obtain feedback. He will certify your competency in each of the objectives, but you will need feedback from him regarding your progress as you work on the competencies. It may also be advantageous for you to obtain feedback from your peers as you progress through the chapters. It is important that you get as clear a picture of your understanding and skill development as you can during the process of your development. This will increase the efficiency as well as the effectiveness of your growth as a teacher of elementary science. In addition to other benefits, this procedure will enable you to be more analytical and critical of your teaching performance and reduce your sensitivity to analysis and feedback by others. Self-analysis and self-correction of deficiencies are probably the most effective ways of increasing your teaching skills as a practicing teacher.

Technician versus Theoretician

Because the skill level you develop in a competency-based program is essentially that of an educational technician, and because it is desirable that you eventually reach the skill level of a theoretician, we must explain at this point the differences between these two levels of competency and attempt to indicate the way toward your personal growth and development as a teacher theoretician. First, let us define what is meant in education by the terms technician and theoretician. A technician is a practitioner who is able to apply specified skills in specified situations. A theoretician, on the other hand, is able to apply theoretical knowledge to a variety of unexpected situations. The technician can function effectively as long as the situations he encounters are reasonably similar. When situations arise which require considerable adjustment, his repertory of skills is insufficient (Broudy, 1972).

Competency-based programs have been criticized because they do not prepare teachers as theoreticians. Their defense has been that training as a theoretician is unnecessary. There is some evidence to support the idea that the teacher need not be able to give a theoretical explanation for the success of his performance. For example, a teacher does not have to understand the principles of operant conditioning in order to influence student behavior through positive reinforcement. She merely has to know that praising students when they engage in desired behavior will result in increased frequency of the desired behavior. What does the teacher do, however, when students do not respond to praise? Limited knowledge will not enable the teacher to cope with unexpected responses. However, if the teacher understood the theory properly, he/she would immediately begin to look for competing reinforcers and attempt to establish reinforcing influences which would bring about desired behavior changes. Without a sufficient understanding of theory, the teacher may begin in desperation to apply procedures that may even encourage students to misbehave. In the complexity of the classroom it is the ability to use theory which will bring order to the act of teaching. Teachers cannot expect that students will always respond in prescribed ways to their ways of dealing with them. Variability of student behavior is likely to be the rule rather than the exception. Consequently, teachers who can apply theory are needed because they can do everything that a technician can do, as well as handle situations which are beyond the capability of the technician.

At this point, the question might well be asked: "If it is so much more desirable to have theoreticians in the school, why do we even consider training technicians as a viable alternative?" The answer to the questions is related to time and money as well as competition for teacher candidates. Training a theoretician is a much more lengthy and costly process. It may well take two or three additional years to train a professional theoretician than someone who is able to carry on as a technician. The theoretician could be expected to spend many more hours learning theory as well as at least two years applying it in a well-supervised clinical setting. It really is a matter of what we think we can afford by way of training teachers. In addition, unless certification were tightly controlled, competition between training institutions might boil down to which one would certify you with the least amount of effort. One possible alternative is to train both technicians as well as theoreticians. Teams of teachers could be organized with theoreticians providing the leadership for individuals who have only a technical training.

Because the contents of this book primarily offer the reader training as a technician, it is necessary to explain just how this may be defended as a viable course to pursue. First, it must be said that the writers have no reservation in offering the competency-based approach as superior to the traditional approach to training science teachers. Traditional programs are characterized by teaching a little theory followed by an unarticulated practical experience called student teaching. Theory and practice in traditional programs have not been articulated at all. Graduates of such programs have learned through their experiences to be imitators rather than users of theory. The problem is that much of the imitation is of poor teaching practices. A competency-based program at least provides trainees with minimum necessary skills in teaching even though they may not be able to bring their behavior under complete theoretical control. At the beginning stages of training, it is likely to be very useful to understand and be able to apply the various skills identified as critical in competency-based programs. With the emphasis on competency, the trainee must be able to demonstrate the skill with a predetermined level of proficiency. This insures that the trainee has sufficient ability to conduct a class with a minimum of skill. The teacher will then be able to build upon these minimum skills, and gradually increase the amount of theory he/she is able to use. At present, this appears to be a promising alternative to traditional teacher preparation programs. In time, perhaps more and more teachers will be able to prepare themselves as theoreticians. Meanwhile, it is critical that teachers master sufficient skill to embark on successful teaching careers. A competency-based program appears to be the most viable means of achieving this.

Theory and Its Uses

To work as a theoretician, it is essential that a teacher must not only understand theory, but be able to apply it in practical situations. Perhaps because it takes so much effort and time to become a skilled theoretician, practitioners have a long standing disenchantment with

A theoretician will understand the child and his world and be able to help him learn and make sense out of the larger world he is part of.

learning and applying theory. Study of theory is usually criticized for being too impractical for application in the normal classroom. Accordingly, the best preparation from this view is to confine oneself to practical situations and attempt to formulate a series of actions which will work in each of these situations.

Actually there is nothing more practical than theory when it comes to understanding classroom processes and how to react to them. The problem with the cookbook approach to learning teaching skills (which means applying a different set of actions to each of a number of classroom situations) is that the teacher becomes essentially immobilized when he is confronted with a barrage of student behaviors for which he cannot produce the appropriate set of actions. The ordinary classroom is very complex. The purpose of theory is to simplify the task of the teacher in assessing what is happening and how to respond to it.

In essence, theory is a set of rules or collection of understandings which guide or control the teacher's actions. Theory should provide three functions: (a) description; (b) prediction; and (c) explanation. Description refers to the fact that theory provides us with a means of classifying knowledge about the field to which it pertains. In essence, knowledge about teacher and pupil actions and behaviors can be classified and categorized into units so that they are more understandable.

Prediction is a particularly useful attribute of theory. This means that a teacher can bring the behavior of students under control through careful execution of his own behavior. The teacher can thus predict what students will do as a consequence of his actions. If the theory is valid, he can depend on the relationship between his own behavior and that of his students to exist almost without exception. Of course, few theories relating to human behavior are 100 percent valid, but the more valid the theory the greater predictability it will have and the simpler it will be for the teacher using it to function in the classroom. One of the greatest difficulties experienced in the classroom is where students behave contrary to our predictions. If the teacher is not guided by theory, of course, he will not be concerned about predictability but rather will try to come up with the solution to each situation and problem as it arises. This greatly complicates the teacher's situation and also reduces his effectiveness.

Explanation is the third important attribute of theory. A theory should explain the relationships that exist between phenomena. In the classroom the teacher may use theory to explain why students are unruly or why they seem unable to learn a particular skill. For example, the theory of behavior modification may help the teacher understand that it is her own behavior that causes her students to misbehave. Once theory has helped her realize the implications of her behavior in terms of student behavior, she can learn to adjust her actions appropriately.

Preassessment and Prescription

In teaching children it is essential that the teacher let her own behavior be governed by the information she has obtained about her class through preassessment. Preassessment is the process of determining students' learning styles, developmental levels in terms of intellectual skills and achievements, as well as psychomotor, social and emotional development, and other information which is related to properly prescribing learning experiences for children. It makes little sense to ask students to attempt to do tasks in science when they are not at the proper readiness level intellectually or when they do not have appropriate prerequisite knowledge. Nor is it useful to ignore appropriate social and emotional development in prescribing experiences in learning.

In diagnosing readiness and prescribing learning activities, theory plays an important role. Theory guides our thinking and reduces the apparent complexity of human behavior to a manageable level. For example, if we are using the perceptual-field theory regarding the growth and development of children, we may diagnose student learning disabilities in terms of poor self-concept. Prescription of learning would have to be coordinated with efforts to improve self-concept. With a theory, our attention becomes focused upon probable causes of learning difficulties in a limited way. This of course reduces the complexity of diagnosis and greatly simplifies the process of prescribing appropriate remediation to accompany learning. In the process of doing this we need to be aware of the fact that other theories may be used, which may take an entirely different view of man and the basis of his growth and development. It is likely that with different theories, different explanations will be made of human behavior. This should not be a deterrent to us, however. Each of the theories may in fact be used as a basis to explain some complex aspect of human behavior. If each theory has been properly researched it can prove useful in understanding the behavior of students, at least in some aspect, and be used as a basis for prescribing learning and/or remediation.

Prescribing appropriate activities for learning is a critical skill for the teacher. In teaching, this is often referred to as strategy and tactics. When using strategy based on theory, the teacher is able to follow through in a consistent way rather than taking a hit and miss approach. Without theory to guide the teacher in the development of strategy she will find herself in the position of teaching by trial and error or engaging in procedures which practice has made respectable. If one thing does not work, another will be tried. Teaching under these conditions becomes very unpredictable. When some particular series of procedures appears to work, the teacher is unable to explain exactly what influence or combination of influences was the basis for her success. With theory, strategy can be designed which fits a particular theory and the teacher can act consistently within the limits of the theory; she can then attribute the behavior of students to the use of a consistent set of behaviors of her own. In this way the teacher can gradually gain a greater amount of predictability with regard to her teaching.

Growth toward Becoming a Theoretician

We hope that you have come to realize how important becoming a theoretician is to your growth as a professional teacher. There is no question that mastering theoretical approaches to teaching is a long process, one which will not be completed when you finish your formal preparation. Mastering the competencies contained in this book will equip you with the basic skills necessary to begin your work as a teacher. You should become committed to the idea that a good deal more growth will be required before you become a truly professional teacher. This growth will depend to a great extent upon how well you are able to learn and master the application of sound teaching theory. This book will suggest the ways and means of improving your level of mastery. You will read about theories of growth and development as well as how children learn. You will also learn how to organize and sequence learning materials. You will be asked to organize and teach science lessons to small groups and make careful analyses of your teaching. Hopefully these experiences will help you formulate a pattern of exploring the meaning of various theories, testing them out as a practitioner and then carefully analyzing your performance and adjusting it as necessary so that your behavior becomes a valid representation of the theory you are trying to apply.

It can usually be assumed that as a teacher you can expect limited assistance in your professional growth. Schools do not have sufficient sources of funds to offer you a continuation of training at the level that would be desirable. In addition, the full time energies of the teacher are required in the ongoing instructional program. Many schools offer teachers a few workshops and a little supervision, but both are grossly inadequate to provide the necessary help to raise the teacher's professional level. The responsibility of professional growth thus depends upon the initiative of the individual teacher. This can be accomplished by mastering the procedures for self-analysis outlined in this book and continuing to pursue an understanding of educational theory and applying it to your teaching. You will find it useful to learn the various schemes for analyzing teaching which incorporate audio- and videorecording procedures. By learning how to analyze your own teaching and its effect on students, you will be equipping yourself to become a real student of teaching and to develop into a true theoretician.

References

Broudy, Harry S., *A Critique of Performance-Based Teacher Education,* Paper presented at the National Convention of the American Association of Colleges for Teacher Education, Chicago, 1972.

Coleman, James S., *Equal Educational Opportunity,* in Editorial Board of the Harvard Educational Review, Mass: Harvard University Press, 1969.

Cooper, James M., Howard L. Jones, and Wilford A. Weber, "Specifying Teacher Competencies," *The Journal of Teacher Education* 24 (Spring 1973): 17–23.

Dodl, Norman R., "Selecting Competency Outcomes for Teacher Education," *Journal of Teacher Education* 24 (Fall 1973): 194–99.

Elam, Stanley, *A Resume of Performance-Based Teacher Education: What Is the State of the Art?* American Association of Colleges for

Teacher Education, One Dupont Circle, Washington, D. C. 20036, March, 1972.

Popham, W. James, "Pitfalls and Pratfalls of Teacher Evaluation," *Educational Leadership* 32 (November 1974): 141–46.

Science Curriculum Improvement Study, *SCIS Teacher's Handbook.* Berkeley: University of California Press, 1974.

Silberman, Charles E., *Crisis in the Classroom: The Remaking of American Education,* New York: Random House, 1970.

Smith, B. Othanel, *Certification of Educational Personnel,* ERIC Document ED 055–975, 1971.

2
Scientific Literacy and Elementary School Science

Why Teach Science

One of the long range goals of this book is to assist you in answering the question "Why should I spend the time and effort teaching science?" This many-faceted question deserves serious consideration by all teachers. Not only will the answer you formulate help you to determine whether or not you will teach science, it will also allow you to determine the goals of your science program and the strategies you will use to accomplish these goals. The answer will not be a simple, short phrase. Rather, it will be an answer which takes into account such factors as how children learn, the needs of children, the nature of man, and the basic information needed to live a rich and full life.

Exercise 2–1 Why Should I Teach Science?

To assist you in making use of the following information, Exercise 2–1 has been designed to help you determine your present opinions about teaching science to elementary school children.

Part A. For each statement below decide whether you Agree (A), Disagree (D), or have No Opinion (NO).
1. Science is too technical for students below grade three.
2. Science knowledge will enable a student to study other topics with greater understanding.
3. Elementary school science should be taught so as to prepare students to take junior high school science.
4. A science textbook occupies a major role in the instruction of elementary school children.
5. It is appropriate to have all students participating in science activities most of the time.

21

6. The development of "proper" attitudes should be a major concern of the elementary school science teacher.
7. It is possible to identify specific knowledge that all students must master during the elementary school years.
8. Elementary school students can "discover" significant relationships through guided processes.
9. The technological aspects of our world should occupy a significant portion of the time allowed to "science."
10. A particular effort should be made to identify potential scientists among elementary school students and provide them with an enriched elementary school science program.

Part B. When you have indicated your personal reactions to the above statements, spend some time in a small group sharing your opinions with others. Try to resolve in your own mind the divergent opinions of others.

OBJECTIVES

The readings and exercises of this chapter are designed to assist you in developing the following competencies:
1. Write a definition for scientific literacy which can be utilized to formulate one's purposes for teaching elementary school science.
2. Synthesize a point of view concerning the question "Why teach science to elementary school students?"

Science and Everyday Life

Teachers have learned from classroom experience that students are most easily motivated to learn about topics that are close to them. Creating interest in a study of the government of Italy will probably be more difficult than a similar study of local government. A physical education instructor may find it easier to teach students the rules of basketball than of rugby. Teachers in the Great Lakes area will be able to teach students about the effects of glaciers on the land formation more easily than teachers in the South Central states. In each instance, the teacher can motivate students when they have some personal attachment to the subject being studied.

In general, science can appeal to students' interests of daily living. A young child, when left on his own, is eager to explore his environment. The constant urge to move, seek, and ask questions is obvious when one observes children. Children often ask questions relating to the "hows" and "whys" of the environment. For example, "Why does a spinning top slow down and stop?" or "Where are the stars in the

daytime?" or "How do plants know when to start growing in the spring?"

Note that most questions, including those mentioned above, originate from the child's daily experiences. The child watches the spinning top slow down of its own accord after he worked so hard to make it go. Observations of the first crocus on a cold spring day prompt the student to wonder why the plant begins to grow in anticipation of the warm days ahead. Obviously, a young child is not ready for discussions detailing characteristics of friction, planet rotation, and the life cycle of a plant. But he is ready for additional experiences that will allow him to expand his view of the environment around him. To squelch this curiosity is to curtail the child's desire for continued learning.

Curiosity about the world around us is not unique to the young child. Young and mature adults continue to seek new answers to questions. One has only to examine the headlines of popular newspapers and magazines to find evidence of this phenomena. The effects of drugs on man, the effects of population growth on the future of man, the desire for more comforts in daily living, the effects of military technology, concern for the effects of new practices on the ecological environment, and the curiosity of the laymen for new information gained from space travel are examples of topics found in adult popular reading material.

Should the schools attempt to educate all students to be scientists? Obviously the great minds of the future are in our elementary schools today, but not all of these people will distinguish themselves in science. In fact, very few will spend any significant portion of their life devoted to such an endeavor. There are many other vocations necessary to the development of our society and the individuals in it.

To really pursue the above question in detail, one needs to recognize what is meant by the term "science." Is science being learned when a child discovers the difference between girls and boys, between plants and animals, between hot and cold, between dogs and cats, or between life and death? Is one learning science when spellbound by the "magical" powers of a Mr. Wizard who is impressing his audience with his demonstrations? Does peering into an active aquarium, listening for the variety of sounds made by a symphony orchestra, smelling the aroma of different plants in a garden, or touching the surface of different rocks found in a ditch along the road constitute scientific learning?

Exercise 2–2   The World of the Child

It is appropriate for you to seek the opportunity to "play" or interact with some children at this time. Getting to know the child's world is the point of Exercise 2–2.

Although each situation will be unique, we suggest that you develop a situation in which students experience some phenomenon that is unfamiliar to them. This can be done with preschoolers or older students. The choice of the topic will, of course, depend upon the student. Again, because each situation is unique, it will be most valuable if you record your observations soon after the event and share them with others who have had a similar experience. It may be possible for you to record your experience with audio or video equipment for a better analysis situation.

Defining Science Literacy

Since science exists in such abundance in everyday living, the question the teacher should ask changes from "Shall I teach science?" to "What shall I select from all that is available to include in a science program?" How much time should be spent on teaching about environmental education? Should the decline in public emphasis in the space program indicate a corresponding decline in the emphasis on study of space related topics? Should students learn to use the microscope? Should students be required to participate in the local science fair?

What a teacher chooses to include in the curriculum will be derived from a combination of several factors. The chief factor will be the textbook or program selected by teachers or the school system. Chapter 12 of this book surveys the common science programs used in schools today. When implementing one of these programs, you will likely capitalize on strengths of science content background acquired through formal and informal training. The actual classroom science program in the elementary school will be influenced by current and long-range interests of both teacher and students, by topics being publicized in the public media, and by the various strengths and weaknesses of the children in the classroom.

In actuality, all of the above mentioned factors operationally define the nature of science. Textbooks for elementary school science simply reflect what the authors feel is the nature of science. The experience a teacher has had as a student in the classroom is a composite expression of the nature of science by that teacher and, to a large degree, the textbook utilized in that course. How one interprets his own needs and interests and those of his students will also reflect the nature of science. For that reason, the rest of this chapter pursues the question of the nature of science.

The teacher's knowledge about the world helps him decide what to include in a science curriculum. In a science course, one learns the many laws, theories, facts, and figures which have been accumulated through the work of scientists. Browsing through the science and technology sections of the local library will show that not only has a great deal of knowledge about our world been written and rewritten many times, but the rate of growth of that knowledge is increasing each year. The larger number of scientists, as well as the greater communication between them, and the increased expertise in analyzing, storing, and retrieving data have all contributed to this rapid rate of knowledge accumulation. It is apparent that we must give children enough of a knowledge base to allow them not only to have an understanding of our vast environment, but also to incorporate changes in knowledge in future years as well.

In a yearbook entitled *Rethinking Science Education,* Hurd (1960) summarized a number of viewpoints on what science education should be. He concluded that one aspect was the knowledge accumulated by scientists and the other was the "enterprise" the scientists engaged in to gain this knowledge. The term " enterprise" means a large number of complex behaviors which are partially described by such terms as problem solving, inquiry, and the scientific method. These terms give rise to images of the scientist in the laboratory among a maze of complex equipment, offices of thick, heavy books, and a group of technicians arduously recording data from experiments. This is hardly the picture we want to convey to an elementary school student. Hurd (1960) and others portray the enterprise as a very positive process.

To gain another viewpoint on the nature of science teaching, let us examine the project conducted by the National Assessment of Educational Progress, which was designed to measure the status of science education throughout the nation. This project sought to assess the knowledge and abilities of four age groups in each of the different subject areas, and to determine the status and progress of education in that discipline. To assess the status of science education, a group of prominent science educators was organized to identify the objectives of science teaching. These objectives were arranged into four areas that represent the purpose of science education:

1. Know fundamental facts and principles of science.
2. Possess the abilities and skills needed to engage in the processes of science.
3. Understand the investigative nature of science.
4. Have attitudes about and appreciations of scientists, science, and the consequences of science that stem from adequate understandings (NAEP, 1975).

In subsequent work on the Project, objectives were translated into test items which were randomly administered to students across the nation.

The four areas above shed further light on the nature of the scientific enterprise referred to by Hurd. Science is also thought of as activities having identifiable processes which will contribute to one's ability to investigate phenomena. Further, it is considered to have a relationship to man, which involves people and the consequences of one's action on another.

The nature of science, then, is more than a reservoir of knowledge; it is a dynamic, ongoing inquiry into our environment. This inquiry has

The nature of science is best learned from personal inquiries of materials in our environment.

produced an abundance of knowledge which technology has made use of in various ways to enhance our life style. It has also brought out behaviors that are conducive to effective inquiry. These behaviors identify skills and attitudes which allow the investigator to proceed using the knowledge already gained from previous investigations. The composite of all these skills, processes, and knowledge, has been termed scientific literacy.

In an attempt to further define the scientifically literate person, Hurd has compiled this list of characteristics:

1. He has faith in the logical processes of science and uses its modes of inquiry, but at the same time recognizes their limitations and the situations for which they are peculiarly appropriate.
2. He enjoys science for the intellectual stimulus it provides, for the

beauty of its explanations, the pleasure that comes from knowing, and the excitement stemming from discovery.

3. He has more than a common sense understanding of the natural world.

4. He appreciates the interaction of science and technology, recognizing that each reflects as well as stimulates the course of social and economic development, but he is aware that science and technology do not progress at equal rates.

5. He is in intellectual possession of some of the major concepts, laws, and theories of several sciences.

6. He understands that science is not the only way of viewing natural phenomena, and that even among the sciences there are rival points of view.

7. He appreciates the fact that scientific knowledge grows, possibly without limit, and that the knowledge of one generation "engulfs, upsets, and complements all knowledge of the natural world before."

8. He appreciates the essential lag between frontier research and the popular understanding of new achievements and the importance of narrowing the gap.

9. He recognizes that the achievements of science and technology properly used are basic to the achievement of human welfare.

10. He recognizes that the meaning of science depends as much on its inquiry process as on its conceptual patterns and theories.

11. He understands the role of the scientific enterprises in society and appreciates the cultural conditions under which it thrives (Hurd, 1960; enumeration has been added).

In order to accomplish the education of an individual to some level of scientific literacy, the science education programs of our schools must include a study of the knowledge generated by science, practice in the use of the processes of science, and the opportunity to develop the attitudes conducive to the study and use of science knowledge and processes. The next sections of this chapter study the three areas of science education.

Knowledge of Science

Most people would agree that the amount of facts and figures in science is overwhelming. The encyclopedic nature of the discipline presents a barrier to learning about it. How does a teacher organize the information to be learned about science in a way that will allow students to develop the desired scientific literacy?

Man's senses provide a means of gathering data about the environment around him. For example, one hears the great variety of sounds emitted by birds. After repeated experiences the sound of a particular bird may be remembered and associated with that bird. A further description of the bird is gained through the sense of sight. One then learns to associate the sound of a bird with particular color markings and shapes. The sense of touch allows further data accumulation about birds. The ardent observer can accumulate a great deal of data about birds in general and about some birds in particular by using his senses. Modern technology has extended the capacity of man's senses to acquire data with such instruments as the electron microscope and radio telescope. The function of the teacher is to help students learn to organize the many bits of information into manageable learning experiences. How does the teacher do this?

The Process of Education (Bruner, 1960) suggests an answer to this question, which is useful in the development of curricular materials for elementary school science. In summarizing the opinions and research of many prominent educators, Bruner has proposed that the structure of the disciplines, that is, the relationships existing among the many bits of data which have been accumulated, must be identified. Correspondingly, learning the structure of a discipline means learning how all of this data is related. The structure of knowledge about birds identifies how the many observations made about birds are interrelated. To gain knowledge about birds we must learn these interrelationships.

Bruner further proposed that in some form the foundations of any subject can be taught to anyone at any age. This does not mean that a college level course consisting of a complex system of factual material can be taught to a primary age student. Rather, it suggests that the beginning levels of a structure of science can be taught to a young child.

In speaking about the advantage of teaching the structure of a discipline, Bruner proposed that learning in science should not only be to gain a greater understanding of part of our natural environment, but it should also be a jumping off point for further study. When knowledge of the discipline is ordered and related, the student begins by learning some of the more easily observed bits of data and the simpler relationships of its structure. It is these simple relationships that aid the further study of the structure. At first, the young child identifies the general shape of a few birds he observes in a zoo cage. Later, walks in the park or forest will provide him with experiences to enlarge the early relationships about the nature of a bird. How then does one find relationships between the bits of knowledge about our environment?

In organizing data about the world around us we find that the bits of information tend to fall into neat little groups. The term "concept" is usually associated with these groups of similar items. For instance, think about a group of furniture pieces. These objects could be com-

bined into smaller groups, according to their function, and then named with such titles as "chair," "table," "cupboard," and so forth. Certainly there are many different types of tables and chairs, but in most cases the characteristics, or attributes, within each group are sufficiently similar so as to be identifiable and not confused with other groups. Also, a new object, such as a porch swing, would be more likely added to the group labeled "chair" rather than the one labeled "table." Thus, the naming of subgroups of objects or events provides a way of identifying, differentiating, and classifying new objects.

Consider for the moment your meaning of the term "fish." The specific attributes you associate with the abstraction will vary with the set of experiences you have had. If your experiences are limited to catching blue gill from a local pond or creek, your abstraction will yield attributes of a relatively short, oval-shaped body, and an upright, dorsal fin. On the other hand, if your experiences have been in a large tropical fish aquarium, your abstraction of the term fish will more likely include attributes that are more varied in terms of color, shape, size, and special features. No matter what your experiences, though, you would have little trouble distinguishing an object with four legs, long tail, and shaggy fur from a fish. Undoubtedly you would not associate any of these attributes with your own particular meaning of the concept of "fish."

If you keep in mind that concepts are abstractions invented for the purpose of studying objects and events, it is not surprising to find that simple concepts have a limited value. One can find objects that tend to fit attributes from two similar conceptual groups. One of the current debates concerns man's attempt to distinguish what is "alive" from what is "dead." A text of elementary biology builds experiences that contribute to the development of the concepts of "life." More advanced study, however, provides sufficient data to ask the question: "When has life been extinguished from a once living organism?"

These examples of concepts that show similarities between objects can be extended to cover more abstract concepts, such as energy, which can then be operationally divided into further areas of study like heat, sound, and light. Grouped another way, heat and light have in common the characteristic of electromagnetic radiation. For the purpose of the practical classroom learning environment we are concerned with the necessity of finding common attributes of objects and providing a label, a concept to aid us in further study of that area of knowledge.

The purpose of this chapter is not to explore the conceptual structure of science. Rather, it attempts to show that one need not master all of the factual material of our natural world in order to study science. Through a study of various phenomena, broad ideas do emerge which

can be used in organizing learning and applying knowledge. Science, then, is the seeking of knowledge on which to develop concepts, such that further study will be aided.

Exercise 2–3   Identifying Science Concepts

1. Define the meaning of concepts.
2. Select an article about science, or a portion of an elementary, secondary or collegiate textbook. Identify the concept or concepts being presented.
3. Combine your list of concepts with those identified by other members of your class.

The Processes of Science

Hurd identified two components of science, knowledge and enterprise. He described the active component as follows:

> Science is a process in which observations and their interpretations are used to develop new concepts, to extend our understanding of the world, to suggest new areas for exploration, and to provide some predictions about the future. It is focused upon inquiry and subsequent action (Hurd, 1960).

Even before this publication, science educators sought to identify the elements of the process so that they could be more efficiently learned by others.

The Nature of Inquiry

Have you ever watched a young child moving about a crib, a playpen, or sandpile? The normal child spends nearly all of his time making inquiries about his environment. He questions, looks, guesses, discovers, tries something again and again, compares, communicates his findings, and sometimes just sits and daydreams. Obviously, the child is learning, albeit by a random, inconsistent process. Sometimes he makes great strides in his learning process and sometimes he seeks the assistance of an adult when frustrated by something that "won't work."

The processes by which adults learn something new are not that different from those of the child. Of course, the adult procedures are more mature and systematic. Most teachers feel that the development of these inquiring processes is a function of someone in the educational system; some refer to it as "learning to think." Somewhere in the educa-

tional system the student is expected to develop the skills of self-direction and become capable of pursuing a topic of study about some problem they have identified.

The skills of inquiry or knowledge seeking are common to a number of disciplines of study, notably the natural sciences and the social sciences. Suchman (1965) has defined inquiry as learning which ". . . is initiated and controlled by the learner himself as a means of expanding his own understanding." Scientific inquiry certainly is concerned with the acquisition of knowledge, but it is also concerned with the process by which this new knowledge is acquired.

The popular image of the scientist conforms to this definition. One imagines him busily moving about his laboratory, making use of all sorts of mysterious equipment. In reality, one finds many scientists sitting at a desk reading computer printouts or just thinking. Other scientists follow different kinds of simple routines with amazingly simply machinery. Nevertheless, they are all "inquiring" of their environment in order to learn more about it. The position of the science educator is to determine what elements of this process can be identified and taught to future scientists.

Suchman (1965) has identified three elements of the inquiry process. He suggests that inquiry begins with the identification of some discrepant event that causes a contradiction with accepted knowledge. To resolve this discrepancy, one must have the freedom to gather information and to test predictions that might provide a solution to the problem. In order to accomplish this, the investigator must have a responsive environment in which to pursue this investigation. Those who would control this situation must provide an element of trust and freedom for the process to take place.

Science educators generally agree that the most appropriate way of learning how to inquire is to be placed in an environment where inquiry can take place. This point of view requires the learner to actively seek data, discover relationships, and resolve discrepancies. To further develop this approach to learning, one must specify the behavior of scientists as self-directing learners. The investigation of the scientific method has been a subject of discussion among science educators for many decades. Lately, the discussion has centered on determining the processes of science.

Identifying the Processes of Science

Most efforts to formulate a scientific method have resulted in some scheme generalized by the following:

Figure 2–1   A Diagram of the Scientists Way: His Methods of Intelligence

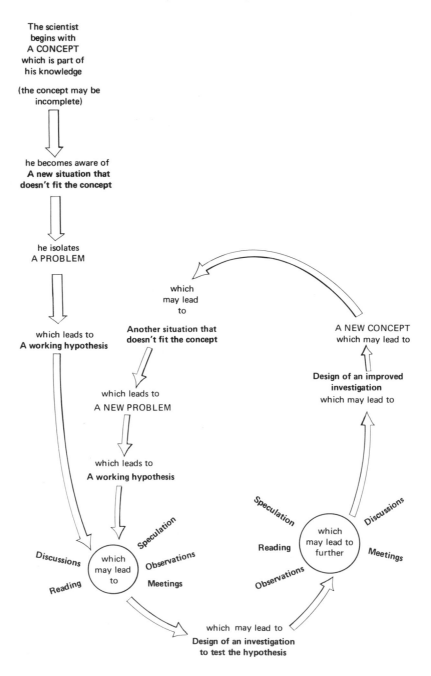

1. Identify the problem to be studied.
2. Design an experiment to solve the problem.
3. Collect the necessary data.
4. Analyze the data.
5. Formulate conclusions and identify new concerns.

The general consensus today is that there is no one method by which the results of science are determined. There is no singular process which is sure to get results. A study of the case histories of successful scientific investigations produces no magical formula by which one can pursue contemporary concerns of science. This is not to say that attempts to determine the processes by which information is determined are futile. Only the effort to find one single design seems fruitless.

Numerous educational projects in the last twenty years have produced great insights into the various components of the investigative nature of science and the procedures by which these processes can be taught to students in the classroom. Figure 2–1 provides an example. Paul F. Brandwein developed this scheme to describe the art of scientific investigation for teachers who are using the science program of which he is senior author. The scheme begins with an identification of a concern based on familiar information. This problem is then examined in a variety of ways by using the contradictory information apparent from early inquiry. Subsequent investigations yield further clarifying results which expand the initial knowledge base. Inherent within this scheme are many steps not specifically identified.

Learning how to control variables in an experiment is a useful process skill.

During the early 1960s, the American Association for the Advancement of Science (AAAS) through its Commission on Science Education began an extensive study of elementary school science teaching with an emphasis on the development of process skills. Whereas most science education programs begin with the selection of a topic of study (for example, magnets, photosynthesis, simple machines) the AAAS-sponsored program based the construction of each unit of study on the development of one or more process skills (observing, hypothesizing, etc.).

The choice of subjects to be studied was often arbitrary since many different subjects studied in the science curriculum can be "observed" or "hypothesized." In the AAAS Program subjects are far less important than process. To emphasize this fact the program was given the name, *Science: A Process Approach* (SAPA); more about the specific nature of the materials for this program is included in Chapter 12 of this book. The process skills identified by this program, which can be taught to students in the elementary school years, are of interest here.

To design a curriculum based on the development of process skills, it was necessary to articulate what the process skills were. The AAAS

TABLE 2-1   THE PROCESSES OF SCIENCE

BASIC PROCESSES

Observing: Using the five senses to obtain information

Using Space/Time Relationships: Describing spatial relationships and their change with time

Classifying: Imposing order on collections of objects or events

Using Numbers: Identifying quantitative relationships in nature

Measuring: Measuring length, area, volume, weight, temperature, force, and speed

Communicating: Expressing ideas with oral and written words, diagrams, maps, graphs, mathematical equations, and various kinds of visual demonstrations

Predicting: Making specific forecasts of what a future observation will be

Inferring: An explanation of an observation

INTEGRATED PROCESSES

Controlling Variables: Studying the influence of changing variables, the factors which influence one another

Interpreting Data: Using data to make inferences, predictions, and hypotheses, the statistical treatments given to such interpretations, and the study of probability

Formulating Hypotheses: Making generalized statements of explanation

Defining Operationally: Defining terms in the context of experience

Experimenting: Larger process of using basic and integrated processes

Source: Adapted from AAAS, *Commentary for Teachers*, 1970.

curriculum development group identified eight elementary and five integrated skills around which the program was to be built (AAAS, 1970). These thirteen skills are listed and briefly defined in Table 2–1, in the order in which they are usually presented to students. Beginning early in kindergarten (Level A of the program), the student has extensive experience with materials that develop skills in observation. Somewhat later in that year, additional experiences teach the child to infer. Integrated skills begin in approximately the fifth grade (Level E).

Early learning experiences in the SAPA Program give students the opportunity of working with many different subject areas. In each one the objective of the lesson seeks to enlarge the capability to use one or more science processes. The students practice the skills of *observing* phenomena to identify what the world around them is really like. The observations must then be *communicated* to others in an accurate and informative manner. To be more specific in their descriptions students must develop the ability of *using space/time relationships.* To further describe just about any phenomena, the students develop skills of *measuring* and *using numbers.* In order to distinguish between what is really being observed and what is an interpretation of that observation, students learn the difference between *observing* and *inferring.*

Consider how practical it is for any individual in our society to have a high degree of proficiency in the above-mentioned skills. The person is better able to enjoy beauty because observation skills have been developed. Process skills of measuring, communicating, and using numbers and space/time relationships provide a basis on which to use those observations. The use of these skills is not limited exclusively to the usual science topics. Certainly an element of mathematics is involved. In addition, communication is taught and learned in several components of the curriculum. Social skills are also developed. To be more specific, any social event is likely to be enhanced by using science skills while participating in it. Being able to distinguish inferences from observations is of practical value in daily living to guard against being taken in by nonfactual statements. The important point is that science is certainly one area of the curriculum where we can begin to develop these skills in primary age students.

In later years students learn the skills of predicting, formulating hypotheses, controlling variables, interpreting data, forming operational definitions, and experimenting. The latter process is cumulative, and students can make use of any or all of their previously developed skills.

Perhaps the reader will be able to appreciate the emphasis on process as opposed to content with an example. A SAPA unit of approximately third grade level deals with the concepts of "Loss of Water from

Plants" and is the sixth lesson that seeks to develop the skill of working with inferences. The objectives of this unit are as follows:

At the end of this exercise the child should be able to:

1. Construct appropriate inferences about water loss from plants based on observations of investigations demonstrating water uptake and loss.
2. Construct situations to test such inferences.
3. Construct predictions from a graph about water loss from plants over a given period of time (AAAS, 1974).

To evaluate the success of this lesson, the teacher will present the class or individual students with situational problems as described in the objective. Suggested test situations concern changing colors of flowers by a florist, picture sequences of potted plants on a balance, and new graphs that the student has not previously seen.

The writers of other science programs, described in Chapter 12, have also concluded that students in the elementary school years can learn the so-called process skills of science right along with the concepts of science. These programs usually do not require the student to learn long lists of facts or memorize statements. Rather, the student learns to "process" with the concepts much like the example from SAPA described above.

The process skills identified by these programs and implemented in the elementary school are important in the total educational program. Secondary school programs have long sought to develop these skills, but students have been unprepared for this experience. There have been few process-based science programs in the elementary schools. Without this foundation work, secondary schools have been unable to teach these basic process skills. Another statement of support for emphasizing science processes is that most of the current elementary school science programs have been developed by scientists who were not directly concerned with elementary school education, but who felt it was most important that process skills be developed. Furthermore, the development of these skills is not unique to the science area. Other subject area specialists, the social scientists for example, have also sought to develop elementary and secondary school programs to develop process skills. To most of the educational community, this is a proper direction of change for elementary school science.

Exercise 2–4   Process Skills in Science Experiences

If possible, visit an elementary school classroom or watch a videotape of an elementary school classroom to observe students involved in a science lesson. If that is not possible, then select an exercise from a contemporary school science program which describes how students are to be involved in a science activity.

Using either or all of the above resources, examine the experience to determine which science processes are being used by students. Consider the list proposed by the AAAS (see Figure 2–2) or some of the process labels you consider more appropriate. Be specific in identifying the part of the lesson in which each process is being utilized.

Developing a Scientific Attitude

A teacher may attempt to "teach" students some specific bit of knowledge or some skills, and then test them to determine how much they actually learned. The teacher feels somewhat sure that the test is a valid assessment of whether or not the students possess that knowledge or skill. Working with attitudes is much more nebulous. It is difficult to pinpoint the existence of an attitude in the same way that one can show that a student knows the definition of a term, or can adjust a microscope or synthesize a hypothesis. Certainly a student can fake an opinion in the hopes of pleasing a teacher, or otherwise behave in a way not consistent with his real attitudes toward a situation. It is easy to see why teachers have traditionally stated that they do not really "teach" attitudes in the classroom.

Several factors seem to contradict this indifference toward the learning of attitudes. Teachers have identified the students who have "poor attitudes toward learning." A short visit to any school's faculty lounge will probably find discussion of one or more of the problem children in the school. They are usually talking about student attitudes as reflected by the child's behavior in school. One child may be singled out because of such behaviors as writing on restroom walls, talking out in class, or not completing assignments in the classroom. Another student may be especially noteworthy because he "could learn if he would only try." The teachers have inferred, and probably correctly so, that students who do not try have a negative attitude toward school. This inference is based on observations of behavior, which the teacher feels was not influenced by him, but was volunteered by the student. This voluntary behavior is considered to be indicative of the student's attitude.

Techniques for motivating students have long been considered by teachers as essential to the learning process. The successful teacher has apparently integrated these techniques into the classroom routine. One can find many classrooms where students are highly motivated to learn. This is evident by the way they attend to what the teacher is doing, by the way they complete assignments, and by the way they voluntarily participate in activities above and beyond what is required of them. Again, their behavior is indicative of their attitude.

The point to be made here is that students do learn attitudes as a result of their participation in classroom activities, and this happens even if the teacher has not planned for it. Developing an attitude toward science takes place as a result of the type of activities used in the classroom. If science instruction is based exclusively on learning facts and concepts, then the student may develop the attitude that science must be accepted as it has been identified and developed by experts. A science lesson stressing the development of process skills, however, develops attitudes conducive to the student's learning about science from personal experiences. Preparation for teaching science should include concern for the attitudes toward science. What, then, are the preferred scientific attitudes?

Some Views On Attitudes for Science

The National Education Association-sponsored Educational Policies Commission has identified seven values as characteristic of the spirit of science:

1. Longing to know and to understand
2. Questioning of all things
3. Search for data and their meaning
4. Demand for verification
5. Respect for logic
6. Consideration of premises
7. Consideration of consequences (EPC, 1966)

The Commission statement points out that these values are not intended for the future scientist but rather to characterize rational thought processes in man's approach to daily living.

If one considers these statements in the light of everyday experience, it soon becomes apparent that these characteristics reflect an operational definition of a mature, rational approach to life. For example, a person who possesses these characteristics is not easily impressed by misleading advertisements so popular in today's media. He/she gives careful, thoughtful consideration to political candidates. Such a person wants to do more than watch life pass before him.

It should be apparent that attitudes associated with the nature of science should not be limited to the natural sciences. The same attitudes hold true in the areas of political science, mathematics, and library science. Even people in the fields of art, music, and literature utilize these values to some extent. The teacher, perhaps more than any other professional, will find occasion to provide for the development of these values.

In 1969, the National Science Teachers Association sought to identify the attitudes which are appropriately developed in the science classroom. After several meetings of science educators throughout the country, a summary statement was prepared which outlined the following attitudes:

1. *Awareness of Conditions*
   a. relates personal requisite abilities, interests, and attitudes
   b. appreciates the interaction of science and technology
   c. appreciates the interaction of science and the arts
   d. appreciates the limitations of science
   e. understands that science is generated by people with a compelling desire to understand the natural world
   f. recognizes that science grows, possibly without limit
   g. recognizes that the achievements of science and technology properly used, are basic to the advancement of human welfare
   h. recognizes that the meaning of science depends as much on its inquiry process as on its conceptual patterns
   i. appreciates the cultural conditions under which the scientific enterprise is promoted
2. *Acceptance of Values*
   a. rejection of myths and superstitions as explanations of natural phenomena
   b. has the habit of considered response
   c. has the habit of weighing evidence to formulate a considered response
   d. realizes that science is a basic part of modern living
3. *Preference for Values*
   a. curiosity
   b. patience
   c. persistence
   d. openmindedness
   e. confidence in the scientific method
   f. searches for truth
   g. sees the importance of science for understanding the modern world
   h. believes that intellectual satisfaction is to be gained from pursuit of science
   i. desires to be creative
   j. enjoys science for intellectual stimulus and the pleasure of knowing (Harbeck, 1969)

Students who are active in the learning process are able to demonstrate their attitudes such as curiosity, persistence and open-mindedness.

None of these ideas was expressed for the first time at this listing. The awareness statements describe ideas that have long been accepted. The problem has not been over the statement of the idea, only over the interpretation of it for classroom use. To be more specific about the meaning of the attitudes requires specification of the behaviors to be expected of students who do possess these attitudes.

To gain insight into the attitudes possessed by others, one can only study their behaviors. In fact, one cannot be sure of the attitude unless there is a great deal of voluntary behavior associated with it. When asked by the teacher, a student may reply that he likes science. However, the teacher should not accept this verbal response as the sole indication that the student really possesses this attitude, unless there is a corresponding increase in the student's voluntary participation over a period of time.

The NSTA Committees sought to define these attitudes more clearly by formulating some classroom behaviors that would indicate their possible presence. Consider the following examples:

1. *Curiosity*
   a. frequently asks questions and challenges statements of others
   b. asks different people the same question

    c. applies multi-resources to one question
    d. often takes a second look
    e. goes out of his way to find answers
    f. reads numerous books and magazines

2. *Appreciates the Limitations of Science*
    a. limits conclusions to present data but verbally recognizes possibility of error
    b. willingness to retest in the face of seemingly conclusive data
    c. frequently challenges classmates or teachers who make authoritative statements, such as "science has proved. . . ." (Harbeck, 1969)

You are cautioned in your interpretation of human behavior as an expression of attitude to realize that a single instance or a short-range series of behaviors may not be conclusive evidence that an individual holds a particular attitude. But, behaviors exhibited by students voluntarily over a long period of time may be considered to be valid indicators of specific attitudes.

Exercise 2–5 Identifying Behaviors for Attitude Development

1. Summarize the point of view for developing student attitudes as a part of elementary school science instruction.
2. Identify an attitude other than curiosity or appreciation for the limitations of science. Then identify some specific student behaviors that would indicate the presence of this attitude.

Responsible Citizenship and Scientific Literacy

Scientific literacy has been defined in the preceding sections as consisting of knowledge, process, and attitude components. Knowledge about the natural world can be organized into structures or concepts. The processes by which these knowledge structures are built can be specified. Furthermore, the attitudes which are reflected by the voluntary actions of a scientifically literate person can be identified. All three components form an integrated whole for the practical implementation of a scientific literacy.

Man's approach to responsible citizenship is, at least in part, an application of scientific literacy. Man exists within the environment, which has been the subject of study for many years. The knowledge gained describes the environment for those who are curious as well as those who make a living using some part of this knowledge. The processes which have been used to develop this knowledge continue to prove useful in increasing our understanding of our environment. The attitudes of science are reflected in the use of both its knowledge and processes.

It is not difficult to find applications of science to modern living, and therefore is not difficult to discuss the application of science literacy to current problems of man. In recent years the public media has devoted a great deal of time to accomplishments of the space age. New propellants have been developed and new materials have been synthesized to withstand the extreme temperature changes encountered in space flight. Certainly these developments made use of previously acquired knowledge, and new knowledge about materials was generated. One would expect that some developments were the result of systematic investigation in a scientific laboratory. One would also expect to find some developments as a result of a "lucky guess" or "intuitive leap." The attitudes toward further exploration, curiosity, or longing to know and understand are further reflected in the dedication of many people. You can gain further insights into the processes by reading chronological accounts of the various space-age programs.

Not everyone appreciates the dedicated work of scientists. In fact, many pressure groups object to the further application of science on the basis of past errors in judgments of some scientific endeavor. Some pressure groups simply resist the extensive amount of money being spent on scientific research and technology. For instance this has been true of space research, where millions of dollars needed to launch a pile of metal into space could be put to use for other, more humane, projects, such as procuring food and other basic needs for the poor and sick. The resolution of these conflicts is difficult due to the side benefits of space-age research and development, such as better materials and processes for industry that have helped man in terms of basic necessities as well as conveniences.

You are urged to discuss with your classmates current concerns of man and the implications of scientific advances. Reading popular literature on the subject may also be helpful. Concerned citizens should read some of the scientific journals to gain a broader understanding of the interests and advances of the scientists. Certainly, the well-informed citizen should seek out both points of view. A recent publication by a scientist turned journalist may be of such value. Some have suggested that the scientific world in which we live is not consistent with the economic and social aspects of life. And the point may be well taken. The implementation of a responsible scientific literacy must therefore consist of a balance between the products and processes of science and the attitudes associated with them.

The average citizen or elementary school child is not going to be concerned directly with such issues as germ warfare and nuclear destruction. However, they will be concerned with the ecological problems that confront their daily living. In fact, the alert elementary school teacher can make classroom learning in science and social studies relevant by identifying meaningful scientific problems and incorporating them in the curriculum. The responsible application of a scientific literacy consists of the appropriate use of knowledge as reflected in the processes and attitudes expressed by the individual. The primary age student may express this by an awareness of accumulation of litter and talk about the relocation of the city airport. It is hoped that older students can make appropriate use of the processes of science through voluntary actions, resulting from a knowledge base appropriate to their maturity level.

Exercise 2–6   Using Science as a Responsible Citizen

Select a contemporary concern of your community and identify what appropriate action could resolve it. Then identify what attitudes, processes, and knowledge would be needed to understand this concern and act on it.

Goals for Instruction in Science

The scientifically literate person should be able to demonstrate the scientific knowledge, processes, and attitudes appropriate to his age level as outlined in previous sections of this chapter. A science education program for any age will include those kinds of learning experiences that will develop an appropriate balance of all three components. This basic guideline still provides teachers with a broad selection of science education experiences and goals. Many different concepts are available, process skills are varied, and the widest disparity occurs in the realm of developing attitudes. The question must be asked: "Why develop scientific literacy?"

General Education

Everyone encounters the concepts, processes, and attitudes of science daily. Facts such as rattlesnakes are poisonous, water boils at 100 degrees Celcius, and wood is not magnetic are of utilitarian value to many people. On a more general level, the concept of a food web is useful for everyone in understanding and appreciating the various ecological problems of our environment. The examples are numerous. Knowledge of our environment is useful to anyone who lives in any conceivable environment. Most people recognize the futility of memorizing all of the facts and are more likely to make use of broader concepts. After all, specific facts can be sought if the basic concepts are known.

Vocational Education

Among the first-grade students of the current school year are the future scientists, technicians, engineers, home economists, and elementary school science teachers. For these people, their first-grade science experiences will turn out to be the beginning of their life's work. The first-grade teacher cannot identify these children nor attempt to teach them all to be scientists. Even with all of the current interest in career education at the elementary school, most educators do not feel that teaching for specific job skills is an appropriate task for the elementary school. *Career awareness* does begin in the primary grades and gradually progresses toward *career exploration* at a later time. The rationale is that all students do make choices in their selection of a career based on the experiences they have had. All disciplines should attempt to orient the student to the careers of that discipline so that more accurate choices can be made.

Leisure Time

The amateur photographer, hunter, ham radio operator, and camper are examples of individuals who can apply scientific literacy to their leisure time. Each involves a knowledge base, some types of process skills, and certainly the attitudes discussed earlier in this chapter. Students can be introduced to a variety of leisure-time activities through the science classroom. The chemistry and physics associated with photography could be taught without reference to practical use. But students are more likely to be motivated when the content is referenced to such an idea as photography.

A careful look at this goal for teaching scientific literacy may provide a key to motivating students to study science in the elementary and junior high school years. Not many students are interested in science as a vocational career per se and they are not going to accept the idea that they need to learn concepts so they can function in daily living situations. If you are able to experience the joy of watching preschool and primary age students actively "playing" with a new toy or some other object, then you can appreciate the motivation most children have to continue with this "playing." Students love to play with animals, mirrors, moving objects, and rocks. Why should we attempt to interest them in other, less apparent subjects when what they are motivated to pursue can also be used to teach scientific literacy?

The Self-Directed Individual

In order for a person to be a self-directing individual, that person must have some combination of inquiry skills. To have these inquiry skills, it is necessary to have a broad base of knowledge, the ability to do specific process skills, and the appropriate attitudes. As stated earlier, the process skills and attitudes appropriate for science instruction are also common to other areas. With the addition of a solid base of conceptual understandings, together with the general and specific process skills and attitudes, the educated individual may be able to function in new situations as a self-directed learner. Although not all methods of learning science will provide this type of development, it is definitely within the realm of good science instruction.

Summary

In a limited way, we have sought to identify reasons for teaching science to elementary school children. Evidence to this point has been found in the nature of science, the nature of the child, and the nature of the necessities for the existence in our world today. The discussion has defined science education as the development of a scientific literacy comprised of the knowledge, processes, and attitudes of science. The previous section suggested that the kinds of activities chosen could be those which would develop career education, use of leisure time, critical thinking skills, and general education. For you as an elementary school teacher, faced with teaching more than ten different subject areas every day, how can you assimilate all of this and develop your own science program?

Most teachers will make use of the locally adopted program as their primary instructional vehicle. They will follow the scope and sequence as outlined in the program. Teachers may, after developing a familiarity with the program, modify individual lessons to make use of particular methods and materials they feel more appropriate. In a practical sense, one cannot really expect most teachers, especially beginning teachers, to do any more than this for the science program. What use is the material presented in this chapter to the teacher who is following a prepared program?

To begin with, the selection of the program by the faculty and administration will reflect their interpretation of what is needed to develop a scientific literacy. This is not to say there is a program available which is the best for developing scientific literacy among students. In fact there is no information to show that one given program is better than the other. But some factors will make a difference. If the school system decides not to purchase equipment, for example, they are saying that it is not necessary for students to have direct experiences for the development of process skills. It is difficult to learn to conduct inquiries with only a picture or mental image to use.

More importantly, the methods for teaching science advocated by the program and made use of by the teachers are generally regarded as being more significant than the selection of the program itself. A program composed exclusively of reading and demonstration cannot hope to develop the skills of process and attitude development that a program involving direct experience with equipment by all students can. To be more specific about the methods found to be most appropriate, subsequent chapters will contain information regarding what learning psychology can do to make learning more efficient. Following that, the variety of methods available for use and the strategies that tie these methods together will be presented.

One point needs to be made before closing this discussion of goals of science education. To be of use in the classroom, the broad goals of science education need to be made more specific. Consider a statement such as the following: The science unit on weather should help the students develop awareness of the effect of daily weather changes, and an appreciation for the difficulty of forecasting daily weather changes. This statement does help the teacher identify some aspects of what to teach the students. But it leaves a great deal of uncertainty as to what learning outcomes can be expected. Since the evaluation of the student's work will be much more specific than this, it is most appropriate to specify the particular intentions of the unit of instruction. This is the focus of the next chapter. Once the specific outcomes of learning are known, then it will be possible to move on to identifying the methods and strategies to be employed.

Exercise 2–7 My Viewpoint for Science Instruction

1. Write your definition of the term "scientific literacy." Your definition should reflect consideration of the readings of this chapter, but should be in your own words.

2. In your own words, respond to the following question: "Why should science education be included in the elementary school curriculum?"

References

American Association for Advancement of Science, *Plants Transpire.* Boston: Ginn and Company, 1974.

Bruner, Jerome S., *The Process of Education.* Cambridge, Mass.: Harvard University Press, 1962.

Commission on Science Education, *Commentary for Teachers.* Association for the Advancement of Science, 1970.

Educational Policies Commission, *Education and the Spirit of Science.* Washington, D.C.: National Education Association, 1966.

Harbeck, Mary Blatt and Albert F. Eiss, *Behavioral Objectives in the Affective Domain.* National Science Teachers Association, 1969.

Hurd, Paul DeH., "Science Education for Changing Times," in *Rethinking Science Education.* Fiftyninth Yearbook of the National Society for the Study of Education, 1960.

National Assessment of Educational Progress, *1969–1970: National Results and Illustrations of Group Comparisons.* Superintendent of Documents, U.S. Government Printing Office, Washington, D.C. 20402.

Suchman, Richard, "Learning through Inquiry," *Childhood Education.* February 1965, pp. 289–91.

3
Determining Viable Instructional Objectives in Science

What the Goals of Science Should Be

For a number of reasons, the process of determining what the goals of science instruction should be is necessarily more complex than formulating the goals themselves. First, a number of philosophical questions must be resolved before anything further can be done in developing educational goals. For example, the basic question in formulating objectives is what kind of educational product do we want to produce (that is, do we want to produce students who can perpetuate the best of the past, adjust to the problems of the present, or alter conditions for the future)?

Secondly, it is necessary to reach agreement regarding the process and nature of the input by students which will be accepted in formulating objectives. It is reasonable to limit student input to those areas where their level of expertise is adequate. At the same time, it is grossly unreasonable to assume that students should have no part in determining the goals which they are expected to achieve. Students will not work to accomplish goals they do not accept as viable for them. As the saying goes, "You can lead a horse to water, but you can't make him drink." Students must have proper incentives. The incentives are most appropriate when the students agree about the usefulness of the goals. Extrinsic motivators may be used when students do not accept the ends of the educational process, but less "real" education is likely to be achieved.

A third consideration, which complicates the process of determining educational goals, is the knowledge explosion. How to deal with the phenomenal growth of knowledge, in terms of implementing new knowledge in the schools, is not very well understood. The related problem of trying to decide which comes first, goals or subject matter, is also a critical question in goal formulation. As courses of study now exist, a teacher is given a body of knowledge to teach to students. Out of this body of knowledge he is expected to form an appropriate knowledge structure that is consistent with pedagogical considerations and develop instructional objectives which articulate this predetermined knowledge structure. Yet, on the other hand, teachers are encouraged to initiate their educational plans with objectives and select subject matter which is necessary in achieving those goals. In sum, formulation of goals in education is not a simple matter of writing instructional objectives which conform to the behavioral format. Rather, it is a complex process of considering issues in philosophy, selecting knowledge, and integrating student concerns along with societal expectations.

And so it is with elementary school science: The goals chosen for elementary science instruction in your school or classroom will be generated from a consideration of the needs of society, the interpretation of the discipline of science which can best serve those needs, and the particular needs, capabilities, and interests of the children in the school. In the last chapter several goals for science education were proposed. In this chapter procedures for developing instructional objectives will be given.

This chapter is divided into two sections. Beginning students should master the section on elementary principles of writing objectives. The advanced objective writing section is designed to bring a greater degree of sophistication to the process of writing objectives and requires a good deal of thoughtful study. Although it is highly recommended, the beginning student may omit the advanced section if he is pressed for time, and yet not experience difficulty in completing the other competencies outlined in the text.

How Objectives Are Generated

Elementary Principles of Writing Objectives

OBJECTIVE: *When presented with a general goal statement and a secondary level statement, the student will generate an instructional level objective that is consistent with the general and secondary level objectives.*

Instructional or behavioral objectives are usually based upon more general goals. In fact, their main purpose is to help in the achievement of general goals. General goals are usually derived from basic philosophical considerations. Instructional objectives must be consistent with the basic philosophy and purposes of the school. It is therefore necessary to generate objectives for instruction which aid in meeting more general expectations.

It is difficult to substantiate common acceptance of general goals by all constituents, but it is generally agreed that schools should prepare students to meet the economic and social conditions of society successfully as well as accentuate personal development. Schools should aid in the development of intellectual processes, social and domestic skills, and personal identification. Translating these goals into specific instructional objectives within the rubric of courses of study is the major curriculum task of the schools. In many cases, the whole task is left up to individual teachers. In others, secondary level objectives are generated and written into curriculum guides with accompanying outlines of curricular content and suggested learning activities. The teacher is expected to formulate specific goals and instructional activities from these. In still other situations, specific instructional objectives are generated by groups of teachers (or perhaps by groups of educators at other levels) and each individual teacher is expected to accept the goals produced by the group and devise learning activities which provide the necessary practice to achieve the objectives. Whatever situation the teacher finds himself in, he must be certain that the instructional intents of his classroom are consistent with the general goals.

A united effort is necessary in schools to insure that all general objectives are appropriately met. This is especially so in cases where the traditional subjects are offered. Not all courses of study contribute equally to the achievement of a particular general goal. The goals of each course must be articulated with all other courses to insure the proper emphasis on all important goal considerations. This is not an easy task, but failure to accomplish this coordinated effort has resulted in excessive emphasis on some goals and neglect of others. In addition, some goals have been attended to but not clearly delineated. This is especially true of such goals as the development of intellectual processes and improving citizenship. There has been a tendency to equate intellectual development with recall skills and citizenship with disciplined school behavior. Developing goals that aid in focusing attention more realistically upon intellectual consideration and citizenship is dealt with later in this chapter. It is sufficient at this point to conclude that the intents of general goals must be validly incorporated into the instructional goals and practices in the classroom.

A clearer picture of how to generate instructional objectives from general goals may be obtained from the following examples:

1. Suppose that the development of knowledge about science for the purpose of investigating natural phenomena is one of our general goals. From this statement, a list of more specific, secondary level objectives could be developed, such as: "Students will learn basic concepts on which investigations can be based." This type of statement suggests

another list of objectives at yet a more specific level for use in planning instruction. One such statement could be: "Students will recall from memory on a written exam the definition of food chain." Another might be: "Given the elements of a complete food chain, the student will place the elements into a sequence and defend his choice based on the definition of a food chain." In both of these examples the student is required to perform some type of behavior which can be observed by the teacher and judged as either adequate or inadequate evidence of achievement. To determine if the secondary level objective has been achieved, many such instructional objectives would be required. And in turn, there would be several other secondary level objectives which would need to be pursued toward the eventual accomplishment of the general goal stated above.

2. If the general goal was the development of intellectual processes, the following secondary level objective would be appropriate: "Students will be able to exhibit evaluation skills." Evaluation is one of the highest levels of intellectual operation because it incorporates a number of other cognitive skills. Mastering evaluation skills is an assurance of intellectual development. A specific instructional objective which may be generated from this secondary level objective is: "From a series of science fair projects students will rank the projects from best to worst and support their rankings by defending their judgment criteria and the application of these criteria to the judgment process." If the student is able to provide a logical rationale regarding his judgment, we can accept this activity as contributing to intellectual development. If the objective had not required the student to substantiate his rankings, we could only assume that the student expressed his preferences, which may or may not have been based upon higher intellectual processes.

It is not readily apparent just how many areas of study contribute to the achievement of general objectives. Consequently, many teachers simply teach the basic facts with little thought regarding how an area of study may aid in achieving general objectives. Usually, these studies consist of a topic-by-topic examination of prespecified areas of knowledge with students being required to remember associated facts and principles. It is essential that every educator examine each subject and determine what contributions he may make in achieving the goals of the school. The overriding fact which most teachers are confronted with is that they do have subject matter to teach. Perhaps it would be better if all subject matter were evolved from prestated goals, instead of assigning teachers specific subjects. Therefore, the subject and its organization must be viewed as a real constraint on the formulation of objectives. The task then becomes one of accomplishing those goals which can be achieved within the confines of a subject. (Certainly, there are instances where this is not the case.) In order to do this, the teacher must first order the area of knowledge so that all components of the subject are organized in their relationships with one another. Care must be taken not to use the topical organization usually found in most textbooks. Rather, knowledge must be structured as its components are related, which generally entails one topic cutting across another so that their meaningful relationships are accentuated.

Once the subject has been structured, the teacher can then formulate instructional goals which are consistent with the general goals and which can best be achieved by an understanding of certain portions of the knowledge structure he has developed. In this way the subject and appropriate objectives can be made to complement one another.

Exercise 3–1   Levels of Objectives

For the example goal statements and accompanying secondary level objectives below, generate at least two statements which would describe appropriate instructional level activities. At this point you need not be concerned with the style of the objective, only that it describe some act on the part of the student which can be observed by a teacher. Sample answers are at the end of the chapter.

A.   To learn the processes of investigation used by scientists.
Secondary Level Objective No. 1: To be able to observe accurately.
Secondary Level Objective No. 2: To be able to seek reliable information to answer questions.
B.   To approach everyday living with an application of the skills of inquiry.
Secondary Level Objective No. 1: To be able to identify problems accurately and specifically.
Secondary Level Objective No. 2: To be able to approach the solution to problems with an open mind.

Issues in Writing Precise Instructional Objectives

OBJECTIVE: *After reading the following section students will be able to recall at least three advantages and three disadvantages of using precise instructional objectives.*

Before discussing the fundamental aspects of formulating instructional objectives, let us first examine some of the issues frequently raised regarding their use. The term first used for a precise instructional objective was "behavioral objective." The use of this term is unfortunate because it has come to be associated with stimulus-response learning theories of behavioral psychologists. Such a view of instructional goals is much too narrow and has caused many educators with more humanistic views of education to avoid serious consideration of the place of precise objectives in the educational process. The use of precise goal statements does not preclude acceptance of objectives which are not specifically measurable, however. Objectives that can be stated in precise behavioral terms and measured can be included with goals which are more experiential in nature. A certain portion of instruction must be given to the pursuit of highly important goals which, although unmeasurable by a particular teacher, are so intrinsically praiseworthy they merit due consideration.

There are a number of advantages often claimed for precise instructional objectives. Among these is the fact that having to formulate such objectives forces the teacher to explicitly identify his instructional intents and measure the extent to which he has accomplished them. Such close scrutiny increases the teacher's accountability for his teaching procedures. Consequently, there has arisen a movement in society to require the intentions of all instructional programs to be explicated so that accountability can be made a reality. It is difficult to argue against any segment of society being made more accountable. Argument can be made, however, regarding the validity of the proposed measures to determine who is achieving appropriate levels of competency. Generally speaking, most human systems are open rather than closed, in that environmental influences outside the institution usually have a potent yet undefinable impact on the institutional processes. This is particularly true of schools. Therefore, a good deal of caution should be exercised when it comes to using behavioral objectives for the purpose of establishing a system of accountability. In time, such accountability may be possible, but for the present, there is dearth of valid measurement instrumentation.

Another advantage claimed for behavioral objectives is that they clearly identify what the student should be able to do as a result of instruction. In many situations, students lack a viable "road map" with which to guide themselves through the instructional maze, which is usually caused by the teacher's neglect to initially inform students of the instructional intent of the course and by his failure to subsequently refer to the goals when necessary to maintain a clear perception. Certainly, a clear view of the goals is needed in effecting the desired closure for a lesson.

Critics of behavioral objectives usually point out that even though precise instructional goals add clarity to instructional intent, they artificially constrain the ends of the instructional process. In the first place, all students are required to achieve the same goal, and in the second place, the goal is a very narrow one. This, of course, may happen when the teacher is either too rigid to differentiate his instructional goals to accommodate a variety of interests and abilities or too insensitive to realize that the sum total of instruction cannot be circumscribed by precise goal statements. As a matter of fact, in practice this has indeed been the case. Many long lists of rather trite behavioral objectives have been generated as a replacement for the traditional nebulous goal statements. Neither alternative is viable; it is necessary to include defensible behavioral goals as well as acceptable nonmeasurable ones.

Precise instructional objectives are good when used as a basis for critical analysis. If a comparison is made between the specific classroom goals and the general objectives, it is easy to determine whether or not general goals are being achieved through classroom instruction. This makes it easier to find out whether or not we are accomplishing what we intend to. This may be a threat to the incompetent, but it is an important advantage to anyone who is serious about the purposes of education.

The use of precise instructional objectives is also more likely to insure the inclusion of defensible instructional materials and procedures. Many learning activities which students are exposed to may be a waste of time. Once students are made aware of specific goals, they are less inclined to engage in activities that do not help them achieve these goals. Teachers are also less likely to provide activities which are inappropriate. One of the difficulties involved here is that limiting the scope of learning activities to conform to specific goals may constrain the creative responses of some students. In addition, it may restrict the field of possible considerations in a learning task and convey a view of simplicity to the student. It also may be that the learning activities designed by the teacher do not coincide with the learning idiosyncracies of some students. These considerations are, of course, important and must be attended to in the overall process of evolving objectives so that some learning does incorporate creative and idiosyncratic possibilities. It is important to emphasize that the position taken in this book is one of attempting to achieve a balance between the considerations of behaviorally oriented and experientially oriented curricula. As previously pointed out, exclusive emphasis on one orientation or the other is not likely to be viable.

Another advantage claimed for precise instructional objectives is that they make evaluation more valid and reliable as well as objective. It is, of course, important that student work be evaluated objectively. Behavioral objectives explicitly specify what is to be considered in evaluation. They hopefully preclude the insertion of certain biasing factors common in many traditional classrooms. Validity, which refers to whether the evaluation instrument measures what it intends to, and reliability of measurement are also increased when precise instructional objectives are used. When intents are clarified through the use of explicitly stated goals, validity is obviously enhanced. When expected behaviors are clearly described in instructional goals, a basis is also formed for more reliable evaluation. Independent evaluators, for example, are more able to provide reliable ratings when the object or process being evaluated is clearly delineated.

There is one danger that should be pointed out relative to measurement. If objectives are selected mainly on the basis of their measurability, many praiseworthy goals will receive little or no attention in the curriculum. This has been the case in many programs based on behavioral objectives. This problem can be avoided if general objectives include all of the necessary goals for a particular area of preparation and if specific objectives are generated whose achievement guarantees the accomplishment of the general goals.

Finally, precise instructional objectives are an important component of the Basic Instructional Model (BIM), which was discussed briefly in Chapter 1. It has been developed from research and development work in experimental psychology, military training, and programmed instruction, and is currently serving as a basis for a great many instructional programs. The model is particularly useful when it is used in a self-instructional, competency format. The BIM is a procedural guide to designing, conducting, and evaluating instruction.

The basic rationale for the BIM is efficiency. Essentially, the goal of instruction is to maximize the efficiency with which students are able to achieve prespecified objectives. Perhaps the one drawback of the model is its emphasis on efficiency and its resultant deemphasis on effectiveness.

Even though the BIM has yet to have its efficiency claim validated experimentally as a total unit, certain principles involved in its development have been derived from empirical studies. It seems evident that clearly specified objectives would help the student focus his study to include only those areas which contribute to achievement of the objective, thus limiting the time which may be spent on unrelated activities.

Exercise 3–2   Advantages and Disadvantages of Precise Instructional Objectives

The preceding section has introduced several advantages of using precise instructional objectives with a discussion of potential limitations. On a sheet of paper write as many of these advantages and limitations as you can recall. Then check them. Continue until you can identify at least three advantages and three limitations of using precise instructional objectives. Suggest additional advantages and limitations not mentioned in the reading.

Additional Exercises

1. Writing precise objectives is a popular topic for articles in professional journals. Review current issues of journals such as *Education Today,*

Science and Children, and the *Instructor* for additional information on this issue.
2. Examine texts on elementary school science for statements of objectives. You will probably find them stated only in the teacher's version. Not all statements will conform to the standards for precise instructional objectives as set forth in sections which follow.

Formulating Objectives

OBJECTIVES

1. Given a list of instructional objectives, students will be able to identify which contain any of the following weaknesses—lacks an observable terminal behavior, lacks a minimum acceptable standard, and lacks appropriate conditions under which the behavior must be demonstrated.
2. For a topic within elementary school science students will be able to formulate precise instructional objectives that contain an observable terminal behavior, a minimum acceptable standard of performance, and conditions under which the behavior must be demonstrated.

The first step in using the BIM to plan for instruction is to formulate appropriate objectives. In doing this, it must be decided what they should be able to do after completing the unit of study under consideration. Finally, the instructor must identify what the available instructional resources are, including his own expertise. Once this has been accomplished, he is ready to formulate his objectives.

In this section, only the basic pattern for formulating objectives will be dealt with. In succeeding sections, additional principles will be added to embellish the basic model with necessary constraints and considerations. These considerations of necessity complicate the process of objective writing but they make the process a more rational and supportable one.

A precise instructional objective is really a statement of instructional intent and is composed of three parts. First, it states in behavioral terms what a student will be able to do subsequent to instruction. Second, it identifies the conditions under which the particular behavior must be demonstrated. Third, it outlines the degree of proficiency with which the skill must be demonstrated.

HOW TO CLEARLY DEFINE OBSERVABLE TERMINAL BEHAVIOR

Traditional objectives usually include such terms as know, understand, comprehend, and appreciate, with no indication of how these goals of learning may be overtly demonstrated. Obviously, these terms mean different things to different people. Consequently, these terms not only miscommunicate to other teachers and administrators, but they also fail to convey to the student what is expected of him after he completes the various learning activities. A student may rightfully feel that he has been misinformed regarding the instructional intent of a lesson when such terms are used, because he has to rely upon his own definition of a rather nebulous term and attempt to respond in accordance with this perception. If it is incongruent with what the teacher expects, the student is always the loser. Even if the teacher understands his misperception, there is still a loss of time and effort which has been applied to a task with no payoff.

Terms which evoke a more common perception of expectation are listed below as well as in Table 3–1.

describes	measures	weighs	arranges
gathers	computes	classifies	sorts
counts	balances	defines	organizes
experiments	segregates	hypothesizes	induces
deduces	structures	compares	extrapolates
translates	interprets	estimates	selects
formulates	writes	recites	debates

These terms are more likely to convey to the learner the way in which he must demonstrate that he "comprehends" or "understands" something. It is not uncommon, nor should it be discouraged, for such terms as "comprehends" and "understands" to be included in a behavioral objective, as long as a more explicit behavioral term is also included to explain how the vague, implied behavior must be demonstrated. Ordinarily, nebulous terms add very little to a behavioral objective, but if the objective writer feels they are necessary to communicate instructional intent, they may be included along with the behavioral term. It should be noted, however, that one behavioral statement usually does not include all that is intended by terms such as "grasp" or "comprehend." The teacher should include all the behaviors which are necessary in "grasping" or "comprehending" if he chooses to use these terms. This subject will be more fully explained later.

It may also be necessary to add "behavioral qualifiers" to the behavioral terms in cases where it is not clear how to report the behavior. For example, students usually report their behavioral responses in writing, because this provides a record which can be more reliably and validly evaluated. Sometimes, however, other types of reporting are desired, such as in cases where a student is required to solve a problem. The important skill is solving the problem; the solution may be reported either in written or oral form. As a rule of thumb, any behavior that can be reported in other than ordinary written form should be so qualified.

The teacher should be cautious of using other forms of reporting unless the nature of the goal makes it necessary. For example, oral

TABLE 3-1   ACTION WORDS: DEFINITIONS AND EXAMPLES

These are the definitions of the action words which name the performances specified in the objectives of *Science-A Process Approach.*

IDENTIFY   The individual selects a named or described object by pointing to it, touching it, or picking it up.
  Example: Which of these shapes is an ellipse? (Student points to the appropriate item.)

NAME   The individual specifies what an object, event, or relationship is called.
  Example: What is this three-dimensional object called? (Student responds with the name of that object.)

ORDER   The individual arranges three or more objects or events in a sequence based on some stated property.
  Example: Order these shapes from smallest to largest. (Student puts the items in the proper arrangement.)

DESCRIBE   The individual states observable properties sufficient to identify an object, event, or relationship.
  Example: Describe this object for me. (Student states that the object is a cylinder, 6 centimeters in diameter and 10 centimeters long, and the surface is red and smooth and harder than my fingernail.)

DISTINGUISH   The individual selects an object or event from two or more which might be confused.
  Example: Raise your left hand. (Student responds by raising left hand.)

CONSTRUCT   The individual makes a physical object, a drawing, or a written or verbal statement (such as an inference, a hypothesis, or a test of any of these).
  Example: Come to the board and draw a triangle. (Student demonstrates the ability to draw a triangle.)

DEMONSTRATE   The individual performs a sequence of operations necessary to carry out a specified instruction.
  Example: Show how you would use a straightedge to decide whether this surface is flat or curved. (Student uses straightedge by laying its edge along the surface.)

STATE A RULE   The individual communicates verbally or in writing a relationship or principle that could be used to solve a problem or perform a task.
  Example: What is the relationship of length and width to the area of a surface? (Student responds that area equals length multiplied by width.)

APPLY A RULE   The individual derives an answer to a problem by using a stated relationship or principle.
  Example: What is the area of this surface? (Student responds 350 square centimeters.)

Adapted from AAAS/Xerox Corporation, *Commentary for Teachers,* 1970, pp. 22–25.

Conditions are important components of objectives in science. Often students make use of specific items of equipment in performing inquiry skills. These students are using a spring scale to weigh unknown objects.

reporting should be used for reciting poetry, where simple memorization and recall are not adequate. On the other hand, oral statements are difficult to handle and evaluate in ordinary classes because of the numbers involved. In addition, the teacher is prohibited from reevaluating responses unless they are recorded. Thus, oral reporting should be used only when it is necessary because of the nature of the behavior to be demonstrated.

APPROPRIATE CONDITIONS

The second component of a behavioral objective which will be discussed are appropriate conditions. Conditions refer to any special constraints under which a behavior has to be demonstrated. Examples of constraints include time limits, use of aids and equipment, and characteristics of equipment. Sometimes a particular condition may apply to most objectives in an area of study. For example, when the student is not permitted to use textbook and notes while demonstrating competency, he is experiencing a constraint. In this case, the common condition need only appear in a preliminary statement which applies to a series of objectives rather than being incorporated into each separate objective. Any conditions which vary from these common conditions should be included within the objectives to which they apply.

Sometimes conditions are so commonly associated with a behavior, or have to be present in order to execute the behavior, that making reference to them in an objective is unnecessary. For example, water is a necessary condition to swimming and baseball bats are essential in demonstrating batting skill, and therefore, there is no need to mention these conditions in an objective.

Some conditions are necessary to communicate to the student exactly what freedoms or constraints will be operable as he demonstrates competency. For example, in a 100-yard dash wind speed and direction constitute a critical limitation upon the speed of the runners. So critical is this constraint that records are disallowed when favorable winds reach a particular speed. An appropriately written objective for this skill might be: *With a tail wind speed of less than 5.8 mph,* students will be able to run a 100-yard dash in under 10.5 seconds. The *underlined* portion of the objective represents the conditions.

MINIMUM ACCEPTABLE STANDARD OF PERFORMANCE

The performance standard is the third component of a behavioral objective. The purpose of this component is to communicate to the student exactly how well the terminal behavior must be demonstrated. In the objective about running a 100-yard dash, the standard is "in under 10.5 seconds." This standard is a quantitative one. Quantitative standards, as the name implies, specifies amount or numbers. Usually, will be able to run a 100-yard dash in under 10.5 seconds. The italicized portion of the objective represents the conditions.

Standards of performance need to be understood by students. For example, if students are required to calibrate a spring scale, they must understand the need to verify their calibration by measuring the weight of unknown objects to within acceptable standards of accuracy.

The more difficult and demanding standards to evalute in a behavioral objective are the qualitative ones. These standards require more than counting. The evaluator must be able to make an estimate of the quality of performance where judgment is not based on an accumulation of a series of discrete units. More will be said about the use of qualitative and quantitative standards later. For the present, it is sufficient that you be able to distinguish the three parts of an objective and write objectives that contain the three elements written in an appropriate format. To help you develop these skills, the following exercises are given.

Exercise 3–3 Basic Elements of Writing Objectives

Directions: Use the responses in List A for the objectives in List B. Select the correct or most correct response. Answers may be found at the end of the chapter.

List A

a. Lacks an observable behavior only
b. Lacks a minimum acceptable standard only
c. Lacks conditions only
d. Lacks behavior and standards
e. Lacks behavior and conditions
f. Lacks standard and conditions
g. Lacks behavior, standard, and conditions
h. Is appropriately written

List B

1. Students will be able to observe the changes in the bottom of an aquarium.
2. The student must be able to correctly name items depicted in a series of pictures of simple laboratory equipment.
3. Without the use of aids, students will distinguish between an observation and an inference on a written examination, including at least one example of each.
4. Students will demonstrate their interest in geology by collecting at least twenty-five different rocks and labeling and displaying them.
5. After observing life in an aquarium, students will be able to identify organisms which eat others in the aquarium.
6. Students will really understand the law of magnetism.
7. Students will be able to name the stages in the life cycle of frogs, fruit flies, and meal worms.
8. Students will understand that certain factors limit the number of plants and animals surviving in each generation.
9. Without the use of diagrams or teacher assistance, the student will be able to construct an electrical circuit.

10. Students will be able to describe how water enters, moves through, and leaves plants.
11. Students must be active participants.
12. Students must be able to demonstrate their ability to identify and describe wedges, screws, and inclined planes in complex machines.
13. Without the use of aids, students must be able to convert a given number of inches to the equivalent number of meters.
14. With the assistance of a timing mechanism, students will know the appropriate time lapse root growth in eight out of ten designated.
15. Students will demonstrate their understanding of hurricanes by listing their places of origin, known paths, and control measures.

The following are possible rewrites for the objectives in Exercise 3–3.

1. After observing life in an aquarium over a period of four weeks, students will be able to name at least three changes that have taken place in the bottom of the aquarium.
2. Given a series of pictures of laboratory apparatus the student must be able to name correctly at least fifteen of the twenty items, without aids, indicated by the teacher.
3. Objective was adequate.
4. Of their own volition, students will demonstrate their interest in geology by collecting at least twenty-five different rocks and labeling and displaying them.
5. After observing life in an aquarium, students will be able to identify at least three organisms that eat other organisms in the aquarium.
6. With reference to notes or text, students will be able to define accurately the law of magnetism and formulate written proposals for experiments which depict how magnetism works.
7. From a diagram depicting the life cycle of a frog, a fruit fly, and a meal worm, students will be able to label the stages in each life cycle with 80 percent accuracy.
8. When shown examples of animals and plants in biological systems, students will be able to name at least one factor that may limit the number of plants and animals surviving in each generation.
9. Without the use of diagrams or teacher assistance, students will be able to construct an electrical circuit and correctly explain the flow of electricity in the circuit.
10. On a written examination, without aids, the student will be able to describe the process by which water enters, passes through, and leaves plants, including the seven points included in class discussion.
11. Of their own volition, students must actively participate in class dis-

cussion by making at least three responses during a fifty-minute discussion period.

12. When presented a picture of a complex machine, the student will be able to point to and describe any simple machines visible in the picture in ten of the possible twelve situations.

13. Without the use of aids, students will be able to convert a given number of inches to the equivalent number of meters in eight of ten problems.

14. With the assistance of a timing mechanism, students will be able to correctly determine the growth rate of roots in eight out of ten designated plants.

15. Given a map of the western hemisphere, students will demonstrate their understanding of hurricanes by listing the places of origin of most hurricanes, tracing their known paths on the map, and correctly outlining five of the basic control measures used.

Exercise 3–4. Writing Precise Instructional Objectives

Write ten behavioral objectives that include all three of the behavorial components. Underline the behavior once, the conditions twice, and put a wavy line under the standards.

Taxonomy Of Educational Objectives

OBJECTIVES

1. Given a set of cognitive objectives, students will be able to select the general level represented (knowledge, comprehension, application, analysis, synthesis, and evaluation) with at least 80 percent accuracy.

2. Given a set of affective objectives, students will be able to select the general level represented (receiving, responding, valuing, organization, and characterization) with at least 80 percent accuracy.

3. Given a body of subject matter, students will be able to write precise instructional objectives for each major level of the cognitive and affective domains (knowledge, comprehension, application, analysis, synthesis, evaluation, receiving, responding, valuing, organization, and characterization) which include the three basic components for acceptably written objectives.

In most any list of general objectives for science education generated by either national commissions or local curriculum committees, cognitive skills usually occupy a prominent role. Even though these skills have been emphasized as general goals, there has been little evidence that they have been operationalized in the instructional process. Schooling still tends to consist essentially of memorization and recall of factual information. With the publication of the *Taxonomy of Educational Objectives* (Bloom, 1956; Krathwohl, 1964; and Harrow, 1972) educators were provided with a system for organizing instruction oriented toward achieving cognitive, affective, and psychomotor goals. The taxonomy is a system of classifications for educational objectives much like those used by biologists for classifying plants and animals. It is composed of a set of general and subcategories of objectives which cover essentially the whole realm of learning outcomes which may be expected from instruction. The developers of the taxonomy have assumed that learning outcomes can best be described in terms of changes in student behavior. Consequently, they attempted to state their objectives in behavioral terms. It should be noted, however, that most examples of objectives used as illustrations lack the specificity necessary to qualify as true behavioral objectives. In this chapter, you will learn how to write specific behavioral objectives which reflect the various levels of the taxonomy.

The taxonomy has three major subdivisions: (a) the cognitive domain; (b) the affective domain; and (c) the psychomotor domain. The cognitive domain is composed of objectives that deal primarily with intellectual skills. The affective domain emphasizes interest, attitude, values, and appreciations. The psychomotor domain includes objectives based upon motor skills such as golfing, tennis, typing, and equipment operation.

Exercise 3–5   Classifying the Domains of Knowledge

Classify each of the following as either cognitive, affective, or psychomotor. (Answers are at the end of the chapter.)

1. Write a definition for force.
2. Draw a circle using a compass.
3. Apply a rule to change inches to meters.
4. Voluntarily check out additional references on a current science subject.
5. Develop a hypothesis for a situation which involves related variables.

It should not be assumed that all objectives can be quickly and easily classified in an appropriate level in one of the domains. Some objectives can be easily classified while others contain elements of more than one of the domains. For example, where would "conducting an experimental investigation" be classified? Obviously, psychomotor skills are involved in using the apparatus but this skill may be of lesser importance than the cognitive and affective components. The knowledge about science and the particular investigative skills utilized would be cognitive in nature; characteristics such as curiosity, use of laboratory animals, and neatness would be affective in nature. Deciding which is more important, the affective or cognitive skills, is not as easy a task. They may be so interrelated that it is nearly impossible to separate them. This difficulty has led some educators to despair and claim that classifying objectives is just an arbitrary activity with little real significance. Admittedly in some cases it is difficult to place an objective in one domain or another, but even so, classification forces us to determine what level of cognitive, affective, and psychomotor skills is involved in a particular activity, and subsequently to develop appropriate and sequenced learning activities that will yield the desired terminal behaviors. If classification is not attempted, the components of some skills may never be discovered. Failure to recognize all components of a particular act usually results in prescription of an inappropriate training model.

Probably one of the most important contributions of the taxonomy has been its effect on helping some teachers to engage students in higher intellectual processes. As pointed out earlier, schooling has consisted mainly of memorization and recall. When teachers asked students to "think," what they really meant was "remember what I said." Now there are more process oriented curricula for elementary school science and other areas in which mental skills are emphasized.

In addition to creating a greater emphasis on complex mental operations, the taxonomy has also generated more interest in the development of affect among students. Little or no attention has been given to systematic ways of helping students develop sound value systems. The taxonomy has helped conceptualize a means for organizing affective instruction in an appropriate sequence. Instruction in the affective area has traditionally consisted of "preaching and admonishing." The affective domain of the taxonomy points out that such input activities are only a beginning in the total process of value development.

When the teacher is considering what his instructional goals should be, it is imperative that he consider the ways in which his subject matter can be used in developing abilities, attitudes, and skills from all levels of each of the domains. Obviously, not all subject areas are equally useful in developing all skills. Some subjects will ignore some levels and, in some cases, a limited number of levels will be emphasized while others will receive only cursory attention. This is as it should be. Science education should contribute to those areas of development which it is best able to influence.

THE COGNITIVE DOMAIN

The cognitive domain consists of goals which have as their purpose remembering and manipulating facts, ideas, propositions, and concepts. As already stated, schools have generally emphasized remembering information and ignored higher mental operations. This has been done in spite of the fact that these higher skills have been identified as desirable outcomes of education. One plausible reason for this is the difficulty in evaluating the achievement of goals at these levels. The taxonomy has supplied suggested means for evaluating these skills. Further information may be obtained by referring to the taxonomy itself (Bloom, 1956).

The cognitive domain is composed of six major classifications: (a) knowledge; (b) comprehension; (c) application; (d) analysis; (e) synthesis; and (f) evaluation.

Some categories are further subdivided into secondary and tertiary levels. In this work, only the major categories will be considered. Again, if further information is desired, you may refer to the taxonomy.

The cognitive categories are arranged in hierarchical order from the simplest behavorial outcomes to the most complex. Thus, the cognitive domain starts with knowledge and then proceeds through the increasingly complex levels of comprehension, application, analysis, synthesis, and evaluation. Each classification is assumed to include the behaviors from all levels below it. Therefore, an objective written to engage students in analysis must also include skills in knowledge, comprehension, and application, and so on. For example, consider the following objective: "Given five articles which outline a position regarding the construction of ecological goals, students will write a position paper that logically supports contentions in the articles with which their position agrees and refutes those contentions contrary to their position. The paper must include the resolution of at least five arguments." The highest level of cognition required by this objective is synthesis. However, the cognitive skills below synthesis in the hierarchy are also involved. Thus, the student must be able to analyze the various positions presented in the five articles, apply basic principles for constructing a position paper, comprehend the meaning of each position, and know the components of the objectives in order to accomplish it. Only a part of the lower level skills necessary in fulfilling the requirements of this objective is identified in this example. In many objectives, there are several implied skills at each subordinate level which are basic to achieving the goal.

Knowledge Knowledge is defined as recall of specifics, universals, methods, processes, patterns, structures, and settings. The important point to remember is that all that is required at this level is to *bring the appropriate information to mind*. No manipulation of the information is expected.

The following are examples of knowledge-level objectives:

1. Without the use of aids, students will correctly define the terms "heat" and "temperature."
2. Without access to notes, students will correctly list at least two of the food chains studied in class.
3. Given a series of diagrams depicting the structure of the common leaves studied in class, students will be able to name correctly at least 80 percent of them.

Comprehension   Whereas knowledge implies simple recall of information, comprehension refers to understanding the meaning of information. Usually, the student demonstrates his understanding by using information in a limited way. The assumption is that if one can use knowledge appropriately, he obviously understands it. At this level, the student is able to make use of knowledge without necessarily relating it to other materials or visualizing its fullest implications.

It is useful to know subcategories of comprehension in order to increase understanding of the major category. These include translation, interpretation, and extrapolation. In terms of translation, comprehension can be demonstrated by accurately rendering from one language or form of communication to another. Translation has been properly accomplished when the rendering is judged to have preserved the intent of the original communication.

Interpretation refers to the skill of explaining or summarizing a communication. While translation involves a part-for-part rendering, interpretation requires a reordering or rearrangement of the communication. Explaining a concept in your own words would be an example interpretation.

Extrapolation involves an extension of trends or tendencies beyond the data which is given and the determination of implications, consequences, and effects which are consistent with the conditions described in the original communication. Extrapolations are often made with research data where experimental treatments are assumed to produce similar effects in populations other than the one receiving the treatment.

The following are examples of comprehension-level objectives:

1. When presented with a relationship of two or more variables stated in mathematical terms, the student will restate the relationship in a complete sentence (translation).
2. Based upon given graphs of temperature, precipitation, and cloud cover for the previous month, the student will write a paragraph describing the weather and utilizing all given information (interpretation).
3. Based upon a graph of average temperatures for the current month over the past 30 years, students will predict the expected average temperature for the month (extrapolation).

Application Application involves the use of abstractions in particular and concrete situations. Here the individual is expected to demonstrate skill in using rules, methods, concepts, principles, laws, and theories in situations with which he is not completely familiar. These situations may be similar to previous experiences but should be sufficiently dissimilar to provide a basis of application rather than recall of previous behavior repertoires. Much of what is done in schools is considered preliminary to actual application. Generally, the focus of education is upon learning and understanding information. Application has to wait until students leave the school. However, it is generally conceded that applying information aids in remembering as well as contributing to the meaningfulness of material. In addition, school experiences where applications are made help bridge the gap between theory and practice. When this is done under the supervision of the teacher, there is a greater chance for properly articulating theory and practice. The taxonomy serves to emphasize the need to include application experience in the school curriculum. The teacher may, however, experience difficulty in making direct applications in a school setting. For example, a preservice teacher may learn theories of child growth and learning but may have to wait until his practice teaching experience to apply these principles in a real situation. Such undesirable gaps in learning can in part be alleviated through contrived or fictitious situations where students can make a simulated application of principles. Needless to say,

Students may be given explanations regarding the use of a particular piece of science equipment like the equal arm balance and are asked to apply this knowledge to weighing unknown objects.

These students have been asked to perform an elementary analysis task. They are trying to determine the relationship between the number of drops of liquid making up a larger drop of the liquid and the diameter of that drop.

these contrived situations should be made as real as possible. The following are examples of application-level objectives:

1. Given information regarding polar coordinates, students will be able to measure polar coordinates of objects in the environment and map their locations.
2. Given samples of appropriate minerals, the student will apply the methods for determining hardness to each sample, to establish the hardness within one point of the correct value.
3. Given the weights of two objects and the length of a rod joining the two, use the "Law of the Lever" to determine where to place the fulcrum for the objects to balance.

Analysis   Analysis makes reference to the ability to break communications down into their component parts so that the organizational structure can be understood and dealt with. In this process, the relative hierarchy of ideas is made clear and/or the relationships between these ideas are made explicit. The purpose of analysis is to identify the subcomponents of a communication so that the intended meaning is made clear, determine the way in which a communication is organized, and conceptualize the way in which the component parts in their relationships convey effects and impressions. The task in analysis is to separate the important from the unimportant, fact from fiction, logical from illogical, relevant statements from irrelevant ones, etc.

Analysis can be made not only of communicated material, but also of such complex things as insect behavior, plant nutritional deficiencies, or an ecosystem. It should be pointed out that the conception of analysis presented here is not limited exclusively to the formal logical analysis of statements. While formal logical analysis is useful in some instances, many educational tasks in the public school require less sophistication. It is convenient to speak of most activities where subcomponent parts of a product or communication are explicated and related as analysis.

The following are examples of analysis-level objectives:

1. Students will be able to explain differences in a set of environmental conditions occurring in a given object or objects in the environment over a period of time.
2. Given data which describe the various stages in the development of a pond, the student will order the information to describe the most probable sequence of events in the development of the pond.
3. Given simple electrical circuits, the student will analyze the circuit to determine the path of electricity.

Synthesis Synthesis is the ability to put parts together to form a new whole. This process involves combining elements and parts into a pattern or structure not clearly evident before. Two points need to be emphasized about synthesis. First, creative expression is generally involved at this level. This creative functioning should not be construed to mean completely free expression since generally the student is expected to operate within given limits, such as particular types of problems, given materials, or some particular theoretical or methodological framework.

The second point that needs to be emphasized is that the product which is formulated in the synthesis process must form a consistent whole. This means that subcomponent parts must articulate with one another even though their arrangement may be unique. For example, a tentative hypothesis regarding the cause of a volcanic eruption, which includes logical support information, would display synthesis skill. Building volcano models where free expression is emphasized rather than consistent structuring is not an example of synthesis skill.

Comprehension, application, and analysis may also involve the putting together of components and formulation of meaning, but these are less complete than synthesis in terms of magnitude. The main difference between these lower categories and synthesis is that with the lower categories a whole is studied in order to understand it better. However, in synthesis, the student must draw upon elements from many sources and put these together into a structure or organization which is unique.

When synthesis occurs, it should yield a product which can be observed via one or more senses and which is composed of more than the materials supplied to the learner. This product can be judged in terms of its consistency and uniqueness of organization. In teaching students synthesis skills, it is essential that the teacher focus the students' attention upon unconsidered constraints and inconsistencies so that the product is a properly organized whole.

The following are examples of synthesis-level objectives:

1. Given a hypothesis concerning a topic about which he is knowledgeable, the student will design a way to test the hypothesis which is consistent with the design procedures established during class discussion.
2. Given the results of an analysis of the local town's air and water resources, the student will develop a statement to be sent to the city newspaper which incorporates the results of the analysis and proposes a plan to insure purity of air and water for present and future populations.
3. Utilizing appropriate materials, the student will construct a model to demonstrate an example of soil erosion. The effects of air and/or water on the materials utilized will be described in an accompanying oral or written report.

Evaluation Evaluation involves the ability to judge the value of material (statements, experiments, essays, conservation programs, etc.) which are used for some purpose. When judgments are made, it is necessary that criteria or standards be used as a basis for determining the quality of the material. Judgments may be made in terms of accuracy, effectiveness, economy, satisfaction, etc. They may be used to determine which of a number of materials is best or which among a number of products meets given standards. The criteria which are used may be either given to the student or evolved by him. If the student evolves his own criteria, it is essential that he be able to logically support them. It is also necessary that the student be able to supply a rationale for his judgments, thus supporting his evaluation and eliminating the possibility that evaluations be composed only of preferences. Evaluation is the highest level in the cognitive domain and as such includes skills at lower levels. Consequently, when judgments are given, it must be based upon comprehension of appropriate knowledge. Judgment also requires the evaluator to examine the subcomponent parts of a product to determine its internal consistency. Because these and other higher cognitive skills are required in evaluation, judgments given exclusively on the basis of personal preferences are entirely affective in nature.

Even though evaluation is primarily a cognitive function, there is an influence of the affective domain at this level. Certainly, values, liking and enjoying, are involved in judgment. However, the emphasis is placed upon cognitive rather than emotive functioning.

The following are examples of evaluation-level objectives:

1. When presented with opinions concerning solutions to local environmental problems, the student will evaluate each opinion to determine which is best according to factual material identified in previous investigations of community problems.
2. By examining each of three science fair entries, the student will assign a rating to each based on the characteristics described in the categories of hypothesis, relevancy of data, completeness of conclusion, and appearance.
3. Given the criteria for judging the quality of public health programs, students will be able to determine which programs meet these criteria adequately.

Exercise 3–6   Classifying Cognitive Objectives

Identify the level from the cognitive domain where each of the following falls. Answers to Exercise 3–6 can be found at the end of the chapter.

a. Knowledge	c. Application	e. Synthesis
b. Comprehension	d. Analysis	f. Evaluation

1. The student will be able to list from memory two characteristics of igneous rocks without reference to outside materials.
2. On a classroom written exam, the student will describe in less than fifty words the relationship of light to the process of photosynthesis.
3. After studying the four basic components for writing a report of an experimental study, the student will utilize these characteristics to write a report of data provided for that purpose.
4. Given a diagram of a cell, the student will orally identify at least four of the parts.
5. Students will be able to identify variables that may affect the outcome of an experiment which involves a simple mechanical system.
6. After watching a television program explaining the effects of soil erosion, the student will write a two-page paper in which he explains the ways in which erosion has affected the economy of the area. Examples from the program must be cited in the paper.
7. After a study of static electricity, the student will correctly use at least one principle learned in developing a demonstration of the existence of static electricity.
8. Given a series of statements about the results of an experiment, the student will be able to identify those which are consistent with given data from those which are not, with 80 percent accuracy.
9. The student will be able to determine the mechanical advantage of simple machines by applying one or more of the basic principles to seven of ten simple machines shown in diagram form.

10. From pictures of various animals, students will be able to classify at least four out of five examples on the basis of what they eat.
11. The student will be able to state the four characteristics by which materials can be identified and described.
12. When presented with a series of common objects, the student will describe the objects using at least four types of characteristics.
13. When presented with a description of an object, the student will choose one of a series of objects which fits that description.

Exercise 3–7   Writing Objectives in the Cognitive Domain

Write an objective for each major level of the cognitive domain which satisfies the conditions of appropriately written cognitive objectives. You may wish to have your objectives checked by a colleague or instructor.

Knowledge
Comprehension
Application
Analysis
Synthesis
Evaluation

THE AFFECTIVE DOMAIN

The affective domain is composed of goals which have as their purpose the development of attitudes, interests, appreciations, and values. There is little doubt that affective goals are considered important by science educators. In 1968 the National Science Teachers Association published a work entitled *Behavioral Objectives in the Affective Domain.* This publication was the culminating effort of several study groups which sought to identify what elements of affective education were useful to science education. (See Chapter 2 for further information on this publication.)

Nearly all sets of science objectives include affective goals. However, even though these goals are considered important, in practice little is done to develop curricula for attitude change, nor are tests available to determine the extent to which attitudes have changed. The problem, it appears, is not so much one of undermining the importance of value development, but rather one of difficulty in preparing appropriate materials and validly evaluating the attainment of goals.

The taxonomy (Krathwohl, 1964) has helped reduce the ambiguity associated with affective goals by outlining categories of value development and arranging them in a hierarchy, much like the one evolved for the cognitive domain. In the case of the affective domain, the arrangement is made in the order in which values are developed—from receiving value information up to the point where values are exhibited as a consistent part of one's life style.

The affective domain is composed of the following five major categories of levels: (a) receiving; (b) responding; (c) valuing; (d) organization; and (e) characterization.

As with the cognitive domain, the major categories are further subdivided into component parts. In the case of the affective domain, however, there are no tertiary subdivisions.

It is particularly important when writing affective objectives that the value, attitude, or appreciation under consideration be part of the goal statement and that the behavior which will be accepted as evidence of attainment of that goal also be included. This is necessary because an attitude can be observed only by some behavioral indicator. In addition, if only the behavior is present in the objective, we are unsure of what the affective goal is. It is possible that a specific behavior may involve more than one value or attitude. The following is an example of the appropriate format to use when writing affective objectives: The students will indicate their *commitment to the value of honesty* (value) by exhorting their classmates *to exhibit honest behaviors* (behavioral indicator). You may find the following procedure useful in writing objectives in the affective domain. First, write down the affect you feel to be desirable (see Chapter 2 for ideas). Examples would include "curiosity toward natural phenomena" or "cooperative approach to investigations undertaken in class." For the statement chosen you would begin by describing behaviors you would accept as indicative of the expression of that affect, as well as those behaviors which denote the absence of that affect. This list can then be utilized in specifying the desired objective.

It should be pointed out that care needs to be exercised in accepting a behavior as evidence of a specific value. This is especially true when the student is aware of what the teacher is looking for. His behavior may be designed to impress the teacher or for some reason other than the expected one.

Receiving The lowest level in the affective domain is receiving. According to the taxonomy, this is the level at which the learner is sensitized to the existence of certain phenomena and stimuli. At this point, the student is willing to receive or attend to value-laden stimuli. The difficulty of forming behavioral objectives at this level is obvious. The question that must be asked is: "What evidence is there to show that the student is attending or receiving?" Some individuals may accept the student's posture or the direction he is facing as evidence of receiving. This assumption is rather precarious, however. Not only is the teacher unable to tell whether or not the student is listening, but he has no indication regarding his understanding. Therefore, as evidence of receiving, it is recommended that the teacher accept verbalizations that show understanding of communicated stimuli. These verbalizations should not be confused with responding behaviors, which will be discussed later. If the value under consideration is, for example, honesty, the student would show evidence at the receiving level by participating in a discussion about honesty where an understanding of the rudiments of honesty is emphasized. The point is that the student must engage in some behavior which indicates an increased sensitivity to, awareness of, or attention to affective information. Simply sitting erect, facing the teacher is not an adequate indicator.

The following are examples of objectives at the receiving level:

1. The student will demonstrate that he is acquiring a sensitivity to present ecological problems by contributing to an introductory discussion on the subject.
2. The student will indicate that he is interested in good classroom discipline by offering comments about the subject in class.
3. Students will indicate an interest in discussing current events in science by bringing newspaper clippings to class.

Responding   Responding refers to active participation by the student. At this level, he acts out behaviors which are consistent with one holding a particular value. However, the element of commitment is not present. The student may respond either on a volitional basis or under obedience or compliance. At the lowest level of this category, the student may not have fully accepted the value even though he responds as if he has; in other words, if certain constraints were not present, the student would probably not choose to conform to the particular value or norm on his own.

At the next higher level of this category, the student must demonstrate willingness to respond. This represents a response based on voluntary choice. While it is not always easy to determine that a student is responding willingly because he holds a particular value, it is not so difficult for a teacher to regulate his behavior so as not to exhibit an expectation of compliance. However, even though he does not display an attitude of expected compliance, there is no assurance that the behaviors are a true indication of values which the student accepts. It can be said, though, that he is responding voluntarily.

At the highest responding level, students may be observed expressing satisfaction regarding a particular response. They exhibit pleasure, zest, or enjoyment. Generally, at this level, it is said that the student has an "interest" or, in other words, he seeks out and enjoys activities of a particular type.

The following objectives are written at the responding level:

1. The student will display an attitude of safety by observing the safety rules specified for use of laboratory equipment.
2. The student will demonstrate good study work habits by turning in his homework assignments on time at least 95 percent of the time.
3. The student will demonstrate curiosity about ecological problems by voluntarily seeking out information on at least one issue of concern to him.

Valuing Valuing refers to the worth or value which someone attaches to an object, phenomenon, or behavior. Valuing develops as a consequence of the individual's own assessment of worth as well as those of society. Through the interaction of personal and social preferences, values are slowly internalized and accepted by the individual as his own criterion of worth. Behavior at this level is sufficiently consistent and stable to be considered characteristic of the individual's beliefs. The individual is viewed as holding a particular value because his behavior consistently indicates this belief in appropriate situations.

This level is composed of three subcategories which represent increasingly deeper stages of internalization. At the lowest sublevel, there is sufficient acceptance of a value by the student for him to prefer being identified with it. However, at this level, the individual still holds out for possible reevaluation of his position. Threrfore, his position is a tentative one.

At the highest level of valuing, the individual exhibits a high degree of certainty with regard to acceptance of a particular value. At this stage, we can say that students are committed. They no longer doubt, but remain firm in their beliefs. A person who displays behaviors at this level is clearly perceived as having the value. Generally, he can be observed trying to further the thing valued, to extend his own development in terms of it, and to increase his involvement with it and things representing it. Often he is engaged in the activity to try to convince others or win converts to his cause. Usually, there is a zeal associated with his behavior.

The following objectives are written at the valuing level:

1. Students will indicate their commitment to cooperating with others by volunteering to be a reading aide to a student needing the assistance.
2. Students will show a high degree of concern for the safety and welfare of fellow class members by actively encouraging one another to abide by the safety regulations set for use of the equipment.
3. Students will demonstrate commitment to a scientific approach to problem solving by attempting to apply the process to science issues involving social problems.

Organization During a student's encounter with possible values, he soon is confronted with the necessity of organizing several values which are relevant to certain situations. This requires that he first conceptualize the value in a form which permits organization. At this level, then, use is made of higher-level cognitive functioning to deal with affective entities. In other words, at this level there is a necessary interaction between the cognitive and affective domains. Usually, the skills of analysis, synthesis, and evaluation are emphasized. Various values are brought together into an internally consistent system by comparing the values and their interrelationships. Then values are hierarchically arranged so that the more dominant and pervasive ones are able to exhibit the greatest potency.

This level has much possible application in the schools. Emphasizing cognitive value organization aids the student in making conscious choices which he can defend if challenged. Values that are carefully organized permit consistent behavior of a permanent nature which is less likely to be weakened by attack. In school, students can engage in learning activities which help them organize their values in a defensible pattern. With properly organized values, the student can increase the reliability of his behavior and at the same time achieve a greater degree of confidence in the validity of his responses.

Even though the organization of a value system is a personal thing, it is necessary to help students perform this task with a clear view of social reality. Values formed in the absence of the realities of social life lack viability because much behavior must be acted out in social situations and consequently must be fairly consistent with it. Because schools tend to be isolated communities with an excessive amount of artificiality, it is necessary to contrive learning situations with as much realism as possible, given the normal constraints of the classroom.

The following objectives are written at the organization level:

1. The student will exhibit his organization of the values of honesty and courtesy by making consistent written responses to fifteen situations contrived to require interaction of these two values.
2. The student will show proper organization of individualization and group action by incorporating both values consistently in a series of group science activities.
3. Students will indicate that the value of using the scientific method is organized into their total value system by using the scientific method where it is deemed to be appropriate and using other means of investigation where they are appropriate.

Characterization   At this level the individual has been controlled by an internally consistent value system sufficiently long to have adapted to behaving in accordance with it. His behavior pattern has become his lifestyle. Executing appropriate behaviors no longer arouses emotion or affect except at those times when his belief system is challenged. Individuals with characterized values are viewed by others as having the characteristics that make up their value pattern. It is relatively easy to predict behavior because it always conforms to the preestablished value pattern. The person simply does not act out of harmony with his "philosophy of life." To have arrived at this level, the individual must have evolved an appropriate balance between affective and cognitive functioning. He must understand what he is and why he has organized his lifestyle the way he has. Ordinarily, such characterization is associated with a high degree of satisfaction. It is likely that the student will leave formal schooling without having characterized his values. This is as it should be. There are still numerous experiences which will be encountered causing altered perspectives and subsequent reorganization of values. The school's purpose is to initiate the appropriate organization processes and help the student conceptualize the way he should proceed toward full characterization.

The following objectives are written at the characterization level:

1. Students will indicate growth toward the characterization of the value of honesty by consistently acting out honest behavior in all their dealings with teachers and fellow students.
2. Students will exhibit consistency in the use of the scientific method by always rejecting solutions to problems which are not founded on relevant data.
3. The student will indicate a consistent attitude toward objectivity by always approaching problems in an objective way.

Exercise 3–8   Classifying Affective Objectives

Identify the level from the affective domain where each of the following falls.

a. Receiving	c. Valuing	e. Characterization
b. Responding	d. Organization	

_____ 1. Students show a consistent display of ethics regarding pollution control by regulating personal and civic life according to a code of behavior based on ethical principles consistent with proper pollution control.

_____ 2. The student will show his interest in a movie on proper science attitudes by taking notes on the film.

_____ 3. The student will show his concern for the welfare of others in the lab by sharing his work materials during class.

_____ 4. The student will show his commitment to artistically appropriate choices and arrangements of science displays in his room by decorating his room in relation to these choices.

_____ 5. The student will consistently demonstrate maturity by being able to adjust to new information regarding population control in a way that does not compromise his value system.

_____ 6. The student will show that he understands the relationship between the energy crisis and pollution control by prescribing a position in an appropriate balance which incorporates both concepts.

_____ 7. The student will show his interest in biology displays by visiting a natural history museum when assigned to do so.

_____ 8. The student will show his interest in tolerance of other scientific views by participating in a discussion of these views.

_____ 9. The student will show his interest in science issues by listening to the videotaped science lecture series whenever he has free time and by encouraging others to listen.

_____ 10. The student will demonstrate a balanced perception of the rights of the individual and the rights of society with regard to artificial limitation of life, as shown by appropriate response to a questionnaire which properly differentiates these two values.

_____ 11. The student will indicate his commitment to science by checking out and reading numerous scientific books at his level and reporting voluntarily on these books to the teacher.

_____ 12. The student will exhibit a high degree of support for extracurricular activities by joining the science club and becoming an active participant.

_____ 13. The student will demonstrate his belief in scientific methods by always using them to devise and conduct his experiments.

_____ 14. The student will demonstrate his interest in science literature by reading all of the assigned material.

Exercise 3–9   Writing Objectives in the Affective Domain

Write an objective for each major level of the affective domain which satisfies the conditions for appropriately written affective objectives.

Receiving
Responding
Valuing
Organization
Characterization

THE PSYCHOMOTOR DOMAIN

The psychomotor domain deals with the execution of motor skills. Even though psychomotor objectives typically contain elements of both the cognitive and affective domains, the dominant characteristic of the student's response is a motor movement. The elementary school subjects in which psychomotor skills receive a major emphasis include

Some tasks in science have important psychomotor components like preparing a wet mount microscope slide.

speech therapy, physical education, art, and music. Other subjects, however, depend on such psychomotor skills as speaking, gesturing, writing, and laboratory skills to some extent.

The taxonomy for the psychomotor domain represents a model for viewing, explaining, and categorizing the movement behaviors of students. It is organized in a hierarchial arrangement along a continuum from low-level psychomotor behavior to the highest level. Its purpose is to help educators categorize relevant movement phenomena so that educational goals and experiences can be properly conceptualized and organized within the curriculum. The psychomotor domain consists of the following six major categories or levels: (a) reflex movements; (b)basic-fundamental movements; (c) perceptual abilities; (d) physical abilities; (e) skilled movements; and (f) nondiscursive communication.

Each of the above levels of movement is divided into subcategories. A more detailed treatment may be obtained by referring to the taxonomy itself. In science education only a limited number of movement categories are ordinarily used as a basis for developing psychomotor skills, which are generally the domain of other curricular areas. For this reason you will not be asked to make differentiations between the various levels as you did in the cognitive and affective domains. It is useful, however, to understand the various levels in the taxonomy and how they are related so that you can see how psychomotor skills you may be concerned with are based on the development of more fundamental movements. It is possible that one of your students will be unable to perform a particular psychomotor skill because he lacks a more fundamental capacity which is ordinarily well-developed in children of a particular age. Armed with a few basic facts regarding the taxonomy, you will be better able to diagnose these problems.

Reflex Movements The first level is reflex movements, which are actions that are ordinarily elicited as a response to some stimulus. These movements are part of the response repertoire of all normal children and are required before more complex psychomotor skills can be developed. You will not ordinarily be concerned with developing these movements unless a particular student has some impairment.

Basic-Fundamental Movements Basic-fundamental movements are another category of movement with little concern to educators. These movement patterns develop during the first year of life and build upon the reflex movements already referred to. Basic-fundamental movements consist of such behaviors as grasping, reaching, manipulating objects, crawling, and walking and are ordinarily learned naturally without training. Again your concern for the development of these skills will be limited to students who manifest an impairment of some type.

Perceptual Abilities Perceptual abilities is the next category and refer essentially to cognitive functioning. It is included in the psychomotor taxonomy based upon the fact that perceptual and motor functions are inseparable. Without proper perceptual skills, students are unable to make adequate motor responses. This level does have application to the science teacher because it involves the ability to make accurate observations which, of course, is a crucial skill in science.

The perceptual abilities category is divided into five subcategories. The first of these is *kinesthetic discrimination,* which consists of the ability to make judgments regarding one's body in relation to surrounding objects in space. It involves the capability to recognize environmental objects and control the body and its parts in movements involving these objects while still maintaining balance. Obviously this skill is critical in the use of science equipment and the manipulation of various environmental objects.

Visual discrimination is the second subcategory. It involves: (a) *visual acuity,* which is the ability to distinguish form and fine details and to differentiate between various observed objects, (b) *visual tracking,* which is the ability to follow objects with coordinated eye movements, e.g., following the movement of an animal; (c) *visual memory,* which is the skill to recall past visual experiences or previously observed movement patterns, such as animal mating rituals; (d) *figure-ground differentiation,* which is the ability to select the dominant figure from the surrounding background, e.g., when a child is able to identify the dominant moving object and respond to it, such as catching insects or other animals during movement; and (e) *consistency,* which is the ability to recognize shapes and forms consistently, even though they may have been modified in some way.

The third subcategory is *auditory discrimination.* This involves the ability of the child to: (a) receive and differentiate between various sounds and their pitch and intensity; (b) distinguish the direction of sound and follow its movement; and (c) recognize and reproduce post-auditory experience, like remembering the call of a bird.

The fourth subcategory is *tactile discrimination.* This involves the ability of the child to differentiate between different textures simply by touching. Being able to determine the slickness or smoothness of an object or surface is essential to properly executing psychomotor movements where the body must come in contact with surfaces in the process. In addition, the sense of touch is important in classifying substances as well as plants and animals. Children can learn much through this sense.

The fifth and final subcategory is *coordinated abilities.* At this level the child is able to incorporate behaviors which involve two or more of the perceptual abilities and movement patterns. For example, movements can be made to intercept an object along its trajectory while at the same time being able to differentiate the object from its background.

Physical Abilities   Physical abilities is the next category in the psychomotor domain. These include endurance, strength, flexibility and agility, and are essential to efficient execution of psychomotor movements. They constitute the foundation for the development of skilled movements because of the demands placed on the various systems of the body during the execution of psychomotor skills. Underdeveloped physical abilities can be a serious limiting factor in developing highly skilled movement. While physical abilities are crucial to the execution of psychomotor movements, science instruction will probably not focus on developing these abilities. There may be instances where some children do not have the necessary flexibility or agility to perform certain manipulations of science equipment. In these instances children may be given special instruction. Ordinarily it can be expected that students will have sufficient physical capabilities to perform the necessary psychomotor movements associated with science.

Skilled Movements   The category of skilled movements consists of two separate continuums—vertical and horizontal. The vertical continuum involves the degree of difficulty or complexity of the particular movement, and horizontal refers to the level of skill-mastery for each of the levels of complexity. The levels of complexity include simple adaptive, compound adaptive, and complex adaptive. Each of these levels of complexity has the following mastery levels: beginner; intermediate; advanced; and highly skilled.

Most of the psychomotor movements associated with science come under this category in the taxonomy. Also, the compound adaptive skills within this level are the most commonly manifest psychomotor skills used by children in science. These skills involve the use of implements or tools in the process of movement. The best example of this kind of movement is using science equipment.

These students are using psychomotor skills to prepare a circuit board.

In executing skilled movements there is a continuum from beginner skill through intermediate and advanced skill levels to the highly skilled. At the beginner skill level the child is able to perform the skill with some degree of confidence and similarity to the movement expected. This stage is somewhat beyond the trial and error or initial attempts at the learning task. When the child can minimize the amount of extraneous motion and execute the skill with some proficiency, he is categorized at the intermediate skill level. Once the individual can perform the movement efficiently and with confidence and achieve almost the same response each time, his skill level is judged to be advanced. At this level, the student's performance is usually superior in quality when compared to similar performances of his peers. Highly skilled performances are usually limited to individuals who use their skills professionally.

Nondiscursive Communication The last major category in the psychomotor domain is nondiscursive communication. This category of behaviors consists of nonverbal communications used to convey a message to an observer, such as facial expressions, postures, as well as complex dance choreographies. This category obviously has limited application to elementary science even though its development is important to the total school program.

The following are objectives written at the psychomotor level:

1. Using an equal arm balance, and the weights provided, students will be able to determine the weight of objects to within 5 percent of the actual weight.
2. Using the sense of touch exclusively, students will be able to differentiate between various objects with different textures with 80 percent accuracy.
3. Students will be able to adequately use the tools necessary to build an operating electrical circuit.
4. Students will be able to assemble the necessary glassware, tubing, and rubber stoppers to perform a simple experiment.

Advanced Principles of Writing Objectives

OBJECTIVES

1. Students will be able to explain what is meant by an if-and only-if relationship between a disposition or understanding and a specific behavioral indicator.
2. Students will be able to determine incongruencies between a disposition or understanding and a specific behavioral indicator in example objectives.

Over the last few years a good bit of zeal has accompanied the movement for writing behavioral objectives and using them as a basis for instruction. Several science curriculum development projects have sought to use precisely stated objectives. The goal has been to alter the prevailing practices in science education of forming vague objectives and then proceeding to confound students with a series of unrelated learning activities. Such a practice is considered pedagogically unsound by proponents of behavioral objectives. In the first place, when goals are stated in vague terms precise evaluation is impossible. Moreover, teachers and students are unable to exercise intelligent choices regarding the means for attaining these goals. Such a situation undermines articulation and coordination of effort and diminishes the effectiveness of the whole operation.

To many ardent supporters of the behavioral objective movement, transforming instructional intents from the traditionally vague statements to a more precise, explicit format is a simple matter of supplementing each announcement of purpose with a stated behavior which is easily observed and measured. This task, however, is not as simple as it first appears to be. It is not easy to achieve a high degree of correspondence between purposes and specific behavioral objectives. For complete correspondence an if-and-only-if relationship must be demonstrated to occur between an understanding or disposition and some specific behavioral performance. In simpler terms, we must be able to say that a particular purpose has been reached if-and-only-if a particular behavior is demonstrated.

Even with apparently simple psychomotor skills complete correspondence between purposes and behaviors is questionable. When higher cognitive skills are desired, an even greater lack of correspondence may exist. For example, if a science teacher desires to teach his students the proper execution in a scientific investigation wherein they incorporate certain skills which help to insure a complete and accurate investigation, he may inform students of his intention in an objective such as: "Without assistance from others determine by investigation the specific boiling point temperatures of a series of five unknown liquids, within two degrees of the actual value." The assumption made is that students can satisfy the objective of a proper scientific investigation if-and-only-if they measure the temperature within two degrees. In the first place this objective does not contain any reference to the subcomponent skills necessary for completing an investigation. Secondly the objective artifically constrains the learning task for the student. It leads him to believe that getting a correct answer is all there is to conducting an investigation. It is unlikely that any wise teacher would advocate getting the right answers as the only consideration. It is true that an investigation must be accurate, but other factors have an effect on developing investigative skills. Consequently, the component skills should receive appropriate attention. Such properly executed components as how to make a correct hypothesis, how to collect the right kind of data, how to analyze the data, and how to reach conclusions based on the data all increase the ability of the investigator. The question which must be asked about any behavior in an instructional situation is: "Can the behavior which the student is asked to exhibit be accepted as an indication that he has the ability or disposition called for in the instructional purpose?" If not, then the objective must be either discarded or altered to increase the correspondence between purposes and behaviors.

If the correspondence between the instructional purposes and behaviors of skill-level objectives is often found lacking, how much more prevalent is the lack of correspondence among affective and cognitive goals? There is little doubt that much incongruence does exist. In fact it may be impossible in some instances to formulate valid and complete behavioral indicators for goals at the higher levels in these two domains. For example, suppose the teacher wants the student to "understand the impact of pollution upon present American life." The teacher may formulate an objective like one of the following to express the behavioral outcome which he would accept as evidence of understanding:

1. Students will demonstrate an understanding of the impact of pollution upon present American life by achieving 70 percent accuracy on a teacher-made test on which students must be able to match effects of pollution with various aspects of present American life.
2. Students will demonstrate an understanding of the impact of pollution upon present American life by visiting industrial areas of the city where pollution has had a derogatory effect, and writing a paper in which the conditions of the area are described.
3. Students will demonstrate an understanding of the impact of pollution upon present American life by writing a research paper in which they include at least six significant sources that deal with this topic.

By examining the above objectives and attempting to determine the extent to which they are valid and complete indicators of instructional purposes, we see that the first objective requires students to demonstrate understanding by responding to items on a matching test. Logically speaking, unless "understanding" is construed merely as the ability to match words or phrases on a teacher-made test, we are in difficulty. Certainly understanding requires the student to grasp and assess an array of possible connections between the industrial processes and their effect on the environment. Skills in analysis, synthesis, and evaluation appear to be necessary in developing a sufficient understanding of the problem. If by understanding we mean more than can be indicated on a matching test, then measurement by this means is incongruent with the actual intent of the goal.

The second objective requires the student to display higher intellectual skills, but it still lacks completeness. For one thing, it does not specifically direct the student to relate the effects of pollution on present American life, nor does it contain an appropriate focus on the nature of pollution problems. In addition, there is no specific direction to the student in terms of things to be analyzed and evaluated. One thing worthy of note is that the objective sets up conditions for integrating appropriate affective data with the cognitive components. Affect is an obvious component of understanding the impact of pollution on present American life and should be considered an important part of this goal. The question is whether visiting an industrial complex will create the appropriate affective condition to bring about understanding. Even though such a visit would increase understanding of the effects of industrial pollution, it is unlikely to help the individual appreciate the nature of life in a polluted environment. Therefore, this objective must be judged incomplete, both in terms of its cognitive, as well as its affective, components.

The third objective is the most complete of the three objectives, but again it does not satisfy if-and-only-if conditions. The student is asked to use sources of information which deal with the impact of pollution on present American life, but is not informed regarding how he must be able to "deal" with the information, except as part of a research paper. Before such a paper is written the student must first have attained an understanding by subjecting the material to analysis and producing possible explanations for any relationships discovered. This objective ignores the affective domain altogether, and must also be judged unsatisfactory in meeting the conditions of completeness.

Another example may help sharpen the focus on some of the potential problems associated with writing behavioral objectives. In his book entitled *Preparing Instructional Objectives,* which incidently has served as the primer for writing behavioral objectives, Mager asks the reader to consider the following objective: To develop critical understanding of the operation of the "target tracking console." (*A target tracking console is a piece of military equipment*). He rightfully explains that no two people are likely to agree as to what is meant by "critical understanding." Consequently Mager rejects this term because it is not directly observable and leaves the learner in a quandary regarding how to organize his efforts in order to reach the objective. He then accepts the following objective as a replacement for the discarded one: When the learner completes the program of instruction, he must be able to identify by name each of the controls located on the front of the "target tracking console." The problem with the replacement objective is that few instructors would accept it as evidence that a student has a critical understanding of the operation of the target tracking console. Yet, it is used as a complete replacement, implying that both objectives are equivalent. If the instructor only wants students to name the controls located on the front of the console no one could object to the obvious gain in clarity and precision obtained in the behavioral statement. But what if "critical understanding" was intended to mean "knowing how a target tracking console operates." Under these conditions, "identify by name" falls far short in meeting the if-and-only-if criterion. A "critical understanding" may imply many things. For example, it may mean "to be able to understand the operation of the machine in order to make appropriate repairs; to be able to properly operate the machine and troubleshoot problems as they develop; or to be able to determine where and when the machine may be used and not exceed its limitations." The point to remember is that we must achieve conceptual clarity regarding what is really intended before behavioral objectives are formulated. Otherwise, it seems inevitable that the complete intentions of the teacher will be perverted by the press for stating his goals in a behavioral format.

The problem of conceptual clarity is particularly troublesome and difficult because too often inappropriate behavioral indicators are accepted as evidence that an appreciation is present. Some proponents of behavioral objectives have flatly rejected the validity of affective objectives because of this. They are reluctant to accept such things as "sighs in ecstasy when performing science experiments" as evidence that a learner appreciates science. No reasonable person would accept such evidence, but we are not consigned to exclusive acceptance of such indicators. The meaning of appreciation must first be understood in terms of its relationship to other concepts. When this has been clarified it will be possible to determine behavioral indicators for appreciation. Perhaps these indicators will not be exhibited on a paper and pencil test, nor will they usually be observable over short periods of time. They may require day-to-day strategy and observation by the teacher to gain the necessary data to make judgment in this area. The fact that achieving affective goals is perhaps more difficult or a little less objective should not discourage us from trying.

There is another problem with attempting to formulate affective goals in behavioral terms. Basically it is again a matter of obtaining conceptual clarity about the meaning of appreciation. A difference exists in the capacity to appreciate, depending upon skills as well as experiences. Appreciating science may depend upon one's knowledge and understanding of the history of the discipline and may require the development of investigative skills in order to come to full fruition. These subjects may be taught not for their own sake, but to provide learners with background and materials with which to appreciate the discipline of science. From this it can be seen that appreciation objectives are necessarily complex. Until such time as greater conceptual understanding can be obtained concerning the meaning of appreciation, formulation of behavioral objectives in this area must proceed with due caution.

It may also be pointed out that in some instances, no educational gain is achieved by transforming general, vague goals into more precise objectives. With some subjects, listing specific objectives helps create an overly restrictive teaching-learning situation. Thus even though the teacher may intend to incorporate a rather broad conception of an area in the learning situation, the student's attention may be artificially constrained by specific goal statements. The student may refuse to go beyond the confines of the behavioral objective even though a greater understanding may be obtained by doing so.

Exercise 3–10 The If-And-Only-If Relationship between Objectives

For each of the following instructional intents write objectives which as a group satisfy the if-and-only-if relationship. (Examples are given at the end of the chapter.)

1. Students will understand the significance of food chains in the balance of ecological systems.
2. Students will understand the impact of the American space program on technological development.

Experiential Objectives

OBJECTIVES

1. Students must be able to describe the differences between behavioral and experiential goals and explain the problems of evaluation inherent in experiential goals.
2. Students must be able to formulate viable criteria which can be used to determine whether or not particular experiential goals should be included in the school curriculum, develop a logical rationale for these criteria, and prepare an example of an experiential objective which is consistent with the criteria.

One of the most viable accusations leveled against behavioral objectives is that they form artificial and sometimes arbitrary boundaries to the learning situation. Of course the learning situation is simplified by specifically naming those behaviors for which the student is responsible. The student is able to address himself exclusively to the behaviors sought because he knows that teacher evaluation will include only the prescribed skills and information. Consequently, the student will not be inclined to pursue any personal interest because there is no reward for this and because most learning activities will be structured to insure accomplishment of the objective. Any learning activities which do not specifically train the student to exhibit the specified behaviors are usually not encouraged because they are viewed as not having any defensible purpose. A strict adherence to behavioral objectives thus not only limits the student's field for learning but also any inclinations to engage in responsible learning for self-gratification. Certainly the danger of teacher input-overload through the exclusive use of behavioral objectives is no less than for input-underloading through excessive permissiveness. Both are likely to create paralysis and ignorance.

It cannot be assumed that learning is somehow equivalent to specific behavior changes. Learning does affect behavior, but our simplistic groping with science curricula strictly circumscribed by behavioral objectives is at best premature and at worst a serious limitation to the learning process. Activities have to be included in the curriculum on broader grounds than simply the efficacy of the activity for specifically changing the behaviors of students. A balance has to be struck between input-overload and input-underload in terms of educational goals. The idiosyncratic preferences and learning styles of students must be taken into account. At the same time sufficient structure should be provided so that profitable learning takes place.

One way to reduce input-overload is to include experiential goals as part of the curriculum, along with the more specific instructional objectives. Not only does this allow for nonspecific idiosyncratic responses by the students, it also helps eliminate teacher stagnation which results from the daily observation of familiar, anticipated student behaviors. Teaching with experiential goals consists of having students engage in activities which are not constrained by limited specific goals. The difference between experiential goals and behavioral objectives is mainly in terms of specificity and measurability. For example, some outcomes, such as flexible teaching and empathy, are extremely difficult to specify completely and measure; yet, they are important skills for the competent teacher to have. Consequently there is justification for including experiences in the curriculum, which will contribute to the development of these skills.

In addition to developing certain skills, experiential goals may be included because they aid the student in organizing his own learning and pursuing personal interests. However, these activities should be engaged in only when they meet specific criteria. Students should not be permitted to engage in nonpurposeful activities or activities which can be accomplished just as successfully outside the jurisdiction of the school. Ordinarily, experiential goals should be pursued by individuals or small groups of students with common interests and/or purposes. The teacher needs to exercise a good deal of skill in listening to students and then helping them to clarify their views and the directions they should take in the instructional program. He must be able to adequately encourage students to reflect upon their experiences and report what they learn in a variety of forms. These forms may include writings, drawings, speeches, discussions, or a defense of a position. This way the teacher will be better able to encourage students to become informed and capable, but in individual ways which are difficult for the curriculum writer to predetermine.

If a particular science activity is to be engaged in by students it is necessary that it be justified in terms of meeting defensible criteria and contributing to the overall goals of the school. It must be worthwhile not only to the student but also to society. It is not sufficient to say that one activity should be engaged in because it is more beneficial than another. Obviously neither activity may be justified. Activities need to be acceptable in a more absolute sense.

The following are examples of criteria which may be used to determine whether or not to accept a particular activity as viable.

1. *Does the activity engage students in higher intellectual processes?* One of the criticisms made earlier concerning educational practices is that schooling is frequently limited to recall of factual information. This is so even though general goals of education usually have development of intellectual processes as one of their basic aims. It is often assumed that teachers avoid the responsibility of helping students develop these fundamental processes because of the difficulty involved in organizing appropriate activities and evaluating the intellectual processes. This indeed is true in many cases, but a good deal of the blame must also be placed on the fact that the nature of intellectual development and the means of its encouragement have not been understood by science teachers. In actual practice many instructors simply imitate the recitation-recall model which has always been in vogue, rather than expending the necessary time and energy required to aid intellectual development. Of course much of the fault must lie with schools and their organization. Classrooms with their present organization and current pupil-teacher ratios make it difficult to individualize to the degree necessary and to provide guidance to the student in his work. Given these problems and constraints it seems justifiable for students to be permitted to engage in activities which we believe aid in development of specific mental operations. It may be difficult or impossible to determine the extent to which the student is successful in developing these skills, but at least he will not be prohibited from developing them because of our inability to validly measure. An example of an experiental objective based upon the criterion of engaging students in higher intellectual processes is as follows: Students will engage in the activity of formulating a written plan designed to reduce pollution in the city. Note that this is a divergent learning activity which permits students some latitude in how to approach and solve a problem. Because the activity is essentially open, prespecification of the particular intellectual skills to be used and the quantitative measure of these skills is inappropriate. At the same time the extent to which intellectual skills were used can be inferred from the results of the activity.

2. *Does the activity cause the child to reflect seriously on his values and to organize his value system rationally?* When dealing with the affective domain it is necessary to involve students in science activities

that have emotive components, so that value development can be pursued in relation to feelings and attitudes. Much that is learned in science is couched only in intellectual terms, even though affective components are present. Avoidance of affect develops persons who are either devoid of feeling or who are unable to deal adequately with their emotions on an intellectual basis. Affect is understandably difficult to measure but situations can be contrived where attitudes, feelings, and values can be examined and properly developed. For example, students may be asked to role play different characters in order to get a better understanding of what various situations are like from different vantage points. This way they can gain insight into the reasons why people have the attitudes and values they do. This insight is basic to developing one's own value system in light of reality. Thus a reasonable rationale can be constructed for including nonmeasurable experiences where the outcomes are presumed to be in line with defensible affective expectations.

The following is an example of an experiential objective based upon the criterion of causing the child to reflect seriously on his values and to organize his value system rationally: Students will visit a forested area where ecological balance has been upset and destructive forces are evident and then write a paper explaining how this experience has effected their value system.

3. *Does the activity require the student to make reasoned choices and accept the consequences for these choices?* Certainly the school is one of the most protective of all our public institutions. Children are shielded from the realities of the outside world and frequently fail when they are unable to adjust to these realities when they leave the protective environment of the school. One way the school shields the student from reality is by not letting the student experience the reasonable consequences of his behavior. This is done usually to protect the child's tender growing psyche from the bluntness of the real world. If the child steals, for example, he is forced to clean the blackboards after school or some other unrelated task. We also shield the school child from many of the ideas or phenomena which he needs to understand in order to make reasonable choices. Then we propose to make up the student's mind for him through impeachments. Such tactics are as shameful as they are ineffective. A student must have the opportunity for free choice in situations where he must show logical reasons for his choices and then reap the logical consequences for these choices. In this type of learning situation the student should be expected to formulate rationale for decisions reached which are consistent with good reason. Through this means the chance is increased that viable choices will be made, thus reducing the frustration which results from making haphazard random responses that are inconsistent with the real world. Activities that increase the student's ability to behave more rationally and

consistent with reality can certainly be supported as important constituents of an educational program even though they may not be specifically measurable.

The following is an example of an experiential objective based upon the criterion of requiring the student to make reasoned choices and accept the consequences of these choices: Students will be required to select a project for the science fair, prepare it, transport it to and from the fair, and be responsible for answering questions about the project and making sure it is secure from damage and theft.

4. *Does the activity require the student to engage in purposeful interaction with his peers and to support and defend ideas in an active interchange?* Some of the most important skills to be learned in a school setting are those of interpersonal interaction. Through the interaction experiences staged in the science classroom students can learn such things as how to clearly state their views, how to make one's ideas understood by others, how to react to the ideas of others, how to get along with others and be sensitive to their feelings, and how to compare, evaluate, and react to the variety of ideas presented in an open forum. Having these skills is an obvious advantage. Our present society is variously crippled by our inability to properly communicate. Communication skills are desperately needed by every member of society because of the increase in social discourse at all levels of social living. The needs in this area extend from personal interaction to the international

If an activity causes children to experiment with and test problems they are interested in, it may be included even though it may be difficult to accurately measure outcomes.

scene. Activities aiding in the development of these skills should be supported as viable constituents of the school program even though their measurability is subject to question.

The following is an example of an experiential objective based upon the criterion of requiring the student to engage in purposeful interaction with his peers and to support and defend ideas in an active interchange: Students will participate in a series of debates regarding the issue of pollution, environmental control, and the production of sources of energy.

5. *Does the activity encourage the student to experiment with and test idiosyncratic problems?* The meaningfulness of schooling depends to a great extent on the student's view of what is learned in terms of its contribution to his understanding of himself and phenomena which impinge on his existence. It is understandably difficult to formulate behavioral goals which cater to individual idiosyncracies. But if the student does not view the learning as personally relevant and helpful, only half-hearted efforts are usually made to master the material. In addition, searching for solutions to personal problems and learning personally interesting information is the accepted mode of learning in the adult world. In the school setting, certain limits must be established but a good deal more latitude is possible. The school cannot permit unlimited explorations by students. Some things are better learned outside of school anyway, but experiences should be offered to students which permit a more personal approach to learning. This procedure will also better serve the student as he grows into adulthood. He will have had experience in dealing with personal learning under expert tutelage and, seeing the importance of a more scholarly approach to living, will continue to pursue this approach. Presently the opposite is poignantly true. School is viewed by many merely as a stepping stone to better employment, not as an environment in which to learn how to deal with life's important problems and questions. Experiences which provide a better connection between school and life generally can be defended even though the specific behaviors may be hard to define and the outcomes impossible to validly and reliably measure.

The following is an example of an experiential objective based upon the criterion of encouraging the student to experiment with and test idiosyncratic problems: Students will participate in a discussion about how science can be used to solve problems in everyday life. They must then prepare a written report about how they have personally used science to solve some specific everyday problem.

The above list of nonmeasurable, experiential goals is, of course, not exhaustive. It does, however, illustrate the necessity of including nonmeasurable goals along with measurable ones in the science program. Experiences such as the ones described increase the scope of the school beyond that of training, into the realm of educating children. Some courses of study, like driver's education, arithmetic, typing, and physical education will draw less frequently upon experiential goals. For the most part, their purpose is to train students in specific behavioral repertoires. On the other hand, courses such as social studies, literature, and science should include both types of goals, as they are appropriate to the intended outcomes of schooling.

Even though experiential objectives are not specifically measurable, these experiences should be evaluated. It is just that measurement will not be as exact. In the first place, students will likely make different, although personal, responses. Common standards are hard to establish for such differentiated behaviors. Second, judgment of performance must be made on a subjective basis under conditions where limited agreement exists with regard to what the standards should be. Under these conditions, it is hard to support specified criterion levels of performance as being minimally acceptable. Adequacy tends in this case to be more relative and less absolute, thus making it necessary to accept competency within wider limits. However, reasoned judgments should be continually evaluated in terms of their contribution to intended purposes with every effort to verify that treatments do meet expectations.

Exercise 3–11 Criteria for Experiential Objectives

Now attempt to formulate at least one criteria of your own which supports inclusion of experiential objectives in the school curriculum. Then write a rationale for the criteria selected and prepare an experiential goal which is consistent with this criterion.

Criterion
Rationale
Experiential Goal

Qualitative Standards, Parameters, and Evaluative Adjuncts

OBJECTIVES

1. Students will be able to formulate parameters for educational objectives having qualitative standards which accurately and specifically describe the intended behavioral outcomes of the objectives.
2. Given an objective with a qualitative standard, students will be able to formulate parameters which adequately elaborate the components of the behavior called for in the objective and provide additional clarity to the educational task.

3. Given an objective with its associated parameters, students will be able to write evaluative adjuncts which indicate the criteria to be applied in evaluating student attainment of the objective.
4. Students will be able to explain what is meant by the level of generality of objectives and give examples of objectives which they can defend as being written at the appropriate level.

QUALITATIVE STANDARDS

Objectives which are written at the knowledge level of the cognitive domain usually lend themselves to quantitative measures. The same is not true with higher cognitive skills and affective objectives. If, for example, we wish students to be able to name the bones of the body it is a simple matter to set a standard of 80 percent correct. However, it is not as easy to establish standards for such goals as writing appropriate conclusions to investigations or evaluating the quality of pollution-control devices. These goals require qualitative judgments by the teacher.

PARAMETERS

When qualitative teacher judgments are necessary it is not adequate to simply inform the student of this in the objective. Yet it is obviously difficult to describe how the teacher will qualitatively judge a particular product. What is needed in the description are explicit statements that tell the student what the elements of his response should be and the criteria by which the teacher will judge his response. These supporting statements will be called parameters—statements which elaborate what the nature of a particular response should be. They are particularly useful in providing direction where responses are expected to be divergent. Parameters help the student behave in a way that is amenable to evaluation by given standards. For example, if an instructor wishes his class to write poetry, he may want to constrain student responses in terms of theme, the use of metaphor, meter, and the like. In addition he may ask students to refrain from the use of such trite rhyming word pairs as June-moon, love-above, and singing-ringing. Even though the student may respond creatively, it must be done within an identified framework. With this added information the student can better visualize teacher expectations as well as evaluation procedures, and adjust his behavior accordingly.

The following is an example of an objective with a parameter: Students will develop a science fair project wherein they make appropriate use of the skills of hypothesizing, data collection, and developing conclusions. The topic should be one other than exemplified in class and should be dealt with in a new and interesting way.

In this objective, each student is encouraged to make an individual response based on certain parameters. These parameters refer the student to those things he must attend to in order to accomplish the objective. The factors mentioned in the goal are the ones the teacher will consider in evaluating the student's work. It is obvious that evaluation of such a project cannot be made on the basis of quantitative standards. In addition there is a limit as to which qualitative standards may be applied objectively. Subjectivity usually enters into judgments of this kind.

EVALUATIVE ADJUNCTS

Many times when students are engaged in activities that require subjective judgment they are completely unaware of how the teacher will evaluate their efforts. The teacher, however, has an obligation to clarify what his criteria are. In the above objective, students are told what must be incorporated into their work: they are not informed of the relative importance of each factor, nor are they told how each factor will be evaluated. In order to communicate this information to the student, it is recommended that *evaluative adjuncts* be added to the objective, where appropriate, in order to clarify intended evaluation constraints and criteria. The following evaluative adjuncts may have been added to the above objective:

1. The most important factor in completing the science project is your ability to prepare an appropriate hypothesis.
2. A judgment will be made in terms of how well the elements of data collection and conclusion are related to the stated hypothesis.

Evaluative adjuncts supply the student with such information as: (a) what the teacher considers to be the most important aspects of a particular goal; (b) any special or unique ways in which evaluation will take place; (c) what the teacher's evaluative criteria are; and (d) how these criteria will be used to judge the quality of student work. Their purpose is to provide the student with as much information as possible regarding the way in which the teacher will evaluate his efforts. Where qualitative judgments involving a degree of subjectivity are required, the teacher has an obligation to clarify his expectations with parameters and to elaborate his evaluation procedures with evaluative adjuncts.

A second example may help clarify how parameters and evaluative adjuncts are used. First, examine the following objective, which has no parameters: Students will study a pond community, a spruce forest community, and a desert community in the field and write a paper explaining the relationships which exist among the plant and animal members of each community.

The following parameters may be added to the objective: The paper must include the food webs and chains which exist in the system and an explanation of the transfer of energy between successive levels in these webs and chains. In addition, explanations must be made regarding the balance of life in the communities and the potential dangers which exist for creating an imbalance.

The parameters stated here are intended to more clearly specify what is meant by relationships and to help the student focus attention on these relationships as they contribute to larger ecological problems.

Evaluative adjuncts may also be added to the above objective: The following are some possible examples: (1) papers will be judged primarily on the basis of the student's ability to identify existing food chains and webs and to explain points where there is potential danger of creating an imbalance in the system; or (2) it is more important to identify the relationship between major members of each community than the various subgroups.

With the above parameters and evaluative adjuncts, students are provided not only with a clearer conception of the task they must accomplish, but also with the criteria the teacher will use in judging the adequacy of their work. It is true that to some degree, at least, parameters and evaluative adjuncts act as additional constraints on student responses. Realistically, however, teachers do have specific expectations which they maintain even though they may not do so deliberately. In addition they ordinarily have standards by which they make judgments. Writing and publicizing parameters and evaluative adjuncts serve the purpose of clarifying what the teacher is most likely to want included in a student response and how he is going to evaluate these responses. On this basis they serve a useful purpose. It should be noted by those who believe that parameters and evaluative adjuncts may artificially limit creative expression that these statements may themselves call for creative expression. Their purpose is not to limit creativity, but rather to provide a reasonable structure in which valid creative responses can be made.

Exercise 3–12 Writing Parameters and Evaluative Adjuncts

The writing of parameters and evaluative adjuncts is essentially an individual matter and depends upon the teacher's knowledge and experience. It is therefore recommended that the reader write several objectives from his own area of interest and then attempt to write parameters and evaluative adjuncts for these objectives. The objectives in the exercises in this chapter may also be used for this purpose. When you have completed your work show it to a colleague or instructor to receive feedback.

Objective 1
Parameters
Evaluative Adjuncts

Objective 2
Parameters
Evaluative Adjuncts

Objective 3
Parameters
Evaluative Adjuncts

Generality

One of the problems encountered in writing objectives is the level of generality at which they should be formulated. In the past, instructional objectives were usually written in a form that was too general and excessively vague. With the advent of behavioral objectives there was a tendency to produce instructional goals that were far too specific. Objectives must be written which are both precise enough to communicate clearly and broad enough to reduce the great numbers of objectives which would have to be generated to cover each infinitesimal item in the curriculum. If objectives do not have a sufficient degree of generality to reduce their numbers to a manageable level, it is not likely that their formulation and use will have much appeal to educators. In addition, reducing the number of objectives will probably have a positive effect on the student's perception of complexity of the instructional experiences.

An example of how to achieve an appropriate level of generality may be taken from the study of simple machines. It would be better to formulate a series of goals which students should achieve with a number of machines than to develop a separate set of goals for each one. Of course, this is possible only to the extent that similar goals are sought in each machine. Specific objectives can be written where selections have goals that are not common to other selections. Examine the following objective: Given a sufficient description of a machine students will be able to write an accurate description of the simple machines which are in use.

It is likely that an instructor may expect students to be able to achieve this objective for several types of everyday machines they encounter. However, having to write a similar objective for each machine considered during a year's study is unnecessarily repetitious. In the example, the instructional intent is sufficiently specific and unambiguous, and at the same time general enough to reduce the number of objectives which need to be generated.

Another example may be helpful. Formulating and testing hypotheses may constitute the major goal of a science course. An objective like the following may be used as the basic goal for most all activities where hypothesizing and experimenting are involved: Given the necessary equipment and facilities students will be able to appropriately formulate and test hypotheses experimentally for any of the science problems presented in the course. Hypotheses must be empirically testable and experiments must be safely and accurately completed.

Exercise 3–13   Writing Objectives at Appropriate Levels of Generality

Write at least three objectives which are general enough to be appropriate for a number of different learning situations and yet precise enough to communicate the instructional intent unambiguously. When you have accomplished this, write a short rationale defending your objectives as being written at an appropriate level of generality.

Objective 1
Rationale

Objective 2
Rationale

Objective 3
Rationale

Answers to Exercises

Exercise 3–1

A. Secondary Level Objective No. 1: To observe and record what happens when sodium is placed in a beaker of water. (Example response) Secondary Level Objective No. 2: Given a list of questions regarding the feeding habits of starfish students will observe a starfish and record the answers to the questions. (Example response)
B. Secondary Level Objective No. 1: Given a problem regarding the effects of pollution on life in a pond students will design an experiment which will supply answers to the problem. (Example response) Secondary Level Objective No. 2: Given several possible solutions to a problem regarding any science situation students will devise an experiment to answer the question which the problem presents without undue emphasis on the suggested solutions. (Example response)

Exercise 3–2

Advantages: (a) Forces the teacher to explicitly identify his instructional intents; (b) can be used as a means to encourage the development of teacher accountability; (c) informs the student regarding what he should be able to do subsequent to instruction; (d) aids in bringing closer correspondence between general goals and the instruction which takes place in the classroom; (e) optimizes the inclusion of defensible instructional materials and procedures; and (f) makes evaluation more valid and reliable.

Disadvantages: (a) May artificially constrain the instructional process; (b) May limit creativity; and (c) objectives may be selected in terms of their measurability rather than their intrinsic worth.

Exercise 3–3

1.	g	9.	b
2.	f	10.	f
3.	b	11.	g
4.	c	12.	f
5.	b	13.	b
6.	g	14.	a
7.	f	15.	f
8.	g		

Exercise 3–4

When you have completed the task of writing ten behavioral objectives in the appropriate format, have a colleague or your instructor check your work.

Exercise 3–5

1.	Cognitive	4.	Affective
2.	Psychomotor	5.	Cognitive
3.	Cognitive		

Exercise 3–6

1.	a	8.	d
2.	b	9.	c
3.	c	10.	a
4.	a	11.	a
5.	f	12.	b
6.	e	13.	a
7.	c		

Exercise 3–7

When you have written an objective for each of the major levels of the cognitive domain have a colleague or your instructor check your work.

Exercise 3–8

1.	e.	8.	a
2.	a	9.	c
3.	b	10.	d
4.	c	11.	c
5.	e	12.	c
6.	d	13.	e
7.	b	14.	b

Exercise 3–9

When you have written an objective for each of the major levels of the affective domain, have a colleague or your instructor check your work.

Exercise 3–10

1. The following objectives are examples which could be considered necessary to understanding the significance of food chains in the balance of ecological systems.

   a. Without aids, students will be able to name the general components of an ecosystem and explain their relationship to one another.

   b. Students will be able to explain the relationships of plants and animals in representative ecosystems (lake, pond, forest, tundra, seashore, desert, alpine, etc.).

   c. Students will be able to define the first and second laws of thermodynamics.

   d. Students will be able to explain the relationship of efficiency to the second law of thermodynamics.

   e. Students will be able to explain how the principle of stability is related to the development of a balanced ecosystem.

   f. Students will be able to correctly name and differentiate between any of the different types of food chains.

   g. Students will be able to explain how a food chain is related to a food web, and draw a diagram showing an example of this relationship.

   h. Students will be able to explain the transfer of energy in a food chain composed of at least four trophic levels and compute the percentage loss of energy at each level with 95 percent accuracy.

   i. Using examples students will be able to explain why differences exist in the potential imbalance of different types of ecosystems.

   j. Students will be able to explain the extent of imbalancing possible through specific disruptions of representative ecosystems.

  k. Students will be able to explain the amount of conversion to biomass which is possible in representative components of an ecosystem based upon size relationships.

2. The following objectives are examples which could be considered necessary to understanding the impact of the American space program on technological development.
    a. Students will be able to explain the relationship between money spent on aerospace and the development of other related industries.
    b. Students will be able to explain the relationship between the advance of science and the development of technology.
    c. Students will be able to name specific technological advances that have been derived from the research program in aerospace development.
    d. Students will be able to list changes in the American lifestyle which have been brought about as a result of the advance of technology.
    e. Students will be able to indetify specific examples of the change in buying habits of Americans which have come about as a consequence of technological development.
    f. Students will be able to relate specific figures which show the amount of increased energy usage resulting from increased technology.
    g. Students will be able to explain the nature of the relationship between technology, energy use, and pollution.
    h. Students will be able to relate specific figures that show the relationship between technology and urbanization.
    i. Students will be able to explain the impact technology has had on the development of values in American society.
    j. Students will be able to explain the impact of technology on the rise of consumerism and the problems it produces.
    k. Students will be able to explain the practical benefits derived from space flights and the concomitant understanding of our solar system.

Exercise 3–11

Your response to this exercise should be different from those given in the text and yet follow the format which the text illustrates. Have a colleague or instructor check your work.

Exercise 3–12

Check your responses with a colleague or the instructor.

Exercise 3–13

Check your responses with a colleague or the instructor.

References

Bloom, B. S. *et al.*, *Taxonomy of Educational Objectives (The Classification of Educational Goals), Handbook 1: Cognitive Domain.* New York: McKay, 1956.

Clark, D. C., *Using Instructional Objectives in Teaching.* Glenview, Ill.: Scott, Foresman, 1972.

Edwards, C. H., "Behavioral Objectives: An Updating," *Contemporary Education* 65, no. 1 (Fall 1973): 23–26.

Fishbein, J. M., "The Father of Behavioral Objectives Criticizes Them: An Interview with Ralph Tyler," *Phi Delta Kappan* 55, no. 1 (September 1973): 55–57.

Gagne, R. M., "Behavioral Objectives? Yes!," *Educational Leadership* 29, no. 5 (February 1972): 394–396.

Gronlund, N. E., *Stating Behavioral Objectives for Classroom Instruction.* Toronto, Ontario: Macmillan, 1970.

Kneller, G. F., "Behavioral Objectives? No!," *Educational Leadership* 29, no. 5 (February 1972): 397–400.

Krathwohl, D. R. *et al.*, *Taxonomy of Educational Objectives (The Classification of Educational Goals), Handbook II: Affective Domain.* New York: McKay, 1964.

McAshan, H. H., *Writing Behavioral Objectives: A New Approach.* New York: Harper & Row, 1970.

Mager, R. F., *Preparing Instructional Objectives.* Palo Alto, Calif: Fearon, 1962.

Popham, W. J., "Objectives '72," *Phi Delta Kappan* 53, no. 7 (March 1972): 432–35.

Raths, J. D., "Teaching without Specific Objectives," *Educational Leadership* 28, no. 7 (April 1971): 714–20.

Sanders, N. M., *Classroom Questions: What Kinds?* New York: Harper & Row, 1966.

Smith, P.G., "On the Logic of Behavioral Objectives," *Phi Delta Kappan,* 53, no. 7 (March 1972): 429–31.

4
Preassessment

Students probably never undertake a new learning task with a completely undeveloped behavioral repertoire. Instead they bring with them a large number of already acquired behaviors, abilities, and interests. Some of these previously acquired competencies and attitudes will have a direct effect on their ability to master the new task. In order to insure that students reach the level of mastery of which they are capable, it is imperative that this body of preinstructional behaviors and attitudes not be ignored. A careful assessment of the appropriate preinstructional behaviors should permit the instructional designer to more adequately direct the learner through the instructional materials and thus adapt the instruction and associated strategies so that instructional objectives are attained in an efficient and effective manner. Many of the principles in science build upon one another. Before a child can understand one concept it is necessary that he learn certain prerequisites. Unless the teacher knows where each child is in terms of this knowledge, she will be unable to prescribe learning that is consistent with the child's present understanding. No teacher should take lightly her need to obtain preassessment data with which to make instructional decisions. Failure to properly use valid preassessment information may result in lack of understanding and confusion, boredom, and failure.

OBJECTIVES

1. Students will be able to name the various components of a comprehensive preassessment program and explain how these components can be used in relation to one another in making a valid assessment of a child's strengths and limitations.
2. Students will be able to preassess a child in a comprehensive way and make a written conclusion regarding their findings.

The key to developing appropriate learning strategies and providing purposeful instruction depends to a large extent upon your ability to preassess or diagnose each child and the learning situation in which instruction takes place. In order to accomplish this most important task preassessment should not be limited exclusively to such devices as achievement and IQ tests. It is best to take a sufficiently comprehensive assessment so that related components can be seen for what they are. For example, a child's lack of academic competence may be related to a poor self-concept rather than intellectual ability.

Sometimes there is a conflict regarding what role the teacher should occupy with regard to preassessment and diagnosis. Many teachers view their role as one of evaluating student performance. This conflicts to some degree with the role of the teacher as one who relates to children and tries to determine their needs. If a teacher perceives himself as an evaluator only, it may be difficult for him to get an authentic analysis of the student. Students are likely to be on guard and attempt to conform to what they believe the teacher wants. They may be afraid to disclose their weaknesses, because they always want to impress the teacher in the judge-like role he occupies.

Much of the difficulty encountered in making valid diagnoses involves the teacher's own view of himself. In the role of evaluator, instead of a diagnostician, the teacher will probably attach a degree of worth to whatever he sees. In contrast, as a diagnostician, the teacher simply tries to identify conditions, situations, or problems by noting signs and symptoms. In doing this the diagnostician must maintain neutrality, or a nonjudgmental attitude, viewing symptoms as neither good nor bad, but as growth-facilitating or growth-inhibiting. This attitude leaves the teacher free to use the preassessment data to work with the various conditions that influence learning in a way that will clear away obstructions, and thus allow students to use their potential to the fullest in achieving educational goals.

You will need to learn to be objective in using the data which comes from your attempts at preassessment. You will need to exercise caution that your own attitudes do not get in the way of proper decision making. This does not mean that you will always have well-founded empirical information with which to work. You may still have to use intuition and hunches, but these should be unbiased and based upon something other than uneducated guesses. Uneducated guessing may lead a teacher far afield and create difficulty for children.

The purpose of diagnosis is to assess a child's individual needs, learning styles, or problems on a qualitative level. Diagnosis is therefore not an end it self. Rather it is a way to bring about more effective and efficient learning. It is a way of helping the teacher understand the child better, so that she can enter into a plan of constructive instruction with the child. As part of this process the teacher should seek not so much to find out what the child knows but rather to discover the extent to which the child can modify himself in order to reach his fullest potential. The teacher thus becomes an interpreter of potential rather than a mere judge.

In developing to their fullest potential, children need more than just the opportunity to progress at their own rates through a set of prespecified materials. Rather, they need individual structures and approaches to learning. There are many qualitative factors involved. Each child will evidence a unique potential, and will be different in attitudes as well as learning styles. The task of organizing instructional experiences which take these differences into account is an infinitely complex task. However, the first step in simplifying this complexity is to make appropriate preassessments. Properly "tuning in to each child" will serve not only to better prepare you to provide appropriate learning, but will also strengthen student-teacher relationships and enhance the whole instructional program.

Diagnostic Information Sought by the Teacher

As indicated earlier, there are many factors which influence a child's ability to benefit to the greatest extent form schooling. Without consulting a sufficiently comprehensive set of factors, it is always possible that the more critical factors will be overlooked. Ordinarily it is wise to view the behavior of children as the product of multiple causation. The child's social, emotional, physical, mental, perceptual, and attitudinal state all influence his behavior simultaneously. At any time, one factor may be dominant, but each may need to be analyzed to determine what role it is playing in the child's educational life.

There are at least five major areas which a teacher must keep in mind when fulfilling his/her diagnostic role. First, he must look at the child's person—his lifestyle, his self-concept, his needs, and the obstacles to his growth. Second, he must determine the child's potential—both those that are apparent as well as those that are hidden. In addition, the child's handicaps and other factors which may lead to dysfunction must be identified. Third, he must examine the child's learning styles. This includes the learning modalities which he prefers, as well as his dispositions or "sets" toward learning. Fourth, he must be able to see the child's abilities and achievements within a developmental and experiential framework that helps him to determine whether or not the child is ready to succeed with the instructional program. Fifth, he must be able to examine the environment itself and determine whether it properly articulates with the child's patterns of growth and facilitates development of full potential (Seaberg, 1974).

The child's concept of his world and his enjoyment of it are generally influenced by a wide variety of pre-school experiences.

The Child's Person

A child's success in school depends extensively upon his personality and associated behaviors. For example, an obnoxious child is unlikely to recieve positive imput from either the teacher or his peers. Each child brings a unique biological structure with him into the world. In addition there may already be certain idiosyncratic behavior tendencies by the time a child is born. In any case, given what he is born with, the child develops his self-concept as a consequence of the interaction between his own unique self and certain unique aspects of the world in which he finds himself. With the great variability thus produced, it is no wonder that such great diversity exists between individuals. As a child grows, his most significant relationships are found in the family setting. The feelings he has about himself are reflections of the feelings that he perceives his parents have toward him. Later on, siblings, the peer group, teachers and other important adults influence the development of his self-concept. Each of these influences has its impact on him and forms the basic behavior patterns which we can observe.

In order to understand a child and prescribe learning for him which satisfies his needs and contributes proper growth in his self-concept, it is necessary to understand him as an individual. What is good for one child, may not necessarily be good for another. In order to find out what will enchance each child's schooling experience, the teacher needs to diagnose the nature of each child's personality.

Self-concept is a very critical aspect of one's learning capability. Poor self-concept results in low achievement and discipline problems. Research in a wide variety of areas supports the need for learners to have a good self-concept. Coopersmith (1967), for example, found that individuals who were high in self-esteem were success-oriented, independent, creative, confident, socially independent, stable, free from anxiety, and able to cope with events. Low-esteem individuals were found to be the opposite. They did not trust themselves, were reluctant to express themselves in groups, were listeners rather than participants, and tended to be self-conscious and self-preoccupied. In addition, low-esteem individuals suffer from feelings of inadequacy and unworthiness, and because of these feeling, they avoid close relationships. Thus they often feel isolated or alienated (Coopersmith, 1967).

The teacher's attitude figures prominently into the child's self-concept. The more positive the child's perception of the teacher's feelings toward him, the better his achievement tends to be, in addition to improved classroom behavior (La Beene and Greene, 1969). These as well as other studies point to the importance of self-concept in diagnosing the educational development of the child. Since achievement levels, as well as general classroom decorum, depends so heavily upon self-concept, teachers must be able to diagnose it and alter the school environment to enhance it. In this way one of the greatest roadblocks to learning can be removed.

Potentials

The schools have traditionally looked only at a limited aspect of children's potentials. In general only a very narrow range of academic potential has been focused upon. Many of these narrow emphases do not contain some of the more important skills which can be developed in teaching science. For example, most intelligence tests simply measure the child's ability to use language as a way of processing and understanding his world. However, such testing procedures do not square many times with the child's actual experience and consequently are not valid diagnostic tools. Human intelligence is multi-faceted, and composed of a host of abilities with an almost infinite number of combinations. No two individuals are identical in their intellectual capacity. In spite of this, children do have some common tendencies, which permit us to group them as necessary. Some children may have a high degree of verbal fluency and yet be low in making divergent responses. Other children may possess many of the creative skills and yet lack analytical skills. Properly diagnosing the presence of these skills provides the teacher with a basis for prescribing the kinds of science activities which various children will find most rewarding to be involved in.

In diagnosing student abilities and prescribing instruction, the teacher should be careful not to have them engage in activities which focus exclusively upon skills that they already have. Many different kinds of qualities can be assets to the individual as well as to society. It is true that people tend to exhibit their strengths and cover up their deficiencies. In addition, it is a good idea to help children become successful using the abilities they are strongest in. However, children also need to develop and gain confidence in using skills and abilities that they are not very proficient in, so that they are able to broaden and enrich their lives, as well as fortify their self-concept. Some children have potentials that they are completely unaware of and may never encounter situations which bring these talents out unless the teacher provides them. The teacher needs to exercise caution in developing children's latent abilities, to insure that they do not experience excessive failure and refuse to pursue developmental activities.

Many potentials are readily apparent to the teacher. Children with strong intellectual capacities stand out immediately and are noticed by all, because they take leadership roles in discussions and are often engaged in reading and investigating. Children who excell socially are usually the center of attention. Their ideas become the basis for group action and other students prefer to be in association with them and to follow their directions. Children with unusual physical skills are also striking. They win the races and games and in this way gain the admiration of all.

It is an easy matter to identify the skills of youngsters who stand out, but what about children whose talents are more or less hidden? Their skills also need to be discovered and encouraged so that they can receive the necessary help and experiences to enhance the development of these talents. It would be ideal if teacher's attempted to discover and encourage some potential in each student. For example, some children may be more adept at one aspect of science experiments than another. The teacher must be sensitive to these differences so that tasks can be assigned appropriately.

Some children learn best by seeing.

Learning Style

Children do not all learn in the same way. Instead, each child learns in the way he has learned to learn. Teachers are prone to forget this fact and consequently are confronted with the frustrations associated with their attempts to use the same teaching-learning strategies for all of their students. It can also be a frustration to have to approach students in such a variety of ways because of differences in learning style. Far too often teachers engage in trial and error in their attempt to find out how a particular child may best learn.

In any classroom, there are probably no two students who learn the same things in the same way. Some have different ways of conceptualizing and organizing information. Some learn best through reading while others benefit more from listening or doing things physically. Some children prefer to work under pressure of deadlines while for others pressure only blocks their ability to learn. Some children also work and learn better when they know that many others are ahead of them. Some children may give up on such situations and can only apply themselves to learning when they feel they are ahead of their peers.

Learning styles may be categorized as visual (reading), aural (listening), or physical (doing). Some individuals may favor only one style exclusively while others may use a combination of them:

> For a long time now, teachers and guidance workers have tended to ignore the concept of different styles of learning. They have instead focused their attention on emotion, motivation, and personality as causes for learning or failure to learn. When confronted with an intellectually able student whose learning fails to measure up to his learning potential, they have tended to attribute this failure to an emotional block or personality conflict. Little attention has been given to how a pupil's learning could be improved simply by concentrating on the way he works and learns . . . a careful analysis of the way a child works and learns is of greater value than speculation about his emotional state. He may indeed feel sibling rivalry or certain irrational fears, but these conditions may not affect his learning as much as the methods the teacher uses to teach him. The important consideration . . . is whether the methods of learning imposed by the teacher utilize sufficiently the strengths in the child's style of learning (Riesman, 1966).

Gould (1964) has reported major differences between children who learn by seeing and those who learn by hearing. The seeing learner acquires knowledge through visual channels and understands and processes his world by visualizing it. The hearing learner, on the other hand, understands by listening and verbalizing about it; he usually translates visual stimuli into words before he can deal with them.

Children's learning styles, seeing versus hearing, will influence how well they score on standard IQ test. A seeing learner, even though he may be bright, will often exhibit clumsiness in his verbalizations and appear to be less intelligent than he really is. In addition, time tests usually distress him, and this may also influence our perceptions of his ability.

The seeing learner does not feel a need to talk problems through. Consequently he is likely to be a quiet child. This type of child readily adapts to new situations. He adjusts well in social situations and generally keeps out of trouble. Because of these attributes, his capabilities may go unnoticed until he is well along in his schooling. It may be junior or senior high before his talents in art, math, science, and descriptive writing are noticed. The teacher will have to insure that his special probelms are dealt with and that he is not ignored and neglected.

On the other hand, auditory learners score well on standard IQ tests. They do not succumb to time pressures associated with testing. In addition, they do well in reading. In fact this is the primary way in which they receive knowledge. However, auditory learners may have trouble with writing and arithmetic, because of their inability to visualize. They will make better progress in math if they can do the majority of their learning on a verbal level.

Hearing learners need to hear themselves in the process of learning. They do not know what they think, at least in an organized way, until they hear themselves say it. You will notice that they talk or at least move their lips when they read. This may at first appear foolish, but should not necessarily be discouraged. So long as they are allowed to learn in this manner they arrive at proper solutions eventually. When they have a problem in their learning, the teacher must discuss it with them. The hearing learner needs to have new situations explained to him before they have adequate meaning. The teacher should therefore explain any new object, situation, or process when it is shown to learners (Gould, 1964).

Some children learn best by hearing as opposed to seeing.

Children also differ in terms of cognitive styles. Despite the lack of research information, many teachers report that students perceive the same task differently. Some students comprehend situations better through discussion rather than by reading and independent study and some are able to analyze and evaluate information inductively, while others are not. Differences among children in styles of perception, cognition, and conceptualization are probably as real as the differences in general intellectual ability and educational achievement. Kagan, (1964) for example, found that some children had a preference for grouping objects on an analytical basis. Two cognitive dispositions appeared to underlie these analytic groupings. The first was the tendency to reflect on alternative solutions or classifications and the other was the tendency to perceive and analyze the array into component parts. Other children seemed to group objects on the basis of either a holistic relationship between the components or by a rapid global inference. The dimension of being reflective (or analytical) versus impulsive (or holistic) was found to be a stable characteristic by the first grade (Kagan *et al*, 1964). It was found that children who were reflective performed better in such situations as reading recognition (Kagan, 1965), and inductive reasoning (Kagan, Pearson, and Welch, 1966).

In teaching science, Kagan's work has particular importance. He views the reflective-impulsive dimension as related to the problem-solving process at three points—when the child initially verbalizes and comprehends the available data; when he selects hypotheses; and when he evaluates the accuracy of the final solution (Kagan, 1966). When attempts were made to instruct impulsive children to be more reflective, it was found that significant changes could be made in learning style. However, it required a reflective teacher as well as positive reinforcement (Yando and Kagan, 1968).

Cognitive styles are in fact information-processing habits which function across a variety of subject areas. There appear to be many styles that can be reliably measured (Messick and Ross, 1962). In addition to reflection-impulsivity, there are large and stable differences between children in their ability to perceive items as discrete from background stimuli. Some children are able to focus successfully on the relevant parts of a visual display while others perceive the display as a unified whole. While one child may be able to overcome the distractions surrounding an object, another may experience difficulty in doing so. The obvious application of this finding is that for some children the phenomenal field must be greatly simplified before they will be able to learn. Others can be exposed, with benefit, to the environment in its complexity.

Children also seem to differ in the size of the categories and concepts they form and use. These range from a few broad and vaguely defined concepts to many precise, but narrow categories. In addition, the amount of ambiguity which may be accepted, as well as the level of abstraction possible, can range from abstract to very concrete in different persons. Even the memory processes appear to be different among different children. Some children process information so that objects tend to merge in the memory and are no longer distinguishable. With other children, differences between events are highlighted in the memory. Obviously with such memory-processing differences, different outcomes may be expected from different children in situations where memory is a factor. In fact, the variety of cognitive styles will moderate the learning that results from educational treatments. No one treatment will be equally effective for all children. Therefore, it is imperative that teachers learn to understand and recognize the cognitive characteristics of children and the nature of process and environments which together produce a particular learning style.

The idea that particular learning styles may be directly teachable is an intriguing idea. This means that children can be taught to approach science problems in particular ways and solve them using specified processes. Because it is likely that habits of learning may be strengthened over time, the early elementary years represent a logical period in which to offer training in learning style development. This assumes, of course, that not all styles are equally productive in dealing with the problems of science. Taba, Levine, and Elzey (1864) made such an attempt to train children in cognitive style. They defined "styles" as the:" ... modes of thought which an individual employs rather persistently in a variety of different cognitive tasks, such as selecting a basis for grouping objects, determining how to label what he sees and how to organize the various aspects of his environment." They conducted an experiment in which children were given training in specific kinds of thought processes and cognitive skills. Instruction was not varied according to the style of the individual. The styles which were included in the instructional sequence were inductive reasoning in concept development and the capacity for analysis and abstraction. Children were measured in terms of grouping and classifying as well as hypothesizing and predicting. It was found that children could indeed be instructed to become better data discriminators and to reduce the amount of overly cautious influence. The teacher asking questions which forced children to use grouping, hypothesizing, and predicting seemed to account for these improvements. The curriculum that was used focused on concepts and fundamentals in an inductive developmental sequence rather than on a multiplicity of specific facts. Children were taught the processes of classifying, inferring, and hypothesizing. This indicates that in teaching the processes of science, the teacher can largely control the student's responses and limit him to memory and recall, or she can help him by forcing him to use analysis, evaluation, and other processes which provide him with styles of learning that are more consistent with the inherent process of learning science.

There are certain implications which can be reached in considering the work of Kagan, Messick, and Taba. First, it may be concluded that instruction can be designed to teach specified learning styles. The child can develop these styles early and they can guide him in many situations. Also, ways of accommodating different learning styles have been suggested. Impulsive children should perhaps be taught to read in groups led by a reflective teacher. A phonics approach may be effective with analytic and reflective beginning readers, while a whole word approach to reading might be superior with children who are impulsive. In teaching science skills, inductive teaching seems to work better for some students while deductive is better for others.

Not only is the cognitive style of the students a factor in the teaching-learning situation, but also that of the teacher. Teachers also have their personalized style of learning and this style certainly is used to influence students to develop habits of processing information. Given the fact that both teachers and students vary in their cognitive style, and that a particular style may be more appropriate in one teacher-student interaction than another, it appears necessary to encourage an eclectic approach in the classroom:

> The same method will not always be optimal as the content changes, and it will not be optimal for all students. By presenting and seeking information in various ways, and perhaps in several ways, one can increase the range of students of varying style who "get the point." At the same time, the necessary variety of presentation will keep the teacher from settling into a cognitive style which may be unlike that of most of her students (Fredrich and Klausmeier, 1970).

The teacher needs not only to use an eclectic approach, but also to be diagnostic and predictive. In other words, the teacher should not simply use a variety of means to cater to a variety of learning styles. She should attempt to determine the learning styles of her students and provide them with experiences that are consistent with their style of learning so that they begin to experience success. She should also provide experiences for children for the purpose of broadening their learning styles to include those which are more viable for learning and understanding science. Children need to experience initial success in learning science so that they do not become discouraged and associate science with negative experiences in learning. At the same time, if a child's learning style is not sufficiently fruitful in gaining what science has to offer in intellectual development, the teacher needs to provide teaching-learning activities which will achieve these ends. A careful blend of these two emphases will need to be determined for each child.

Another set of factors which relate to how children learn are social class and cultural background. A study completed by Fort, Watts, and Lesser (1969) made an attempt to determine what differences existed between diverse social and cultural groups. They developed an instrument to measure ability in four areas: verbal; reasoning; numerical; and space conceptualization. Children used as subjects in the study were first graders from lower-and middle-class homes of Chinese, Jewish, Negro, and Puerto Rican origin. The measures did not require the children to read or write, but consisted primarily of a number of pictures and games which the child was asked to manipulate or label.

The results of the study indicate that: (a) middle-class children were more able to perform on all tasks than lower-class children; (b) children from different ethnic groups show different constellations of abilities as well as different levels of performance for various tasks; and (c) middle-class children from different ethnic groups in general perform more like each other than do lower-class children from different ethnic groups.

Chinese children showed higher ability in spatial tasks than they did in any of the others. They performed verbal tasks least well, even though the test was administered in their native dialect and/or English, whichever was prefered by the child. Performance in both reasoning and numerical areas was nearly as high as performance in spatial tasks. Cultural influences which may account for this are: (a) the Chinese language is a highly spatial one and is often taught to preschoolers, (b) games played most frequently in Chinese homes are spatial ones; (c) more Chinese professionals are employed in occupations which require the use of strong spatial skills, such as architecture and engineering; (d) there is relatively little reinforcement of verbal skills; in fact, a highly verbal or talkative child may be considered a problem in a Chinese home; and (e) Chinese students are more frequently found in the natural science areas than in such areas as psychology and education.

By contrast, the Jewish children show greatest proficiency in the verbal area. They were next best in numerical concepts and poorest in spatial skills; reasoning skills are only a little better than spatial. In keeping with this finding, Jewish homes are more likely to emphasize verbal skills. In addition, Jewish parents are found more frequently in occupations such as teaching, law, and psychology, which require verbal capacities. Jewish people are also often found in occupations such as business and stock-broking areas, which require a high degree of skill in manipulation of numbers and the use of numerical concepts. This may explain the high numerical scores which Jewish children achieve on the skills test instrument.

Negro children evidenced the greatest amount of skill in the verbal area. They performed least well in the numerical area, with reasoning and spatial scores coming somewhere between these two. The preliminary observations made in the study suggest, contrary to what has been heretofore suspected, that verbal interaction in Negro homes is frequent and encouraged. Also, Negro parents of the children sampled were more likely to be employed in such "verbal" occupations as teaching and law. The lack of Negro parents in occupations requiring manipulation of numbers, may perhaps explain why Negro children displayed a poorer grasp of numerical concepts.

Puerto Rican children evidenced the least difference among the four abilities. The best area was spatial and the worst was verbal concepts. Again, causal information indicates that spatial skills are reinforced by the culture. Puerto Rican women engage in such tasks as close and intricate needlework, while men are often engaged in technical jobs which emphasize and strengthen spatial skills. Again the evidence of the connection between cultural and skill development is more circumstantial than empirical and needs verification. However, preliminary observations tend to confirm that a child's culture and social class markedly influence the capability he has to do different tasks which are related to learning.

Development in terms of stability and origin of patterns of ability are of immense interest to educators. Knowledge about development helps us fit the child's pattern of mental abilities to the content and timing of instruction. It also helps us to answer such questions as: How can instruction be adjusted to the child's particular strengths and weaknesses, or the child's abilities modified to meet the demands of instruction? If patterns of intellectual development depend heavily upon culture, different means of instruction can be devised to meet the differentiated capacities of children. In the elementary school, teachers need to consider such differences in capacity in organizing the experiences for children.

A fourth category of diagnostic tasks which must be performed by the teacher is that of determining readiness. The teacher needs to see the child's abilities and achievements within a developmental and experiential framework that helps her to determine whether or not the child is ready to succeed with any new specified experience. Readiness implies that a child may enter into new experiences equipped with all of the requisites necessary to cope successfully in specific learning situations. As a teacher you will need to know the child's state of readiness so that he may be exposed to learning situations in a way that will be most beneficial to him. Factors such as the child's past experience and achievements, his interests, attitudes, special aptitudes, and developmental growth—including intelligence, auditory and visual perception, emotional maturity, social status and peer relationships, physical dexterity, and coordination—all need to be considered in determining a child's readiness.

If the teacher fails to properly diagnose each child's level of readiness, many children may be asked to accomplish tasks for which they are unprepared. This lack of readiness may be for any of a number of reasons. A child may, for example, lack some necessary prerequisite experiences. The teacher cannot assume that children have had all of the prerequisite activities associated with learning and understanding a particular science concept or skill. Nor should he assume that all of his/her students have or have not had a particular experience. Ordinarily some children have had certain experiences, while others have not. Some require extensive review of what they have previously learned, while others require little or no reviewing. For this reason, it may be helpful if preassessment is in a form which will determine the students who have had prerequisite experiences, as well as what they remember from these experiences. In determining which students have had experiences with prerequisite knowledge or skills, a simple procedure is simply to ask them or talk with their previous teachers. After this the teacher will need to determine to what extent they have sufficient knowledge of prerequisites to enable them to achieve the goals of instruction that she has.

In addition to determining the prerequisite experiences which her students have, she will also need to determine their achievement level in terms of which students are high achievers and vice-versa. This knowledge helps her to better individualize her instructional procedures. Children who do well in science may be able to work more independently than those whose achievement level is low. The teacher will obviously find a variety of levels of achievement among his/her students. This fact should force him to consider offering a variety of experiences to students according to their ability. It may be difficult to give instruction specifically for each individual student, but certainly some differentiation in learning should be provided for students whose achievements differ markedly. Perhaps only three or four different kinds of experiences for students need be provided. Anything the teacher can do to take into account the differences in ability levels of students will enhance the science instruction of the classroom.

The developmental level of students should also be taken into account. Knowing what children at various developmental levels are capable of intellectually will be of great assistance in planning science lessons. It makes little sense to expose children to experiences for which they lack the necessary intellectual development. Chapter 5 shows what children can be expected to be able to do at different developmental levels and how to prepare instruments for measuring these levels of development. As you study that chapter, you will find that children go through the same set of developmental levels, but they vary with regard to the time they reach these levels. In the late elementary years you are likely to find children with a good deal of variability in their intellectual capacity. Some children, for example, may be able to abstract readily while their peers may be unable to do so.

Finally, in diagnosing, it is imperative that the educational environment itself be assessed. We need to know what effects the school experience is having on the child and to determine what the actual learning outcomes are and then compare them with the overall goals of self-development of the child in order to insure proper correspondence between expectations and achievements. Teaching methods need to be examined in light of the intellectual and social growth of students to insure that the methods which are used are bringing about the desired results. Academic growth as well as social development need to be examined in relationship to the methods used so that alterations can be made which will bring greater assurance that our expectations will be achieved. The learning environment needs to be examined critically. It is true that a child is in school primarily to learn, but he also needs to feel good about what he learns and about himself as a learner during the educational process. We cannot assume that if a child is not doing well in school it is only because of such personal problems as poor self-perceptions or other dysfunctions; it may be the instructional setting that is mostly at fault. The diagnostic process is not complete until the total constellation of factors operating within the child's life space are examined and analyzed. Cause and effect hypotheses should not be made without identifying all possible factors and how they may be related in producing the kinds of behavior patterns we observe in students. Only then can intelligent changes be made in the child's environment which will offer him a better means of growing properly in the school experience.

The school environment itself must be analyzed in order to provide optimum learning conditions.

The Tools of Preassessment

There are a variety of means for preassessing learning in the classroom. Because there may be many factors affecting student performance, a comprehensive means of diagnosis must be utilized. Limiting the diagnostic operations in the classroom will only reduce the amount of data available with which to make educational decisions. There are formal as well as informal means for diagnosing children in the instructional program. Informal diagnosis should be going on all of the time, and may be used to make decisions which will help children think, determine new interests, and avoid the unpleasantness of becoming entangled in a learning task for which they are unprepared.

Sometimes the teacher wishes to look more deeply into areas of personal and educational concern. To do this it may be necessary to make a formal diagnosis of the students and their learning environment. The teacher may, for example, sense a problem by informally observing a child in various circumstances during a period of time. Just observing that something is amiss in a child's academic, social, or personal life may prompt the teacher to observe more closely and formalize the diagnostic process.

If a child's behavior is particularly puzzling, the teacher may decide to prepare anecdotal accounts of the child's behavior. He/she may also decide to use self-report forms, sociometric devices, and so on. Through these means various patterns may begin to emerge, which can be used in formulating a plan to help the child individually. Sometimes the teacher may learn that the problem is beyond her area of expertise and will then refer the child to specialists for appropriate action.

Informal Observation

Informal observations may well be as valid a means of determining a child's readiness for learning as most formal instruments. Informal observations focus primarily on the child's personal adjustment to the school curriculum as well as to his peers and teachers. Such things as his goals, aspirations, behavior patterns, mechanisms for coping, and learning styles may be observed in this way. Observations made by experienced teachers can accurately determine a child's readiness for an activity, such as learning to read, or why he may be misbehaving in order to capture the attention of the class. She may also observe behaviors informally which indicate that a child's self-concept is suffering and needs to be bolstered in some way.

By being a careful observer the teacher can become aware of the child's interests, potentials, and physical and mental sets, and can use these facts in guiding the child's learning. The teacher should properly look for answers to such questions as the following: What are the interests of individual children? Given a choice, what kinds of activities does the child prefer? What kinds of books does he/she choose? What kind of material does he bring from home? What does he talk about when engaging in conversations with his peers? What subjects does he bring up in class discussions? How does the child express himself creatively?

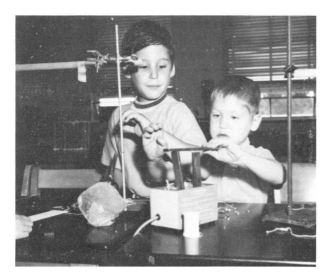

Informal observation is a crucial factor in diagnosing students.

What is his most common and fluent mode of expression—talking; writing; painting; or drawing? Does he work well with his hands? What does the content of his creative works tell you about his interests and conceptions of himself? When he creates, does he reflect himself? Under what conditions is the child creative?

You may also wish to consider questions regarding the child's work habits: How does the child approach problems? Is the child impulsive, confident, or fearless? Does the child need to be coaxed before he works well? Can he work independently? Does he require group activity in order to succeed? Does the child need a great deal of guidance? Can he solve problems well? What kinds of questions does the child ask and what depth of thought do these questions imply? Does the child seem to come up with most of the ideas in class? Does he hang back and never assert his ideas?

In your questioning of children you may also wish to consider thinking of the following kinds of informal diagnostic questions: What levels of thought does the child exhibit? Can he deal with abstract ideas? How well does he comprehend? What language patterns does the child use in discussions? What kinds of assistance does the child seek? Does he require extensive explanations? Is he able to proceed with only hints and suggestions? Does the child appear frustrated when questions are asked? Does he seem to have a poor memory? Does he have trouble making associations in learning?

In working with children you may think of the following kinds of questions: When a child is being helped, how does he respond? Is he quick or slow to understand? In discussions, does the child catch on quickly? Does he get discouraged and mentally drop out? Does the child appear to have great tenacity and stick to tasks until they are completed? Does he usually give up in the middle of a task? Is he short-tempered, frequently venting his frustration? Does he have a very short attention span? Does the child show difficulty in visual perception? Does he have difficulty copying? Is the child having auditory difficulty as evidenced by his inability to hear phonetic combinations or to follow instructions? Does he lose interest when required to listen? Is the child interested only when allowed to manipulate objects? Does he rebel at the formality of classroom work? Does the child have a high energy level or does he seem to be in poor health or appear sleepy in class? Does he have poor motor coordination and dexterity?

The teacher may also wish to ask similar questions about attitudes which children's behavior may be an indication of? Does the child feel comfortable with his own appearance? Does he appear to have confidence in his abilities? Is the child outgoing, reserved, or withdrawn? Is the child hostile to authority or simply compliant and accepting? Does he constantly seek teacher and peer approval? Is he consistent in his behavior from one situation to another? Are the remarks he makes about himself consistent with the way he really is? Does he appear tense? Does he grit his teeth, grimace, bite his nails? Does he cry easily, pick fights, retaliate? Does the child readily escape your notice, and "fade into the woodwork?"

The social relationships in the class are also worthy of the teacher's attention. As a teacher, you may well ask such questions as: Is the student a leader? Is he a leader in most situations, or does the activity make a difference? Is the child popular? Is he usually left out or without friends? Is social acceptance a predominant value? How are social problems solved? Does the child value good clothes and grooming, school success, sports, or what? Is the child swayed by other's values? To what extent do the values of the group influence the child's individual behavior? Is he becoming an independent thinker? How does the student perceive his peers? Is he perceived as being better than others or does he occupy a social role such as a bully or a scapegoat? Does he appear to occupy a social role that is interpreted by the group as deviant? What social circumstances seem to precipitate poor student behavior? How does the group handle the emotional upsetting of one of its members? What similarities or differences exist in individual behaviors of children in academic, social, creative or physical activities? What is the meaning of these differences?

Formal Diagnosis

Obviously a multitude of questions may be asked regarding the behavior of children, which are useful for diagnostic purposes in an informal way. These questions may be used as a basis for making more formal appraisals at some future time. For example, as a consequence of informal questioning, the teacher may decide that data needs to be collected using a more comprehensive and formal means. He/she may decide in a situation where the student's behavior is somewhat puzzling to record descriptions of his behavior in varying situations over a period of several months. Perhaps quite divergent situations are used for the purpose of observation and a variety of observational schemes incorporated into a comprehensive diagnosis. All these data may be taken by the teacher and analyzed to determine whether there are commonalities that indicate some positive action which may be taken to solve a student's learning problems. If the teacher takes extensive notes on a student's behavior, she may later go over her notes and perhaps see connecting links in the child's behavior that she has heretofore missed. These links may yield important clues to the child's self-concept, goals, interests, or they may uncover information about his social, personal or intellectual needs which are not being met. *Anecdotal records* provide a means of accumulating this type of data. A good anecdotal record may give a fairly valid picture of a child's behavior from which to prescribe means to accentuate his learning experiences. Anecdotal records should probably contain the following information in order to be complete:

1. Setting
2. Date and time
3. Actions of the child
4. Reactions of other people involved and the child's responses to these reactions
5. Quotations by the child and others
6. Nonverbal information such as posture, gestures, voice qualities, and facial expressions, which give clues to the child's feelings during the episode
7. Description of the episode in sufficient detail that an accurate picture of the happening can be constructed later

Formal appraisal of *students' interests* may also be determined by the teacher in the classroom. Of course, every child will not be interested in the same science experiences at the same time. However, the interest of one student may generate similar interests in his peers. Therefore, it should not be assumed that simply obtaining interest data in a one-shot survey will suffice for the whole year. This data needs to

Creative activities can tell us a lot about students.

be collected periodically as children have an opportunity to experience science and observe their friends doing the same. Interest often is a transient entity requiring continuous monitoring. Sometimes it "flits" from one subject to another while at other times interest in one topic subsides only to be rekindled later on. In spite of this, it is useful to formally survey the science interests of students and use this information as a basis for curriculum development. Possible survey questions include the following:

1. What science subject most interests me?
2. What subject in science do I know most about?
3. What animals are most fun to read about?
4. What plants are most interesting to study?
5. What aspects of the human body are most interesting?
6. Where would I go in the forest?
7. What would be the most fun to visit—a chemical plant or a pond?
8. Which of my friends like science?

Much can be learned about children and their interests by observing them in a variety of conditions while they are involved in different kinds of tasks. A child may behave differently working on a science project at the science worktable than when he is on a field trip outdoors. He may behave differently, too, when confronted with creative tasks to perform versus more structured work. One of the best opportunities for finding clues to the child's self-concept or his creative and mental sets is through observing him work with materials that require his creative efforts. As a teacher, you may wish to structure situations in which creative possibilities prevail. Children may be asked to use creative dramatics, art, or role playing for some aspect of the science curriculum. They may be asked to prepare a bulletin board, design an experiment, or create stories illustrating the principles of science. Opening up the experiences of children in this way provides an excellent opportunity to make observations regarding the interests and potentialities of children. While participating in such learning activities the teacher may observe the following kinds of things:

1. Interests
2. Intellectual skills
3. Skill in using the tools of science
4. The care with which children do their work and the neatness of the work they perform or products they create
5. The persistence of students in redoing work that is unsatisfactory
6. The attitude of children who refuse to try
7. The extent to which children will destroy their own work so that others do not see what they have done
8. The spontaneousness of children and their ability to be creative
9. The extent to which specific children need to engage in social interaction in order to benefit very much from instruction
10. The extent to which a child's work can be used to gain insight into how he feels about himself, the school, and his school experiences, or, the child's personal feelings toward him/her, if the teacher is sufficiently observant

Another way to formally preassess children in terms of social relationships is through *sociometry*. Sociometry is the study of interpersonal relationships in group settings. Ordinarily the data with which to formulate a sociogram (which is a graphical representation of social interrelationships) is to ask students such questions as who they would most like to work with on a special science project. Usually they are required to state at least three preferences. Additional information may also be obtained by asking the class to name the three children they would least like to work with on a science project. The first question will help you determine who are the social stars and social isolates. The second question may help obtain information regarding the extent of isolation that some class members may feel. For example, in a sociometric study completed by the authors it was found that two students were disliked by every class member. Each student was asked to indicate, in order, the three students that he would least like to work with on a science project. These two students were placed in first and second

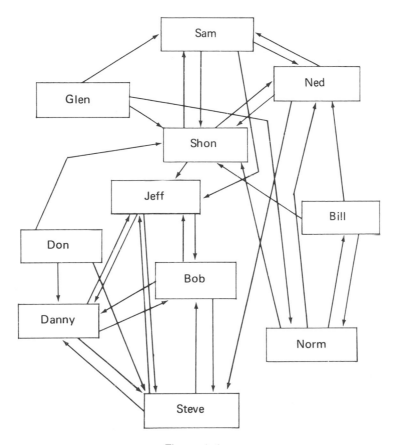

Figure 4–1

position by every single student in the class. They were preferred only by one another (Edwards, 1975). Until the teacher was provided with this sociometric information, he was completely unaware that such isolation existed.

Whichever question the teacher wishes to ask, he can prepare a sociogram like the one depicted in Figure 4–1. In this case, let us assume that students were asked to indicate which of their classmates they preferred to work with. Note that Shon is the social star. A number of students want to be associated with him. Jeff is the second most frequently chosen individual. Note that Jeff, Bob, Danny, and Steve constitute a clique of mutually chosen friends who are apparently not striving to enter any other social group, nor encouraging any other boys to join their group. Sometimes a sociogram will show relationships where small groups of students constitute a clique, but are not chosen by any one else. It should not be hastily assumed that sufficient social support is being given to the members of such groups. They may in fact be rejected by the rest of the class and band together out of necessity. This is the reason that it usually pays to construct a sociogram based upon unliked peers as well as liked peers.

In order to improve social relationships the teacher will ordinarily want to structure situations in which isolates are placed with social stars or with other people of high acceptance, and will integrate students who are members of cliques into other groups. This can be done easily by involving students in group work such as group experiments and projects in configurations which will expand the social life of children. This way, children will come to realize that there are others they can enjoy working with. Friendships fail to materialize because current configurations or friendship groups constitute a safe arrangement, one which is comfortable and where there is little felt need of change. Altering these groups to include social isolates will enrich the lives of all children and save some children from a long history of ostracism and impoverished self-concept.

Care should be exercised in rearranging social groups. Students who like one another should not be torn apart and asked to associate exclusively with classmates they dislike or are unfamiliar with. Children may have a tendency to "tease" one another and create even greater social distance between one another. In addition, the teacher should put his findings to use so that he cannot be accused of asking questions that are too phony or nosy. To avoid this, the teacher may say to the class: "Name three people, in order, with whom you want to work. I cannot promise to give you all of your choices, but I will give you one of them if I can. I want to form some new groups so that you will have an opportunity to work with other students and learn from them."

An additional source of preassessment information is *standardized tests.* You need to be aware of the limitations of such tests as well as their potential usefulness in revealing information necessary for proper diagnosis of children's academic potentialities and achievements. Most schools periodically administer IQ tests, achievement tests, reading inventories, and psychological tests. In addition there are some standardized interest inventories which are often used for diagnosis.

The teacher may also prepare his own *teacher diagnostic materials.* These may, in fact, be better than the other materials which are available. If the teacher wishes to determine the extent to which a student has mastered a specific skill, such as utilizing science equipment to perform experiments, he has only to make systematic observations. The extent to which a child has mastered certain concepts of science can be determined from a teacher-made test. Tests can be developed which lead a child through the step-by-step process of a complex concept or operation and by checking the child's work, the teacher can determine exactly where a child experiences difficulty.

One of the problems with teacher-prepared materials is that they may be just as invalid as standardized tests in determining intellectual capacities and learning difficulties. Most teachers do not have the time or skills necessary to construct tests which measure the various components of the intellect. They also lack training in preparing diagnostic materials which will pinpoint specific learning disabilities. However, because they may be unable to find instruments which have already been prepared, they will likely have to resort to developing their own materials in spite of deficiencies they may have. If they are constructed for specific situations, their validity in all probability will exceed other available materials.

Some science programs for elementary children contain associated preassessment instruments with them. An example of one of these is the *Individualized Science Program* put out by Imperial International Learning Corporation. This program contains a tape which is used to instruct students in the use of sets of printed materials as well as science objects. Before children begin the instructional phase of the program they must do a preassessment test. The accompanying teacher's manual contains the answers to the preassessment questions, which are designed to place children at a level in the program that is commensurate with their ability. The preassessment instrument is easily scored by the teacher. Student answers are compared with a key and lessons which the preassessment indicates the student need not do are crossed out. Once this has been accomplished, students complete the assigned lessons in a self-paced format.

Assessment of Diagnostic Data

Once all of the preassessment data have been accumulated, the teacher must next attempt to make an analysis of each child's work and related personal components and attempt to make judgments upon which to base corrective plans. The judgments which the teacher makes, however, should not be hasty or based upon insufficient data. Valid interpretations come from looking at a variety of growth factors and noting how they are interrelated. There are an infinite number of errors that may be made. Some of them may never even arouse our suspicion. For example, some children, though progressing satisfactorily or even doing very well when compared with their peers, may in fact be underachievers.

As a teacher you must become skilled at examining a child's developmental growth patterns and identifying the interrelationships between physical, social, emotional, and intellectual factors. If children are having academic problems you need to ask yourself whether they are due to poor self-concept or are a matter of poor attitude or learning disabilities. There are a variety of questions that may be asked in such analyses: Is a child's apparent frustration due to materials which are too difficult or do they lack in terms of interest? Does a child's poor performance involve a physical or health problem? Is the hyperactive child emotionally disturbed or is there neurological damage? Is the child's performance in class consistent with what could be expected, given how well he has scored on standardized tests? Does the child favor a particular learning modality—visual, auditory, kinesthetic? Do the materials used in the class fit the learning style of the child?

Some experts emphasize that in making a diagnostic analysis, it is important to observe the differences within an individual which precipitate learning problems. For example, a child may suffer difficulties in one or more of the following: (a) receptive processes; (b) expressive processes; or (c) organizing processes. Learning problems usually involve problems in one of these areas. A particular child may have good abilities in one of these areas while experiencing difficulties in another. The consequence of this may be a great difference in ability in subcomponents of academic tasks. In diagnosing, you must decide which impairments are related to other impairments. You may, for example, discover a child who has difficulty in reading because of inadequate oral language experience. On the other hand, his inadequacy may be related to visual-perceptual problems (Kirk and Kirk, 1971).

Once a comprehensive diagnosis has been performed and some conclusions have been reached regarding the implications of these findings, the teacher is prepared to formulate plans to capitalize on strengths and minimize the effects of weaknesses of children in the instructional process. Strategies for instruction must adequately reflect what has been learned in the preassessment process so that the learning activities which occur in the classroom take this knowledge into account.

Exercise 4–1   Preassessing Students in Science

1. Attempt to make an assessment of one or more elementary school children. Select children from several different levels if you can. Make as comprehensive an assessment as you are able to, including standardized test information, as well as estimates of self-concept, social skills, personality variables, etc. In completing this exercise it would be well to work with a fellow trainee. This way you can make independent appraisals which you can later discuss and evaluate.
2. Prepare a sociogram for a group of elementary school students and explain how you would reorganize the class for a specific set of learning activities in science.

References

Coopersmith, Stanley, *The Antecedents of Self-Esteem*. San Francisco: Freeman, 1967.

Edwards, Clifford H., "Variable Delivery Systems for Peer Associated Token Reinforcement," *Illinois School Research*, 12 (Fall 1975): 19–28.

Fort, Jane G., Jean C. Watts, and Gerald S. Lesser, "Cultural Background and Learning in Young Children," *Phi Delta Kappan* 50 (March 1969): 386–88.

Fredrick, Wayne C., and Herbert J. Klausmeier, "Cognitive Styles: A Description," *Educational Leadership* 28 (April 1970) 668–72.

Gould, P. "The Seeing Learner and the Hearing Learner," mimeographed speech, 1964.

Kagan, J., "A Developmental Approach to Conceptual Growth," in H. J. Klausmeier and C. W. Harris, ed., *Analysis of Concept Learning*. New York: Academic Press, 1966.

Kagan, J., "Reflection-Impulsivity and Reading Ability in Primary Grade Children," *Child Development* (1965): 609–28.

Kagan, J., L. Pearson, and L. Welch, "Conceptual Impulsivity and Inductive Reasoning," *Child Development* (1966): 583–94.

Kagan, J., B. L. Rosman, D. Kay, J. Albert, and W. Phillips, "Information Processing the Child: Significance of Analytic and Reflective Attitudes," *Psychological Monographs: General and Applied*, 78, Whole No. 578 (1964).

Kirk, Samuel A., and Winifred D. Kirk, *Psycholinguistic Learning Disabilities: Diagnosis and Remediation*. Urbana: University of Illinois Press, 1971.

La Benne, Wallace D., and Bert I. Greene, *Educational Implications of Self-Concept Theory*. Pacific Palisades, Calif.: Goodyear Publishing Company, 1969.

Messick, S., and J. Ross, *Measurement in Personality and Cognition*. New York: Wiley, 1962.

Seaberg, Dorthy I., *The Four Faces of Teaching: The Role of the Teacher in Humanizing Education*. Pacific Palisades, Calif.: Goodyear Publishing Company, 1974.

Taba, H., S. Levine, and F. F. Elzey, *Thinking in Elementary School Children*, (CRP 1574) San Francisco: San Francisco State College, 1964, p. 207.

Yando, R. M., and J. Kagan, "The Effect of Teacher Tempo on the Child," *Child Development* (1968): 27–34.

5
Using Knowledge about Learning and Development

In order to teach science to children it is necessary to have an understanding of how children grow and develop. It is generally agreed that science curricula should be geared to the developmental level of the students for which it is intended. It is assumed that students will benefit most from experiences in science for which they have the requisite level of readiness. Exposing students to materials for which they are unprepared is not only uneconomical in terms of time, it is also likely to lead to discouragement and lack of involvement by students.

One difficulty may be encountered in planning science curricula according to the developmental level of students. This is the tendency to view learners according to patterns which are standardized for each group. This is especially true with regard to characteristics and patterns which are shared by a large percentage of children. It is necessary to create group experiences which cater to group tendencies, but allowances should always be made for the idiosyncratic growth patterns of each individual child. Group experiences are useful and necessary in most instances and when planning for them, the teacher needs to incorporate the best information available regarding the common growth patterns of children. However, because successful learning may depend upon how the curriculum nurtures each child's uniqueness, it is the responsibility of the teacher to develop materials which will accentuate the differences between learners rather than stamp everyone in the same mold.

The majority of schools still start and advance students through the school grades according to their chronological age. This, of course, is inconsistent with what we know about how children vary in their growth patterns. The science teacher will undoubtedly find herself in the position of having a wide variety of developmental levels in the classroom. This will necessitate the ability of not only being able to properly diagnose the capability of each child, but to also design learning experiences which reflect these differences.

Present struggles in the education of so-called culturally deprived children have sharpened the focus on the complexity of the developmental patterns of children. There appears to be a greater willingness to accept the premise that students cannot benefit by being forced through the same set of school experiences. Their growth patterns are unique because each child is endowed with a different set of genetic tendencies as well as unique experiences. Each child also has his own set of perceptions regarding himself and his world and his own idiosyncratic style of learning.

There are a number of different viewpoints about how children grow and learn. Each of these views has its own assumptions regarding human nature and needs. In order to determine upon which of the views to base your own teaching, you will find it necessary to reach your own conclusions regarding human nature. Your first attempt at this will probably consist of a best guess and be based upon what you believe man to be. You will want to keep your initial impressions tentative until such time as you have made a more indepth search and satisfied yourself that your assumptions regarding human nature are consistent with whatever evidence can be obtained.

First, is the psychosexual-personality view of learning and development, which is traced back to the work of Sigmund Freud in psychoanalysis. From this viewpoint man's behavior is governed primarily by his irrational impulses, particularly as related to unconscious motivation and conflict. The child passes through certain psychosexual stages as he grows into adulthood. Each of these stages is critical in the sense that failure to meet the needs associated with each of them may result in various types of dysfunctions later in life. The educational implications are twofold. First, understanding that behavior is based on unconscious phenomena leads one to explain present behavior on the basis of prior experiences, which we must come to understand. Secondly, in order to avoid contributing to unacceptable behavior in children, the teacher must keep the child from experiencing trauma. According to this view man's primary drives are sex and aggression.

The second view of learning and development is behaviorism, which includes the reinforcement-learning theory of B. F. Skinner, the developmental behavior-analysis approach of Bijou and Baer, and the cumulative learning model of Gagné. The primary point of this theory is that man reacts to external stimuli. Accordingly, behavior is externally rather than internally directed. Learning takes place through a conditioning process where certain random stimuli in the environment are seen as sufficiently reinforcing for the individual to continue specific related responses when they are present. Motivation is brought about by the presentation of a stimulus not by some internal director. Behavior is thus governed by external stimuli exclusively, rather than by predetermined purpose. Prior conditioning and physiological drives interact at any particular moment in time to force the individual to select among possible responses.

Cognitive-field and perceptual-field theories represent the third general category of learning and development. This approach views man as a naturally active, seeking, adapting being who learns and is shaped through continual transactions with the environment. Most of these transactions are initiated by the individual himself. This group of theories generally views man as purposeful in his interactions with his environment. He seeks for competency in dealing with the world as he perceives it, and originates his own directions rather than simply reacting to a bombardment of stimuli.

In the following pages, each of the above groups of theories will be explored in greater detail, with applications to science education being delineated. You will be asked not only to understand the various theories but to also apply some of them in practical situations. In some cases a good deal of detail will be used to give operational definitions so that there will be a clear indication of how to proceed in making your application.

Man is an active, seeking and adaptive being.

OBJECTIVES

1. Students will be able to explain the basic assumptions and the operational principles for each of the learning and developmental principles discussed in this chapter.
2. Students will be able to explain how they would apply the various learning and development theories outlined in this chapter in specific case-study situations.
3. Students will be able to select among the theories presented in this chapter the one they would use in specific situations and give a rationale for their choice.

Psychosexual Theory

Because of an almost exclusive emphasis on affect, psychoanalytic theory is probably the least fruitful of the theories to apply to learning in the schools. For this reason it will receive only a cursory treatment here. At the same time, there are trappings of psychoanalytic thought in much of present school practice; thus, if you understand it, it can be very useful.

As previously indicated, from a psychoanalytic point of view, a child is thought to be governed primarily by irrational impulses in the form of basic drives and appetites. Freud assumed that a person's overt behavior could not be understood without knowing his motives, fears, feelings, and thought processes at the time of action. Simply focusing on the behavior of the individual does not give sufficient data to really understand the behavior.

One of the fundamental concepts of psychoanalytic theory is that of instinctual drive. The term "instinctual," as used here, should not be confused with the specific behavioral patterns associated with animals. Rather, instinctual drives are basic motivators of an almost infinite variety of behavior. Chief among the drives associated with the human species is the libido, which is a term used to describe sexuality and all of its associated meanings. Freud used the term "sexuality" in a broader sense than is customary in common usage. In the human species, many sorts of feelings and pleasures, besides sexual pleasure, have become integrated into the pattern of mating and child rearing. It is by no means easy to decide where the purely sexual element leaves off and some other related element enters in (Baldwin, 1967).

Although the libidinal drive is the most important drive from a personality organization viewpoint, psychoanalysis also recognizes a number of other drives, such as hunger, thirst, and escape from pain. Freud grouped these drives together under the rubric of ego-instincts and explained that they operated much the same way as the libido except that they were based upon self-preservation rather than species preservation.

Finally, psychoanalytic theory focuses upon hostility and aggression as an important kind of human behavior. In practice, much more time is spent in helping the patient express and accept hostility as a part of human nature than is spent in the exploration of the patient's sexual feelings. There is little disagreement that anger and hostility are components of human personality, but there is less agreement, however, regarding their instinctual roots. At first, Freud seemed to believe that sex and aggression were somehow related to one another. Indeed, aggression could be viewed as a normal and customary aspect of sexual feelings; quarrels and hostility are often part of love affairs. Later on, however, Freud came to believe that hostility was a separate instinct, the death instinct, which lay at the root of all destructive activities. This latter view has not had wide acceptance among Freud's followers, but there is general acceptance that aggression does play an important role in understanding the motives and behavior of humans.

The assumption that behavior is based on the instinctual drives is fundamental to psychoanalytic theory. In fact, according to the theory, *all* behavior and all other psychological functioning are determined by the instinctual drives. Every perception, thought, feeling, and action ultimately stems from these drives. All personality mechanisms are propelled by psychic energy based on instinctual drives and their enactment constitutes the necessary reduction in that energy.

Transactional Analysis

One of the most fruitful adaptations of psychoanalytic thought is transactional analysis. In recent years there has been a growing impatience with psychiatry's high cost, debatable results, and vagueness. As Harris (1967) has indicated: "to many people it is like a blind man in a dark room looking for a black cat that isn't there." Transactional analysis is a simplified way of understanding and dealing with the conflicts inherent in man's psychological existence. This is a great boon to teachers who can use it not only to understand the behavior of their students, but also to better understand and govern their own behavior.

Penfield's (1951) work has formed the scientific information base upon which transactional analysis is founded. In his work, Penfield provides evidence that everything which has been in our conscious awareness is recorded in detail and stored in the brain and is capable of being brought into consciousness at any time. He reached this conclusion when he found that by stimulating various areas of the brain with a galvanized probe he could force recollections which were clearly derived from the individual's memory. The brain probe could bring to consciousness memories of specific experiences and images as well as sensory experiences and feelings associated with them. In fact, it was found that an event and the feeling which was produced by the event are inextricably locked together in the brain so that one cannot be evoked without the other.

One of Penfield's conclusions was that the brain functions as a high-fidelity recorder, recording, as it were, permanently in the brain cells every experience and its associated affect from the time of birth, or perhaps before, to the present. These recorded experiences and feelings associated with them are available for replay today, in as vivid a form as when they happened. They provide much of the data which determines how we will act in our daily transactions with others.

Transactional analysis involves the study and understanding of the transactions which occur between individuals. It is assumed that these transactions involve related information and experiences which are recorded in the brain. A basic transaction is when one person does something to someone else, who, in turn, does something back to him. What each of these parties does is based upon the three multiple parts of his nature—*Parent, Adult,* and *Child.* These are not abstract components of personality, rather they are phenomenological realities—states of being which are produced by the playback of recorded data of events in the past involving real times, real people, real places, real decisions, and real feelings.

The Parent is a huge collection of recordings in the brain of unquestioned or imposed external events perceived by a person in his early years. Everything the child saw his parents do and everything he heard them say is recorded here. Parent is specific for every child, and represents the set of early childhood experiences unique to him. The data in the parent is taken in and recorded without modification. Because of his lack of experience the child is unable to construct meanings with words and thus modify, correct, or explain what is recorded in the parent. For example, if parental actions result from extreme trauma the child is unable to modify his perceptions of the actions in light of this information.

The Parent also contains all of the admonitions and rules which are laid down by the child's parents, in terms of verbal as well as nonverbal communication. All kinds of attitudes and beliefs are transmitted to the child by the parents: for example, never tell a lie, if you get ahead it will have to be on your own, and you must always eat everything on your dinner plate. It is significant to remember that these rules and attitudes are recorded as truth whether they are good or bad in terms of a reasonable ethic, because they come from the source of all security, the parents.

While the external events referred to as parent are being recorded, another recording is being made simultaneously. This recording is referred to as the Child, and consists of the internal events and responses the child makes to what he sees and hears. It is important to remember Penfield's observation that the child feels again the same emotion that the situation originally produced in him. It is a reproduction of what the child saw and heard and felt and understood. Because of the child's limited vocabulary and experience at the time these experiences first took place, most of his reactions are affective. He has no words with which to construct meanings and consequently is unable to cognitively alter the perspective held regarding the feelings that he is experiencing. Without cognitive alterations, the very same feelings the individual had as a child are elicited in situations similar to those which originally produced the feelings.

During the period while the child is growing he is confronted with an infinite number of total and uncompromising demands which are made upon him. On one hand, there are the child's urges, based on genetic recordings, to explore, to know, to express emotion, and to do things freely. On the other hand, he is confronted with the constant demands of the environment, especially the parents, who require him to give up basic satisfactions for the reward of their approval. This series of transactions usually proves frustrating to the child and creates feelings of inadequacy. The child comes to view himself as "not OK." This conclusion and the continual experiencing of the unhappy feelings which led to it and confirm it, are recorded permanently in the brain and cannot be erased. This permanent recording is the residue of having been a child, even the child of kind, loving, well-meaning parents. It is the condition of childhood and not the intentions of the parent which are responsible for the problem.

The basic information recorded in both the Parent and Child are accomplished essentially by the time the child is five years old. By this time he has already been exposed to nearly every possible attitude and admonition of his parents. From this point on, further communications by parents or other adults are essentially a reinforcement of what has already been recorded. The question is, if in fact we emerge from childhood with a set of experiences which are recorded as permanent, what hope do we have of getting off the hook of the past? The answer to this lies in the development of the Adult, which is the third component of our multiple personality. Beginning as early as the tenth month a child finds that he is able to react from his own awareness and original thought. This is the beginning of the Adult. Adult data accumulates as a result of the child's ability to find out for himself what is different about life from the concepts which are taught to him (the Parent) and how he is made to feel (the Child).

During these early years, the Adult component of personality is fragile and tentative and is easily subverted by commands from the Parent and fear in the Child. The child, for example, who is admonished not to touch a vase, may draw back at first and perhaps cry, but at the first opportunity will touch it anyway in order to satisfy his curiosity. If the Adult is given sufficient opportunity it will assert itself despite all the obstacles thrown in its way. It will thus survive and continue to function more and more effectively as the maturation process goes on.

The Adult is a data-processing entity, which formulates decisions after determining the comparative information from the Parent, the Child and the data which the Adult has gathered and is gathering. The Adult is primarily concerned with transforming incoming stimuli into information which can be stored and related to previous experience. In other words the Adult is the rational aspect of the personality which processes information in light of experience and brings rationality to behavior. It is very different from the Parent, which is imitatively judgmental and seeks to enforce standards which are borrowed and previously recorded in the brain. It is also different from the Child, which tends to react abruptly on the basis of the emotional content of previous experience and poorly differentiated or distorted perceptions. One of the important functions of the Adult is to examine the information in the Parent and the emotion in the Child to see whether or not they are true and accurate for present situations. The child doing a science experiment, for example, may conclude that it is better to follow the safety precautions outlined by the teacher.

The function of the Adult is to act as the data processor and executor of behavior. Its purpose is to maintain behavior which is sufficiently consistent with the real world. Under stress, however, the Adult can be impaired to the point where emotions take over inappropriately. The boundaries between Parent, Adult, and Child are often fragile and indistinct, and vulnerable to strong incoming signals which tend to automatically initiate the same type of reaction we made in situations we experienced in the helpless, dependent days of childhood. The Adult is sometimes overpowered by information which is so overwhelming that it is reduced to a position of "onlooker" in the transaction. The consequent acting out of "juvenile behavior" may be disdainful to the individual but he feels in retrospect that somehow he was unable to help himself.

If things go smoothly and there is a relative absence of conflict between what has been taught and what is real, the Adult is free to become involved creatively. This creativity is born from the curiosity of the Child and the capable handling of data by the Adult. So long as this process is not cluttered by conflicts introduced by the Parent, everything goes along smoothly. In conflict with this idea is the notion held by some that the undisciplined child who is unhampered by limits is more creative than the child whose parents set limits. To the contrary, unless restrictions are extreme, a youngster will have more time to create—to explore and invent—if he is not wasting time in a futile decision for which he is unprepared. The restrictions of parents can set useful parameters for the child which allow him to expend his energy in useful pursuits rather than the inefficient and ineffective practice of trying to determine directions. In science, the child may be provided with basic directions and cautions by the teacher as he works with science materials. In fact the type of materials provided offers some structure within which the child can work. He is likely to find this a more rewarding and fruitful experience than trying to originate his own directions completely. A greater amount of autonomy can be encouraged as the child shows the ability to use it constructively.

Exercise 5-1   Transactional Analysis

Make observations in an elementary school situation and record the following information:

1. Expressions by children which are parent in nature.
2. Expressions by children which are child in nature.
3. Expressions by children which are adult in nature.
4. Expressions by the teacher which are either child or parent in nature.

Behavioral-Environmental Theory

The behavioral-environmental view of man, often referred to as behaviorism, encompasses the views of development and learning which characterize man as a reactor to incoming stimuli. At first, the child's behavioral responses and the environmental stimuli which occur around him are random and unassociated. As the child grows, some of these stimuli and responses inadvertently become associated and if the individual finds the stimuli satisfying, he will repeat the associated responses in the hope that the stimuli will be forthcoming. If the response does result in producing this reinforcing stimulus with some regularity the strength of the response will increase. In other words, if the individual finds the stimulus reinforcing he will tend to repeat the responses with which it is associated more frequently. This process of influencing responses through manipulation of associated stimuli is referred to as operant conditioning. Operants are behaviors which are functionally related to their consequences in the environment. Operant behavior is essentially trial-and-error behavior which is strengthened or increased in frequency because it is rewarded somehow by the environment or those who manipulate it.

If behavioral responses as well as the stimuli which reinforce them are random, the proponents of behaviorism believe that the aims of enlightened society will be subverted. The result will be wars, hunger, crime, pollution, etc. According to behaviorists it would be much better if responsible people were allowed to manage the reinforcing stimuli in such a way that human social behavior would improve and the ills of society would be done away with. It is assumed that without control, people are unlikely to be influenced by reinforcers which will insure appropriate social growth and development. B. F. Skinner, who is one of the chief spokesmen for behaviorism, has said:

> . . . if we are not to rely solely upon accident for the innovations which give rise to cultural evolution, we must accept the fact that some kind of control of human behavior is inevitable. We cannot use good sense in human affairs unless someone engages in the design and construction of environmental conditions which affect the behavior of men. Environmental changes have always been the condition for the improvement of cultural patterns, and we can hardly use the more effective methods of science without making changes on a grander scale. We are all controlled by the world in which we live, and part of that world has been and will be constructed by man. The question is this: Are we to be controlled by accident, by tyrants, or by ourselves in effective cultural design? (1955)

One of the logical places to implement the controls which behaviorists advocate is in the schools. Here students can learn to respond in ways which later will prove effective in social living. Behaviorists believe that the behaviors which students engage in while in the school are a consequence of the conditions set up by the teacher. In other words, the reason that children behave the way they do is because the teachers reinforce them for so doing. This includes the bad behavior as well as the good. Many inappropriate student behaviors can be traced specifically to the influence of the teacher.

It is the belief of some educators that children who are permitted sufficient freedom will somehow learn to govern themselves and engage in school activities which are useful and constructive. This is a departure from the traditional assumption that the only way to insure that children learn is to make the consequences for not learning sufficiently aversive. Years ago this was accomplished most frequently through the teachers' use of a cane. The cane came to be as much a tool of the teacher's trade as a hammer is to a carpenter's; so much so, in fact, that teachers were often depicted in medieval sculpture with cane in hand. Even though behaviorists would not condone punitive or coercive treatment, neither would they advocate any significant amount of freedom being offered to students. Those who advocate the "free and happy student" believe that students themselves should determine what school experiences are most likely to adequately prepare them for the future. Regarding this Skinner has said, if the student selects his own school experiences, "certainly they will reflect his idiosyncracies, and that is good, but how much can he know about the world in which he will eventually play a part? The things he is "naturally" curious about are of current and often temporary interest. How many things must he possess besides his "hot rod" to provide the insatiable curiosity relevant to, say, a course in physics?" (Skinner, 1973).

In the school, the elementary science teacher will be faced with two types of problems as she prepares her science materials and attempts to execute her teaching plan. The first of these has to do primarily with planning. How can learning be arranged in an efficient and effective manner and what principles apply in this organization? The second problem has to do with managing student behavior in the teaching-learning process so that the student's time is effectively used and a minimum number of disruptions occur. From an operant conditioning point of view, there are very specialized ways both to organize learning as well as to manage pupil behavior in the learning process.

Organizing Learning

Organizing learning with the use of behavioristic principles consists of tightly arranging sequences of learning increments. Skills or understandings are broken down into small parts and arranged in learning sequences with each part being reinforced as it is learned. Tight control of learning is essential: when inappropriate responses are made the learner is ordinarily directed to learning designed to correct his misunderstandings. Appropriate responses are rewarded with knowledge of results and the learner is directed to the next component of the learning sequence.

From the behavioristic viewpoint there are various classes of learning. Gagné (1965) distinguishes eight types. The first of these is what he calls *signal learning* or *classical conditioning*, where responses are diffuse and emotional, and the learning is involuntary. Common examples of signal learning include a dog salivating at the sight of food, and a person withdrawing his/her hand at the sight of a hot object. In essence the individual responds automatically to a signal from the environment.

A second type of learning is *operant conditioning*. The basic difference between classical conditioning and operant conditioning is that with classical conditioning there is an automatic response to a stimulus which is essentially inborn. In operant conditioning, particular responses are learned in association to reinforcing stimuli. In this case the individual responds in a certain way because he finds it reinforcing. For example, a child may be praised for actively pursuing his school work. Because praise satisfies his need for recognition, he will therefore continue to study.

The third type of learning outlined by Gagné is *chaining*. This category is reserved for nonverbal sequences. The basic condition for this type of learning is a reinstatement of the stimulus-response units into a proper order. In the elementary school, children learn many chains. They learn to tie, button, paint, draw, write, etc. They also learn to throw, catch, and kick balls of various sizes and shapes. Stimulation for each stimulus-response link is at least partly kinesthetic. This means that a chain of psychomotor movements is executed in sequence based on "feel." Our internal feedback mechanisms tell us as we execute a motor movement whether each component has been properly done. Initially a greater amount of thought must accompany the execution of psychomotor movement. After we become more skilled we rely more on kinesthetic stimulation and feedback to guide our behavior. There is a gradual change from reliance on external cues to reliance on internal cues in most skill learning.

In skill learning there are three phases—cognitive, fixation, and autonomous (Fitts, 1962). In the cognitive phase the students are asked to conceptualize the skill they are to perform. The teacher attempts to describe to the student verbally how to perform the skill and what to expect during its execution. In this phase it is appropriate, especially with young children, to model or demonstrate how the skill is to be executed while giving verbal descriptions. Most of us, but particularly young children, are unable to visualize verbal descriptions of psychomotor movements. A concrete referent, such as a demonstration, is needed to properly visualize the movement. The teacher should not only explain the nature of the movement, but should also point out possible difficulties which may be avoided and ways to maximize one's efforts to learn the movement.

In the fixation phase the proper behavior patterns are practiced until the chance of making incorrect responses is reduced to zero. This consists of a process of gradually linking together the components of the chain into an overall pattern. Many hours and days of practice, with coaching as appropriate, are necessary to gradually produce nearly error-free performance.

The autonomous phase is characterized by increasing the speed of performance while at the same time increasing the accuracy of performance. In this phase the individual is able to perform without undue interference from outside stimuli. The individual is in every sense an expert for whom the performance of the skill has become involuntary, inflexible, and locked in. A minimum amount of conscious control is required at this point for performance.

Either the part or the whole method may be used in training for skill development. In the part method, students practice subtasks one at a time in sequence, gradually building until the complete skill with all its subcomponent parts can be executed. In the whole method, trainees are first asked to observe an entire sequence of subtasks; then they must practice all of the subtasks together. Generally speaking, for skills that are not difficult and are not highly organized, the part method is the most efficient procedure for practicing those parts in which the student is weakest. On the other hand, for skills that are of moderate and high degrees of difficulty and are highly organized, the whole method is the most efficient (Naylor, 1962). It is essential that the teacher of young children examine each subtask to insure that no component is beyond the student's capacity. A certain amount of success is necessary for the student to continue to actively pursue skill development. For example, a small child may find it impossible to use a cork borer effectively because he does not have the physical strength to handle it.

Scheduling practice is also an important consideration. It is usually better to have distributed practice, which allows for rest periods, rather than massed practice which provides little or no interruption. The length of the rest period necessary for maximum efficiency depends somewhat on the nature of the skill to be practiced. A few seconds or minutes are probably all that are required. With distributed practice it is possible to reduce the total practice time and yet achieve better performance (Duncan, 1951).

The fourth category of learning outlined by Gagné is *verbal association*. This is a type of chaining, only the links are verbal units. In its simplest form the chain involves just two links, such as when the child learns to name an object. When the child can also provide characteristics of the named object the response chain is three units long. For example, if a child properly identifies a tree and then adds a description of its size, the three component chain would be "the little tree" or "the big tree." Among all the conditions of verbal learning, probably the most important is that of meaningfulness. This condition has the strongest influence over the rapidity of learning as well as the ability of the child to retain what is learned. Usually meaningfulness depends upon experience. Children who have limited experience find a good deal of difficulty learning and remembering because the symbolic language of the classroom has little meaning for them. A broad wealth of experience is obviously critical to meaningful verbal learning. In teaching science to children this means that it is helpful if they have had experiences with a wide variety of natural phenomena. It would be good if children, prior to their school experiences, had the opportunity to handle plants and animals, batteries, rocks, etc. If children have not had these experiences it is imperative that such experiences be provided for them at the beginning of their schooling.

The next level of learning identified by Gagné is *multiple discrimination.* Here the student must be able to learn different responses for stimuli which might be easily confused. In other words, the student learns to discriminate between the chains of motor and verbal learning he has already acquired. For example, some children have not properly discriminated between "evergreen tree" and "pine tree." In fact there are broad leaf evergreen trees as well as the coniferous type with needle-shaped leaves. In addition "pine tree" is just one of the major types of coniferous evergreens. Thus in learning how to differentiate between "evergreen trees" and "pine trees" children have to learn to make two different discriminations.

The sixth type of learning outlined by Gagné is *concept learning.* A concept is a class of things which has common characteristics. These things may be objects, events, or persons. Usually each concept has a name, such as plants, animals, chemicals, bacteria, and rocks. Some things are not concepts, because they are particular instances of a concept. For example, Douglas fir, bald eagle, oxygen, typhoid bacillus and limestone are specific examples of the above-named concepts. In learning concepts children show an ability to abstract characteristics of something as opposed to its concrete physical properties. For example a child may at first learn to call cubes and similar objects "blocks." Later he may come to learn the concept *cube* and discover that cubes can vary in size, color, or the material that they are made from. He is able to visualize cubes made of a variety of materials or of varying sizes and colors and at the same time retain the basic class characteristics of objects that can be called cubes. Obviously he is able to differentiate cubes from three dimensional, rectangular objects and the like.

Concepts usually have attributes which differentiate them from other related concepts. *Lake* is a concept with certain attributes; chief among these is size. It is usually smaller than an ocean or a sea and larger than a pool or pond. Concepts vary in the number of attributes they have. The concepts of pollution, energy, and conservation all have many attributes. As the number of attributes increases the difficulty of learning the concept increases. In order to simplify learning for the child the teacher may have to limit the number of attributes. Simplification may also be accomplished by combining a large number of attributes into a smaller number of patterns. For example, animals may have physical, biochemical, and behavioral attributes.

A seventh type of learning according to Gagné is *principle learning*. The learning of principles involves understanding the relationships between two or more concepts. For example, the volume of dry gas is directly related to the temperature and inversely related to the pressure it is under. This means that gas expands when it is heated and its volume is reduced when pressure is increased. Hence, the concept of gas volume is related to the concepts of temperature and pressure.

Learning concepts and principles is a source of economy of learning for the child. It brings about a greater sense of understanding and helps him organize his perceptions and master his environment. If we were unable to organize our experiences conceptually and had to respond uniquely to each environmental stimulus the complexity of the world would overwhelm us.

Because schooling is concerned with helping children conceptualize it is important to properly assess how much they understand when they enter school. What the teacher can and cannot teach children depends by and large upon the child's previous experiences and what he/she has learned as a consequence of them. Even though a child may have a wide variety of experiences his conceptual knowledge is likely to be incomplete basically because direct experience is always limiting and a good deal of misunderstanding is possible. The school must take the child with incomplete and inaccurate concepts and add relevant attributes and eliminate irrelevant ones. As previously mentioned, a child may believe a pine tree is equivalent to the concept "evergreen tree." This illustrates how inaccurate and incomplete a child's conceptions may be. He must come to understand that a pine tree is an example of an evergreen tree of the coniferous type and that there are other examples of coniferous trees which look much like pine trees but which are not and that there is a whole group of evergreen trees with broad leaves.

In teaching concepts and principles there are some useful procedures that will enhance student learning (DeCecco, 1968). With regard to teaching concepts the following steps are recommended:

1. Describe the performance the student will be expected to exhibit after he has learned the concept.
2. Reduce the number of attributes to be learned in complex concepts and make the important attributes more dominant than the unimportant ones.
3. Provide the student with the name of the concept he is to be taught.
4. Provide examples and nonexamples of the concept.

5. Ask the student to define the concept.
6. Ask the student to provide examples and nonexamples of the concept.

For teaching principles the following steps are recommended:

1. Describe the performance expected of the student after he has learned the principle.
2. Indicate which concepts or principles the student must recall in learning the new principle and offer assistance to the student in making this recollection.
3. Help the student organize the subcomponent concepts and principles into a proper order or assignment.
4. Have the student apply the principle in a specific situation.
5. Require the student to state the principle and explain its meaning.
6. Verify that the student has learned the principle.
7. Provide appropriate practice.

The last type of learning indicated by Gagné is *problem solving*. Problem solving involves a form of principle learning in which lower-order principles are applied in learning higher-order principles. Included in problem solving are creative thinking, critical thinking, and learning by discovery. Problem solving can be taught by first determining what concepts and principles students will need to solve the problem. Next, the students need to be given some direction and adequate cues as they proceed in the solution of the problem. All of these efforts should stop short of giving away the actual solution. Once one example problem has been solved, additional problems can be used for verification of student's learning and as additional practice.

Creativity and learning by discovery require less structure by the teacher than problem solving. Originality is encouraged. Students are asked to attempt to think of the unusual and unique rather than predetermined ways of proceeding. The teacher will want to provide conditions which increase flexibility, fluency, and originality of the student's solutions to various kinds of problems. Problems will have to be formulated which permit a good deal of divergence on the part of students.

Exercise 5-2   Procedures for Teaching Principles

Outline the procedure you would use to teach a specific science principle.

Cognitive-Field and Perceptual-Field Theories

In contrast to the behaviorist-environmental view of man, cognitive-field and perceptual-field theories see man as a naturally active,

Children are naturally curious and learn and are shaped through interactions with the environment.

seeking, adapting being who learns and is shaped by interactions with the environment, most of which he initiates himself. As has already been pointed out from the behaviorist viewpoint, man is seen as a reactor to environmental stimuli. In addition human reactions are at first random and are repeated only if the individual finds that he is pleasurably reinforced for his reactions. The assumption is that man's actions are not purposeful. This is just the opposite of what is assumed from both the cognitive-field as well as the perceptual-field viewpoints. From these positions man is attempting to master his environment and subdue it so that he can live meaningfully in it. In essence man is trying to master his environment rather than being completely shaped by it. As a teacher it is imperative that you examine each of these positions carefully so that as you teach you will be able to fully comprehend what assumptions about man are implicit in the procedures you use.

Piaget's Cognitive-Field Theory

The most representative theory in this category of theories is that of Jean Piaget. According to Piaget, a child is born with a set of responses which he uses to get to know his environment and himself. In addition, as a child grows and develops he increases the number and complexity of the transactions which he is able to make with the environment. This increase in complexity enables the child to greatly enlarge his ability to deal with and make sense out of his experience. These complex capabilities are internalized so that they can be carried on mentally and are tied to language symbols and systems so that greater abstract manipulation becomes possible. For Piaget, development is in the form of increasing the intellectual capabilities of children through the growth of structures in the brain which he refers to as *schema*. These schema provide the basis for adaptation or adjustment necessary to cope with the environment (Baldwin, 1967).

The growth of schema in a child is a gradual process. Piaget has broken this process down into four main periods or stages: sensorimotor, preconceptual and intuitive thought, concrete operations, and formal operations.

THE SENSORIMOTOR STAGE

The sensorimotor period of development corresponds in time to the period commonly called infancy, the first two years of life. The most important feature of this stage is that the child is acquiring skills and adaptations of a behavioral kind. The child becomes able to coordinate information from various senses and behave consistently with this input of information. Thus the infant is able to look at what he is listening to, and his walking is guided by auditory, visual, and tactual cues.

A second major capability which arises in the sensorimotor period is the infant's ability to operate as if the external world were a permanent place, not one whose existence depends upon his perceiving it. For example, even the youngest infant will track interesting objects that appear within his field of vision. However, if it goes out of his field of vision repeatedly and then immediately returns he will not wait for it. His glance will focus on other things. Later on, however, he becomes able to search for objects that have disappeared and to search for them on the basis of information about where they went. He can take a different pathway to find an object which has been hidden from that which the object took. He somehow has developed a sense of surrounding space that permits him to take a variety of paths to the same point.

Another related capability that a child is able to exhibit toward the end of the sensorimotor stage is that he comes to realize that objects have permanence, are independent of his perceptions, and that things happen in a cause and effect relationship, not by his willing them. Before he realizes this, objects that are out of sight are out of mind. Objects no longer in view no longer exist. For example, if a toy is placed behind a pillow, even while the child is watching, he will simply turn his attention to something else. Later on, he will realize that the toy is behind the pillow and will continue to focus his attention on it. In addition, the child comes to learn that things happen that are not caused by him.

Finally, toward the end of the sensorimotor stage, children are able to exhibit goal-directed behavior. They are able to put together two or three actions into a sequence designed to reach a particular goal. At this time they are able to construct new actions to reach objectives that are otherwise unattainable. Thus they can spontaneously and deliberately vary their actions in order to experiment with new objects and learn new behaviors. However, they are still handicapped by the fact that they do not develop the conceptual structures to correspond with their behavior. Even though they seem to be very adaptive, their behavior is still very concrete and this seriously limits how far ahead they can plan a sequence of actions.

THE PRECONCEPTUAL STAGE

The preconceptual stage occurs between two and seven years of age. During this period there is a gradual growth in the child's internal cognitive picture of the external world and its many relationships. He becomes increasingly more able to associate specific objects with the class to which they belong. For example, by the age of five or six a child may be unable to tell you whether there are more red roses or more white roses in a flower bowl, but he does understand that all the flowers in the bowl are roses, and that some are red and some are white. According to Piaget, the mechanism at work is very much like that in the first stage. By the child forming things into classes and dividing them again, his mental activity begins to tie together the separate labels for things and to place separate groups of things into organized hierarchical frameworks. Through this process the child between the second and seventh year of life builds on objects to form concepts and on concepts to form classes of concepts. He accomplishes this by grouping and regrouping, naming things, and continuing to explore (Case, 1973).

THE CONCRETE OPERATIONS STAGE

The third stage takes place approximately between ages seven and eleven. Piaget reports that at about age seven children undergo a profound reorientation in thinking. Formal thought processes become much more stable and reasonable. This is probably best illustrated by the idea of conservation. Before age seven if a child is shown two balls of clay, which he agrees are equal in size, and then one of these clay balls is rolled into a sausage shape, he will think that the long sausage-shaped ball contains more clay. By age seven he will not think that the the long one has more clay than the short one, but he will still think that the long one weighs more. The concept of conservation develops in the following order: number, substance, length, area, weight, and finally volume. These capacities are in the process of development during most of the course of the concrete operations stage.

An interesting experiment involving the concept of conservation was conducted by Smedslund (1961) with five- to seven-year-old children. The implications for teaching elementary science are evident. The children were given a pretest of weight conservation, which consisted of placing two balls of clay on a platform balance so that their equivalence in weight could be demonstrated. The children were then asked if they would still weigh the same when one of the balls was changed into a sausage shape. By this means two groups of children were identified, one that could conserve and one that could not. Next, training was given to the group that was unable to conserve. Constancy of weight was demonstrated in a number of ways. After this training the children readily concluded that weight remained constant even though the form of objects was changed. After a short time a posttest was given to both groups of children, those who could originally conserve and those who were trained to conserve. The posttest was conducted in exactly the same way as the pretest. All of the children now believed that the clay pieces could continue to weigh the same. However, at this point, without the children seeing, the experimenter removed some clay from one of the changed pieces so that they did not balance when they were weighed. The children were then asked to explain this unexpected event. All the subjects who were trained to conserve quickly reverted back to their preoperational answers, such as "it's skinnier, so it doesn't weigh as much." The majority of the children who had acquired conservation on their own, however, resisted this type of explanation. They felt that there was something "fishy" and that some of the clay must have been removed or that something was wrong with the balance. Among other things, this experiment points out the difficulty in trying to advance capabilities more rapidly than they naturally occur.

THE FORMAL OPERATIONS STAGE

The final stage is formal operations. The beginning of this stage occurs at about age eleven. At this time the child is able to operate on the basis of a hypothetical system in which the form of the logic can be independent of the particular content of the problem at hand. For example, consider the riddle, "which is heavier—a pound of feathers or a pound of lead?" In the concrete operations stage, reason may dictate that a pound is a pound, but the difference between feathers and lead may still interfere with the reasoning. Significantly, neither the child nor the adult ever entirely abandon earlier ways of thinking. Rather, earlier thinking patterns appear less frequently for problems where they would be inappropriate (Chittenden, 1970).

In the formal operations stage the individual comes to understand the basic principles of causal thinking and scientific experimentation and can perform experiments and deduce the proper implications in many instances. At this stage the child is ready to begin relating things such as the concepts of mass and number, in terms of such higher order things as scientific laws. The child is also able to think about what might happen and to envision the various changes that are possible. In other words, he is able to think in terms of probability and to hypothesize. He is thus able to visualize in advance of experimentation. He learns to do all this abstractly, without the use of visual props. At this stage children can do many of the things which are basic to learning science. Before this stage is reached much of what science is all about has generally eluded them.

To further illustrate the formal operations stage, consider the following problem. The child is shown a spinning wheel having holes of various sizes in it and marbles of varying sizes on it. He is asked to figure out why some marbles fall off before others and then to test to see if he is correct. In the concrete operations stage the child can readily classify the holes accurately and can see that there are big and small holes and that in both categories there are some near the center and some near the edge. He has a primitive, intuitive notion of causality, but he appears restricted to noting what actually occurs, rather than thinking in terms of probability. If you ask why the big marble fell off first, he will say, "Because it's bigger." Then, if it is arranged so that the small one falls off first, he will often say, "Because it's smaller," without being overly upset by the contradiction. If you ask him to prove that big ones fall off first, he will not always bother to keep other variables constant. Apparently the child at this age has not internalized a system in which any relevant attribute may vary and in which different combinations of possibilities can all produce the same result. To him one thing must produce a given consequence. The child sees a big marble in a small hole near the edge and concludes that it fell off so soon because it was big. He does not imagine that one could put a small marble in a small hole near the edge and that it might fall off too. He does not see the need to control other factors before he draws a conclusion about size. In other words, he is still bound by the concrete things that he sees before him. His intellectual capabilities are not yet complex enough to represent conditions of the world accurately which are not before him.

It may be observed at this point that little has been said regarding whether or not all children go through the stages described by Piaget. Actually it has been found that there is a good deal of uniformity in the order of the intellectual development of children. There is a remarkable consistency in the sequence of things which children can and cannot do. The exact age at which an individual child goes through each stage is another matter, however. There is a good deal of variability between children regarding when they go through the stages, but the order of the stages is relatively constant. For example, the age at which the child may begin to appreciate that weight does not change if nothing is added may vary, but it never occurs before he learns that objects have permanence; nor does it occur, in sequence, after he learns that all other things must be equal or controlled in a scientific experiment before cause and effect relationships can be identified. Within the subcomponents of any stage the same is true. A child will always learn the conditions under which weight remains constant before he learns the conditions under which displaced volume remains constant and after he learns the conditions under which number and amount remain constant.

There are a number of implications which can be drawn from the ideas of Piaget. First, as has already been indicated, it does not appear to be particularly fruitful to attempt to accelerate the child's development in terms of intellectual capacities. These will grow at their own rate. Not only is it not fruitful, it is likely to be a waste of time to expose children to certain kinds of experiences before they are prepared to benefit much from them. To illustrate, if we consider the characteristics of preoperational thought, we might conclude that any extensive use of instruction which attempts to prove some principle through appeals to logic or scientific experiment would be wasted on children who are at this stage of development. As Piaget has remarked, children do not learn conservation of quantity through being shown that quantity is constant. In fact, from the point of view of Piaget, this is basically impossible because, if the child possessed the capacity to understand the implications of such a demonstration then in all likelihood he would already understand the principle. The ability of an older child to demonstrate conservation is really a symptom of the development of schema or logical structures and one cannot create these structures through teaching the symptom. You cannot make a child have a capacity by trying to teach him to do what he could do if he had that capacity (Chittenden, 1970).

A second implication of Piaget's work relates to what can be done with children given the fact that they grow in stages with defined limits. What can be done to organize learning which fits the intellectual capacities of the individual children you are teaching? It must be concluded that children in the concrete operations state should not be given experiences which required them to think in terms of probability. Nor would preoperational children be asked to accomplish tasks which make conservation of volume a necessity. Children simply will not be successful in these activities. This indicates that a child should be permitted to practice the use of the intellectual capacities which he has on a variety of tasks. If children are given materials to use they will practice on their own without too much teacher direction. They seem to want to master environmental materials with the use of their present capabilities.

A third implication of the stages outlined by Piaget is the formulation of instructional strategies for individuals rather than for groups of children. As indicated earlier, even though children all go through the stages in a sequential pattern, they do not necessarily all go through the various stages at the same time chronologically. This makes it necessary to determine where the child is in his intellectual development and provide experiences which are consistent with that development. Conceivably teachers in the elementary school may be confronted with thinking patterns from a variety of developmental levels. Even in adulthood some people never reach the level of formal operations. Estimates of adults who do not reach this stage vary between 30 and 90 percent. Certainly at the upper levels of the elementary school children are present whose thinking patterns vary from preoperational through formal operations. This all implies that the elementary science classroom should have a wide variety of materials designed for children with a divergent set of capacities. In addition, it assumes that the science teacher will have to work simultaneously with the children who have these varying capacities. Children will have to work individually and in small groups with specially designed materials to enable the teacher to profitably help on an individual basis. Therefore, the teacher will have to conceive of himself in a helping role rather than as a dispensor of information about science.

The elementary science teacher must not only understand what curriculum materials are appropriate for students at various levels of development, but also be able to assess what levels a child is operating on so that the materials can be appropriately prescribed. The following set of tasks is an example of the items that may be used to assess the developmental level of children:

1. CONSERVATION OF NUMBER. Have the child count out five beads in one row and then five in another row alongside the first row. Ask him if there are the same number in each row. If he can tell you that there are the same number in each row, ask him to spread out one row a little farther so it looks longer and ask him if there are still the same number in each row. If he indicates that there are more beads in the longer row ask him why. Inability to indicate that there are the same number of beads in both rows indicates that the child is unable to conserve number and is still likely to be in the preoperational stage.

2. CONSERVATION OF SUBSTANCE. Give the child a ball of clay to handle and observe. Then take the clay and roll it into a long cylinder. Ask the child if the elongated piece of clay has more, less, or the same amount of clay as the ball. When the child responds ask him why he thinks the elongated piece of clay is bigger, smaller, or the same. The child who indicates that there is more clay in the elongated piece shows an inability to conserve matter or substance.

3. CONSERVATION OF LENGTH. Use a whole straw and one that has been cut into sections. Start with both straws lined up in parallel form. (See Figure 5–1a.) Have the child agree that both straws are the same length. Now move the straws so that they are not parallel to one another, but with the sectioned straw still having its parts laid end to end in a straight line (Figure 5–1b). Ask the child if a bug started walking through one straw and then through the other one, all the time traveling at the same speed, which straw would it take the longest time to walk through. Then ask if they would travel the same distance and ask why. Finally move the sectioned straws into a jagged position (Figure 5–1c) and repeat the same questions. The inability to conserve length is indicated by the child saying that changing the arrangement of the straw sections alters its length.

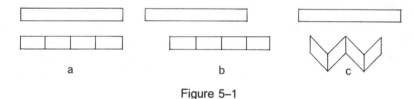

Figure 5–1

4. CONSERVATION OF AREA. Give the child two identical pieces of green construction paper and two toy cows. Have him place one toy cow on each piece of paper. Then ask the child to compare the fields, making certain he notes that they are the same size. Indicate to him that because the fields are the same size each animal will have the same amount of grass to eat. Next tell the child that you are going to use blocks to represent barns. Place the blocks on each field in the manner indicated in Figure 5–2. Ask which cow will have the most grass to eat or if the amount of grass will be the same. Ask the child to explain his answer. Continue adding equal numbers of blocks to each field, asking each time which cow will have the most grass to eat. A child who believes that different arrangements of barns give differing amounts of grass to eat in spite of the fact that the number of barns remains equal, is unable to conserve area.

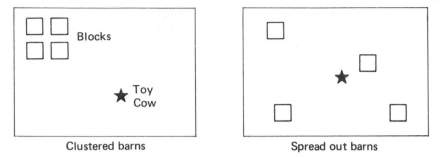

| Clustered barns | Spread out barns |

Figure 5–2

5. CONSERVATION OF WEIGHT. Take a piece of clay and alter its shape in the following ways, each time asking the child if the weight of the clay increased, decreased, or remained the same: (a) transform it into a sausage shape; (b) a pancake shape; and (c) into several little pieces. If the ability to conserve weight is present, the child will indicate that the weight of the clay remains the same no matter what its shape.

6. CONSERVATION OF VOLUME BY DISPLACEMENT. Show the child a tall cylinder that is three quarters full of colored water and two metal blocks of the same size (volume) but of different weights. Let the child handle the blocks and compare the weights. Then ask the child to predict where the water level will be if the lightweight block is lowered into the water and to place a rubber band around the cylinder at the predicted level. Have him next lower the lightweight block into the water and adjust the elastic band to the level of the water at this point. Finally ask the child where he thinks the water level will be when the heavier block is lowered into the cylinder. Then ask him why he thinks this will happen. The child should indicate that the volume of displacement would remain the same if he has developed this conservation ability.

The above list represents a convenient way to assess the level of development of children. If a child is unable to perform any of the conservation tasks he is probably still in the preoperational stage. If he is able to perform some of the tasks but not others, he is in the concrete operations stage. If he succeeds with all of the tasks you may wish to check to see if he can perform tasks at the formal operations level. The exercise referred to earlier regarding the spinning wheel with various sized holes and marbles could be used to determine the extent to which a child is able to perform formal operational tasks. Roughly what can be expected of children in terms of their conservation abilities is as follows:

Conservation of Number	About ages 6–7
Conservation of Substance	About ages 7–8
Conservation of Length	About ages 7–8
Conservation of Area	About ages 8–9
Conservation of Weight	About ages 9–10
Conservation of Volume	About ages 11–14

Thus far it has been shown that the development of intellectual capacity goes through a number of stages whose order is constant, but whose time of appearance may vary with the individual. Each new level of development consists of a new coherence, a new structuring of elements in the mind of the child which until that time have not been systematically related to each other. The appearance of these capabilities can be measured through a series of tasks which the child can be directed to perform. The question that remains is "Now that we know that children develop in stages and can determine which stage a child is in, what difference does this make in the formulation of the curriculum?" This question can be answered, in part, by considering the four factors which Piaget (1964) believed contributed to intellectual development: (a) nervous maturation; (b) encounters with experience; (c) social transmission; and (d) equilibration or auto-regulation.

While development would be impossible without nervous maturation, it does not fully explain how the intellect grows. One indication of this is the fact that the average age at which the stages of growth appear varies a great deal from one society to another. Again, however, the ordering of the stages has been found to be consistent in all societies studied. This has been proved through studies of Africans, bushmen, Iranian villagers and city dwellers, Americans, Canadians, as well as the children in Geneva, Switzerland where Piaget did his initial work. Differences were obtained in terms of when children of different societies pass through the various stages. For example, average ages in Geneva are different from those in the United States, but about the same as those of Iranian city dwellers. On the other hand, Iranian villagers were generally two years behind their city dwelling counterparts. In Canada a delay of four years was found to exist between children in different parts of the country. Thus it can be observed that nervous maturation does not explain everything with regard to intellectual development.

What about the role of experience? Experiences with objects and other phenomena are obviously a basic factor in the development of cognitive structures. Again, however, they do not provide us with a complete explanation. Piaget has noted that there are some concepts which appear at the beginning of the concrete operations stage which can not be explained on the basis of experience alone. Specifically, conservation of substance seems to appear without the influence of experience. Conservation of weight and volume are apparently dependent upon the child's ability to conserve substance. In the experiment with the clay ball where its shape is transformed the child seems to sense that something is conserved even though he is not sure exactly what.

The third factor that contributes to development is social transmission. Social transmission includes social in addition to linguistic or educational transmission. Piaget does not believe that this factor explains development entirely either, even though he believes it is fundamental. Its insufficiency is based upon the fact that a child can receive valuable information via language or education which is directed by an adult only if he is in a state where he can understand this information. In other words, in order to receive the information or to learn, he must have the structures which will enable him to assimilate this information.

Equilibration is the fourth factor which has been identified by Piaget as contributing to development, which he feels is more fundamental than the other three. Equilibration is a process of self-regulation. In the act of knowing, the individual is active and, consequently, when faced with an external disturbance, will react in order to compensate or adjust until a state of equilibrium is achieved.

While the first three factors do indeed play a role in the development of the human organism they are not nearly as fundamental as the process of equilibration, where the individual's intellectual development depends primarily upon his own activity and coordinated efforts. What the first three factors have in common is that they come about in a passive way. Something is done to the individual—his physiological system matures, or he is presented with physical or linguistic material to absorb. However, intellectual development is not passive. A child comes to view the world as coherent and organized to the extent that he acts upon it, transforms and manipulates it, and succeeds in properly coordinating these actions and transformations. Development advances as the child's rudimentary understandings are revised, broadened, and related to one another.

The idea that the intellectual development of children is most fundamentally related to individual activity is extremely important. It is by far the most useful idea about teaching that comes from Piaget's work. In essence it is a plea to allow children to do their own learning. This does not mean that you should let a child do whatever he wants whenever he wants. Nor does it mean that intellectual development will proceed at its own pace no matter what you do. It does mean, however, that schools as they are presently organized can be pretty ineffectual. Much of what we do in school is to transmit information. We become involved in telling things to children much of the time, instead of presenting them with situations in which they are involved experimentally, where they can see what happens when they act upon objects. They need to manipulate things and symbols, to pose questions and seek their own answers, reconcile what they find one time with what is found on another occasion, and to compare findings with those of other children. Simply telling them will not contribute to their intellectual development; allowing them to become active learners will.

At this point you should be able to visualize more clearly the comparisons between Piaget's view of learning and that of the behaviorists. Remember that the behaviorists believe that man is basically a reactor to stimuli from the environment, who responds randomly until he inadvertently finds that a particular response satisfies some need that he has. Also remember that Piaget sees man as an active participant in purposeful activity. Children then actively search their environment with the purpose of organizing and controlling it. Piaget believes the stimulus-response notions purported by the behaviorists to be an inadequate explanation of how learning takes place. When you think of stimulus-response schema, says Piaget, you usually think that first of all there is a stimulus and then a response that is set off by this stimulus. However, he believes that the response was there first.

> A stimulus is a stimulus only to the extent that it is significant, and it becomes significant only to the extent that there is a structure which permits its assimilation, a structure which can integrate this stimulus but which at the same time sets off the response. In other words, ... the stimulus response schema should be written in the circular form—in the form of a schema or of a structure which is not simply one way.... above all, between the stimulus and the response, there is the organism, the organism and its structures. The stimulus is really a stimulus only when it is assimilated into a structure and it is this structure which sets off the response. Consequently, it is not an exaggeration to say that the response is there first, or if you wish at the beginning there is the structure (Piaget, 1964).

You may have wondered at this point, that if the proper intellectual growth and development of a child depends upon his being able to manipulate objects in a personalized way, then what is the role of the teacher besides providing the child with these objects. This has led many who believe that education should be of the "progressive type" to conclude that Piaget's findings support what they have already determined to do. What they propose is that children should be provided little or no guidance in the educative process. What Piaget really suggests is that children during their early schooling should be provided with experiences which have a concrete base, but which can, nevertheless, be internalized. This, of course, necessitates that children have the opportunity to deal manipulatively with their environment in order to obtain meaning which is consistent with their development patterns. In addition, it is essential that this concrete experience be laid down as a basis for the development of abstract thinking which follows. In the development of concrete thought it should not be assumed that there is no place for structure. It is true that materials must be used in a personalized way by children, but the teacher must be on hand to talk to the child about his thoughts regarding the material he is working with. The role of the teacher becomes even more involved and critical when the child reaches the stage of formal operations. Here the teacher will need to question children about their thoughts in order to aid them in developing skills in abstraction and thinking in terms of probability. It is not the purpose of the pupil-teacher interaction to help students to understand concepts or principles, but rather to question them regarding the thought processes they use in manipulating first concrete objects and later abstract ideas.

Later in this book, illustrations will be made of various science programs that are currently available for the elementary school. Chief among these are *Elementary Science Study (ESS), Science Curriculum Improvement Study (SCIS),* and *Science: A Process Approach (S-APA).* It should be of interest to note what principles of learning and development are claimed by the authors as underpinnings for each of these programs. The ESS program has been developed largely on an intuitive basis, rather than a theoretical one with well-defined theories of learning and development implied. Materials were not developed on the basis of any specific theory of how children learn, or on the logical structure of science or upon any concept of the needs of society. Rather development followed a trial and error kind of process. If the materials failed to turn children on, affectively and cognitively, they were discarded and other directions were pursued. However, in spite of the fact that the program was not deliberately based upon any particular theory of learning, at least two of its aspects are supported by Piaget's ideas on intellectual development. These are the extensive use of concrete things for children to work with and the active involvement of children in the learning process. It is assumed by the ESS developers that children learn more when they are doing what they want to do instead of what someone else wants them to do. Supposedly, such self-directed learning has more meaning for them. Much of ESS is, therefore, consistent with the basic ideas of Piaget (Rogers and Voelker, 1970).

The developers of SCIS state emphatically that the ideas of Piaget constitute the psychological bases for their program. SCIS is committed to the intellectual development and scientific literacy of children. Scientific literacy is pursued through concrete experiences whereby children acquire the concepts and communication skills essential to its development. Concrete manipulation and interaction among students

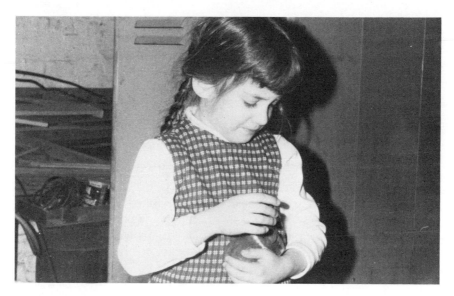

Children should be actively involved in learning.

and teachers are essential components of this program and well organized into their laboratory approach. It can be seen that this program, just like ESS, is based on the ideas of Piaget. However, it should be pointed out that with SCIS, a good deal of emphasis is given to the understanding of the concepts or "big ideas" of science. The emphasis then is to use a manipulative means to obtain an understanding of specified content. Intellectual development is important, but it appears to take a "back seat" to learning specified concepts. It would seem that to more strictly follow Piaget, children's intellectual development would receive greater emphasis and the concepts of science would be relegated to a secondary position. In this position, there would be a good deal of variability regarding which concepts each child would learn as a result of his intellectual pursuits (Thomson and Voelker, 1970).

S-APA is more closely allied with the work of Gagné. Gagné exerted a strong influence on the structuring of the hierarchy of the curriculum and the evaluation system of S-APA. What resulted from this influence is a much more highly structured program than the other two. In this program, students are able to manipulate materials, but this is done with well-defined purposes. The whole program is organized around performance objectives with tests for determining when children are able to properly exhibit the skills called for in the objectives. All skills are organized into a highly structured sequence. Children's experiences in this program are controlled so as to efficiently meet the expectations of the objectives. The objectives are evolved upon the basis of what the processes of science are determined to be. There is probably no course of study for any level of instruction or for any subject matter that includes behavioral objectives which have been so specifically and comprehensively stated and so carefully arranged into a hierarchial sequence (Mayer and Livermore, 1969). S-APA thus is based upon a behavioristic foundation, while ESS and SCIS more closely approximate the ideas of Piaget.

Exercise 5–3   Stages of Intellectual Growth

1. The best way to become well acquainted with how children respond during each of the stages of development is to work with them as they attempt to perform specified tasks. Using the tasks outlined earlier in the chapter to preassess intellectual development, determine the level of development of at least six elementary school students. Select students from various grade levels.
2. Design and use a new set of tasks which can be performed by children who are able to conserve length, volume, substance, weight, number, and area.
3. Design and use a task which can be performed by children in the formal operations stage.

SCIENCE EXPERIENCES FOR YOUNG CHILDREN

Young children are particularly eager to try out various things through immediate and direct manipulation to see how they work. If you observe children you will notice that their curiosity prompts them to explore every possible way that a particular object may operate. They turn the knobs, pull the levers, twist the objects around or attempt whatever manipulations will lead to a further understanding. Children are also fond of asking "how and why" continuously. Because of these traits children usually enjoy beginning science experiences, particularly if they are permitted to handle materials and do more free exploration. In addition children are more likely to enjoy short-term investigations where they have tools available to pull, poke, open, and take apart. Consequently, the kind of experiences which children are best equipped to handle in the early elementary years are those where they use the tools of science to observe, measure, and gather information.

Included below are some experiences young children can be encouraged to engage in which are consistent with their intellectual capacities and which provide a stimulus to the development of these capacities.

1. *The volume of a liquid is conserved, regardless of the shape of a container; volumes of different containers are measurable.* To deter-

mine whether children have reached the stage of intuitive thought at which they can comprehend that the volume of matter is conserved, the teacher arranges four different shaped glass jars, with each containing the same volume of water (Figure 5–3) before a group and asks the class, "How does the amount of water in these glass jars compare?" Once the children have responded the teacher then asks them to think of a way to test to see if their responses are correct. Probably the children will decide to pour the water from each jar into a measuring cup. The children will obviously be surprised to discover the results since their judgments will likely be based upon observation rather than on tested knowledge.

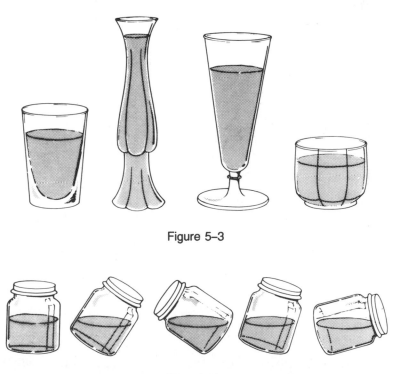

Figure 5–3

Figure 5–4

Next have children observe identical amounts of water in several identical jars which are fitted with screw-type lids and slanted in different positions (Figure 5–4). Ask the children to compare the amount of water in these jars. Then place all of the jars in the same position so that the children can compare their responses with what is actually the case.

Finally set up in various places around the room a variety of different containers of water with a graduated cylinder at each location. Have individuals or small groups of children walk from station to station, filling the various containers and measuring their volume.

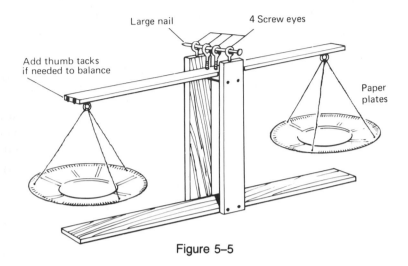

Large nail

4 Screw eyes

Add thumb tacks
if needed to balance

Paper
plates

Figure 5–5

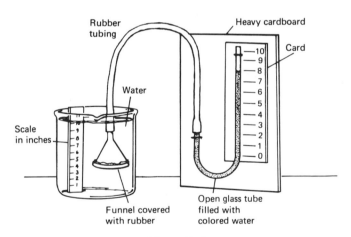

Rubber
tubing

Heavy cardboard

Card

—10
—9
—8
—7
—6
—5
—4
—3
—2
—1
—0

Water

Scale
in inches

Funnel covered
with rubber

Open glass tube
filled with
colored water

Figure 5–6

2. *Objects have weight and may vary in weight.* Students will need
to either construct their own balances or have access to one purchased
from a commercial supply house. Balances can be prepared like the one
depicted in Figure 5–5. Give the children the experience of weighing
a wide variety of things such as coins, seeds, rocks, straw, plants, and
animals. Beads, buck shot or paperclips can be used as the unit of
measure which is placed in the counterbalancing cup of the balance.
Animals can be weighed at intervals to determine their increase in
weight. Children can be asked to indicate what they expect different
objects to weigh. Modeling clay can be formed into different shapes and
weighed by the children to help them understand the conservation of
matter.

3. *Measuring water pressure.* Children can be taught that water exerts pressure that can be measured and that this pressure is exerted equally in all directions. This can be done by constructing a manometer or pressure-depth gauge (see Figure 5–6). Children can measure the pressure of water at varying depths by moving the funnel up and down in the graduated jar of water and noting the changes in the colored water column in the glass tube. Have the children record the relationships they note between differences in depth and manometer readings. Now have them hold the funnel pointing upward and sideways as well as down and note what they observe. Have the students construct a bar graph depicting the relationships between readings and different depths.

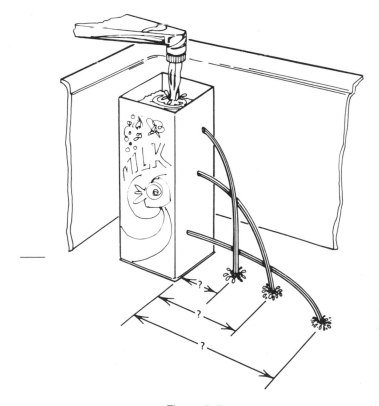

Figure 5–7

Children can construct their own device to measure the pressure exerted by water. Have them take an empty milk carton in which holes are cut at measured heights along the side of the carton as indicated in Figure 5–7. Plug the holes while the carton is filled with water. Leave the carton beneath a running tap so that it is continuously filled with the water while water is being emptied through the holes in the side of the carton. Have the children measure, record, and then graph the number of inches each hole is from the top of the carton and the distance the water spurts from each opening.

SCIENCE EXPERIENCES FOR CHILDREN IN THE UPPER GRADES

Children in the upper grades have usually mastered the intellectual skills associated with the concrete operations stage and are ready to begin using their developing capacity to engage in formal operations. Hopefully children of this age will continue to explore, seek and examine in order to increase their knowledge. However, they should be able to take a more reasoned point of view in their learning. Children should continue, at this level, to learn through direct experience, but with their growing capacities to abstract and to think in terms of probability, they should be given experiences which require them to explain events on the basis of indirect evidence and to hypothesize in instances where multiple factors may influence cause and effect relationships. The following experiences are illustrative of the kind of experiences which are appropriate for children at this level:

1. *Volume of matter is conserved when matter is changed from one physical state to another.* Have students fill paper cups with water and then cover them with foil to prevent any escape of water molecules. Then have them weigh the cups and put them in the refrigerator to freeze. When they are frozen ask students to predict how the weights of ice and water compare. Then have them weigh the ice. To verify the measurements, have them melt the ice and compare the weight of the resulting water with the weight of the original liquid.

Because ice appears bigger it is an interesting phenomenon for children to investigate. Have them carefully mark the water level in a paper cup which is then covered with foil and placed in the refrigerator. When the water is frozen have them mark the level of the ice. Finally, have them melt the ice and measure the level of water. Then ask the children what they found out.

Show the children the demonstration illustrated in Figure 5–8. The water in Container A is vaporized and channeled into Container B which is set in a jar of ice water. The weight of the water when it is in Container A should be compared with the weight of the condensed water in Container B.

2. *A piece of iron surrounded by an electric current becomes an electromagnet.* Students are asked to construct electromagnets like the one shown in Figure 5–9. They are then supplied with a number of objects, such as a small compass, nails, paperclips, iron filings, copper

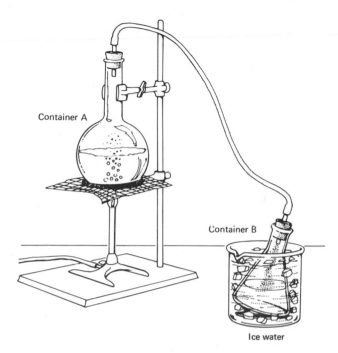

Container A

Container B

Ice water

Figure 5–8

wire, and other items. First instruct students to move the small compass to various locations around the electromagnet to verify that it does indeed have a magnetic influence. Have the children hypothesize regarding what effects the electromagnet may produce and to devise ways to investigate these hypotheses. Some possible activities which can be done include putting the wrapped nail under a sheet of paper or thin glass to see if the nail is surrounded by a magnetic field. The lines of force can be observed by placing iron filings on the sheet of paper and shaking it gently.

Further explorations can be made by having students try several different kinds of rods as electromagnets. Such materials as aluminum, copper, rubber, and glass can be used.

Ask children to explore the relationship regarding the number of turns of wire about the nail and the strength of the electromagnet. They may experiment using up to say twenty turns of wire for each of the objects that they are checking. The strength of the electromagnet could be determined by the number of nails that it can hold.

3. *Plants depend on animals.* Have students place Elodea plants in two large jars filled with water. To one jar add animals, such as snails

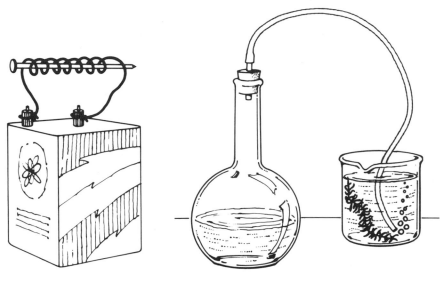

Figure 5–9   Figure 5–10

or guppies. Keep the second jar free of animal life to act as a control. After several weeks have the children make observations. They should observe that the plants in association with animals show better growth.

Next have the children artificially supply carbon dioxide to the jar containing only plants by putting yeast in a flask containing tepid water and a small amount of sugar and transmitting the resulting gas into the jar through rubber tubing (see Figure 5–10). Increased growth of plants is evidence that carbon dioxide is essential to plant growth.

THE GROWTH OF AFFECT

In science education, teachers often ignore the teaching of affect, believing that science deals almost exclusively with the cognitive skills. However, affect is crucial in the teaching of science in at least two ways. First, it provides a reciprocal relationship with cognition, which enlivens and gives meaning to learning. Secondly, science needs to be infused with the values and attitudes which make it a viable and useful subject. What is learned in science cannot be separated from related social values. For example, balance in nature must be related to the implications which ecological unbalance can produce in current society. Affect and cognition therefore cannot be treated as if they were mutually exclusive areas for learning. Rather they have a close dependence upon one another.

With regard to affect and cognition, Piaget and Inhelder made the following statement, "There is no behavior pattern, however intellectual, which does not involve affective factors as motives. . . . Behavior is therefore of a piece . . . The two aspects, affective and cognitive, are at the same time inseparable and irreducible" (Piaget and Inhelder, 1969). The human being is a meaning-seeking species and as such has a strong need to order and organize the environment so it can be effectively dealt with. The child is constantly engaged in activities designed to organize experience. The existence of dissonance created from the transactional relationship between internal growth and external social pressures acts as a motivator for development. The personality and its development is really dominated by the individual's search for coherence and meaning, which comes about as a product of cognitive and affective interactions. At all ages, cognitive organization and development are inspired and fed by a search for meaning which is affective in nature (Gordon, 1970).

The conclusion that may be drawn from knowing how cognition and affect are related is that in any good classroom these two elements will not be separated and focused on individually. The teaching-learning act must contain an inextricable mix of these components. The child must be viewed as an active agent who will seek out, master, and devour intellectual activities when they are approached with his own personal resolve to understand and obtain meaning. This desire for meaning is created from disequilibrium which is in essence affective. Without it learning is sterile and uninteresting.

As indicated earlier, values and attitudes are an important component of teaching science. Whereas cognitive science is devoted to discovering knowledge, values concentrate on the appropriate use of that knowledge. Present society is fraught with moral dilemmas brought on, essentially, by scientific and technological advances. Through our ever-increasing store of scientific knowledge it has become possible to do many things which in the long run may not be in the best interests of society. Some of these dilemmas include artificial insemination, creating life in a test tube, ecological balance versus energy production, industrialization and pollution versus a lower standard of living, emphasis on space exploration versus feeding our growing population, and the advisability of using nuclear weapons. Children need to become increasingly aware of these and other science-related problems as they study science in the elementary school.

In order to properly insure that the moral development proceeds in an orderly fashion, it is important to determine the extent to which children can be taught and expected to understand and incorporate moral ideals into their lives during various stages of their development. As previously mentioned, Piaget believes that moral thinking cannot be separated from intellectual develpment. The assumption is that moral development follows a pattern of growth similar to that of intellectual development. This creates an interesting problem. Ordinarily we do not expect a six-year-old child to make the same intellectual decision as an adult. Consequently, we should not expect him to be making the same kinds of moral decisions. Often we fail to adequately consider the relationship between intellectual development and moral thinking when we ask a child to justify his moral action. The tendency is to impose adult standards upon moral thinking, but not upon intellectual thinking (Jantz and Fulda, 1975).

Piaget has identified two major levels of moral thinking found in elementary school children, which may "coexist at the same age and even in the same child but the second gradually succeeds in dominating the first" (Piaget, 1965). These two levels are *morality of constraint* and a *morality of cooperation.* Morality of constraint is characterized by the blind, unquestioning obedience to rules imposed by someone in authority. On the other hand, following the rules because of a conscious knowledge of the need for cooperation and because the reasoning behind the rules is believed to be sound and valid characterizes the morality of cooperation.

Morality of constraint is most characteristic of students in the primary grades. During this period children are taught to view teachers as authority figures who must be obeyed. Dedication to teacher expectations frequently leads students at this level to engage in "tattling." If such behaviors are encouraged the moral development of children is likely to be hampered. The teacher must avoid the temptation to totally restrain her students by dictating and enforcing all of the moral decisions. Otherwise, children under her direction will likely make slower progress in moving to the next stage, morality of cooperation.

Children in the upper elementary school (grades 4–6) normally make moral judgments that are consistent with the morality of cooperation stage. At this age, students are engaged in activities and experiences which encourage reciprocal respect and sympathy with their peers. Consequently, there is a gradual replacement of the morality of constraint by the morality of cooperation. This shift to the second level of moral thinking can be exemplified by children's concepts of control, justice, and responsibility.

A young child's concept of *control* is essentially that of obeying authority. The purpose of the rule is not as important as simply obeying it. Children at this level (morality of constraint) do not question or analyze rules. Rules are regarded as being revealed as well as imposed by adults. In the second stage of moral thinking the perception of control or authority changes. It is either agreed upon with one's peers or rationally agreed upon with an adult. At this level children become concerned with the question of mutual control and the modification of rules: rules can be changed by mutual agreement, and are no longer sacred but rather negotiable.

Within the morality of constraint, *justice* is viewed in the letter rather than the spirit of the law. According to Piaget, children consider violations of the law as serious transgressions. They are very quick to judge, without taking into account any circumstances. During this first stage of moral development the young child can readily identify his/her own unintentional violation of rules. They find it easy to rationalize and often make such statements as "I didn't do it on purpose" or "I didn't mean to do it." These children are able to use their intellectual skills to determine unintentional versus intentional behavior. But, because of their high egocentrism, these children often have difficulty in applying this same principle to the actions of others. They use their intentions to explain their own misbehavior but they judge others' actions by the results rather than the intentions. When a child moves from morality of constraint to morality of cooperation, the conception of justice changes from a punitive view to one of permitting restitution. Instead of each improper behavior having an immutable application of punishment, adjustments are permitted to make the application of punishment more consistent with intentions as well as actions.

Within a morality of constraint, the young child's understanding of the meaning of *responsibility* is in terms of exact conformity to established rules. Again, motives or intentions are not considered. Moral judgments are made only on the basis of consequences of actions. For example, suppose Bill and Bob are preparing for a spelling bee and Bob stops practicing his spelling in order to play baseball with his friends. The following day, when their team loses the spelling bee, Bill may be

When a child begins to show consideration for others, he is demonstrating reasoning at the conventional stage.

inclined to blame Bob for the loss because he did not study hard enough. Bob may explain that he did not intend the team to lose, but Bill will be unlikely to accept his explanation. Bill thus makes a moral judgment based upon the consequences of the action exclusively without even considering Bob's intentions. Gradually, as children grow, they develop the ability to accept the right of others to their opinion, and to make moral judgments concerning others by examining their intentions as well as their actions (Jantz and Fulda, 1975).

Kohlberg (1970) also suggests that moral thinking occurs in developmental stages. In his research he found that cognitive moral development proceeds through the same invariable sequence of stages that mental processes do. He indicates that the increase in maturity involves the development of a more rational system of reasoning about situations involving moral conflicts. According to Kohlberg, children go through this series of stages without skipping any steps, and that some individuals might remain in the lower stages of moral development throughout their lives.

Kohlberg's theory of moral development consists of three levels, each including two stages:

> Level 1: Preconventional
>   Stage 1: Obedience and punishment orientation
>   Stage 2: Naively egoistic orientation
> Level 2: Conventional
>   Stage 3: Good-boy or good-girl orientation
>   Stage 4: Authority and social order maintaining orientation
> Level 3: Postconventional
>   Stage 5: Contractual legalistic orientation
>   Stage 6: Conscience or principle orientation

In Level 1 (Preconventional) an individual's moral reasoning comes essentially from the consequences of actions and from the physical power of those in positions of authority. In the first stage of this level decisions about moral issues result from a blind obedience to those in authority in an attempt to avoid punishment or seek rewards. In the second stage, a reciprocity develops between the individual and others. Decisions come from a desire to satisfy one's own needs first and the needs of others second. There is an attitude of "you scratch my back and I'll scratch yours." Reasoning involves little or no consideration of loyalty, gratitude, or justice. In this stage the child behaves in a way that will bring rewards and result in personal pleasure regardless of whether these actions conflict with the rights of others.

In Level 2 (Conventional) an individual's moral reasoning takes on a new dimension. The child begins to involve the consideration of the interest of others such as family and peers in his moral reasoning in an effort to maintain respect and support, and to justify the existing social order. At the third stage of this level the child is characterized in his moral reasoning by role conformity. His behavior is greatly influenced by social praise or blame and he tries to obtain social approval and maintain good relationships with others. The concept of right is expanded to include the idea that no one has the right to do evil. Behavior of others is frequently judged by what are assumed to be their intentions. The child will accept the idea that someone at least means well. In the fourth stage moral decisions result from a desire to maintain the existing authority, rules, and social order. Right behavior consists of doing one's duty. Children in this stage are motivated to escape feelings of guilt or blame by avoiding actions that might be disapproved of by recognized authority. A right becomes a privilege which is earned through appropriate behavior. It is a payment for doing well.

The child's moral reasoning in Level 3 (Postconventional) incorporates moral values and principles that have validity and application beyond the authority of groups. Moral reasoning becomes more comprehensive and analytical and reflects universal principles. In the fifth stage of this level, moral development is based upon self-acceptance of moral principles that control one's actions. Moral decision making results from recognition of an individual's rights within a society that has social agreements. Consequently the individual's reasoning on moral issues emphasizes the legal point of view while at the same time holding to the possibility that laws can and need to be changed. Motivation of the individual at this stage is sparked by the approval or disapproval of actions by the greater community. In the sixth stage there is an enlargement of the base for deriving principles. Whereas in the fifth stage, principles were derived primarily from community, this final stage is reached when the individual learns to make moral decisions based upon an obligation to universal ethical principles that apply to all mankind. The basis for individual reasoning on issues of morality incorporate the principles of justice, reciprocity and equality of human rights, and respect for the dignity of human beings as individuals no matter what their racial or cultural origin. The dignity of man emerges as the primary principle of morality. Feeling good about oneself and one's involvements with others becomes the motivation for all moral action. Rights, then, take on a broader meaning. They reflect a genuine concern for individual life and respect for human dignity.

It was determined that all individuals in the studies made by Kohlberg progressed through an invariable sequence through each of the stages of moral development. Early studies involved American males exclusively. Later cross-cultural studies involving middle-class urban males in the United States, Taiwan, and Mexico, and lower-class peasants living in villages in Turkey and Yucatan confirmed the development theory. Even though there was a divergence of cultural, social, and religious backgrounds, the subjects all moved through the same stages of moral development, in the same sequence. Results indicated that while the rate of movement varied between cultures the evidence for sequential moral stages was readily apparent.

Kohlberg's work also established a clear relationship between chronological age and the level of moral reasoning. As with Piaget's levels of cognitive development, all children do not move through stages of moral development at the same rate. However, preadolescents usually attain a preconventional level while adolescents achieve the conventional level. It is not until adulthood that the level of postconventional reasoning is finally reached. In addition, as with the development of the formal operations stage of cognitive functioning, not all individuals attain the highest level of moral reasoning. Actually, less than 20 percent of the adult population reasons at the postconventional level (Kohlberg, 1971). Individuals can become "frozen" at any level and remain there for the remainder of their lives. You may recall that a similar number of individuals fails to obtain the formal operations stage of intellectual development. Although it has not been conclusively demonstrated, it appears that the growth of moral reasoning depends upon the development of the intellectual processes.

Kohlberg's research has also indicated that students who participate regularly in discussions of moral dilemmas usually begin to show evidence of reasoning at successive stages of development. Apparently the exchange of reasoning during a group discussion of moral dilemmas stimulates moral development through the stages. "A good group discussion of a moral dilemma depends on three variables: a recognized moral dilemma, a leader who can help to focus the discussion on moral reasoning, and a classroom climate that encourages students to express their moral reasoning freely" (Galbraith and Jones, 1975).

A dilemma presents the class with a moral problem. It usually involves a story or situation that presents a central character faced with a choice. The dilemmas are moral in nature because students are encouraged to think about the rightness or wrongness of the various actions taken by the central character. A good moral dilemma usually has three characteristics: it presents a real conflict for the central character, it includes a number of moral issues for consideration; and it generates differences of opinion about what the appropriate responses should be in the situation. An example of a moral dilemma for an elementary science class is: Bill lived in a small farming community near the steep slopes of the Rocky Mountains of northern Idaho. One day while hiking in the mountains he observed a cougar dragging a young lamb into its lair. As he watched he noted a pair of young cubs bounding out to meet their mother. They looked no more than about three to four weeks old. As he watched, he thought about what he had recently learned about the balance of nature and the strategic place large carnivores played in maintaining this balance. He reflected again on the problems that were created in the great Kiabab forest when bounty hunters slew several hundred of the big cats. The deer population increased so dramatically that their browsing soon stripped the land clean of much of its vegetation. The ravages of nature out of balance were soon manifest. Without vegetation to hold the soil, much of it was washed away by the seasonal rains. With the undergrowth gone the vastly increasing deer population finally resorted to stripping the trees of their bark. When no more food was available the deer died by the thousands. Bill thought about how glad he was that there were cougars in the mountains. Finishing his reflections, Bill decided it was time to start home. As he slowly climbed down the steep slopes, he observed someone walking toward him. As he drew closer he could readily discern the familiar form of his best friend Jim, who had his high-powered rifle slung over his shoulder. As the two friends approached one another, Bill jokingly chided Jim for hunting at least two weeks before the opening of the regular season. There was anger on Jim's face. "I'm not looking for deer," he said. "I'm looking for that old female cougar who just killed one of our lambs; you haven't seen her, have you?" If I could only find her lair she wouldn't be able to feast on our flock any longer." Bill's mind was reeling. He certainly knew where the cougars' lair was. However, he could not get out of his mind how important the big cats were in maintaining a balanced environment. He thought of the two young cubs who were still dependent upon their mother. What was he going to say? He did not want to lie, nor did he want to jeopardize his friendship with Jim. Friends should be able to trust one another. If he lied, how would he ever be able to look Jim in the eye again? Killing the cougar was not illegal. In fact the ranchers in the area had succeeded in getting a law passed in the state legislature authorizing a bounty of $100 on cougars. He also knew, however, that the number of sheep and cattle taken as prey by cougars was extremely low, and that even where deer were concerned the old and sickly were the most likely to be killed. It seemed to Bill that this was small payment for ensuring that ecological balance was maintained in the mountains he loved. What should Bill do?

There are a number of issues involved in Bill's dilemma: obligation to friends, concern that the balance of nature be maintained, knowledge regarding erroneous conclusions often drawn about the potential detriment of large carnivores, and an obligation to his own conscience with regard to honesty. In the discussion generated with the class, students should be brought to an awareness of the existence of these issues and their inherent conflicts. There are a number of possible strategies for accomplishing this, but one example should be sufficiently illustrative:

1. Distribute the dilemma to the class in written form. Read the dilemma together, making sure that it is understood by all. Ask the class for some expression regarding how they feel about what Bill should do.

2. If almost the entire class agrees on what action should be taken by Bill, attempt to provoke disagreement by asking such questions as, "What if Bill plans to go away to school and would not be seeing Jim for at least a year?" or "What if Bill had some other friends who knew the location of the cougar's lair and there had been some agreement to keep this knowledge a secret?"

A child's understanding depends upon how he perceives his world.

3. Probing questions can be asked to increase the depth of understanding of the issues. The following are examples of the type of questions that may be used: (a) What is the most important thing one friend owes to another? Why? (b) Should a person ever risk friendship for principles he believes are right? Why? (c) From the point of view of all members of the community, what should Bill do? (d) What would most likely serve Jim's best interests? How does this alter what Bill should do?

4. Ask the students to take a position on the dilemma. Give them

a few minutes to think and then ask them to write down both what the character should do and why he should do it.

    5. Divide the class into groups of about five students each and instruct them to discuss their responses to the dilemma. This procedure will enable students to generate additional reasons and start them focusing on what the best responses may be. Next involve the entire class in a discussion of the issues. This gives the members an opportunity to test their reasoning against the thinking of others and to clarify and organize their position.

Exercise 5–4   Using Dilemmas to Teach Values

1. Use Bill's dilemma with a group of elementary school children.
2. Devise a dilemma of your own and try it out with a group of elementary school children.

Perceptual-Field Theories

    Even though Piaget does not say much about perception in his theory regarding intellectual development, it obviously plays an important part in this growth process. Perception is a direct sensory experience where information about our environment is received and stored in the central nervous system. Cognitive growth depends to a great extent upon the nature of this perceptual process. The quality of perception can be significantly altered by a number of factors and the resulting cognitive understandings can be adversely affected. It is crucial that teachers help children make realistic and accurate perceptions of their environment so that concepts and associated behaviors are consistent with the realities of that environment. In order to do this it is necessary to know how the perceptual processes operate and what specific assistance a teacher can give to children in keeping their perceptual channels free from factors which limit the effectiveness and accuracy of perception. The science teacher is in a particularly significant position to insure that students are able to perceive accurately. In working with science materials in a manipulative way—measuring, weighing, observing, etc.—children are trained to focus carefully on the real attributes of phenomena. This helps the child to develop not only his perceptual skills, but also to come to a realization of how important accurate perceptions are.

    Behavior is almost completely determined by the interaction of the individual's conceptual framework and how he perceives his environment at any particular moment in time. From this point of view, education consists of changing the perceptual field. However, just altering the perceptual field will not insure that all children achieve the same understanding of, nor attach the same meaning to, what they perceive. Common understanding requires common perception, which is almost never possible. The factors which alter the way we perceive are usually present to some degree in everyone at all times and these factors reduce the commonality of perception. This, of course, is a great handicap to the teacher who tries to communicate with students, because communication is possible only for those things for which a common perception is held. Many times teachers and students assume that they are communicating when in fact they are not. They may be discussing common subjects but their understandings may be vastly different. Obviously, the way to increase communication and understanding between individuals is to reduce the effects of the above-mentioned inhibiting factors. Efficient and effective behavior also depends upon accurate perceptual experiences. The more completely open children are to their total experience the more likely they will be to make accurate perceptions.

One category of factors which affects perceptual accuracy is needs. Any event which seems to the individual to be related to the satisfaction of a need will have a strong effect upon the rest of the perceptual field. What happens is that the person's perceptual attention becomes focused upon phenomena which have potential for satisfying his needs. In addition the strength of that need will also have an effect. For example, the accuracy and speed of learning may be unaltered so long as the strength of a need is sufficiently low. If the strength of the need increases, however, and becomes the focus of attention, learning may come to a standstill. Maslow (1959) has organized the needs of man into a hierarchy based upon their relative order and strength. He believes that the needs of man include physiological comfort, safety, love, self-esteem, and self-actualization, and that these needs are hierarchically related. Thus the most fundamental need (which is physiological comfort) has to be met or satisfied before the next higher need in the hierarchy emerges, which means that an individual must satisfy his physiological needs before he feels any need to insure his safety.This is significant in that children will be unable to perceive with any accuracy many of the phenomena placed before them in the school setting unless those needs further down in the hierarchy are first satisfied. For example, it is well known that children who come to school hungry are greatly handicapped in their learning. From the point of view of Maslow's hierarchy, their perceptual attention is focused primarily upon physiological need satisfaction and therefore they are unable to focus their attention on the school curriculum.

Personal adequacy is another important category of factors which influence perception. Behavior becomes meaningful when it is explained on the basis of each act being an attempt by the individual to preserve or to fortify his perception of his personal adequacy. The assumption here is, of course, that man has within him a great driving force to become adequate to cope with life. Apparently we need to feel that we are worthwile or, in other words, we must have a good self-concept before we are free to make accurate perceptions. In order to maintain the self-concept, perception may need to be distorted. The individual may defend himself against any threat of alteration of his concept of self by not perceiving those meanings in his experience which contradict his present self-image (Rogers, 1962). On the other hand, if the person is confident about himself, he becomes more willing to be open to his experience and receive every stimulus from the environment without distorting it first by passing it through a screen of defenses. The hypothetical person who is fully open to his experience would have access to all of the available data in a situation on which to base his behavior: the social demands; his own complex and possibly conflicting needs; his memories of similar situations; and his perception of the uniqueness of this situation. The information available to him would be very complex indeed. However, he would have the benefit of permitting his total self to consider each stimulus, need, and demand, its relative intensity, and importance, and out of this complex weighing and balancing, he would be able to discover the course of action which comes closest to satisfying all of his needs in the situation. In addition, he would increase his growth by being able to understand all of the components of situations and how to best predict consequences of various possible actions. Thus the individual could become more completely governed by rational thought instead of fear.

A child's experiences in the school can either be fulfilling or self-defeating. Which of these two alternatives has the greatest influence depends on both the child's previous experience and his self-concept, as well as how he is treated in the school. If the child has a strong self-concept he does not have to devote his full attention to it. Problems can be dealt with more objectively because the child's self is not at stake. He does not feel that he has to prove himself to others and reassure himself that he is sufficiently adequate. When problems are being solved, solutions can be sought solely as "good" answers to the problem at hand, rather than in terms of their immediate contribution to the enhancement of self. The person with the adequate self-concept can thus focus his attention upon the subject matter in an objective way and visualize what is being learned in its widest possible context without filtering out important components. In addition, when the person is basically fulfilled he tends to forget himself and become more concerned about the needs of others. This way he is able to further expand his social world and receive input from others that he is a worthy human being. A weak self, on the other hand, must be forever nurtured and cared for. It intrudes in every situation.

The science teacher should be aware that children need to feel that they are liked in order for their self-concept to grow. Self-concept is something that is learned. Children learn who they are and what they are by the way in which they have been treated by those surrounding them in the process of their growing up. They develop feelings that they are liked, wanted, and accepted from having been liked, wanted, and accepted. Children need to be accepted for what they are in a genuine way. It is a temptation for teachers to accept children only on their own terms. The child whose behavior and values do not coincide with those of the teacher often feels that somehow he is inferior, and that the teacher disapproves of him as a person. Frequently the child caught in this type of situation, where his self-concept is "on the line," will behave inappropriately in the classroom.

Many teachers, as well as people in general, believe that since the world is a very hard place, where people often fail, children should be introduced to failure early. If education is supposed to prepare children for life, it must prepare them properly by giving them a few "doses" of failure before they have to confront the world more directly. This attitude presumes that children are then prepared to face failure if they are ever confronted with it. Many children, however, learn how to fail from their experiences in the school and continue these patterns of behavior throughout their lives. Actually, the best guarantee that a person will be able to deal with the future effectively is for him to have been essentially successful in the past. People learn that they are capable, not from failure, but rather from success (Coombs, 1962).

Children with a poor self-concept find it difficult to succeed in any school subject, but particularly in the study of science, because the child is asked to make observations, experiment, and draw conclusions. Not only can accurate observations be curtailed by a poor self-concept, but the child may also experience difficulty in drawing conclusions. In order to feel good about himself, the child with the poor self-concept cannot afford to be wrong. Only when he is right is he able to soothe his troubled self. Therefore, rather than make a wrong conclusion, he makes none at all. He is afraid to even attempt to explore various possible answers. Since science encourages children to explore, the child with a poor self-concept misses much of what the study of science can offer. When forced, these children often feign difficulties of various kinds: they complain that they do not understand what is expected, or indicate that they simply cannot do anything right. They simply do not want to try for fear of being wrong.

Some of the problems which poor self-concept creates in the teaching and learning of science can be diminished by the teacher. First, the teacher must insure that each child is accepted, by the teacher as well as his peers, on his own terms. As children are in the process of developing they often belittle one another in an attempt to make themselves feel more worthwhile. They need to be taught that it is impossible to feel good about themselves at the expense of a classmate. Next, the teacher should provide a classroom atmosphere where wrong answers do not indicate failure. Only in this way will children be encouraged to explore meanings and to assert themselves without fear of the damning effects of criticism. Before a child will be willing to check out his own perceptions with those of others, he has to feel safe. He needs to have some guarantee that what he thinks, understands, or believes will not be attacked or ridiculed. So long as the individual keeps his perceptions protected within, he will not have the opportunity to measure them against the facts in the case. In other words, he will be unable to compare his perceptions with those of others and adjust them as necessary to be more consistent with reality. Without these cross comparisons the individual will assuredly develop behavior patterns which are inconsistent with social propriety.

Not only should the classroom environment permit children to come up with "wrong" answers, but it should also be a place where all children can achieve some measure of success as judged not only by the teacher and themselves, but also by their peers. What peers think is important to a child, and he will most always use it as one means of determining his feeling of self-worth. It is not an easy matter to provide experiences for children where each participant is able to be successful. This is particularly true of children who have had a long history of failure both in the school as well as at home. However, if the "failure syndrome" is allowed to continue unchecked during the elementary school years even more problems will be created for the individual as time goes by. The success that a child finds in school should not be fabricated. Instead it should be the genuine consequences of his efforts, recognized by all to be a successful response. There are, of course, differences in the abilities of children. This means that for all children to find genuine success, a good deal of individualized instruction is necessary. When group projects are used, tasks will need to be assigned on the basis of student capabilities. On a field trip, for example, children may be asked to perform different tasks. The more able child may be asked to devise questions to be researched, while less capable children carry out the details of the research. This does away with the necessity for all children to compete on the same basis when they have vastly different capacities. Each is able to feel that he has participated in and contributed to the project without feeling that he has to compete in a dog-eat-dog atmosphere. When a child sees that the competition is a little tough he may retreat into his shell. If we can keep him occupied in a project and gradually increase our expectations as he demonstrates that he is able to comply with them, the child will come to understand his own capabilities more realistically and be satisfied with the efforts he is able to make. All the while this is going on it is imperative that the child be shown that his efforts are accepted and that he is also accepted personally. Otherwise his efforts to fortify his ailing self-concept will occupy his time and he will only verify what he has suspected all along, namely that he is inadequate. The preponderance of the available research indicates that success is a necessary constituent of how students feel about themselves and how they perform. Unsuccessful students, whether underachievers, nonachievers, or poor readers, are likely to hold attitudes about themselves and their abilities which are pervasively negative. They see themselves as less able, less adequate, and less self-reliant than their more successful peers. It is not clear, however, whether children see themselves negatively because of their poor school performance, or whether they perform poorly in school because they see themselves negatively. In either case teachers must intervene and attempt to alter this course of development (Purkey, 1970).

One of the most important interventions a teacher can perform is to give a good opinion of his students. The almost unavoidable conclusion is that the teacher's attitudes and opinions regarding his students have a significant influence on their success in school. It is more or less a self-fulfilling prophesy. When the teacher believes that his students can achieve, the students appear to be more successful; when the teacher believes that the students cannot achieve, then their performance is usually inadequate (Rosenthal and Jacobson, 1968).

Organizing curriculum from the point of view of perceptual-field theory is not inconsistent with the principles advocated by Piaget. In both cases, however, it is possible to carry permissiveness to the extreme. Advocates of perceptual theory may take permissiveness to mean freedom to create physical chaos, to upset or destroy property and the decorum of the classroom. This course of action is, of course, untenable. Permissiveness should be taken to mean freedom to have ideas, beliefs, and values and to be able to pursue personal interests which are likely to have greater personal meaning for the individual. From the point of view of Piaget, a similar practice would be advocated. Students would be given the opportunity to deal personally with things that catered to their interest. The question from both points of view is: What is the extent to which children should be permitted to decide upon the subject matter, given the fact that their curiosity and interest should be catered to in order to make learning a personalized experience? Balanced against this question is the consideration of just how much a child can contribute to the decision of what he should do in the

Figure 5–11

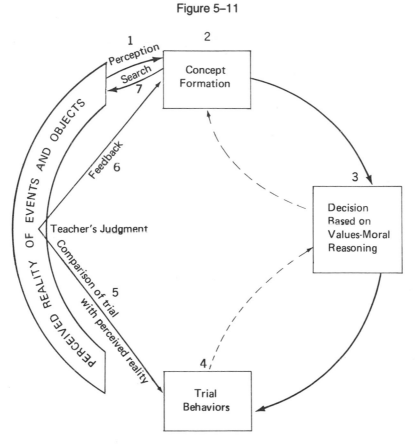

Adapted from Woodruff, Ashael, "The use of Concepts in Teaching and Learning," *The Journal of Teacher Education,* March, 1964, pp. 81–89.

classroom. Certainly there are limits which must be employed to ensure that permissiveness does not produce chaos. In addition, children cannot be expected to know in each instance what would be best for them to learn. What is indicated is a very personalized approach to teaching where the teacher maintains a dialogue between each student, which allows them a genuine chance for input. The teacher will have to suggest what a child should do at the same time the child makes his suggestions. Adjustments can then be made as necessary. This procedure requires the teacher to monitor the activities of each child and have a good deal of assistance from a vast array of self-instructional materials. These self-instructional materials need not be excessively prescriptive either. A simple set of suggestions may be all that is needed to get a child started. The teacher can then engage in various follow-up activities to keep the child working toward reasonable ends and to provide encouragement and help as needed.

A Model for Perceptual-Cognitive Growth

There are obvious relationships between perception, cognition, and the growth of moral reasoning. Figure 5–11 portrays these relationships in a model. Note from the illustration that the reality of events and objects in the environment are perceived through sensory intake, by the various sense organs of the body. This perception process is subject to all the biasing constraints discussed earlier. The perceptions are then registered in the central nervous system and related to the present stock of concepts contained there. The ability to understand the perceptual information taken into the central nervous system depends on the cognitive development level of the individual. When new perceptions are received they are used to alter concepts or to change values regarding the concepts. In other words moral reasoning is initiated, using the cognitive abilities that the individual has. The concepts with their associated value components are then used in a decision-making process. The child decides how the new concepts will be acted out in terms of behavior. He then proceeds to act out his changed conceptions by making trial responses which he believes are consistent with these changes. As the child makes his trial responses he attempts to determine how consistent his behavior is with perceived reality. This may be done with or without the assistance of the teacher. The perceived congruity or incongruity is then fed back into the central nervous system where a decision is made regarding the need for additional information in order to correct behavior and make it more congruent with perceived reality. If additional information is required, the individual continues to search the environment and the entire process of perception, cognition, moral reasoning, trial, and feedback takes place again. This proceeds in cybernetic fashion until the child reaches the point where his behavior is consistent with perceived reality. The teacher, of course, assists the child in this process as it goes along. (Adapted from Woodruff, 1964.)

References

Baldwin, Alfred L., *Theories of Child Development.* New York: Wiley, 1967.

Bijou, Sidney W., and Donald M. Baer, *Child Development I: A Systematic and an Empirical Theory.* New York: Appleton-Century-Crofts, 1961.

Chittenden, Edward A., "Piaget and Elementary Science," *Science and Children,* (December 1970): 9–14.

Coombs, Arthur W., "A Perceptual View of the Adequate Personality," in *Perceiving, Behaving, Becoming: A New Focus for Education,* Yearbook, Association for Supervision and Curriculum Development. Washington, D.C.: NEA, 1962.

DeCecco, John P., *The Psychology of Learning and Instruction: Educational Psychology.* Englewood Cliffs, N.J., Prentice-Hall, 1968.

Duncan, Carl P., "The Effect of Unequal Amounts of Practice on Motor Learning Before and After Practice," *Journal of Experimental Psychology* 42 (1951): 257–64.

Fitts, Paul, "Factors in Complex Skill Training," in *Training Research and Education,* R. Glaser, Ed. Pittsburgh: University of Pittsburgh Press, 1962, pp. 177–97.

Gagné, Robert M., *Conditions of Learning.* New York: Holt, Rinehart and Winston, 1965.

Galbraith, Ronald E., and Thomas M. Jones, "Teaching Strategies for Moral Dilemmas: An Application of Kohlberg's Theory of Moral Development to the Social Studies Classroom," *Social Education* (January 1975): 16–22.

Gordon, Ira J., "Affect and Cognition: A Reciprocal Relationship," *Educational Leadership* 28 (April 1970): 661–63.

Harris, Thomas A., *I'm OK — You're OK.* New York: Avon Books, 1967.

Jantz, Richard K., and Trudi A. Fulda, "The Role of Moral Education in the Public Elementary School," *Social Education* (January 1975): 24–28.

Kohlberg, Lawrence, "Education for Justice," in J. Gustafson, *et al., Moral Education.* Cambridge, Mass.: Harvard University Press, 1970.

Kohlberg, Lawrence, "The Concepts of Developmental Psychology as the Central Guide to Education: Examples from Cognitive, Moral, and Psychological Education," in *The Proceedings of the Conference on Psychology and the Process of Schooling in the Next Decade: Alternative Conceptions.* Washington, D.C.: U.S. Office of Education, p. 41.

Maslow, Abraham H., *Motivation and Personality.* New York: Harper & Row, 1959.

Mayor, John R., and Arthur H. Livermore, "A Process Approach to Elementary School Science," *School Science and Mathematics* 69, (1969): 411–16.

Naylor, James C., "Parameters Affecting the Efficiency of Part and Whole Training Methods: A Review of the Literature" in NAVTRADEVECEN *Technical Report,* N. 950–1. Port Washington, N.Y.: United States Training Devices Center.

Piaget, Jean, "Development and Learning," *The Journal of Research in Science Teaching* 2, (1964): 176–86.

Piaget, Jean, *The Moral Judgment of the Child.* New York: Free Press, 1965.

Piaget, Jean, and Barbel Inhelder, *The Psychology of the Child.* New York: Basic Books, 1969. 1–159.

Purkey, William W., *Self Concept and School Achievement.* Englewood Cliffs, N.J.: Prentice-Hall, 1970.

Rogers, Carl R., "Toward Becoming a Fully Functioning Person," in *Perceiving, Behaving, Becoming: A New Focus for Education,* Yearbook, Association for Supervision and Curriculum Development, Washington, D.C.: NEA, 1962.

Rogers, Robert E., and Alan M. Voelker, "Programs for Improving Science Instruction in the Elementary School: Part I, ESS," *Science and Children* 7, no. 5 (1970): 35–43.

Rosenthal, R., and L. Jacobson, *Pygmalion in the Classroom: Teacher Expectation and Pupils' Intellectual Development.* New York: Holt, Rinehart and Winston, 1968.

Skinner, B. F., "Freedom and the Control of Men," *The American Scholar* 25 (Winter 1955–56).

Skinner, B. F., "The Free and Happy Student," *Phi Delta Kappan* 54 (September 1973): 12–16.

Smedslund, J., "The Acquisition of Conservation of Substance and Weight in Children, III: Extinction of Conservation of Weight Acquired 'Normally' and by Means of Empirical Controls on a Balance Scale," *Scandinavian Journal of Psychology* 2 (1961): 85–87.

Thomson, Barbara S., and Alan M. Voelker, "Programs for Improving Science Instruction in the Elementary School: Part II, SCIS," *Science and Children,* no. 8 (1970): 29–37.

Woodruff, A. D., "The Use of Concepts in Teaching and Learning," *Journal of Teacher Education* 15 (March 1964): 81–99.

6
Organizing Subject Matter

The classroom teacher of science or any other subject faces two major questions: What shall I select for the subject matter to be learned? How should I arrange the approach to learning so that the objectives will be achieved. The two questions are not the same. For example, one can teach about birds in different ways for different purposes. Also, there is more than one approach or strategy to learning about electrical circuits. The reason for the inadequacy of a lesson may not have been the approach to teaching. It may have been that the particular subject matter was not the most appropriate one for study by these students at the time. Or perhaps the way in which the subject matter was arranged did not suit the needs of the learner. In this chapter we will take up the issue of what subject matter should be taught in the school. In later chapters we will deal with the issue of how to teach the selected subject matter.

In this chapter, when we speak of the organization of content for learning, we will not be concerned with the minute by minute order of classroom learning. For the most part, we are focusing on the organization of subject matter in a course or program frame of reference. We will be dealing with both the scope and sequence of the course or program, the scope being the identification of the elements to be included within the program, and the sequence being the order in which the elements are arranged. The scope and sequence of a program comprise the total outline of the subject matter to be achieved and the order in which it is presented.

The frame of reference for selecting topics for study in science is provided in Chapter 2 in the definition of scientific literacy. Scientific literacy is composed of three components: (a) the concepts to be developed, i.e., the "big ideas" of science, (b) the process skills by which science study is accomplished, and (c) the attitudes conducive to science knowledge development and use. Together, these three provide an operational definition of what science education should be and form the basis upon which a program can be assessed for effectiveness. Concepts, processes, and attitudes are all outgrowths of an investigative learning environment in which students are involved with their natural world.

The question then becomes: Which subject matter shall I select that will allow for the full development of a scientific literacy. Certainly there is no shortage of topics. Rather, there is a shortage of time in which to deal with all of the subjects. The purpose of this chapter is to develop a point of view about the selection of subject matter for elementary school science.

OBJECTIVES

The readings and exercises of this chapter have been designed to develop the student's ability to:

1. Develop criteria by which subject matter can be selected for an elementary school science program.
2. Develop a knowledge structure for a portion of an elementary school science program which indicates a continuity between conceptual statements.
3. Identify patterns of subject matter sequences in contemporary science programs.

Guidelines for Selection of Subject Matter

In mid-1971, the National Science Teachers Association-sponsored Committee on Curriculum Studies: K–12, comprised of prominent science educators, prepared a position statement on "School Science Education for the 70s." This statement was created to reflect the change in thinking of science educators who responded to correspondence from the Committee. The statement dealt with general goals, curriculum, and learning of science, and some recommendations to the Association for improving science education. Several parts of the study provide direction to us in selecting appropriate subject matter for science. Among the statements are the following ideas:

> Science is a K–12, sequential curriculum.
> A variety of topics should be included in science.
> The mass of knowledge should not be overwhelming to students.
> There is a relationship between the sciences.
> There is a relationship between science and other subjects.
> Children should have first hand experiences to learn science.
> Science should contribute to the student's concept of himself.
> The topics to be studied should be an authentic picture of science.
> Learning in science should be relevant to the student.
> Science education is a part of the broad school goals. (NSTA, 1971)

Teachers and students are individuals. A teacher who is working with a few students for a period of several months tends to think only in terms of the development of these students for this time period. In terms of the goals being sought by this teacher, she often finds that previous learnings have not been sufficient and remedial steps must be taken. What these students do in years to come will be beyond her control and up to the next teacher. In such a situation, the learners are not being afforded the opportunity to make maximum use of knowledge and skills which they have learned in order to increase their educational opportunities.

Unfortunately, students do not learn in a piecemeal fashion. Their abilities gradually develop to incorporate new ideas into their present understandings. To be able to do this, the program being presented to them must be arranged to allow for continual growth in the knowledge, processes, and attitudes of science. The scope and sequence of the science curriculum, the master plan, is necessary for a successful science program. This type of organization is not an easy task for the faculty of a building or system to construct by themselves. Some commercial programs have a scope and sequence already established. However, before science programs are adopted, they should be examined to see if the scope and sequence are acceptable to the teachers.

Topics of study in science can be chosen which will increase the motivation of the learner. One way of accomplishing this goal is to offer the student a variety of topics during the school year. There is no end to the number of possibilities from which the teachers can choose. Years ago, elementary school science was primarily a nature study course. Now, experience has indicated that the range of possibilities is much wider. Curriculum materials of the last few decades have included everything from nuclear reactions to simple machines and from theories of the solar system to the behavior of mealworms. If you are not familiar with this variety of topics, you should spend some time reviewing contemporary science programs.

Some programs can be categorized as general science in their scope and sequence. These programs were designed to indicate the variety of topics available under the heading of science. The table of contents of such a textbook might look something like the following:

Chapter	Title
I	Our Vast Universe
II	How Weather Affects Us
III	Simple Machines We Can Use
IV	Life in the Pond
V	Atoms and Molecules
VI	Rocks and Minerals

Unless added by the teacher, there was no underlying thread of thought developed by the program. There was little information about machines that aided the study of the pond, and little there to help the study of atoms and molecules. This is not the kind of variety of topics we seek, nor is this the kind of program which will allow for the development of our science goals.

Such general science programs are too often guilty of a concentration on the little ideas of science. These programs stress the factual, particular nature of science. The student learns to respect, or perhaps fear, the overwhelming mass of knowledge contained in the discipline. This type of program does not show science as it really is, consisting of concepts, processes, and appropriate attitudes.

The scope and sequence of the science curriculum should depict the interrelationships within the discipline. This is accomplished by developing the big ideas of science. For example, throughout the environment, one can find applications of the idea that energy is conserved through changes from one form of energy to another. This is in contrast to the development of energy exchanges among each of the many different situations. The student who sees each individual occurrence as an end in itself, is not in as good a position to develop a scientific literacy as the student who sees each occurrence as the reflection of the broad idea of conservation of energy. The interrelationships among the ideas of science should be reflected throughout the scope and sequence of science. This point will be more fully explained later in this chapter.

A closely related guideline for selection of subject matter for science concerns the relationship of science to the other school subjects. For learning to be relevant, it must include popular issues of the day. Typically these issues are not unique to a single discipline of study. The problems of ecology, for example, are not just the concern of science. Applications of ecology can also be found in the social sciences and mathematics. For example, there are two sides to the issue of getting the necessary legislation to implement effective conservation practices. Students can be helped to see both sides through field trips, role playing, and guest speakers. It is difficult to study problems like ecology without relating them to the disciplines other than science.

The study of other school subjects often suggests aspects of study for science. Throughout literature there are references to science-related topics. The practical arts courses are filled with influences from typical science subjects. For example, science concepts are evident in the oxidation of fuel in a combustion engine or the use of pulleys to change the amount of force being applied to an object. The mathematics class solves word problems which are often an application of some science-related topic. For example, problems can deal with the acceleration and velocity of moving objects and the amount of energy of the

The ability to provide first hand experiences for students should be of primary concern in selection of content.

object. A study of science must relate at least by reference to other school subjects.

A science program which restricts study to written descriptions about the environment is needlessly increasing the difficulty of the study of science and may be misrepresenting the nature of science. There are a great variety of topics in science which students can study by first-hand experiences. Students have difficulty appreciating the vast size of the universe, but have less difficulty learning about solutions. There is little a student can do to personally experience the nature of an atom, but he can learn first-hand about animal behavior. As will be explained more fully in another chapter, children at a given level of learning are restricted by the amount of abstract thinking they can do. Suffice it to say at this point that guidelines for the selection of content should take into account the opportunity the subject provides for first-hand experiences by the students.

There are two more important benefits which are related to first-hand experiences. The first of these is the development of process skills of the study of science and other subjects. Students who are investigating a phenomenon have the opportunity to learn the process skills necessary for that investigation. Students learn to observe individual happenings and then later to generalize these single occurrences to make a hypothesis to describe the phenomenon.

A second benfit of using first-hand experiences is the increased understanding the students may have of themselves as people. One obvious subject which leads to better self-concept is the study of the human body as a living organism and as an entity within the environment. But in addition to the actual subject matter are the issues of how the material is presented and the role of the learner in this presentation. With regard to this, there seems to be some continuum regarding the purpose of education. At one end are those who say that it is the subject matter which must be learned and at the other end are individuals who are primarily concerned with the image the learner has of himself and not at all concerned with a body of knowledge being acquired. Somewhere along this continuum is a more reasonable position which provides for the acquisition of knowledge without losing sight of the nature of the individual learner. There is a need to transmit to the next generation what the field of science has learned thus far. There is also a need to instill in that learner the desire to pursue the study further. It seems unlikely that this can occur without some concern for the learner as a person.

The subject matter selected must represent an authentic view of science. This view should be consistent with the practicing scientist's view of his field of study. In recent years, this has become a reality for most science curricula, especially those produced with National Science Foundation funding. These curricula have been set up by scientists, usually from university science faculties, and generally reflect science as visualized by the scientists themselves.

And last, but perhaps most important, is the concern for science as a part of the total school curriculum. As such, the study of science should indicate its relationship to the overall goals of the school. For example, a general goal of most schools is to teach students communication skills. This can easily be developed as a part of science. When students learn to describe what they see in their environment their communication skills are increased by the new vocabulary and the practice of precisely defining phenomena which are new to them. As mentioned earlier, self-concept skills can be developed through personal involvement in learning. Each of the goals must be kept in perspective. For example, many would agree that one primary function of school in general and science in particular is to teach some general information about the student's environment. But this is not the only goal of science and should not be the sole factor in the selection of content.

The process of selecting content for science instruction should be thoughtful, incorporating the guidelines suggested here as well as possible local constraints which might occur. Not every school will be able to provide its teachers with the resources by which a local curriculum can by synthesized. Some schools will depend solely on the purchase of a program with a built-in scope and sequence already provided. This should not be taken for granted and should also be examined in light of the guidelines suggested here. It should also be expected that the selection of content for science is a continuous process. Each year will bring new advances in science, and new ideas from the school and community as to what should be included in the science curriculum.

Exercise 6–1 Identifying Criteria for Selecting Subject Matter for Science

Instructions: Based on the readings of this section, class discussion, and other pertinent readings, construct an evaluation scheme for selecting subject matter for science. Identify each characteristic to be evaluated. For each characteristic, write a description of that characteristic which explains it well enough to allow someone else to use the evaluation instrument.

Exercise 6–2 Evaluation of Subject Matter of Contemporary Science Programs

Instructions: Select one of the contemporary science programs which you have access to. Use the evaluation scheme developed in Exercise 6–1 and rate the selected program on each of the characteristics.

Patterns of Subject Matter Organization

When one examines the myriad science programs now in use by schools, several patterns of organization appear. These patterns might be categorized and labeled as separate discipline, integrated science, and unified science. The categories are not finite since some programs may incorporate more than one organizational pattern. The categorization is done on the basis of how the authors of the program arranged the subjects covered by the program.

In a program which carries the label of a separate discipline approach, the content of the program usually covers only one of the disciplines of science. For example, it is common to see a middle school or junior high school program in science which has *life* science taught at one level, *physical* science at another, and *earth* science at yet another. Of course, in the high school, the curriculum is likely to include courses in chemistry, physics, botany, astronomy, zoology, or geology. In each of these instances, the study was limited to subject matter of a separate discipline within the total field of science.

However, the science program may include more than one discipline in science. A year of study might include something from earth, physical, and life science. This "general science" approach is currently on the decline, although current science programs usually include at least some type of integration in which the study of one subject includes topics from two or more disciplines. For example, a course may begin

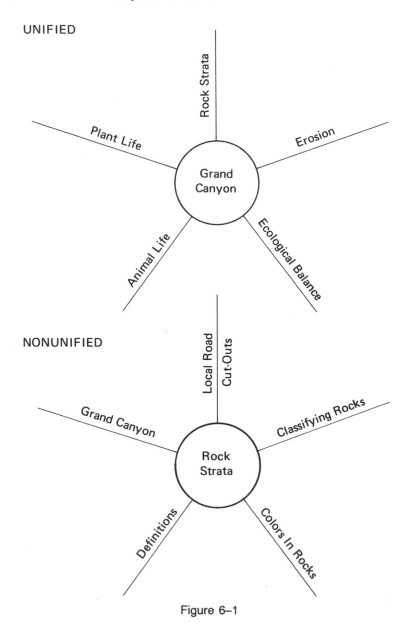

Figure 6–1

with a physics topic which then leads into a topic from chemistry. This background may provide the material necessary to the study of some earth or biological topic. The difference between this approach and the general science approach is that topics are sequenced as they are related rather than having several disciplines studied in one course.

A unified science approach represents a third category of subject matter patterns in science programs. In this category no distinction is made between the disciplines of science. For example, a student might have the Grand Canyon as a focus of instruction, taking into account the geological, physical, and biological aspects of the topic. In this way the student learns a topic in its entirety rather than a discipline in its entirety. Without a unified approach, the student might learn the physical science application of the Grand Canyon in one year, the biological science aspect in another, and perhaps never have the opportunity to study the geological factors because it is not one of the courses ordinarily taught. This approach would provide for the study of a local river, wildlife area, industry, or other phenomenon without necessarily segmenting the study into separate courses.

Figure 6–1 contrasts a unified approach and a nonunified approach to teaching a geological topic. A unit which deals with the Grand Canyon can touch upon many different facets of science. A unit which deals with rock strata or the like can develop the learning activities around rock strata from several different locations. Some of the very same specific instructional objectives could be used in each unit. However, the overall outcomes of the units would be different.

Unified science has become much more prevalent in recent years. A group of science educators who wanted to develop the unified approach banded together and formed an organization called the Federation for Unified Science Education (FUSE). This organization has conducted workshops, developed instructional materials, and otherwise disseminated the concepts of unified science. In one of their newsletters, criteria for unified science were given as science units which included more than one discipline of science and provided continuity between units (Showalter, 1973).

The three patterns of science curriculum organization can be seen at the total program level, the course level, and the unit level of the curriculum. For example, at the total program level or course level, one might find a curriculum organized around an outdoor education center. Within the center operation, one could study topics from botany, zoology, limnology, geology, weather, chemistry, and physics. All of these disciplines would be dealt with as the topics studied required information from that discipline. A program organized in an integrated pattern would have topics from all, or many, of the disciplines alternated throughout the program. These topics would be articulated from one unit to the next. To illustrate a program or course organized around a separate discipline approach, one can imagine a program which consists of separate courses in the sciences. A program such as this might look like the following:

Grades	Science (each course dealing with
K–6	three to five units, each with a separate
	topic, unrelated to each other).

Grade 7	Life Science
Grade 8	Earth Science
Grade 9	Physical Science
Grade 10	Biology or Physical Science II
Grade 11	Chemistry or Biology II
Grade 12	Physics, Chemistry II, or Biology III

For most teachers, it is more appropriate to deal at this time with the patterns of organization of individual units. A unit which had a unified approach would be based on broad topics which would allow for the study of several disciplines related to that topic. One unit might be a study of a creek adjacent to the school yard. This would provide for study of such topics as the force of water, animal and plant life, and the relative affects of the weather on the water flow. In a second unit, the teacher might deal only with forces, a topic from physics. In this unit the teacher would only be concerned with the study of the forces, without interrelating it to any other discipline of study. This would be an example of a separate discipline. In a third unit, study of a type of chemical reaction could lead into a biochemical relationship as applications to the life sciences are found. This would exemplify the integrated science category.

Exercise 6–3   Identifying Organizational Patterns of Science Programs

Instructions: Examine the organizational patterns of several science programs. Attempt to classify each into one of the three categories of separate discipline, integrated science, and unified science. Expect that some programs will employ more than one pattern.

Conceptual Structures of Science

Chapter 2 focused on the idea that the multitude of knowledge generated by scientists over the years need not be as overwhelming as it may seem at first. Too many people today have the image of science as being an encyclopedic presentation of factual material. The term "concept" is used to denote a grouping of factual information having common characteristics. Figuratively speaking, one could imagine all of the information gleaned from the years of scientific progress in one huge pile. Subsequent sorting of that pile into smaller piles of like items would develop conceptual groupings, such as "animals," "plants," "forces," "energy," and so forth. These piles might also be subdivided into smaller groups, for instance, "animals" would then be separated into "birds," "mammals," "reptiles," etc. One's concept of "bird" would be described as a generalization of all items in this pile. The more birds one would see, the better developed this concept would be.

One could generalize about the nature of a "concept" in science by saying that the concepts to be learned are those one-or two-word items listed in the index of the science text. As examples of concepts, one might make up an elementary school science curriculum to include the following:

Acid	Cell	Efficiency	Gas
Air	Chemical Reaction	Egg	Gravity
Atom	Climate	Electron	Heat
Bacteria	Density	Fission	Humidity
Battery	Digestion	Force	Hybrid
Bird	Dispersion	Free Fall	Insulator

Without going further with this list, it is apparent that science has many concepts. Granted that the number of concepts which could be learned is much less than the facts making up these concepts, it is still overwhelming to think that any elementary school science curriculum can possibly deal with all of the concepts available. Is there yet another scheme for organizing the concepts into a more manageable form?

Exercise 6–4 Grouping Science Concepts

Instructions: As an individual, or preferably in small groups, identify groups of concepts that have some common attributes. For convenience, copy the concepts listed above and other such topics easily obtained from the index of science texts on to small cards or sheets of paper. Then arrange the terms on the cards into groups which have one or more common attributes. Write out the phrase which best describes each group.

Developing Conceptual Schemes

Just as groups of factual material are related through common characteristics, groups of concepts are also related in much the same way. For example, one can generalize by saying that energy can change from one form to another. This statement partially summarizes a great number of concepts including those of chemical reaction, sound, light, heat, and motion. The question becomes: Can conceptual schemes be identified which would summarize the total field of science?

The Curriculum Committee of the National Science Teachers Association produced an often quoted statement identifying the use of concepts in planning for instruction in science. In an opening statement, the chairman presented several points of view regarding science instruction including the statement that teachers must build curriculum based on the significant concepts of science. These concepts so chosen should be useful for understanding the structure of science. To assist curriculum developers and teachers, the Committee proceeded to identify seven statements as "conceptual schemes" for the development of science curriculum (NSTA, 1964).

1. All matter is composed of units called fundamental particles; under certain conditions these particles can be transformed into energy and vice versa.
2. Matter exists in the form of units which can be classified into hierarchies of organizational levels.
3. The behavior of matter in the universe can be described on a statistical basis.
4. Units of matter interact. The bases of all ordinary interactions are electromagnetic, gravitational, and nuclear forces.
5. All interacting units of matter tend toward equilibrium states in which the energy content (enthalopy) is a minimum and the energy distribution (entropy) is most random. In the process of attaining equilibrium, energy transformations or matter transformation or matter-energy transformations occur. Nevertheless, the sum of energy and matter in the universe remains constant.
6. One of the forms of energy is the motion of units of matter. Such motion is responsible for heat and temperature and for the states of matter: solid, liquid, and gaseous.
7. All matter exists in time and space and science interactions occur among its units; matter is subject in some degree to changes with time. Such changes may occur at various rates and in various patterns.

Each of these statements was *not* meant to define separate units of study. Rather, they were to pervade the entire curriculum, kindergarten through secondary education. One might attempt to teach the "statements" as they are written. That is, one could tell the students about the statement, provide some examples, and ask them to repeat the statement in their own words or in the original form. Again, this was not the purpose of the statements. It would require a great many experiences over a long period of time to really develop the ideas behind the statement.

Most likely students enter school in the kindergarten with some rather simplistic understandings in one or more of the conceptual schemes. Carefully designed instruction would then continue to build upon previous learnings to enhance these basic ideas. Consider statement No. 2 in the above list. Students in the primary grades can learn to classify objects by color and shape. Later study would broaden the concept to include rocks and minerals found in nature. Plants and animals are easily classified in a similar manner. Later on students begin to assign names to groups of plants or animals yielding eventually the structure of living organisms so useful in the study of biology.

To provide another example of the conceptual schemes approach, we will examine the program developed under the direction of Paul F. Brandwein (1972). Early research by Brandwein and others to determine a workable conceptual schemes approach led to the identification of six statements which together were thought to envelop the entire scope of the area of science. For example, one statement, " a living thing is the product of its heredity and environment," was designed to include such concepts as reproduction, environmental influence, cells, life cycle, and the interrelationships of living things.

Brandwein and others have developed a complete elementary school science program based on the conceptual schemes approach. The structure of their program is depicted in the chart in Table 6–1. The six conceptual schemes are identified across the top of the page as items "A" through "F." The Concept Levels would approximate the typical grade of the elementary school (K–6). To view the development of a conceptual scheme, begin reading at the bottom of a column toward the top. Thus, "A force is needed to start, stop, or change the direction of motion" is a description of a set of experiences and understandings developed in the first level of the program. This provides the basis for the eventual development of the Conceptual Scheme "A."

Note that each statement is rather broad, and is then the basis for one or more units of study at that grade level. For example, the statement "There are seasonal changes on earth" is further broken down into the following statements:

1. Light energy from the sun can be changed to heat energy.
2. All planets and their satellites received energy from the sun.
3. The temperature of an area of the earth is affected by the amount of energy it receives from the sun.
4. Life on earth depends on energy from the sun.
5. All planets and their satellites receive energy from the sun.
6. Our knowledge of the moon is related to the sun's radiant energy.

When viewing bits and pieces of an elementary school science program, an observer may not recognize the existence of the conceptual schemes being used. The difference is not so much in the way science is taught, but in the way it is organized and selected. The use of conceptual schemes will provide

> a framework within which the teacher can provide experiences that will lead students to participate in the processes of science—in observation and in interpretation—and emerge with the products of science, which are testable explanations of the workings of the material world. (Brandwein, 1972)

The use of a conceptual scheme does not impose rigidity in the curriculum. Rather, it allows for selection between many different topics

TABLE 6-1   A STRUCTURE FOR CONCEPTS IN SCIENCE

	CONCEPTUAL SCHEME A	CONCEPTUAL SCHEME B	CONCEPTUAL SCHEME C
	When energy changes from one form to another, the total amount of energy remains unchanged.	When matter changes from one form to another, the total amount of matter remains unchanged.	The Universe is in continuous change.
CONCEPT LEVEL VI Brown	The amount of energy gotten out of a machine does not exceed the energy put into it.	In nuclear reactions, matter is converted to energy, but the total amount of matter and energy remains unchanged.	Nuclear reactions produce the radiant energy of stars, and consequent change.
CONCEPT LEVEL V Purple	Energy must be applied to produce an unbalanced force, which results in a change in motion.	In chemical or physical changes, the total amount of matter remains unchanged.	Bodies in space are in continuous change.
CONCEPT LEVEL IV Orange	A loss or gain of energy affects molecular motion.	In chemical change, atoms react to produce change in the molecules.	The Earth's matter is in continuous change.
CONCEPT LEVEL III Green	The Sun is the Earth's chief source of radiant energy.	Matter consists of atoms and molecules.	There are seasonal and annual changes on Earth.
CONCEPT LEVEL II Red	Energy can change from one form to another.	A change in the state of matter is determined by molecular motion.	There are regular changes in positions of the Earth and Moon.
CONCEPT LEVEL I Blue	Force is required to set an object in motion.	Matter commonly exists as solids, liquids, and gases.	There are daily changes on Earth.
BEGINNING CONCEPT LEVEL Yellow	A force is needed to start, stop, or change the direction of motion.	Matter is characterized by certain properties by which it can be identified and classified.	Things change (implicit within the development of Conceptual Schemes A and B).

by which the schemes can be accomplished. The conceptual schemes are the guideposts which assist in monitoring the growth of the students throughout the science curriculum.

To exemplify another use of concepts to organize a curriculum for elementary school science, we can examine the materials produced by the Science Curriculum Improvement Study (SCIS). The authors of the SCIS program identified a central point of view that objects and organ-

CONCEPTUAL SCHEME D	CONCEPTUAL SCHEME E	CONCEPTUAL SCHEME F
Living things are interdependent with one another and with their environment.	A living thing is the product of its heredity and environment.	Living things are in continuous change.
Living things depend basically on the capture of radiant energy by green plants.	Man is the product of his heredity and environment.	Changes in the genetic code result in changes in living things.
Living things are adapted by structure and function to their environment.	The cell is the unit of structure and function in living things.	Over the ages, living things have changed in their adaptation to the changing environment.
Living things capture matter and energy from the environment and return them to the environment.	A living thing reproduces itself and develops in a given environment.	Living things are adapted to particular environments.
The Earth's different environments have their own characteristic life.	Living things are related through possession of common structure.	Living things grow and develop in different environments.
Living things depend on their environment for the conditions of life.	Related living things reproduce in similar ways.	Forms of living things have become extinct.
Living things are affected by their environment.	Living things reproduce their own kind.	There are different forms of living things.
Environments differ (implicit within the development of Conceptual Scheme F).	Living things may differ in structure, but they have common needs and similar life activities.	Living things grow (implicit within the development of Conceptual Scheme E).

isms *interact* and thereby bring about change. To develop this central point of view, eight concepts were utilized. The four major scientific concepts are matter, energy, organism, and ecosystem. The four "process"-oriented concepts were property, reference frame, system, and model. Toward the development of these eight concepts, more specific concepts were identified and used as the basis for the development of thirteen semester-long units of study.

The identification of one set of conceptual schemes which would describe all of science may be a futile effort. This problem is compounded by the constant changes being made in the knowledge of the world. But just the sheer task of assimilating all of the knowledge about science into a few statements may not be the most appropriate effort for science educators. This does not keep us from making effective use of the conceptual schemes which have been identified. These schemes have allowed for the development of science curricula in a way which is advantageous to developer, teacher, and student. In general, the usual result is a greater articulation of learning sequences, leading toward a more effective learning environment.

Exercise 6–5 Identifying Conceptual Structures of Science

Instructions: In previous exercises you were asked to examine contemporary science programs for their overall organizational pattern, and the extent to which it exemplified certain characteristics. At this time, you are asked to examine the conceptual structure of one or more programs of science. You will need to examine the teacher's guide for the program in order to determine the conceptual structure in most cases. To derive the structure from reading the entire student portion of the program is possible, but not desirable. For each program investigated, note the existence of any conceptual structure, seek to identify the concepts and conceptual scheme being used, and determine the way in which the program makes use of the concept statements.

Developing Knowledge Structures

Teaching science should reflect a structure based on identified conceptual schemes. One difference between the science teacher as a technician and as a theoretician is the ability to formulate the structure of knowledge for a unit of study, course, or program. We are not naive enough to suggest that every unit taught by a teacher should be developed from scratch through the derivation of an appropriate knowledge structure. This is a highly improbable process due to the constraints of time and resources for the typical school teacher. What we are proposing is that each teacher have the capability to develop the structure of a unit of study and be able to recognize whether or not a given unit of study has a structure to the knowledge presented within it.

When a teacher begins to develop a unit of study for a given body of knowledge, he must first determine the limits of that body of knowledge. This is accomplished by identifying the key ideas within the subject to be taught, which are stated in the form of conceptual statements. The statements provided in Table 6–2 from the *Concepts in Science* program provide good examples of what is needed. The statement should reflect the area being studied, one that is acceptable to the scientific community. Such a statement as: It is important to conserve energy is not a good example because it does not summarize an area of study; it merely enters an opinion.

The second step in the development of a knowledge structure is to break down a major idea into its component parts. A unit of study which is based upon one major idea will develop it through a number of smaller steps. These smaller steps, subcomponent parts to the one main idea, are also conceptual in nature. They, too, are statements of substance rather than statements of opinion. If the main idea of a unit was: The earth is continuously changing, then a component statement would be something like: Earthquakes are a result of internal stress within the earth or Mountains are in a continuous state of change. Each of the component parts builds toward the major idea.

It is important to keep in mind that conceptual statements are not something that students should learn to remember or simply recognize. To learn a concept is a never-ending process emanating from many experiences. Statements of a knowledge structure, being conceptual statements, have this characteristic. You could tell a student that "mountains are changing" and he could learn to parrot it back to you, with the factual material supporting this statement. That is not the idea behind a conceptual statement. To really develop, this idea would require broad experience such that a student could recognize this concept being used, use the concept in making application to some specific event, or use it in some other higher intellectual way (see Bloom's Taxonomy described in Chapter 3).

The first and primary characteristic of a knowledge structure is continuity of conceptual development. Developing the central conceptual thought of a unit of instruction requires the development of the component concepts, which requires that learning of one concept lead into the development of a second, the second into a third, and so on, until the main idea of the unit is eventually attained. The teacher must prepare a knowledge structure which defines this element of continuity in addition to listing the concepts to be developed. A knowledge structure is defined as *not* being merely an outline of some related concepts. Good experiences in the classroom must be cumulative, leading toward the development of long-range conceptual goals of the program.

An examination of textbooks reveals many of them arranged more in a topical fashion than in a way that would reflect a structure for the body of knowledge being taught. The general science type of textbook described earlier in this chapter would usually fit this description. The arrangement of the topics is almost random, in that there is a lack of specified relationships between units of study. In and of themselves, these units of study are often very good; they lack only the cumulative learning characteristic of a good knowledge structure. Most would agree that a series of unrelated learning experiences which are well done in other ways are a great deal better than some forms of instruction. But to overlook the obvious interrelationships of the subject area is imposing an unnecessary burden on the learner. It is expecting that the learner will make the appropriate connections between the subjects being taught. To expect this to happen is certainly an impractical approach to instruction.

Consider the example knowledge structure provided in Table 6–2. The intent of this knowledge structure is to relate several process concepts which provide a basis for studying our environment. The statement in Numeral I provides a summary of the main idea of the structure. We could have said "Systems are important for studying the environment" or "The study of systems." The first statement merely begs the question of why it is important and the second is not a complete statement. The statements of a knowledge structure should be complete, free-standing statements.

Note the cumulative effect of the three main statements. The first defines the term in relation to study of the environment. The second talks about how the study is done by analyzing the changes within the system, and the third statement refers to those changes as being the result of interactions.

The points under each of the three main headings serve to extend and specify the meaning of the three key statements. These statements are more useful in the actual planning of instruction. For example, for Numeral I, students would spend some time learning to name systems and identify parts within systems (statement I–1). To extend this the

TABLE 6–2 KNOWLEDGE STRUCTURE: STUDY OF SYSTEMS IN THE ENVIRONMENT

   I. A system is a specified part of the environment which facilitates study of that part of the environment.
      1. To define a system requires naming each of the parts of the system.
      2. Systems remain the same until some part is taken away or an additional part is added to it.
  II. The parts within a system may change without changing the system as a whole.
      1. The relationship of the component parts of a system are indicated by the effect of one part on another.
      2. Parts within systems change as a result of one part affecting the other.
 III. Changes within a system are caused by the interaction of one object on another.
      1. Interactions are usually the cause of some observable change which can be described as the evidence of interaction.
      2. Some interactions may be such that a change is kept from occurring and the absence of the interaction would allow the change to occur.

Source: Based on *Interactions and Systems* (Chicago: Rand McNally, 1970).

students would learn that to change a system means changing the parts within a system (statement I–2).

The program on which this knowledge structure is based (SCIS, 1970) has students begin with the development of the concept of *interaction*. Then students develop the idea of *evidence of change,* and finally the total concept of *system.* One could approach this structure in another way by beginning with a broad study of systems and then study the interactions within the system. The point is that all of the learning specified by this knowledge structure fits together as a whole.

The relationship of the knowledge structure to the actual learning situation is through the objectives derived from the knowledge structure. The learning activities are then chosen to help the student achieve the stated objectives. The derivation of the objectives should reflect knowledge by the teacher of the capability of the learners to be involved in the unit. That is, the same knowledge structure could be used with more than one ability level, and the development of the objectives should reflect this point. In addition, most uses of a knowledge structure as the source of planning for a unit will provide for the development of higher cognitive skills during the unit. The objectives developed for a knowledge structure should, therefore, include some higher cognitive skills.

Some possible objectives relating to the example knowledge structure on system are:

1. When given a system of objects, identify at least two examples of interaction between the objects which would not affect the system as a whole.
2. When presented with examples of interactions, identify the evidence which shows that an interaction is taking place.
3. When presented with a list of objects, construct a system of some of the objects, and identify two ways that the system can be changed to become a different system.
4. When presented with a set of objects making up a system, be able to describe that system.

Exercise 6–6   Developing a Knowledge Structure

Instructions: You are to build a knowledge structure for a unit of science instruction. This knowledge structure should consist of at least three main ideas and each main idea should have at least two components. The ideas given by the knowledge structure should demonstrate a cumulative relationship to the concepts of the body of knowledge identified.

For the knowledge structure developed, construct at least five precise instructional objectives which could be used for the students you have selected. These objectives should include the three parts (observable behavior, conditions under which it will be performed, and the criterion level to be demonstrated) as well as development of some higher cognitive learnings.

Sequencing Subject Matter

The *sequence* of the elementary school science curriculum refers to the order in which the concepts of the subject matter are developed. Because of the complexity of science, not many individual teachers will attempt to develop or modify the scope of a program. Rather, they will attack the program's sequence. This is usually done to accommodate some local needs which suggest a schedule for learning activities. Teachers should recognize the importance of sequence as well as the scope of the program and make modifications only in the light of a knowledge about all of the factors.

Basically, two factors affect the sequence of subject matter in science. One of these factors is the nature of the learner. Not all concepts can be taught to elementary school students. Students develop through a series of intellectual stages. The early years require concrete experiences in order to learn successfully. In later years the ability to handle abstract ideas will develop. Sequencing subject matter requires an understanding of this and other concepts developed by learning psychologists. Chapter 5 dealt with this issue in more detail.

A second factor in the sequencing of instruction is the nature of the subject matter itself. The nature of the subject matter has a structure as does the nature of science. As developed in the preceding two sections, relationships do exist between the various pieces of the disciplines of science and a good science program will reflect this.

Other local factors will also be reflected in the sequence of instruction. Certain live specimens will only be available for study during some portions of the year. Enough microscopes or other specialized equipment may not be available for particular grade levels. The availability of adequate learning resources for a given age group may be a factor. In summary, it may be fortunate that a single sequence for learning science is not available since we are not always able to follow some externally prescribed sequence.

Four Approaches to Sequencing Subject Matter

Within almost any science program a variety of approaches to sequencing subject matter can be found. This is due to the author's view of the purpose of the lesson, the nature of the subject matter, or some other reason. It may be that the author simply wanted to present some variety to the organization of the textbook. A description of each of four types of organization follows (Taba, 1966).

Some subject matter is sequenced from the simple to the complex. This is a very logical approach. It resembles the building of a house. One first learns to put together simple joints of wood and simple wiring circuits. Only later does one take on the complex task of building a house. So it is with some science topics. One can begin by teaching the simple steps and lead into the more complex topics. The study of life may begin with the study of one-celled animals. This study then works into simple multicellular animals, and finally culminates in the study of man. In this way every detail of the one-celled animal can be thoroughly studied. As more complex animals are studied, more details of living matter are also added to the study. Comparisons to lower animals can be made as each new, more complex animal is studied. Note, the study could have been begun at the human animal level, but this would likely require studying characteristics in less depth. Then as each animal of less complexity is studied, the learner can be asked to be more specific about the nature of each of the parts.

The reverse of the simple to complex procedure for sequencing subject matter is what might be termed the whole-to-part type of organization. In this case, the learner is led from the most general to the most specific. This type of approach would begin with the study of humans and end with the one-celled animal, or, as in the study of ecology, it is common to begin with the whole area of a nature center, and then become progressively more specific about the parts of the whole. One student might culminate by conducting a specialized research study of one of the plant-animal relationships in the area. A study of weather could be done in this type of organization. Students would begin by taking daily readings about the conditions in the atmosphere. Study of the data in the form of graphs would yield some generalizations about the total phenomena. Subsequent learning situations would involve the types of clouds, the formation of a cloud, the humidity in the air, and the water cycle of evaporation and condensation.

Another organization for sequencing content is by the hierarchical method. In this method, learning experiences are sequenced by the prerequisite learning needed to master each subsequent objective. An anaylsis of the learning task would show that certain behaviors must be learned prior to learning some terminal behavior. For example, the ability to make use of the periodic chart of the elements requires the ability to understand the various concepts illustrated on the chart. One would teach about the atomic number, the atomic weight, and isotopes as well as some knowledge about the bonding of atoms within molecules. The exact behaviors would depend upon the nature of the culminating behavior. More generally, it is necessary for students to be able to make use of the individual process skills prior to demonstrating the ability to conduct a complete experiment.

A fourth way of sequencing subject matter is through a chronological approach. The history of science as a total approach may not be the most appropriate way to teach science, but to ignore the history of the discipline completely does seem to be as much in error. One might use a chronological approach to teach about the structure of the atom. The study could begin with the early concepts of matter, which today seem comical to students. Experiments done by the early scientists could be recreated by the students. Attitudes toward the nature of science could be developed as the fluid nature of knowledge becomes apparent. A similar process could be used to study the structure of the universe. The ancient study of the heavens would provide an entertaining way to begin the unit. The sophisticated study of today could be used to show the actual simplicity of the universe. In contrast to the previous method of sequencing subject matter, one could also use the historical approach to the study of the periodic table. This could begin with study of early knowledge about the elements and continue by adding new information in chronological order.

Exercise 6–7   Subject Matter Sequences in Science Programs

Instructions: Through a study of contemporary science programs, identify examples of at least two of the four methods of sequencing subject matter. Through group discussion with your classmates, attempt to identify or develop a contrasting approach to sequencing the same subject matter.

The Spiral Curriculum

In this chapter we have spoken of the need for a science curriculum to consist of units of instruction which have internal continuity. The knowledge structure to be taught should demonstrate a cumulative effect leading toward one or more of the big ideas of science. In addition we have spoken of the use of conceptual schemes as a way of providing continuity to the entire curriculum. There remains one other characteristic of curriculum design which is also necessary in the science curriculum. This characteristic refers to the relationship between units of instruction.

Most can readily agree that learning something once does not insure that knowledge will be retained. Those of you who have taken a foriegn language course in high school and have not had the opportunity to practice the skills since then have probably lost a significant amount of the competencies you once had. Retaining learned skills requires repetition, reinforcement, and continued use. For example, you may teach your first-grade students to classify materials based on characteristic properties. First of all, it makes little sense to teach this skill at all unless there is to be some use for it in later units. Secondly, one would not expect these children to retain the skill unless additional use is made of it. For example, when second-grade children are learning about plants, they could classify them according to properties not studied at the earlier age.

The need for periodic review and extension of competencies holds true for concepts, process skills, or any mental operation. A curriculum which is organized around the idea of periodic review and extension is referred to as a spiral curriculum. To provide a concrete image of this idea, imagine two blocks of wood joined by several dowel rods. When placed in an upright position, the lower block would represent the child entering school, the upper block, his capabilities at the end of the school years. The wooden dowels would represent conceptual schemes, process skills, and the like taught throughout those years. The instructional path from the base to the top could be represented by a strand of yarn spiraling up from the base to the top. The yarn would intersect the dowels several times throughout the spiral to demonstrate how each conceptual scheme or process skill would be included at several points throughout the curriculum.

The key to the development of a spiral curriculum is the articulation process used in the local school system. Within a given grade level, one may find a number of instances where appropriate repetition can be provided. For example, the use of the metric skills taught during the first unit of the year would be used throughout the other units during the year as appropriate. But to maintain this same kind of of appropriate repetition and continuity throughout the curriculum will require the cooperation and expertise of all teachers concerned.

References

Brandwein, Paul F., *et al., Concepts in Science,* Teacher's Ed. New York: Harcourt Brace Jovanovich, 1972.

Ford, G. W., and Lawrence Pugno, *The Structure of Knowledge and The Curriculum.* Chicago: Rand McNally, 1964.

National Science Teachers Association, *School Science Education for the Seventies.* Washington, D.C., 1971.

National Science Teachers Association, *Theory into Action.* Washington, D. C., 1964.

Science Curriculum Improvement Study, *SCIS Teacher's Handbook,* Berkeley: University of California, 1974.

Shamos, Norris H., "The Role of Major Conceptual Schemes in Science Education," *The Science Teacher,* January, 1966, pp. 27–30.

Showalter, Victor, "Unified Science Terminology and Variations," *Prism II,* Center for Unified Science Education, Winter, 1973, pp. 11–12.

Taba, Hilda, *Curriculum Development, Theory and Practice.* New York: Harcourt, Brace & World, 1962.

7
Science Teaching Methods and Their Use

Anyone who has gone through the regular educational programs has spent many hours participating in learning experiences arranged by a classroom teacher. The majority of these experiences were probably enjoyable and beneficial. You will soon be in the position of choosing what students should do during their formal learning experiences that will allow them to learn the subject at hand. Elsewhere in this book the possible goals of science education have been discussed, and the various strategies for accomplishing those goals will also be covered. In this chapter we will define and illustrate some of the methods used for learning science. The chapter should be used as a reference of available methods which can be integrated into an effective strategy for learning. You are cautioned that the order of the methods presented here or the length of explanation does not indicate priority in their use or effectiveness. Nor should one infer that these methods are the only means by which students learn science.

The methods of learning science are presented in two sections. In the first section you will be reminded of the variety of means by which information can be accumulated by the student. These methods include reading, experimenting, taking field trips, and watching movies. No matter what strategy is being employed by the teacher, the student must be presented with information for learning.

In the latter section of this chapter you are shown methods of data expression. These methods provide the means by which students make use of the information gained through one of the methods of the first part of this chapter. The primary data expression mode is through verbal and nonverbal interchange between teacher and student and between students. In addition to verbal and nonverbal expression, you will be reminded of the variety of reporting devices that students need to make use of.

OBJECTIVES

The reading material and exercises of this chapter are designed to assist you in developing the following objectives:

1. The student will be able to describe methods for learning science (reading, demonstration, experimentation, exploration, projects, media, field trips, discussion, and reports). Each description will include the purpose to be achieved and the techniques for use of that method.
2. The students will be able to describe categories of verbal classroom behavior and identify examples of these categories in written or oral classroom dialoguo.

Reading

One way of categorizing instruction in elementary school classrooms is by observing how reading is used for learning about science. On one end of the scale is the type of instruction where children take turns reading from a textbook which is written and designed for a specific grade level. Most of the information is gained from this book; very little demonstrating or experimenting is done and then only from the topics covered in the book. On the other end of the spectrum is the classroom where students spend virtually all of their time working with materials to gain information, and where no reading is done either in a textbook or from supplementary sources. Although the latter description may appear to be more in line with current thinking about the most effective ways to teach science, one must conclude that both ends of this continuum are probably wrong. Rather, children should use their skill in reading to further their understanding of phenomena that have been observed and they should learn to use the particular reading skills needed to understand science-related reading materials.

Variety of Sources of Reading Material

Textbooks for elementary school science are available from several commercial publishers. Generally speaking, elementary school science texts are published in series spanning grades K–6, K–8, or 1–6. The textbooks of a given series are usually written by the same author or authors and are designed to be used consecutively in each grade. Although the organization varies, most grade level texts will deal with four or more topics from science.

Textbook series usually have a teacher's guide which includes a variety of resources for designing the instructional plan for the units of study. These teacher aids are likely to include objectives for instruction, background for the teacher in the concepts being studied, suggested time schedules for the units and lessons, and suggested evaluation measures. The teachers guide will also include the pages from the student text so that the teacher need only make use of one book in planning and implementing the units of instruction.

The National Science Teachers Association (NSTA, 1973) publishes a listing of available commercial programs for instruction in science entitled *Bibliography of Science Courses of Study and Textbooks-K–12*. This publication also includes listings of materials available from state and local school departments.

The second most abundant source of reading material for science is trade books. These books are not textbooks, but would more appropriately be termed "library books." Many textbooks will provide a bibliography of related supplementary reading materials. The local library and the school library will, of course, contain many such books.

In addition to these two most obvious sources of reading material for science, other printed materials should be noted for their value in enriching classroom learning situations with regard to current happenings in the field of science. Older children can make use of the local and regional newspapers for items of information about current news in science and for feature articles of local or topical interest. Some periodicals are published especially for children (e.g., *Ranger Rick*), and are often reviewed in the National Science Teachers Association monthly publication *Science and Children.*

Reading about Science: Use and Misuse

Learning how to read is a primary function of the elementary school educational program. This is evident in statements of goals developed by elementary schools and by their actual expenditures of time and resources. To make any effort to reduce the emphasis on learning how to read would cause alarm from many sectors of the community. On the other hand, many science educators today are developing and implementing science curriculum materials that have virtually no reading materials for students and suggest that the traditional textbook-oriented science programs are not effective for elementary school students. What, then, is the relationship of reading to the elementary school science program?

Consider that a "typical" approach to science instruction in a classroom focuses on a textbook approach. Every student has a copy of a textbook and the teacher has a teacher's guide which includes student pages. Even though science "kits" may be provided and purchased for each teacher, there is probably not enough equipment in the kit to allow students to work in small groups. Each science class consists primarily of students reading silently or aloud from the science text, with the teacher giving demonstrations or additional information intermittently. The textbook is the primary source of information discussed in the classroom and phenomena are demonstrated by the teacher to support what has been given in the textbook.

Compare this "typical" lesson to basic elements of just about anyone's learning theory, as indicated in Chapter 5. In the early elementary school years children are in the "preoperational" level of learning. Consequently they do not have the ability to deal with abstract ideas. If that is so, then it seems difficult for the students to read about such complex, abstract phenomena as the atom, sound waves, and light energy without the personal, concrete experiences of an individual, hands-on learning approach. Does this type of experience rule out reading about science? No, not at all. The following paragraphs will identify the reasons for which reading can be used in the teaching of elementary school science.

Certainly, when the child does read science-related material, there is an additional opportunity to increase comprehension skills. The various reading skills developed during the elementary school reading program can be practiced and extended in reading about science. A second related reason deals with the development of science vocabulary. This need not be limited to formal, textbook materials, or to those materials which can be supplied to each student. In fact, each student could be reading a different text or tradebook and accomplishing these same purposes.

Another reason for having students read about science-related material is to seek information not available to them through first-hand experience. Students can learn about the nature of series and parallel circuits of electricity by direct experience with dry cell batteries, electric wires, and light bulbs. They cannot find out all there is to know about the uses and characteristics of the application of such information by direct experience, at least not in a way that is practical to the elementary school student. But the motivated student can, and should, be encouraged to read further about household circuits, the type of material which could be used, or other such specific information. It is in this way that a teacher can personalize the instruction in science to accommodate the student's varied interests. The teacher should not expect to test the students on such knowledge, but could very well involve the student in an activity which shares this information with other interested students.

Reading about science-related material also insures that current information is available to students. Current events in the field of science are, for the most part, simple extensions of basic relationships studied in the classroom. For example, students who have spent some time developing the concept of community relationship among plants and animals, and the concept of food chains and energy transfer will be able to use current information about ecological problems to enlarge their concepts.

Techniques for Reading about Science

The following guidelines for using reading as an avenue of learning science information are provided.

A variety of resources should be available. Basically, the pay-off for the teachers who spend the extra time to develop a variety of resources is being able to accommodate the reading levels and interests of the students.

Difficult vocabulary terms, which are likely to give the student trouble, should be identified. Assist the student in learning how to pronounce the terms prior to the time they are expected to read the material. In some cases the students only need to be reminded of the meaning of the terms based on past experiences. When a new term is fundamental to the understanding of the main points of the material to be read, it is probably most effective to arrange some type of classroom experience which concretely depicts the meaning of the term. For example, the reading material concerning characteristics of various *organisms* should probably be preceded for most students by classroom experiences in which the students identify organisms they already know about and describe or listen to others describe properties of those organisms.

Students are more likely to profit from reading if a purpose is clear in their mind prior to beginning the reading exercise. If a student chooses to read a selection, then his own pleasure becomes the overriding purpose. Most reading associated even informally with classroom learning ought to grow out of some need to seek information. After experiences of watching and experimenting with the classroom hamsters, the students might seek specific information about the animals that is not evident through direct experience. After finding out that electrical energy can be produced through some types of chemical reactions, a few students may decide to read to find out what materials make up the flashlight and automobile batteries. There are few instances when a student can profit from an assignment like: "Read pages 20 to 28 and we will discuss them tomorrow."

To gain full meaning from a reading experience, students must have the opportunity to integrate new information with the old information. After reading about hamsters, the children could discuss the new information in connection with their recorded observations of the classroom animals behaviors. After reading about the commercial batteries the students could share that information with the rest of the students and then compare the common characteristics of the commercial batteries to what was observed about the classroom constructed electrical cells.

The role of reading is shown in the following diagram to depict its relationship to other classroom experiences:

Preliminary   Reading   Follow-up
Experiences ⟶ Experiences ⟶ Experiences

The preliminary experience could be something as simple and spontaneous as a question raised by a student or it could be the result of a series of experiments and demonstrations.

The reading experience builds or explores the ideas brought out by the preliminary experience. In making the reading assignment the teacher should attempt to show students the relationship of this reading to the early experiences. The follow-up experiences should be designed to integrate the preliminary experiences with the reading experience, and to allow further exploration of the ideas presented. In this way maximum use is made of the reading as a learning experience.

Specific Reading Skills

Reading science-related material will be different from what some students are used to. In addition to the usual paragraph construction, students will encounter other ways of giving information in the forms of charts, graphs, tables, formulas, and symbols. A teacher should not assume that students are going to gain from these forms of data presentation in the same way that they can gain from the usual paragraph construction. Students will better understand the histograms, for example, after they themselves have developed histograms to display data they have collected. In fact, the general format for using reading described above does indeed apply to reading with these other types of information display.

When a text is being used as a data source, students should be able to utilize the aids available in the reading material to find information. Many texts will include the usual table of contents as well as an index and a glossary. Exercises should be provided that will enable students to use these tools. Even in the most nontextbook type of science program, there is still the need to look up specific information about the phenomena being studied.

Another aspect of reading is being able to read and follow directions. Again, even the most nontextbook elementary school science program does make use of student worksheets to guide students through the expected exercises. To develop the student's ability to follow directions the teacher should begin simply and proceed to more detailed instruction. For the benefit of the nonreader, pictures should be utilized as much as possible. In the use of instructions in the classroom, students should be held progressively more responsible for their actions based on the instructions presented. Obviously this would be more true of seventh graders than for fourth graders. To implement this, the teacher would encourage an appropriate concern for detail. Early in the primary grades students should be given exercises in observing and accurately describing their observations. Students can draw pictures of what they observe and then verbally describe these pictures to others. This concern for appropriate levels of specificity at each grade level continues until most seventh-grade students would be expected to build a battery according to the directions presented in the laboratory manual without constant teacher direction. Consider the feeling of accomplishment for the student who can "do it himself."

Reading can and should form an integral part of learning science. However, it should not be the only, nor even the primary, means by which students learn. What are the other ways of learning science? Some of the methods are described in the following sections.

Exercise 7–1   Reading To Learn Science

Answer the following questions:

1. Write a statement which summarizes the rationale for using some techniques other than reading as the only or primary source of learning about science.
2. Identify learning situations in which reading about some phenomena would be more appropriate than some other method of learning.

Demonstrations

In this text and throughout the professional education literature today, much has been said to promote a more student-centered, "hands-on" approach to teaching science in the elementary school. These efforts are aimed at reducing the amount of teacher-centered classroom activities, with the intention of gaining more effective learning for students in the classroom. At first glance these efforts may seem to discount the role of the demonstration as a learning technique. In reality, many of the new curriculum programs in elementary school science which promote a hands-on approach to learning, do in fact recognize the usefulness of the demonstration and build this technique directly into the classroom routine.

The classroom demonstration, although often used in conjunction with other learning methods described in this chapter, is separately defined as the exhibition of some selected phenomena to one or more other people. The demonstration is generally used in conjunction with experiments, discussions, and/or related readings. The purpose of the lesson will help the teacher identify when the demonstration method should be used and the relationship it will have to other methods. A review of some purposes of using demonstrations follows:

Purposes of Demonstrations

CONSERVING TIME

Allowing students to individually and directly observe a particular phenomenon may require a large amount of time by the teacher in assembling necessary materials. In this case it may be more expedient to prepare one set of materials and then demonstrate these phenomena to the rest of the students. For many teachers, the preparation of almost any equipment in sufficient quantity for individual student use appears to require too much time. Caution is urged in consideration of this purpose of excluding direct experience in favor of demonstrations. Rather, one must consider the objectives of the learning experience in terms of the concepts, skills, and attitudes being developed by students.

As another consideration for time conservation, one needs to take into account the time needed for students to manipulate the equipment compared to the time needed for the teacher to demonstrate the phenomenon. Some techniques require practice in manipulating the equipment before the phenomenon can be observed. The student's time can be conserved if the teacher does the demonstration. Caution should be exercised in overly using this factor as a reason for doing a demonstration in lieu of a more student-centered method.

DEVELOPING INTEREST

To begin a lesson, it is necessary that the students be "tuned-in" to the subject at hand. To get the needed attention of the students a brief attention-getting demonstration may be useful. A favorite demonstration of teachers beginning a study of air pressure is to collapse a metal can, seemingly without any forces being exerted. This is accomplished by heating a can containing a small amount of water with a lid removed. After the water begins to boil, the heat source is removed from the can and the lid is screwed onto the can. In a few moments the sides of the can collapse. The pressure is usually sufficient to distort the shape of the container. Care must be taken that the can is air-tight when the lid is attached and that no flammable materials are within or attached to the container. Within minutes students' attention can be turned toward a discussion of reasons that the can collapsed.

STUDENT SAFETY

A vital factor to consider is the safety of the student in the classroom. The teacher is directly responsible for the children entrusted to his/her care and must exercise due caution for their welfare. Without doubt, there are many pieces of equipment used to observe phenomena in a science classroom that have the potential to injure the children. This concern for safety should not be used to exclude any participation by the students in the use of equipment. Where it is deemed to exceed the reasonable limits of safety, a demonstration by the teacher may be in order. To judge the limits of students' safety, one must consider the nature of the experience, and the nature of the children themselves. Certainly junior-high students are more likely to handle equipment safely than are primary-age students.

COST OF MATERIALS

Placing a copper coil in a solution of silver chloride solution will produce some interesting effects due to the chemical reaction between the copper in the wire and the silver in the solution. Having commercially prepared slides of particular specimens available in quantity for individual student use may be useful for students to observe appropriate phenomena at their own rate. However, in both instances, it is possible that the school budget may not be able to realistically provide these materials in sufficient quantities for all students. In this case, it is likely that the students can adequately observe the rather slow reaction of one or two containers of solution and that the teacher can either use a micro-projector if it is available or set up stations in which microscopes are focused on individual slides. In both cases various arrangements can be made to insure that all students can observe the phenomena in question.

MODELING

On occasion, it is appropriate that students have the opportunity to watch someone "show" them how to do something. The most apparent example is when the teacher wishes to demonstrate the technique for using a piece of equipment such as the microscope. The student could probably work out the technique on his own, but this may take time and cause unnecessary damage to the equipment. Prior to beginning the lesson the teacher, perhaps with small groups of students, can go through the procedure for using the equipment.

Teacher demonstrations provide a means by which a teacher can lead a group through a problem solving situa-

GROUP PROBLEM SOLVING

There is another type of modeling that may be appropriately utilized which includes the demonstration method. This type of modeling is of the "process" used by the teacher to investigate new phenomena. The dialogue includes particular kinds of questions and subsequent manipulation, with or without student input, to the eventual acquisition of more information about the phenomena. As an example, consider the instance where a student raises a question about some seemingly "new" problem. The teacher becomes a co-investigator of the phenomenon by leading the children directly or indirectly to a solution to the problem. In this way the students have the opportunity to watch someone else "solve" a problem.

Techniques for Using Demonstrations

As noted earlier, the demonstration will probably be used in conjunction with one or more of the other methods mentioned in this chapter. The techniques to be noted in carrying out demonstrations successfully require some consideration of these other contingent methods. In general, however, the following points will assist the successful implementation of the demonstration.

1. Try the demonstration before performing it with the class. Some "textbook" ideas are not at all what they first appear. The wire you have selected for the electrical demonstration may be too heavy to carry the needed current. The type of can you choose to collapse in the air pressure demonstration may be of a rigid construction that will not be affected by the air pressure.
2. Make sure that all elements of the demonstration are visible to the students.
3. Have the purpose of the demonstration clearly in mind. Is it only for the experience? Are students to be using only the proper vocabulary? Is a concept being developed? Are process skills being developed?
4. Avoid the "magic" effect. Science is the study of observed phenomena and cannot be pursued if there is a sleight of hand or if pertinent facts are withheld from the inquirer's view. In some cases, the study of a phenomena may be beyond the student's ability, which leaves them with a concept that science is a mysterious, abstract study of all of the things we cannot understand. Some study of chemical or nuclear phenomena in the primary grades is an example.
5. Begin from the students' experience, if possible, including related units of study and experiences from outside the classroom.
6. Involve students in manipulating the equipment if possible.
7. Do not hesitate to make use of students' comments and questions if they will not lead too far afield of the task at hand. In consideration of the time available and the availability of resources, depart from the agenda to work with the students in the investigation of some related question.
8. Reduce the amount of teacher talk and increase the amount of student talk as appropriate. In some instances, the demonstration might be done in total silence with a post-demonstration discussion of what was observed by the demonstration.
9. Make use of demonstration failures. One might expect a number of failures of equipment due to changing conditions. The temperature and humidity have an effect on the static electricity reactions which can be observed. Again, make use of the students' reactions rather than just dropping it as a bad experience. The unintentional learning may be just as valuable as the original intent of the lesson.
10. Use sparingly. The temptation is there for the very busy teacher, operating from a very tight schedule, to rely more and more on teacher-directed demonstrations as the source of information for learning science. Care should be taken that the teacher carefully consider the purposes mentioned above, the means by which students learn, and the objectives of the lesson.

Experimentation

To many, the word experiment is synonymous with science. The image of the scientist is someone working away with a maze of apparatus in an "experiment" to identify some tid-bit of information at the frontier of man's search for knowledge. A traditional gift for children is a chemistry set which contains an assortment of substances, some apparatus, and a book of "experiments" which can be performed. The user of this kit is said to be emulating the role of the scientist. For many years, a high school has not been considered complete until a "laboratory" has been constructed in which students can "experiment" to learn about science.

Upon closer examination, the meaning of "experiment" as applied to the common image of science has not been clear. Experimenting may be associated with the process of working with apparatus. It is the connecting of circuits, pouring one chemical into another, dissecting a frog, or looking through a telescope or microscope. In another sense, experimenting may be considered the act of completing a laboratory exercise in which a particular phenomenon, fact, or generalization is found to exist. In the past, textbooks for science have been known to have students complete exercises such as the following:

1. Add the blue solution labeled A to the yellow solution labeled B to see if there is a color change. Write the color of the mixture here ____ ____

2. To the green solution produced in step 1 above, add the white powder labeled C to determine if the reaction took place. Describe what you observe in this new mixture._____

3. Why would you say the bubbles produced in the interaction of materials in step 2 above be an indication of a chemical reaction taking place?_____

All students in the class would typically be doing the above steps at the same time with appropriate sharing of information after each step. Little creativity or critical thinking is going to be taking place during either of the above types of "experimenting." It is difficult to imagine that the true purposes of studying science are encouraged by this type of experimentation. It is unlikely that either routine use of laboratory exercises or recipes, or the mechanical process of manipulating equipment, is going to be of interest or educational value to elementary school students.

The concept of *experimentation* is complex and not easily defined in a way satisfactory to all who use the term. For the purpose of our study of teaching science to elementary school children, a number of positive and negative characteristics can be identified. An experiment usually seeks an answer to a question through an investigation of some observable phenomena. This investigation has originated through past experiences of the student or has been posed by someone other than the student. The investigation centers on the formal or informal manipulation of variables associated with the phenomena. Throughout the investigation the student utilizes several simple processes such as observing, recording data, formulating hypotheses, and measuring. Answers to the question are arrived at by an interpretation of the information gleaned from the experience. The result can generally be reproduced by repeating the same investigation in just the same way. The investigation may have been orderly in that predetermined steps were followed or it may have been through a more spontaneous procedure.

Learning through Experimentation

Learning science through experimentation has changed during the past twenty years as evidenced by the available commercial programs for teaching science. Beginning in the early 1960s programs advocating a "hands-on" approach to teaching elementary and secondary school science became available from commercial publishers. Many of these were developed through extensive funds provided by such sources as the National Science Foundation and some other similar organizations. The nature of these programs and their development is exemplified in Chapter 12 of this text.

Whereas past science education sought to use the laboratory to verify statements made by the textbook and other references, the new programs basically differ by providing experiences through which students could determine the relationship themselves. In the past, students were told about the characteristics of electrical circuits, for example, by the teacher and the reading materials. Students were then taken to the laboratory to see if the textbook was correct when it stated that a wire was needed to connect the second part of the bulb to the other end of the battery. In the new programs for science education, the student is given the battery, bulb, and wire and asked to see if he can figure out how to light the bulb. The source of the information in each instance differs even though the objective of the lessons might have to do with developing the concept of a circuit. There are a number of purposes for teaching science through this type of method. Perhaps most importantly, the students learn how to deal with finding solutions to problems of concern. Such skills as the following are possible to develop:

1. Making problem statements in a specific manner
2. Constructing hypotheses
3. Identifying pertinent variables
4. Recording data
5. Distinguishing observations from inferences

Certainly, these process skills are not unique to science, but have application to other school subjects and to concerns in everyday living. Although no one problem-solving pattern emerges, the student does learn to appreciate and utilize unique approaches to dealing with problems which can be specifically stated.

Another purpose of using the experimental approach to instruction is the potential that students will develop attitudes which are appropriate to a dynamic approach to living. When the students have developed the process skills as indicated above, they are not as likely to shy away from a problem and consider it to be too much for them. They are not as likely to accept preliminary evidence of other students' experiences without verification. They are likely to increase their curiosity about daily experiences. In general, this technique may provide opportunity to develop a "scientific" attitude toward the person's image of his/her daily living.

Even though the objectives of instruction may suggest otherwise, students will learn a number of technical skills involved in pursuing a topic. Using measuring devices such as a balance, a metric ruler, and a graduated cylinder for volume measurement will increase the students' ability to gather data. Students will learn to appreciate the need for a "fine touch" in the use of such apparatus as the microscope and telescope. They will also learn that very simple apparatus can be used to gather information. For example, a very inexpensive pan balance can be constructed with washers or paper clips used as mass units.

Social skills may also be developed through experimentation when done as a group process. In most classroom learning situations using an experimental method of learning, students will share data, exchange means of stating the problem, discuss results of investigations, and organize and share equipment to conduct the investigation. For some situations, this may be the most important goal for teaching science in an experimental manner. When involved on a day-to-day basis, the student broadens his concept and skills of individual and group action.

Techniques for Learning through Experimentation

The background for developing an experiment by and for elementary school students will most often occur through some type of experience by the students. The teacher may structure these activities to lead to a desired problem or may let the problem arise from some unstructured exploratory activities. Students who have been keeping careful watch on the classroom aquarium may question why the aquarium needs to have water added periodically. Classroom discussion may be used to identify students' knowledge of evaporation and may provide the background for asking questions for further study. If students are not able to identify appropriate problems of study, the teacher can provide other experiences that may help them expand their experience base to the point where questions could be asked. Other containers of water can be observed to see if they too "lose" some of the liquid.

A key to the technique of using the experimental method of learning is the involvement of students, usually all students, in the procedures of the investigation. Although a teacher should never expect all students to participate to the same extent, all students would be expected to be involved at their level of readiness to pursue the problems. Some students lead the way in identifying the problems to be pursued, while others are more inclined to observe patiently. Second graders conducting an experiment will not be as adept as sixth graders at controlling the variables being explored. However, both groups can and should be fully involved in the investigation and both groups may gain a great deal from the experience. For example, both of these groups of students could pursue the study of water evaporation and arrive at quite different levels of conclusions.

A problem needs to be identified from the experience of the children and with their involvement. The statement of the problem may have been prompted by activities provided by the teacher or through some unexpected discovery by one or more students. To provide a basis for investigation, this problem must be stated in such a way that all students can pursue it with full understanding of the task at hand. "Does salt water evaporate as rapidly as fresh water?" may be the question resulting from discussion about tropical fish aquariums and the containers of fresh water observed by the students. A question such as "Why does water evaporate?" is going to be a difficult one for students to pursue at the elementary school level. The teacher in this classroom may be able to help the students rephrase the problem into one which can be explored by students in the experiment. In order to be used, the problem statement should be understood by all students, stated in a way that students can collect data from experiences in the learning environment, and one that the students can handle at their level of maturity. The usual pattern will result in students discovering some concepts and relationships, not merely proving what a textbook author has stated as being true.

Once a question is posed, the student then seeks, under the teacher's guidance, the appropriate variables to be investigated. The variables of a system are those factors which, when modified, will produce some change on the system. Consider an example in which students are led into an investigation of pendulums. Through experiences with the swings on the park playground and by observations of the grandfather clock in the hallway, students may formulate the question "What makes the pendulum swing faster or slower?" To proceed, the teacher may lead a small group discussion to brainstorm possible variables which could affect the rate at which the pendulum swings back and forth. Such variables may include: (a) the length of the string supporting the pendulum; (b) the weight of the pendulum; (c) the volume of the pendulum bob; and (d) the distance the pendulum bob is pulled before it is released to swing. Students then must identify four possible "variables" that could affect the number of swings per time interval. Students who have difficulty determining these variables are going to have difficulty conducting experiments because they lack a necessary skill. They will not be able to understand conclusions reached by the class after the experiment is concluded.

Identifying variables of a system leads the student directly into the situation of being able to "experiment." In the example of the pendulum, those students who have identified that there are at least four possible changes that could be made to speed up or slow down the pendulum can then begin to experiment. The level of maturity of the students will determine just how they might go about the experimentation. The end goal of the elementary school science program may be to teach a systematic approach. Early attempts at experimenting may be hit-and-miss. At later times the student can be led to see the efficiency of a more systematic approach.

The student could begin with a given pendulum. In an attempt to speed up or slow down the rate at which it swings, he either: (a) changes the length of the string; (b) puts on a heavier or lighter bob; (c) puts on a smaller or larger bob; or (d) varies the distance the bob is pulled back. In the course of the experiment the student could be doing a variety of individual processes as identified in Chapter 2. He could be observing, recording data, measuring, communicating, and predicting.

Students throughout the room will be collecting data, recording it, and then will be eager to compare notes with other students. Students will undoubtedly find that they have not obtained exactly the same data and may not have reached the same conclusions. A systematic means of organizing the class data should be developed. Students will thus be able to determine whether they have been consistent in collecting their data and may be able to spot errors in technique.

Another important experimental characteristic may also emerge from the data. Experimental error, the errors which are to be expected because of limited equipment and technique, will usually be present in classroom experiments. For example, measuring the temperature of the same liquid with several different thermometers may not produce the exact same thermometer readings. Instead, the readings will cluster around the "correct" answer with some being more and some being less. This is due to the inconsistencies of the equipment and to slight inaccuracies in reading the thermometers. Most of the time, the small experimental error will not interfere with the conclusions to be reached by the students regarding the questions answered.

The student began this investigation with the statement of a problem. The identification of variables, the recording of data, and the mutual exchange of data provide a basis on which to reach an answer to the original question or problem. It is appropriate that the teacher be sure that students did indeed reach the point where they determine an answer to the question and/or reach out for some other problem as an extension to the original situation. To determine whether the students have reached an answer to the problem, the teacher can develop applications to the solution of the problem. For example, if the students in the pendulum problem were to conclude that it was only the length of the string supporting the bob that made a difference in the rate at which the pendulum swings back and forth, the teacher could set up situations in which the students would predict the relative speed of two pendulums of specified lengths.

Systematic storage of equipment is a necessary factor for having an efficient laboratory based science curriculum.

Problems to Be Anticipated

An elementary school science program consisting of reading a textbook and viewing demonstrations done by the teacher and the bright students is a very safe program. Safe from discipline problems which might result if students are getting up to share data, obtain equipment, or manipulate apparatus; safe from potential accidents which are always possible, ranging from scratches by the sharp point of an object to being scorched by a lighted match; safe from accidents such as spilled water and broken equipment; and safe from being an expensive program. By comparison, a program which centers around experimentation, with all students being involved, is going to be "un-safe."

First of all, it does cost money to purchase equipment for all students. If you want all students to have extensive experience with the use of a good balance, then you will be purchasing apparatus likely to cost twenty dollars or more apiece. On the other hand, much science experience can be had with very inexpensive apparatus. For approximately five dollars, a double pan balance can be purchased. One could purchase or have made expensive pendulum bobs and apparatus to support the swinging bobs, or locally obtained objects and string being swung from the end of rulers across the end of a desk could get the job done. Individual teachers and schools have to weigh the cost of purchase against the time teachers would spend collecting the materials.

Storage, retrieval, and replacement of materials is another problem. Some schools will use shoe boxes and label them with the name of the materials contained within. In this way equipment can be stored as like items (all thermometers in one box) or by the experiment to be done (pendulum bobs and string in one box). Stored in such a way it is more convenient to inventory and to replace worn out and broken materials at the end of the year. Sometimes equipment is stored in a central distribution point in the school and in other schools each teacher has charge of his or her own equipment. To the inexperienced, these problems may seem large, but very satisfactory solutions have been found.

Once the equipment has been purchased and is organized and available, some problems of classroom management do remain. It is relatively simple to have the students reach in their desk to procure their science text for reading about science and watching demonstrations. It is more cumbersome to arrange twelve sets of materials before class, set them out for students to use, replace broken materials as needed, and then clean up the apparatus after the lesson. In the long run, it is not as complicated as it may sound. Students themselves can learn to do much of the busy work of setting up equipment either before class or as needed. Student involvement in set-up and clean-up activities also may support the development of responsibility and organization on the part of the student. This problem may seem to be almost insurmountable, but it too has been overcome by elementary school teachers and should not discourage you from use of an experimental approach to instruction.

One other problem in teaching elementary school science with experimental methods merits attention. A busy classroom is often a noisy classroom. An activity-oriented classroom should be expected to be more noisy with twenty active students than if the teacher alone is demonstrating or if one student is reading aloud.

An activity-oriented classroom requires the support of the administration for the purchase of equipment, provision of storage facilities, and certainly for helping to facilitate the type of activities described here. Even the custodian needs to be made aware of the nature of activities and be prepared for the messes that are bound to occur throughout the day. The experimental method of learning is not only likely to cause some trouble to the teacher, but is going to require others to be understanding as well.

Exercise 7–2   Comparing Three Methods of Learning Science

Three primary methods for learning science have been discussed thus far in this chapter: reading, demonstration, and experimentation. Although each is important in its own right, there are useful distinctions made between the three. For each of the methods of learning science listed above, write a description which distinguishes the use of that method from the other three. In writing this description, consider each of the following:

1. How does the student behave during the use of each method?
2. What is the role of the teacher during the use of each method?
3. How does the preparation time differ for the use of each method?
4. Is one method better than another?

Exploration

Children are different. They are different in their readiness to learn as well as in their ability to learn. The latter characteristic relates to the students' rate of learning and level of accomplishment. That is certainly one concern of the teacher. The student's readiness to proceed with a given learning activity is yet another.

Students vary greatly in the kinds of learning experiences they have had prior to the time you will have them in your class. Some of these differences are due to their father's occupation, the location of their home, their vacation experiences, and their hobbies. These vast differences make it very difficult to plan lessons with a common starting point for all. In fact some elementary school science programs suggest that a common starting point for a lesson should not be assumed, and the lessons should be made to accommodate these differences.

The *SCIS Teacher's Handbook,* which is designed to help teachers implement the Science Curriculum Improvement Study curriculum includes "exploration" as an initial part of the learning cycle. The Handbook (SCIS, 1974) defines this stage as when " . . . children explore new materials and/or ideas with minimal guidance or expectation of a specific achievement." Lessons in this program begin with an activity that allows students to have a time in which they "play" with some apparatus to check out their own understandings of some phenomena. This activity allows the teacher to determine the students' familiarity with the phenomena and their readiness to continue with the lesson.

Another program which promotes use of this technique of learning is the Elementary Science Study. Writing about this program, Hawkins describes a learning experience involving the pendulum. Assuming a limited background of experiences with pendulums, the teacher wisely chose to begin the experience with an exploratory phase. The rationale of this choice is explained in the following two-point statement:

> First, because in our previous classes we had noticed that things went well when we veered toward "Messing About" and not as well when we held too tight a rein on what we wanted the children to do. It was clear that these children had had insufficient acquaintance with the sheer phenomena of pendulum motion and needed to build a perceptive background, against which a more analytical sort of knowledge could take form and make sense. Second, we allowed things to develop this way because we decided we were getting a new kind of feedback from the children and were eager to see where and by what paths their interests would evolve and carry them. We were rewarded with a higher level of involvement and a much greater diversity of experiments. (Hawkins, 1970)

Exploration may be used to initiate a unit of instruction as well as to allow students to make use of previous learnings to demonstrate their interests and initiative as they apply ideas to new phenomena of their choosing. The important thing is that use is made of learning that is "independent" of strong teacher direction. The reader is cautioned to realize that exploration does not mean a completely unstructured learning experience. The teacher does focus the attention of the student on a narrow range of experiences and then allows exploration within that range. The teacher might place a number of objects on a tray and then ask the students a question about the objects that is divergent enough to allow students to come up with several ideas. The teacher may take students on a field trip and allow them to explore a small plot of ground and ask them to record what they observe. These explorations may lead into a number of topics of study. The very flexible and creative teacher may be able to allow the students to completely chart the course of study, but more than likely the teacher will use a prepared program and will want to build a specified unit of study upon these explorations.

Field Trips

The idea of taking a field trip to enhance learning is neither new nor unique to the field of science. Most field trips taken by elementary school students turn out to be largely interdisciplinary experiences. Both natural science and social science concepts and processes are likely to be encountered in trips to visit industrial and governmental installations. Mathematics and economics are also very likely to be encountered. The material of this section may serve to remind the reader of the obvious characteristics of field trips, but may also extend the concept of field trips to be more broadly interpreted.

The "field" begins just outside the classroom door. To some teachers the idea of a field trip conjures up images of buses, administrative paper work to get parental permission, long trips, box lunches, getting released from other teachers, and many disciplinary problems. Although there is more truth than fiction to that image, the concept of the field trip mentioned here need not be that way. The hallway or gymnasium of the school provides a natural environment for the experimentation of variables of paper airplane flight. The cluster of weeds around the two power poles near the edge of the asphalt playground, if left relatively undisturbed, may provide a natural environment for studying populations of animal life. A walk around the neighborhood at two-day intervals in the spring provides evidence for a study of relative growth of plants' buds and flowers. Depending upon the situation, these field trips may not prove to be the "hassle" that the above image of field trips portrayed.

In contrast to the schoolyard field trips, which may last only fifteen minutes, other field trips have been utilized with elementary school children that occupy the greater part of a week in time. Some outdoor education facilities have been developed and personnel hired to permit as many as several hundred school children of approximately fifth-grade level to spend several days at the sight. Students might arrive on a Tuesday noon, sleep and eat in the facilities provided during the week, and leave the facility on Friday noon to be back in their home town by the normal school closing on Friday. The week's activities may consist of field experiences and perhaps some of the regular subjects of study treated with an outdoor flavor. Although the teachers are generally included in the week long trip, they may or may not do the instruction.

Purposes of Field Trips

Whatever the location of the field trip, from schoolyard, to industry, to extended camp experiences, there are a variety of purposes to be served by the experience. One of the primary reasons for including field trips as a method of teaching science is that it provides an additional source of information to support the development of process skills, concepts, and attitudes. There is a limit to how much information can effectively and realistically be included in the printed materials provided students. There is a limit to how much information the students can take from classroom exercises that simulate real-life situations. There is a limit to the student's ability to transfer concepts and information from classroom dialogue concerning practical applications to modern living. In short, there is a definite advantage to classroom learning in the first-hand experience of the field trip.

More specifically, field trips may provide information regarding careers for the field of science and other disciplines. In a publication entitled *Career Education,* a position statement by the U.S. Department of Health, Education, and Welfare, total career education is said to begin in the elementary school years with the development of career awareness. The adolescent years continue the trend by including more specific career exploration, and the high school years are to include entry level job skill training. Although elementary school teachers cannot possibly educate their students to the many job possibilities that will exist in the future when the students will enter the job market, students can learn that there are many different types of work available and learn something about the amount of training involved. When visiting a sight, students can be shown the diversity of jobs that are necessary to make any installation function and be shown that all of these jobs are respectable.

With many field trips comes a greater community awareness. Students learn to appreciate that their community is made up of a variety of elements and that a number of these elements are concerned with some aspect of science. Students also learn of the abuse some people give to elements of the community. The interplay of governmental, industrial, and educational forces can usually be illustrated. These types of field experiences can often be referred to again once the children are back in the classroom.

Techniques for Using Field Experiences

Whatever the reason for choosing to use field trips to gain firsthand experiences, various options are available in the way that the experience can be utilized as a teaching method. The most fundamental guideline to the use of a field trip is that it ought to have a purpose, and the purpose should contribute to the development of concepts, skills, and attitudes of one or more science units. Field trips are often used as a break from the routine of the classroom, as a special treat for the students. As such, the full utilization as a learning device is not realized if the students are in a holiday mood rather than an inquiring or, at least, receptive mood. This is not to say that students must be taking notes or asked to memorize factual material about the trip. But the purpose should be such that it does actually provide the student with at least an awareness of information pertinent and appropriate to the students and to the subject being studied.

A second guideline for use of a field experience is that it be planned. A trip in which the teacher is as naive as the student regarding what might happen may not be the best way to handle an extended learning experience. A trip which utilizes someone else as a leader is certainly an exception, provided that this person does have a plan which is consistent with the teacher's purpose in taking the students on this field trip. Some types of field trips may be taken with the expressed purpose of "exploring" the particular environment. Usually the students should have some type of focus as to what is to be "explored." A focus might be to look for examples of living materials that have a coloration which causes them to be difficult to see in their environment. Students might be challenged to count the number of different living materials found in a specified segment of ground.

Students taking a field trip may require specialized equipment and/or observation skills in order to make good use of the learning experiences available. A trip to study living materials in some outdoor area may be enhanced by use of some collection and handling equipment. A trip to visit some industrial applications may require previous experience with terminology and/or processes in order to understand the industrial applications being explained.

Just prior to the field experience, students should have the opportunity to preview the activities in such a way that: (a) the purpose of the trip is clear to them; (b) the special limitations on their behavior is explained; (c) appropriate training and equipment is provided; and (d) the logistics of the trip are explained. The way in which this orientation would be handled would differ somewhat, depending upon the placement of the field experience in the unit of study. The orientation would be more divergent if the field experience was early in the unit and was intended to raise student motivation toward study of the unit. On the other hand, if the field experience occurred at the end of the unit, then the focus of the orientation might tend to be more convergent toward the identification of answers to particular questions.

Problems to Be Encountered

Several problems for the teacher are often present in taking field trips and are reasons that field experiences are not included as often as their usefulness might warrant. The first of these is the extra time needed to arrange a field experience. Unless it is a simple excursion around the schoolyard, the trip may require special arrangement for transportation, meals, parental permission, and on sight arrangements for guides or facilities. Most likely, the first trip to a given sight will be tedious in terms of details and unexpected problems which will create additional time needs. Suggestions for reducing the preparation time include the use of parent volunteers or the school secretary to make arrangements and input from teachers who have previously taken field trips to this sight.

Another important concern is for the safety of the students. A teacher is best advised to check local school and community regulations that might be appropriate. The school principal should be able to take care of special insurance needs and to alert the teacher to special hazards present in the field experience. The experience of other local teachers may also help here. In general, the teacher must remember that due caution should be exercised to alleviate all forseeable dangers to the student. Certainly accidents will happen and the wise teacher is prepared to deal with them. The local school administrators should have a plan as to how to deal with emergencies while on a trip.

Projects

Science Fairs are popular throughout elementary, junior, and senior high schools. Social science and mathematics fairs are often held jointly with the science fair. In each instance students exhibit their individual or small group projects, often in competition for ribbons or trophies. Although usually local in nature, some science fairs do provide for students who excel to take their projects on to a regional, state, or national contest. Science Fairs International and the Westinghouse Science Projects are two such organized science fairs which provide for large prizes for national winners. Whether or not the projects are asso-

Science Fair projects for problem solving involve investigations which reflect process skills, attitudes and concepts.

ciated with any kind of formal exhibition, projects are a popular way of learning about science.

Why should students do science projects? Answers to this question would include: (a) students individually apply concepts and skills learned in class; (b) students exhibit and develop their individual interests and skills; and (c) students can win prizes. Although most teachers would not put much emphasis on the third response, the first two answers do hold some educational potential for the student. Perhaps the ideal situation occurs when a student voluntarily becomes interested in some aspect of the regular classroom instruction and begins an individual project to pursue his interest. Since this does not often happen, science projects are usually begun as a regular assignment.

Science projects usually consist of one of two types: reporting projects and discovery or problem-solving projects. Reporting projects occur when the student exhibits information which has been acquired through reading one or more sources. This information is then exhibited in some attractive form as a booklet, poster, or three-dimensional model. In some instances, the three-dimensional model or poster is the focus of attention. One means of doing this is for the student to buy a model to put together from a hobby store. Another source is to find some object such as a cow's eye, some industrial apparatus, or some object found around the home and then write up a report to explain the model or object.

Problem-solving projects begin with a question to be answered from the collection and interpretation of data. Problem-solving projects differ from reporting projects in that the student can show the "answer" in terms of information that was collected. The emphasis is on the problem-solving approach and the use of skills of collecting data, observing, interpreting information, measuring, and exhibiting information collected in this way. Questions to be answered would be exemplified by the following:

1. What kind of automobiles pass the corner of Main and First street during the time of 8:00 AM and 8:30 AM?
2. What kinds of dyes can be made from plants? Will these dyes be water resistant on types of cloth such as wool and cotton? On types of cloth such as polyesters?
3. What concentration of salt in water will produce the most appropriate living conditions for brine shrimp?

Stating the question or problem to be pursued is a large factor in the study. Students should not be expected to do this without practice and without assistance from others.

There are advantages and disadvantages in both types of projects. A teacher may wish to use both types of projects at times during the school year. There is a strong argument that the problem-solving type of project is more representative of the nature of science. The student is practicing and demonstrating that he has acquired various types of process skills. Students should not be expected to do this type of project until they have had instruction in the use of these skills. As in any other method, the teacher must decide which project type is to be used based on the goals of instruction and on the characteristics of the student.

Media

Due to the many advances of modern technology, a teacher can make use of a wide variety of media with which to supplement the classroom learning environment. For those classrooms which use textbooks and demonstrations as the primary methods of teaching, the many other forms of conveying a message promise an enriching atmosphere. Unfortunately, some teachers go to the opposite extreme and will use any type of mediated instruction, no matter what the subject, in order to occupy the instructional time for science. Somewhere between these two opposites of too little and too much is a point at which mediated instruction can prove beneficial to students.

In this brief section, an exhaustive treatment of the benefits and possibilities of mediated instruction cannot be given. Instead, an effort will be made to illustrate the diversity of materials and purposes by which one is able to enrich the learning environment for elementary school science. Some familiarity with the equipment and media is assumed. To update and extend this treatment of media possibilities, one need only read through current issues of educational periodicals such as *Science and Children* and *Today's Education.*

Two-Dimensional Static Projections

"A picture is worth a thousand words," or so the old saying goes. The most obvious way to supplement the textbook and other printed material is to bring in pictures which tend to enrich and/or focus the student's attention toward the world's environment around them. These pictures can come from science-related journals, news magazines and newspapers, as well as commercial agencies which sell pictures for the specific purpose of enriching the classroom. Commercially prepared slides and filmstrips can be purchased or homemade slides and filmstrips may also be of value.

In addition to the usual pictures of wildlife, unusual phenomena, and current events, teachers should not shy away from using charts, graphs, tables, histograms, or posters. These too contain useful information for classroom discussions. Students may not always understand the complete meaning of a chart or graph, but often the general point may be understood.

To display pictures, charts, and other flat visuals, a number of options are open to the teacher. If a single item is to be discussed by the entire class, then an opaque projector may be of use. This projector will accept any flat work up to approximately one inch in thickness and, by reflected light, project the image on a screen large enough to see. Usually the room must be in complete darkness in order to see details of a picture or other visual.

No one who has ever been in school has missed seeing many different kinds of bulletin boards. The bulletin board of the elementary school classroom is often regarded as a decorative element of the room or something that carries a good message. The bulletin board is also a valuable learning tool. Students studying the parts of a pond can progressively develop a bulletin board to represent the information being collected. Students learning the concept of a "solution" can assist a teacher in putting up key characteristics of the concept as they develop. Vocabulary development can be assisted by a bulletin board. The bulletin board can be the focal point of the lesson, or a convenient aide to supplement the dialogue.

A rather new process is one that is able to "lift" the color from some types of paper and transfer the color to a clear piece of plastic. This translucent "picture" can then be projected onto a screen by the use of an overhead projector. More commonly, one can purchase commercially prepared pictures and diagrams which will supplement a lesson. The overhead projector can also be utilized as is the chalkboard to allow the development of diagrams and the writing of others before or during the classroom discussion. The overhead projector is becoming one of the most widely used means by which teachers support instruction with media. The versatility of being able to project prepared or spontaneous pictures, diagrams, charts, graphs, etc., has proven to be successful for most teachers.

One of the more traditional means of projecting pictures is by the use of the filmstrip projector. This machine projects a thirty-five milli-meter slide onto a screen of sufficient size for classroom viewing. The filmstrip is produced by a special camera which takes "slides" approximately one-half the size of the usual 35mm slide camera. With the use of this special camera, a teacher can produce his/her own filmstrip. More commonly teachers will utilize commercially prepared filmstrips to supplement their science instruction. Many filmstrips come with audio tapes or records to provide a narration to the filmstrip. Teachers may choose not to use the prepared audio track and to use the pictures for another purpose or at a pace more suited to their students.

A teacher's experiences are often the basis of instruction in the science classroom. Today the 35mm slide film is a popular pastime which can be turned into useful classroom instruction. Slides taken of camping and hiking experiences can be used to illustrate biological and geological concepts. Visits to industrial sites may also prove to be of value to the study of science and social science. The 2 X 2 slide projector is becoming more common in the elementary schools. Some filmstrip projectors also have an adaptor for slides. Newer projectors have some type of holder for keeping the slides in a special order for projection.

Two-Dimensional Dynamic Projections

"Movies" are the highlight of any child's day. The good artist can capture more on a few minutes of animated or live action filming than a good teacher can explain or demonstrate in a much longer period of time. Technology today provides the teacher with a variety of types of "moving pictures."

The most traditional form of mediated instruction is the 16mm film. Both black and white and colored films are available for use in the elementary school either by being purchased or rented from distributors. Some school systems will even have purchased a number of more popular 16 mm movies even though the purchase price may be over two hundred dollars. This form of media is best used to display something that cannot be appreciated by a static projection. A film in which a narrator holds various forms of plants or rocks and tells the listener about them is not an appropriate use of the media. A film which demonstrates a phenomenon which is difficult or impossible for the teacher to set and perform because of time or equipment may be a more appropriate use of the 16mm film.

In recent years two other forms of moving pictures have become popular, both involving 8mm film. Some distributors have made use of the 8mm film in much the same way as the 16mm. The only difference is that the film is only one-half as wide and does not produce an image of the same quality as the 16mm when projected to the same size. The more unusual use of the 8mm film is in the cartridge form. The single-concept film loop runs continually in a special projector, never needing to be rewound. Usually lasting only a few minutes, the projector and cartridge are very small compared to other moving picture projectors and have found use in small group activities and in study centers. The best use of these film loops has been for the demonstration of a phenomenon which requires motion to show the effect, but lasts only a matter of seconds. The simplicity of the machines make 8mm film loops usable by individual students.

Techniques for Using Media

The above paragraphs have provided a very brief overview of the many types of media which are available for use by the classroom teacher to supplement instruction in elementary school science. The reader should not infer from the above comments that a teacher must use any or all of these materials in order to insure a good lesson in science. On the contrary, use of these materials will not insure an effective lesson. Research into the use of mediated instruction does not support any claim that use of some material such as 16mm films will naturally increase learning in science. The effectiveness of the material for learning science is not in the material itself, but in the way in which the teacher makes use of the material.

Although it is difficult to generalize about use of the materials in a way which will apply to all situations, there are some ground rules which usually apply. The first of these is that the media must have an integral purpose in the lesson. Too often a teacher regularly schedules a 16mm film, any film, for showing at a given time on Friday. The routine of this practice tends to put down the purpose of learning the film might have and tends to develop habits of nonattention on the part of students. The purpose of using media may be only to provide enrichment to a lesson or unit in progress by saying the same thing in another way. Most appropriately, the purpose of using a particular media form is because it is the best way to portray the phenomenon being studied.

The second general rule is to be sure to introduce the student to what it is that is going to be shown. The teacher need not give away the "punch line" of the film or filmstrip. What is to be seen may be in the form of a question to be asked. In some way the teacher should focus the student's attention on the media. After the use of the media, the purpose of using the material should be discussed in a way that every student has the opportunity to find out if that purpose has been accomplished. The third rule, the follow-up portion, is a very necessary component. Without it, students are left hanging, unsure if they found out what the teacher intended them to find out, and without the concept really being explored.

A fourth point to the use of any type of material is to consider the potential for reshowing a particular mediated form. If the demonstration being done through a single concept film loop is somewhat complex, students may profit from, or in fact need, a second showing. This applies equally to the reshowing of a media form used by a teacher one year or more ago. With a slightly improved focus, even more may be gained from the second showing.

The problem which often prohibits use of mediated instruction is that a filmstrip costs over twenty dollars and a 16mm film costs over two hundred. A 16mm projector will cost over several hundred dollars. The elementary school teacher who is having trouble gaining enough money to purchase equipment for use by the students for experimentation should carefully consider the purpose of the total program in determination of priorities for purchasing learning aids.

Exercise 7–3   Selecting Methods for Accumulating Information

In this exercise you are asked to select methods for accumulating information discussed in this chapter to be appropriate for the following hypothetical situation. For each of the methods, you are asked to indicate why it would or would not be a means by which students could develop the necessary information to achieve the goals of the lesson.

The situation: A fifth-grade teacher is designing a unit in the life sciences which has a general goal of developing the concept of interdependence between living organisms. The teacher seeks to allow students to develop the concept from their experiences and to be able to express this information about interdependence in situations other than the one used in the study of the unit.

Instructions: For each of the following methods of learning, provide a rationale as to the purpose, if any, each might serve in accomplishing this teacher's goals.

1. Reading
2. Experimentation
3. Demonstration

4. Exploration
5. Media
6. Projects
7. Field Trips

Data-Expression Methods of Learning

Previous sections of this chapter have dealt with the means by which students obtain information. The student can make use of textbooks, films, demonstrations, and television to obtain a great deal of factual material. Our knowledge and experiences with how children learn require us to make use of other methods in conjunction with the data-gathering methods so that learning can take place. These other methods are termed data-expression methods and are presented in the following sections. The verbal dialogue and completion of reports are such commonplace occurrences in the classroom that many teachers take them for granted. Teachers will carefully select a film, reading, or demonstration and then decide to "discuss" it afterward and have the students "write down what they saw." The selection of methods for data expression should deserve at least the same, if not more, careful consideration than the data-gathering methods.

Discussion

The term discussion is often applied loosely to any kind of verbal dialogue in the classroom. But the discussion is much too significant a learning device to allow it to be an ambiguous part of the learning methods being used. Verbal dialogue takes place during almost any learning situation. But to learn something via a discussion is in itself a distinguishable part of the learning environment. Some would regard it as *the* point of learning in the classroom. Before we can really study this method of learning, we must define the many parts of verbal dialogue and then study the interrelationships of these parts. The next few paragraphs outline the elements of classroom dialogue.

One system of categorizing teacher verbal behavior was developed by Ned Flanders (1970). Because of its simplicity and versatility a great deal of work has been done with the system as research into the structure of dialogue in learning environments. A number of inservice programs have been developed to assist teachers in improving their classroom dialogue. Because of this widespread appeal to researcher and practitioner, the Flanders Interaction Analysis System (FIAS) will be used as the beginning point in our discussion of classroom dialogue.

Lecture

The part of classroom dialogue which first comes to mind is the teacher imparting information to one or more members of the class. The category "information giving," or, more commonly, lecturing, is the most highly used verbal behavior by the classroom teacher. The lecture given by a teacher may last for only a few moments or may go on for several hours over consecutive class meetings. The lecture may be done at the initiation of the teacher or it may be done in response to a question being given by students.

Studies of learning tend to discount the learning potential of the traditional classroom lecture. This is not to say that students cannot learn from listening, but that listening should not be the only source of learning. For this reason, no great deal of space will be devoted here to a discussion of how to lecture. Obviously, some common sense points are pertinent. A lecturer must take into consideration the listener and his readiness to receive what is being given. The lecture should be well organized and be done in a clear and concise manner. Just as with other methods of learning, the listener will profit from numerous examples of the concepts being discussed. In general, the elementary school science teacher will do well to make any type of lecture brief and to tie it in with a more direct, concrete means by which the students can obtain the necessary information.

Questions

The second most used category of verbal behavior is the question. Typically a teacher will ask questions of students to see what they remember or understand from the lecture they have listened to, the textbook they have read, or the demonstration they have watched. Everyone lectures and asks questions in their daily conversations. The new car owner enthusiastically tells his friends and neighbors about the shiny new car and the neighbors and friends ask questions to learn still more about the purchase. These two behaviors are so commonplace that teachers may overlook the various types of questions and the subsequent effect they have on students' activities, especially classroom dialogue. It is appropriate to consider the various ways questions can be categorized.

A simple way of categorizing questions is by the effect the question has. Convergent questions are those which tend to narrow the thoughts of the student to eventually bring him to the point being sought. Following an experiment in which students recorded data on the colors of writing which could be seen through various colored sheets of plastic, a teacher might ask one of the following questions to converge on appropriate conclusions:

1. What were the colors which could be seen through the green filter?
2. Could you detect any color which could be seen through all filters?
3. What general statement can you make as a result of this investigation?

In each case the teacher's purpose in asking that question is to converge the student's thinking to a designated point of learning.

The opposite type of question is the divergent question. In this type the teacher seeks to open up the topics of discussion to those students might select. In this way students can share opinions, exchange past experiences, and demonstrate their attitudes toward the subject being discussed. Divergent questions are generally used to begin discussions and will initiate responses which are neither right nor wrong. The effective teacher then makes use of these responses to develop further discussions, experiments, etc. Examples of such questions would include the following:

1. What types of interactions can you create using the materials on this tray?
2. What examples around your home can you suggest as evidence of chemical or physical changes?
3. How would your life be limited if you did not use water as a solvent?

Not all questions fit into one of these two categories of questions. For this reason other ways of categorizing questions may be useful. The Taxonomies of Educational Objectives studied in Chapter 3 of this text provide one means of categorizing questions. Questions can be asked at all levels of the cognitive domain in just about any subject area. The following examples illustrate this point:

Knowledge: What are the parts of the digestive system in the human body?

Comprehension: Mary, in your own words, can you give us a description of the meaning of the word ecology?

Application: If the rock weighs 100 grams and its volume is found to be 30 cm³, what is its density?

Analysis: The list of data for the four variables in your experiment are listed on the board. How can we make use of graphs to help us interpret this data?

Synthesis: Who can formulate a new statement which summarizes what we have learned about matter?

Evaluation: Of the four statements formulated by the students for summarizing what we have learned about matter, which one best summarizes the data?

The teacher should be aware of the nature of the question being asked so that the level of thinking is consistent with the plans and objectives for the lesson.

Many other ways could be found for categorizing questions, some of which may be more appropriate or convenient for a specific purpose. For example, one study (Seagren, 1972) of inquiry teaching developed the following categories:

1. Content Level Questions
2. Decision-Making Questions
3. Analysis Level Questions
4. Affective Domain
5. Structure or Process

The distinction between types of questions has been introduced here to remind the reader that questioning is an important determiner of the nature of classroom dialogue. In the formulation of strategies for learning in the next chapter, the nature of the question will take on an appropriate level of importance as the teacher decides just what series of methods will best accomplish the goals of the lesson.

Student Talk

Student talk in the classroom is an integral part of the learning process. The learner cannot occupy a passive role, and in order to be actively involved, the learner must be participating in the exchange of information. This exchange of information on the student's part can be analyzed in a number of ways. To begin with, the Flander's system divides student talk into that which has been solicited by the teacher through some question or direction, and that talk which is being initiated by the student.

Generally, student talk in the classroom will be due to some solicitation by the teacher. The teacher asks for some type of recall of information and the student or students respond with the information. The teachers ask the students to perform some type of mental operation which requires the application of a rule and the student replies with a response that indicates he has done so. In some classrooms the student's primary verbal dialogue is as a result of solicitation of ideas by the teacher. These ideas are those of someone else (textbook, lecture, film, etc.) and the students are to respond in a way that indicates that they have acquired these ideas.

Student's self-initiated ideas occur in the classroom in a variety of means. Unfortunately some student-initiated comments are not desirable at a given point in time. The student who says, "But I don't like doing homework!" or "Mrs. Jones, Larry hit me!" is probably doing so at his own initiation. The learning situation in which the student's own ideas are being allowed and desired as a part of the learning process is generally more profitable. The teacher who asks "What are your thoughts about the current space program and the amount of money being spent on it?" is probably going to receive a number of different responses which are those of the student and not those of someone directly connected with the learning process.

As another way of looking at student responses, a scheme for analyzing teacher questions can be utilized to analyze student responses. For example, making use of the inquiry analysis scheme mentioned in dealing with questions, student responses can be found to be an analysis, a decision, a statement of attitude, or the recall of information. When the teacher asks, "What conclusion can we make from the information gained in this laboratory exercise?" a number of different responses could be made by the students:

1. Mary told our group yesterday that we would find out that all things float in water. (recall of information)
2. It seems to me that our information is not very complete and that we cannot make any conclusions as yet. (analysis)
3. I didn't like doing this exercise and I can't seem to make myself get anything out of it. (attitude)
4. Our group's information leads me to think that all things float in water except metal objects. (decision)

If we are concerned with developing the mental capabilities of students, we must take note of the mental process being implied by the student's response. Analysis of student comments such as done above provides some information about this process.

The bulk of the student-teacher dialogue in the classroom, almost any classroom, consists of the above-mentioned categories: teacher lecture, teacher questions, student responses, and student initiated talk. A teacher who plans a discussion will consider: (a) What shall I tell the student?; (b) What kinds of questions should I ask to see if they understood what they heard (or read or saw); and (c) What kinds of responses do I expect from students? But to really expect a discussion to be successful, a teacher should expect some other types of verbal behaviors to be used.

Exercise 7–4   A Simple Classroom Dialogue

Instructions: A short dialogue of teacher-student interaction follows these instructions. Based on the categories of (a) information giving; (b) questions; (c) student responses; and (d) student initiated talk, analyze the conversation. Before each sentence, place a letter to indicate which of the above cateogires is being exemplified. (Answers are provided at the end of the chapter.)

_____ Teacher: The aquarium we are viewing was provided for us by Michelle.
_____ What do you see in this aquarium that is similar to the other aquarium? Yes, Johnny!
_____ Johnny: I can see each of the kinds of plants and animals that we put in our aquarium.
_____ Mary: But there is something else. It looks like some kind of black sand on top of the white sand.
_____ Teacher: Michelle, did you put the black material in your aquarium?
_____ Michelle: No, we didn't. That black stuff just started appearing a short while ago and it seems to be increasing.
_____ And we also noticed that the green color in the water seemed to come in later also.
_____ Teacher: Those are good observations, students.

Reinforcement

Reinforcement is an important category of the Flanders system. In this system, this category covers any type of verbal comments by the teacher which are likely to be complimentary to the student. Typical reinforcing comments would include, "That is a good idea you have given us, Johnny!" "Yes, Mary, that is correct." "Yes, Jimmy, go on!"

Merely repeating a student's comments may also be reinforcing. Research indicates that most people react positively to reinforcing behaviors expressed by others. A sequence of teacher question–student response being repeated over and over again without intermittent reinforcement by the teacher or other students is not as likely to encourage further student contributions as when reinforcement is being used.

Another and related category of teacher verbal behavior is the "use of student ideas." What does a teacher say about a student's idea that will encourage further contributions by the student or will convey the message to the student that enough has been said. The Inquiry Analysis System (Seagren, 1972) identifies several kinds of responses. The first is repeating the student response. This has the advantage of making sure that all students have had the opportunity to hear the response, is reinforcing to the student who gave the response, and gives the other students more time to absorb the idea being given and to make appropriate additional comments.

After a student has given a response, it may be appropriate for the teacher to refer that comment to another student for elaboration, clarification, or discussion. In this way the teacher is acting as only a "gatekeeper" to the conversation, neither endorsing nor denying the comment. Another method of gatekeeping is to ask a question about the comment that will cause that student, or another, to extend the idea or to see the fallacy of the reasoning.

With the use of the categories of verbal behavior mentioned above, most classroom dialogues would be complete. Other, more minor categories do exist. One such category is a teacher discussion of an attitude expressed by a student. The teacher is likely to discuss a student's cognitive ideas, but not as likely to discuss the feelings being expressed by the students. Such comments might include: "I can see how you are becoming frustrated getting this piece of apparatus to work correctly," or "Mary, you seem very upset that so few students are participating in the Ecology Club Project!"

These types of comments are rare in many classrooms, but their use may need to be increased in order to more successfully develop the attitudes of students.

Another small category is teacher directions. This category includes all of the comments which will result in the student making some overt response. "Will all of you open your books to page 21?" "Johnny, please go to the chalkboard and write out your calculations to the problem," and "Gather around the two terraria so that we can all watch the animals and plants," are all examples of such directions. Some directions are really reprimands for the student. Such comments fall into the category of criticism. They would include, "Mary, return to your seat!" and "Will all of you please lower your voices so that we can hear what Mary has to say!"

A last category is silence. This category is simply the absence of talk by either teacher or student. This is the time when some or all of the participants in the discussion are thinking about what they are going to

TABLE 7-1 SUMMARY OF CATEGORIES FOR INTERACTION ANALYSIS

TEACHER

INDIRECT INFLUENCE

1. ACCEPTS FEELING: accepts and clarifies the feeling of one of the students in a nonthreatening manner. Feelings may be positive or negative. Predicting and recalling feelings are included.
2. PRAISES OR ENCOURAGES: praises or encourages student action or behavior. Jokes that release tension not at the expense of another individual, nodding head or saying "uh huh" or "go on" are included.
3. ACCEPTS OR USES IDEAS OF STUDENT: clarifying, building, or developing ideas or suggestions by a student. As teacher brings more of his own ideas into plan, shift to Category 5.
4. ASKS QUESTIONS: asking a question about content or procedure with the intent that a student answer.

DIRECT INFLUENCE

5. LECTURES: giving facts or opinions about content or procedure; expressing his own ideas; asking rhetorical questions.
6. GIVES DIRECTIONS: directions, commands, or orders with which a student is expected to comply.
7. CRITICIZES OR JUSTIFIES AUTHORITY: statements intended to change student behavior from nonacceptable to acceptable pattern; bawling someone out; stating why the teacher is doing what he is doing; extreme self-reference.

STUDENT TALK

8. STUDENT TALK RESPONSE: talk by students in response to teacher. Teacher initiates the contact or solicits student statement.
9. STUDENT TALK INITIATION: talk by students, which they initiate. If "calling on" student is only to indicate who may talk next, observer must decide whether student wanted to talk. If he did, use this category.
10. SILENCE OR CONFUSION: pauses, short periods of silence, and periods of confusion in which communication cannot be understood by observer.

be saying. If indeed we are teaching students to think, to reason, to inquire, then such "thinking" time should be provided at appropriate times in the conversation. A teacher is often very concerned about what to say following a given student comment. In some instances "saying nothing" may be the best response. A short pause may give the student time to rethink his answer, give another student the chance to respond, or give the teacher the opportunity to think of a more appropriate response. In general, this category denies the apparent assumption that someone must be talking at all times if learning is to be taking place.

The ten categories of student and teacher verbal communication are summarized in Table 7–1 for your convenience. Note that with this arrangement, the categories of teacher talk break down into those of "direct" and "indirect" influence on student behavior. That is, the verbal behaviors of giving directions and lecturing very directly influence the kind of behavior that a student is going to exhibit. Whereas, if the teacher repeats a student idea, asks another student about the idea, or compliments the student about the idea, the next verbal communication from the student is not going to be as predictable. The next time you have the opportunity to observe classroom behavior, note the behaviors of the teacher as either direct or indirect and then note the resulting student behaviors. A teacher who is using a more indirect approach will tend to have a more open, more student-centered classroom environment.

The Flanders System of Interaction Analysis is concerned only with the verbal aspect of a classroom dialogue or discussion. The other significant aspect of the discussion is the nonverbal communication going on between student and teacher. A teacher who frowns at a mischievous student may do as much to squelch that behavior as if the teacher had said something. The teacher who is frowning while complimenting a student or smiling as he delivers criticism may be contradicting himself and confusing the student. In addition, the teacher who exhibits no emotion may be taking away from an otherwise motivating classroom environment.

The above presentation of categories of verbal and nonverbal behaviors has been given in this section to provide you with a means for examining the actual implementation of the other methods discussed in this chapter. For example, during a classroom demonstration or experiment, the verbal behavior of the teacher should be noted. Is the teacher using a more direct approach (telling information and giving directions) or is the teacher using a more indirect approach (asking questions about student ideas, referring student questions to others, complimenting student's ideas). The teacher's verbal behavior will usually be found to have a significant influence on what the students are doing.

Aside from the other methods, the display of verbal behaviors was introduced here to aid you in identifying the nature of dialogue in a discussion. A discussion concerning the factual material presented in a film, book, or field trip is not the same as a discussion which is intended to elicit student ideas and to work on the clarification of those ideas for students. One will be more teacher centered than the other. In the discussion of student ideas, the teacher will need to utilize more indirect behaviors as a general rule and will need to refrain from presenting information and asking very direct questions.

The continuum is depicted in Table 7–2. On the right is the open end of the continuum and on the left is the restricted end. No attempt

TABLE 7-2 A DISCUSSION CONTINUUM

	RESTRICTED	OPEN
5 Lecture	Frequent, factual, teacher-initiated topics	Infrequent, if any; may be as answer for student question
4 Questions	Often, usually short, convergent, low or high cognitive	Few, longer in each instance, more divergent, high-level cognitive
8 Student Talk Response	High use, narrow response to teacher-initiated points	Low use; may be in response to other students or teacher
9 Student Talk Initiation	Limited use, may be in form of question of teacher's intent	High use; may be in response to teacher's or students' questions or may be original with student
3 Use of Student Ideas	Clarifying of student comments toward point of conversation	Referring comments to others, asking for extensions of student ideas
2 Praise	Praising correct responses	Praising students' original ideas
0 Silence	Very little, but usually followed by 8s	May be used, usually followed by 9s

has been made here to quantify the occurrence of the categories of FIAS along this continuum. The type of discussion which can occur at either end of the continuum could take different forms and as such would have different combinations of categories. It is not within the scope of this chapter to identify the variety of discussions which could occur. Rather, the point of this presentation is that the classroom discussion is a classroom learning method which can be specified. You are encouraged to make use of the FIAS system or some similar system to become more aware of the discussions taking place in classroom which you observe.

A discussion at the other end of the continuum would be found at the time of discussion of an assigned reading. The teacher would be seeking student knowledge about specifics given in the reading by asking low cognitive questions (4s) and would anticipate receiving student responses (8s) based on the reading. The type of question would influence the degree students departed from the readings to express their own ideas (9s). The use of student ideas (3s) would be limited to helping students clarify their responses about the reading. If silence (0s) did occur it would most likely be followed by 8s rather than 9s. This conversation would be a teacher directed discussion and would be toward the "restricted" end of the continuum.

The usefulness of a system such as Flanders Interaction Analysis can be seen in exploring various types of discussions. To say that a teacher is going to "discuss" some topic is rather ambiguous. Discussions can be viewed on a continuum with the extremes being primarily student talk with little teacher intervention on the one end and on the other teacher talk with little student contribution. At the midpoint of this continuum would be a conversation not dominated by either students or the teacher. To explore various types of discussions along this continuum we will make use of the FIAS system. The numbers for the categories are taken from the chart.

A unit of study might open with a divergent, open discussion which seeks to identify student ideas and present knowledge of the subject. The analysis of the dialogue would find a few instances of extended questions by the teachers (4s) with very little information given (5s) or directions (6s) being given. Student talk would consist more of student initiated ideas (9s) than responses to questions (8s). Silence (0) is very likely to have occurred as "think time" was being allowed. A closer look at the questions would find them to be of higher order cognitive types, and have a wide possible range of answers. Not many instances of the teacher using the student's ideas (3s) would be evident, but a good amount of reinforcement was used. In summary, the teacher influence was found to be more indirect (more of categories 1 through 4) than direct (categories 5, 6, and 7). This discussion would be at the open end of the continuum.

Exercise 7–5   Observing Classroom Dialogue

The novice teacher, the experienced teacher, and the prospective teacher can all profit from observing other teachers as they conduct science lessons. As indicated in the preceding paragraphs, these observations can be enhanced by a systematic recording of the interaction between students and teachers and between students and other students. Under the direction of your instructor, visit a classroom to observe a science class in progress. Prior to visiting a classroom, decide what aspect of the dialogue you will be studying in this observation. For example, you may wish to watch for the type of questions being asked by the teacher. Or you may want to focus on what kind of responses the teacher makes after students respond to questions. Obviously, this preplanning is easier when you know something about the lesson to be taught. Your instructor will provide more directions for this activity based on the particular situation you will be observing and the form in which you are to report results.

Communication through written laboratory reports can be an effective method of learning.

Reporting

The ability to communicate with others is a vital skill. To some this ability is a way of earning a living. To others communication of information is just part of their general education relating to daily living situations. In general, all must be able to communicate to convey an idea and to understand the communication of the ideas of others.

Science reporting is an appropriate, if not essential, part of the science curriculum. The kindergarten child tells the others in the class about the large bug his father found while gardening last evening. The second-grade student draws a picture of the aquarium before and after the addition of the plants. The third-grade student creates bar graphs to represent the temperature of the respective systems being studied. The fourth-grade student writes conclusions to the experiment just conducted. The fifth-grade student constructs coordinate graphs to represent the time it takes for a pendulum to swing for several different lengths. The seventh-grade student writes a lab report including five separate sections.

When the student is reporting about some type of experience, the teacher has the opportunity to carefully examine the thinking of the student. Responding to short questions posed by the teacher may not display errors in thinking by the student. An activity of organizing thinking into a concise and understandable form does provide the teacher with greater knowledge of the students' present understandings and their ability to organize and use those understandings.

The development of these skills requires instruction over a long period of years. Early primary years should use types of reporting appropriate to the abilities of students, such as drawing pictures of events and making bar graphs to represent relative amounts. Some programs include these skills as a regular part of the program and in others these skills can be easily added. Later grades continue this development with longer written reports, more complex graphs, and appropriate oral reports.

Most contemporary science programs, especially those which stress a process approach, include reporting as a regular method of instruction. Other programs using an experimental approach can easily be made to accommodate the report method of learning. Do not be misled by the type of "workbook" which is included in some programs as the means of reporting. Too often these workbooks are merely fill-in-the blank types of questions which require very little higher level cognitive thinking skills.

No effort is being made here to provide instruction in the variety of reporting techniques. Use of the process-oriented science programs will provide a more viable means by which you can learn these techniques.

Answers to Exercise 7–4.

1–a, 2–b, 3–c, 4–d, 5–b, 6–c, 7–d.

References

Hawkins, David, "Messing About in Science," *Science and Children,* February, 1965.

Sanders, Norris M., *Classroom Questions—What Kinds?* New York: Harper & Row, 1966.

Science Curriculum Improvement Study, *SCIS Teachers Handbook.* Berkeley: University of California, 1974.

Seagren, Alan T., *et al. Inquiry Behaviors,* Instructional Staff Development Program, M-D Con E Lab, KCMO, 1972.

U.S. Department of Health, Education, and Welfare: Office of Education. *Career Education,* Washington, D.C.: Government Printing Office, 1971.

U.S. Department of Health, Education, and Welfare: Office of Education. *How to Provide for Safety in the Science Laboratory,* Washington, D.C.: National Science Teachers Association, 1968.

Bibliography of Science Courses of Study and Textbooks—K-12, Washington, D.C.: National Science Teachers Association, 1973.

8
Strategies in Science Education

In order to meet the goals of science education it is essential that the teacher formulate appropriate strategies, which involves planning for and using various techniques designed to achieve these goals. Because of the great variety of situations under which science education takes place as well as the variability in the nature of science goals each situation and purpose requires individual strategic planning. Some science goals require children to conduct experiments. Others expect children to measure, or observe, or perhaps explain concepts. Each of these different purposes requires a different type of learning experience for students. Situations differ from one another in many ways too. Different children have different levels of cognitive development, different interests, different reading abilities, different learning styles, different problems with regard to self-concept, etc. Success in achieving your goals depends on how well you learn to use carefully planned strategies which incorporate knowledge about these factors.

Strategy requires taking into account the purposes of instruction and all of the constraints which may limit the achievement of the goals as well as any elements which may enhance this achievement. From this perspective it is absurd to think of teaching only in terms of using various methods to learn about science. Many methods must be used with variations as necessary to achieve goals. The important thing is to focus upon the goal and make plans which outline defensible means for achieving these instructional intents. Much of the teaching presently being done in the schools permits the methods or means of instruction to become ends in and of themselves. In these cases instructional goals are usually ambiguous and no thought is given to strategies for achieving them. Teaching-learning consists of the teacher providing learning activities and students trying to remember the facts associated with them. With properly defined goals for instruction, strategy becomes a greater imperative. Immediately the focus is upon how the goals can be achieved.

Strategy, then, is the plan generated by the teacher for achieving instructional goals given the ordinary constraints in the classroom. Classroom constraints consist of student interests, ability levels, reading skills, self-concepts, and other learning disabilities. In order to achieve the objectives, the teacher must be able to provide learning activities for children which reduce the influence of constraints. For example, younger children are unable to deal with abstractions. Their interest and learning will be greatly enhanced if concrete materials are used in instruction.

The most important thing to remember when planning a strategy is to focus continuously on the objective as you plan. If the objective is the purpose for which the strategy is devised, it should be the ever present guide in determining what the strategy should be. Methods, materials, and experiences should be selected which efficiently and effectively aid students in meeting instructional expectations. The teacher should avoid the temptation to engage students in learning situations which are not particularly useful in achieving objectives. For example, it may be easier but less fruitful to have students simply read about "life in a pond," rather than taking them on a field trip to a pond where they can really learn from first-hand experience. Certain aspects of life in a pond cannot be effectively taught from books. For one thing, books are less concrete and consequently less effective in teaching children in the concrete operations stage. In addition, interest is likely to be greater if children can explore an actual pond rather than having to get all of their sensory data from pictures in a book. Finally, there is usually a better opportunity to individualize in a real situation because the interests of children will be manifest and the teacher will not have to guess at what they might be.

Because of the complexity of the classroom, even the best laid plans can fail when they are put into practice. This is where tactics comes in, which will probably accompany any strategic plan. Unforeseen contingencies can greatly alter the effects an instructional plan may have on a class, and therefore a teacher needs to be prepared to change his original plan as necessary. He/she should make alterations in order to achieve the objectives. Again, the objectives serve as the guide. In fact, it is the objectives which make it necessary to revise plans. When a particular method or procedure does not appear to be working toward the desired ends of instruction, the teacher must make a tactical maneuver and change the plan appropriately. Some of this tactical maneuvering must be made quickly, without much previous thought. Some tactics can, however, be planned for in advance. A teacher may have a number of contingency plans which can be drawn upon just in case conditions in the classroom are different from what is anticipated. With experience, you will learn what changes may be useful in different situations. You must remain flexible so that changes can be readily made as they are needed. Carrying a strategic plan to its conclusion in spite of what is happening in the classroom as a result of it is a very poor teaching procedure.

OBJECTIVES

1. Students will formulate written strategies and rationales for these strategies based upon specified objectives which clearly indicate how each of the following principles have been incorporated within the strategy: Preassessment, Entry Behaviors, Perceived Purpose, Revealing Objectives, Feedback, Individualized Instruction, Enroute Behaviors, Analogous Practice, Equivalent Practice.

Preassessment as a Basis for Strategy

The preassessment process can provide much of the information that is needed to develop an appropriate teaching strategy. One thing that can be checked is reading level. In science, students will come in contact with a number of new terms. In addition, if the science program is individualized at all, students will need to be able to follow written instructions precisely. Even though much of a properly conceived science program at the elementary level must involve working with tangible materials, there are still many very interesting and useful printed materials. If the reading level of children is below that necessary to handle appropriate printed materials the teacher must prepare audio tapes and the like, until such time as reading skills are developed. Some advocate permitting children to learn exclusively in the way they find easiest. Thus the nonreading child may be provided with all nonprinted materials. A much better strategy is to initiate instruction using the child's favorite learning mode but gradually shifting emphasis to a more balanced approach. If a child is encouraged to learn only with one mode, he will be unlikely to use other learning modes later on. Because learning is available in a variety of modes, children will be handicapped if they are unable to use them all. Those who feel that a child should accentuate the one learning mode he is best able to use fail to comprehend that learning is to a great extent learning how to learn and to a lesser extent amassing content. Exclusive emphasis upon one learning mode carries an implicit assumption that learning is indeed simply a matter of accumulating knowledge.

Another body of useful information which can be provided through preassessment is the level of cognitive development that each child has attained. Because cognitive ability is developmental, it can be expected to change over time. In addition, part of the growth process may be influenced by the nature of the learning experiences that children have. Piaget's stages of development serve a very useful purpose in planning curricular experiences for children. It does no good to ask students to perform intellectually beyond their level of cognitive ability. Likewise, dwelling upon skills which have already been mastered may be boring to the child because he needs a challenge to keep him interested. One likely outgrowth of preassessing cognitive abilities is an individualized science program. Children in most any classroom will be in various stages of development and require different kinds of experiences. The teacher needs to properly diagnose the child's intellectual abilities and follow subsequent growth to determine how the child is advancing so that appropriate materials can be provided. An example of a diagnostic tool for intellectual abilities was given in Chapter 5.

Strategy should always include consideration of students' interests.

The level of knowledge about science that children have is an important preassessment activity. Strategy cannot be planned for children in the absence of this information. It will be difficult to generate interest when the science material chosen is already familiar to the children. Also, the teacher must know if certain areas of knowledge are basic to the understanding of other important concepts but are unfamiliar to the children. Many times science teachers assume far too much about what children know. This can often be attributed to the superficiality of the evaluative measures. Students find that they can memorize information and succeed in testing situations but never truly understand the concepts the test is supposed to measure. Later the teacher may find that the children are unable to apply the knowledge they have been taught. For strategies to be truly successful it is necessary that we obtain accurate information regarding the understanding children have about the concepts we plan to teach. Failure to do so will doom our efforts before they begin.

Student interests constitute one of the major components of a teaching strategy. It accomplishes very little to have students engage in science activities in which they are uninterested. Sometimes it may appear to the teacher that some students are simply not interested in anything, at least not anything that is happening in the school. There are, of course, a number of different reasons why children manifest disinterest. Many times the apparent lack of interest is really fear of failure or a long history of no success. Children can become interested in a number of topics if they can be assured success in working with them. Most normal children have a high degree of interest in the world around them. For them science is an intriguing area to learn about. Problems arise, however, when all children are asked to do the same kinds of things as if their interests were somehow simultaneously the same. Student interests will probably never be the same. The teacher needs to arrange the learning activities for children in a way that caters to this variety of interests. One way to do this is to bring a large number of different science materials into the classroom and let children select those things which interest them. Each of these materials should lead naturally to learning science principles and processes. The children will need to be helped by the teacher individually to use the materials in an educative way. If the teacher does not provide the child with some structure and direction, the child's interest may decline and he will shift his attention to other objects before he has gained the educational benefit from the first set of materials. Left to themselves, children may wander aimlessly from one set of science materials to another. At this early age some guidance is needed to show them how to learn—they must learn how to ask questions and how to determine some means for answering these questions.

It should not be assumed by the teacher that a child's interest in a particular aspect of science will remain unchanged. Some children's interests change frequently, while others sustain an interest for long periods of time. For example, some children may develop and maintain an interest in space studies because of the support often given such studies in popular television programming. In fact it may seem that a child is interested in nothing else. There is no need to become distressed by this solitary interest. It would be much wiser to capitalize on it. If a child is preoccupied with space travel and finds it difficult to become interested in other subjects, the teacher may be able to bring in other topics by association. For example, in interplanetary travel there is need for food. The problem of how to supply food on long voyages is a critical one. A child may be asked to try to figure out some means of supplying food on such long space voyages and thus enhance or broaden his science interests. The child will thus find it necessary to consider principles of biology. How to sustain life in a spaceship for long voyages may also raise questions about physical and chemical principles. With his interest in space studies to sustain him a child may learn much of science.

It is often said that children do not know what they are interested in, and that they have difficulty maintaining an interest in anything for very long. This indecisiveness is usually due to fear of failure. The child believes that if he shows no interest he will not have to do anything at which he might fail. The strategy in this case is to provide experiences which children can succeed at and gradually increase the difficulty until success is attained at tasks comparable to those accomplished by other class members. Once children recognize that they can be successful they will become interested in a greater variety of subjects. Children who fear failure tend to want to repeat the same activities over and over again. They will draw the same picture repeatedly or engage in the same experiment several times. Little good is accomplished by forcing such children to extend themselves beyond what they feel comfortable doing. Rather, you may wish to design experiences which insure success for them until they reach a point where failure is not so traumatic.

The listening skill, which has been given little attention, is a most important skill in our formal educational system, and can be advantageously preassessed. Students develop very poor listening capabilities. Behind this widespread inability to listen lies a major overshift in our program of instruction in the classroom. Attention has been focused on reading as the primary source of learning. Speaking and listening have been essentially ignored. Interestingly, studies show that 70 percent of our waking day is spent in some form of verbal communication of which the greatest part is listening. Of the total time spent in verbal communication, 9 percent is spent in writing, 16 percent reading, and 30 percent talking, while 45 percent is spent listening. Nearly three times as much time is spent listening than reading and yet listening skills are implicitly relegated to a position of nonimportance in the schools (Wright, 1971).

The basic difficulty involved in listening comes from the fact that we think much faster than we speak. Psychologists believe that the basic medium of thought is language. Our brains are made up of billions of cells which process words at a fantastic speed. With the rate of speaking averaging around 125 words per minute the brain is asked to accept information much more slowly than its capacity. This, of course, proves to be distracting to the listener. This may explain why we routinely think of something else while listening to others. The problem then is that we have spare time in our receiving process. The way in which we use this time determines our listening effectiveness.

If our students have poor listening habits (and most of them do) then we must attempt to correct them as best we can. One thing which limits listening skill is the tendency to evaluate. Children can be taught to withhold judgment while a statement or opinion is being conveyed. They should be taught to comprehend each point made by a speaker and reserve judgments and decisions until after the speaker has finished.

Another barrier to effective communication is emotional filters. Figuratively, we reach up and mentally turn off what we do not want to hear. On the other hand, we are also inclined to hear and accept as true those things we would like to hear, even though they may be false. It is not an easy matter to teach youngsters to avoid focusing on what they hear in terms of prejudices, convictions, mores, or values. When we listen we often mentally plan a rebuttal to the speaker's comments while he is speaking. One useful counter measure is to make up our minds to seek out the ideas that might prove us wrong, as well as those that might prove us right. If we teach children to do this they will be in less danger of misunderstanding or missing what people have to say. Children may be asked to write down ideas which support the speaker's contention and save thinking about any rebuttal until after the speaker is finished. This will help them develop listening skills at a high level.

Finally, listening only for details is a block to effective listening. This may seem incongruent to what is ordinarily thought regarding good listening. However, focusing on details and facts often results in viewing the learned facts out of context. While one fact is being assimilated, the whole, or part of the next fact is almost certain to be missed. When listening for specifics the listener is likely to catch only a few facts, garble many others, and completely miss much of the remainder. Children need to be taught to focus upon the ideas that are being expressed. Facts should be listened to for what they contribute to the understanding of ideas. If the ideas are understood, the listener will be surprised to learn that supporting facts are more effectively remembered than when attempting to learn facts exclusively.

Although the above discussion of preassessment is not intended to be exhaustive it does show how important it is that teachers find out about their students before planning strategies for instruction. It should be increasingly clear that there are a number of reasons that children may fail in the instructional process if their current abilities and interests are not taken into account in the planning stage. On the other hand there can be much greater assurance that instruction can be properly planned if important abilities and interests are preassessed. If deficiencies are discovered in student abilities, steps can be taken either to increase ability levels or make learning activities consistent with abilities. Learning of children's interests can greatly increase the teacher's effectiveness in selecting among the great variety of materials possible.

Perceived Purpose

Properly formulating instructional goals is only part of the solution to the problem of how to teach science effectively. It is also necessary to engage in instructional procedures which maximize learning and lead students to goal achievement. It is the conviction of some supporters of instructional objectives that once an objective has been properly formulated in precise terms and clearly communicated to students that little else remains for the teacher to do except sit back and wait for them to demonstrate the behaviors called for. This may be true if the only difficulty in teaching and learning was inappropriately stating objectives. Such, of course, is not the case. Humans behave as individuals and exhibit a variety of responses to stated objectives. In spite of this tendency, it may be conceded that there is a direct relationship between the clarity of stated goals and the enthusiasm with which students pursue related learnings. Where confusion exists there is likely to be little commitment to learning.

Even though clarity of science objectives may enhance learning, students must agree that the stated goals are meaningful and important to them or it is unlikely that they will learn enthusiastically. Consequently one of the most important components of any teaching strategy is to help students not only have a clear view of the learning task but to also agree that it is a worthwhile pursuit. This is called perceived purpose (Popham and Baker, 1970). No amount of badgering or coercion will substitute for genuine interest in achieving objectives. This is the reason that it is necessary for the teacher to develop strategies designed to help children have perceived purpose.

In many instances the teacher will formulate what he believes to be viable goals only to find that students do not agree with the proposed importance of these objectives. Many teachers react by telling students to "learn it or else" or "learn it because I told you so." This is done unfortunately because the teacher is unable to understand why students cannot comprehend the importance of the learning tasks he proposes. On the other hand, students fail to see why an instructor should require mastery of such irrelevant material. Both parties share in the responsibility for blocking the instructional process by taking such one-sided irrational stands. The student's error is in not realizing that an instructor is in a better position to judge the strategic importance of a particular area of study. At the same time instructors many times do not have sufficient reason for teaching some topics. They are often guided by personal interest only. In addition instructors often expect students to simply accept their word regarding the importance of an area of study. Not only should the teacher have a well-formulated rationale for all the topics he teaches, but he should also invite students to formulate their own reasons for studying these topics. Through this means students and teacher may reach agreement regarding the relative importance of possible areas of study.

Revealing Objectives

Generally it is a good policy to clarify the objectives for students at the beginning of a lesson, as needed during the lesson, and at the close of a lesson in order to guarantee that the instructional purposes are always sufficiently visible to direct learning. This is because the visibility of the goals sometimes become obscure during the instructional process or students sometimes do not recognize the relevance of a particular learning activity to the stated objectives. In addition it forces the teacher to periodically justify the activity in the classroom. Perhaps an illustration will help clarify this point. Let us say, for example, that the teacher's objective is "to teach his students to recognize plant and animal relationships in a natural environment." The teacher must organize strategy which hopefully will result in the achievement of the objective. He must assess the present skill level of his students, the learning disabilities that they have, the motivation problems that he is likely to encounter, etc. These constraints are then incorporated into a plan of action which he is confident will help achieve the objective. This is the strategy, but keep in mind that achieving the objective should be the focus of attention. As the teacher begins to develop his lesson, it is likely that he will have to make adjustments because problems encountered in achieving the objective can rarely be completely determined in advance. For example, he may find that he has overestimated the ability of the class to make astute observations of natural phenomena. Consequently, tactical maneuvers must be made to adjust to these problems as they occur. Thus we have both *strategy or preplanning* and *tactics or on-the-spot adjustments* both designed to achieve the objective. In a sense the objective is reached "by hook or by crook" and in large measure this depends on the ingenuity of the teacher. In the classroom situation the teacher must be a strategist as well as tactician. This means that he must organize student activities which result in achievement of defensible purposes and follow through until the objectives are realized. Otherwise much valuable time may be lost and no viable goals achieved. In the event that the teacher desires students to reach experiential goals, less specific teacher direction is indicated. In this case student idiosyncracies are encouraged so long as they are within given parameters. In either case, students should have the goal in mind and be able to visualize how the activities he is engaged in contribute to its achievement. Thus learning activities may be viewed as means to an end, not as ends unto themselves.

Feedback

To determine how well instruction is proceeding the elementary science teacher must be able to observe responses from his students in order to determine their progress in meeting goals. Otherwise he will be unable to make tactical adjustments when it is necessary to redirect their efforts or clarify their misconceptions and erroneous actions. Thus an essential part of any strategy is the communications system. Such a communications system must be a two-way process so that all contingencies and obstacles are accounted for as the students proceed through their learning. There are, however, a number of problems associated with the communications process itself. Primary among these is the lack of a common perceptual base between students and between students and teachers. This is brought about through the difference in experiences of teachers and students. Because communication is possible only to the extent that common perceptions exist, a great deal of miscommunication occurs. For example, a child may never have seen what effects water pollution can have on the wildlife in an area. Full appreciation may be lacking until he has had personal experiences with this. This problem can be alleviated, in part, through a series of interactions between the parties involved. This way mutual response and feedback can be engaged in until there is agreement regarding meanings.

Another barrier to effective communication is the variety of meanings associated with words and symbols. Some words have several meanings and depend upon context for understanding. For example, the word small when referring to the size of micro-organisms is entirely different than when used to describe the relative size of mammals. Other terms mean different things to different people. Still other words have no usage outside particular ethnic groups, cultures, or subcultures. The uninitiated may never capture the meaning of verbal transmissions when they are couched in specific cultural idioms. The teacher must understand the meaning of the terms used by different cultural groups in the classroom to not only understand the communication himself but to also insure that students understand one another. It is essential that the teacher always take communication problems into account when he plans his strategy. Failure to do so can cause subversion of the whole instructional process.

Because of the problem experienced with misperception and miscommunication, there is a need to have a feedback system for providing students with knowledge regarding the appropriateness of their responses in the learning situation. Ordinarily students respond in terms of the perceptions they take in and that are registered in the central nervous system. Here in the central nervous system perceptions are used by the individual to change his concepts prior to making a decision regarding how to behave in terms of this new information. The decision regarding how to behave usually contains value components as well as cognitive ones. Once a decision is reached the person proceeds to act out his changed conceptions by making a trial response while the teacher provides feedback. If the trial according to the teacher's judgment shows that the individual has a misconception, he is able to assist the student to correct this misconception by providing additional experiences or altering the objects or events in the environment which have contributed to possible misperceptions. The student can then be asked to make another decision and alter his behavior accordingly. This process of altering precepts, cognition, decision making, trial, and feedback thus continues in a cyclic fashion until the teacher is satisfied that the student is performing in the expected way. It is not uncommon in schools, for a portion of this learning cycle to be omitted in the process of teaching and learning. Commonly, students are engaged in sensory intake and retrieval with little or no time given to decision making, trial, and feedback. The student is often evaluated on his performance with no opportunity to receive feedback beforehand. Thus, the teacher has little information concerning whether or not the student is prepared for final evaluation until after the evaluation is given. Ideally, the student should, through the feedback system, increase his skills to the point where he is reasonably confident that in the testing situation he will be able to achieve the objectives.

Individualizing Instruction

Another important principle in the formulation of learning strategies is that of individualizing instruction. Individualizing instruction may take one of two basic forms. Either the objectives can be differentiated in terms of ability levels and interests, or different students may be assigned different means to achieve identical objectives. Conceivably both practices could be used separately or together. If we plan to use identical objectives for students with different abilities it is imperative that our strategy reflect these differences. Not only may students have different abilities, they may also differ in terms of interests as well as previous experiences and achievements.

It is not always evident how one should proceed in dealing with problems associated with individual differences. There are a few basic principles which do apply, however. For example, less able youngsters may require more attention to be given to proper prerequisite activities. In addition, the less able student will likely require more time and attention to be given by the instructor. Special exercises may have to be developed for the slower student so that he may have added practice. The more gifted student may also require specialized learning experiences in order to avoid boredom and challenge his abilities. In addition, the more capable student may be able to more adequately plan some of his own activities. Students with varying interests may be assigned different materials which may result in achieving similar objectives.

Sequencing Instruction

One of the most important responsibilities a teacher has as a strategist is that of properly analyzing the prerequisites for and subcomponents of a terminal goal and providing learning experiences which are organized in a proper learning sequence for achieving the goal. The teacher must be able to optimize the chances for the student to succeed in spite of the enormous number of different student aptitudes and readiness levels. In addition his own personal teaching style must be integrated into the total instructional plan. It is obviously difficult to obtain control of all the variables which operate in the instructional process. However, an increased orderliness is possible. The first task in organizing for instruction is analyzing the desired outcomes and identifying the subtasks for the objective. This, of course, requires that goals be stated in precise terms so that specific *en route behaviors* can be identified. An en route behavior is any activity which a student must master as a prerequisite to performing the terminal behavior. For example, if the goal is for students to be able to describe the relationships between plants and animals in a natural environment, they must first be able to explain what ecosystems and food chains are. Knowledge about ecosystems and food chains are en route behaviors and are prerequisites to learning how to determine plant and animal relationships. In determining prerequisites it is essential that the instructor ask himself the following questions: What must the learner be able to do before he can successfully perform the terminal behavior? Can a student successfully demonstrate the desired behavior without being able to demonstrate his mastery of subcomponent skills? What is the order in which the subtasks should be learned? With subtasks identified, instruction can be sequenced so that these prerequisites are mastered before students attempt to practice the terminal behaviors sought. For example, the following topics are organized into a sequence with the prerequisites preceding the terminal behaviors:

1. Energy can be transformed from one form to another. For example, the light from the sun is converted to sugar which can be used as energy for the movement of animals.
2. Transformation of energy is not 100 percent efficient.
3. When energy is transferred in a food chain from plants to animals and from one animal to another, a lot of energy is lost as heat.
4. Longer food chains lose more energy as heat than short ones do.
5. Shorter food chains have a greater amount of energy which can be stored.

It is logical that learning about the efficiency of energy transformation (2) should be preceded by a consideration of the nature of energy transformation itself (1). Obviously, the efficiency of energy transformation (2) comes before any consideration of heat loss as a result of inefficiency (3). Once it is understood how energy is lost (3), the next logical step is to show how the length of food chains determines the extent of the loss (4). Finally, once the relationship between the length of the food chain and energy loss is understood (4), the concept of how greater amounts of energy can be accumulated in shorter food chains (5) can be successfully taught. In each case the concepts are related to one another in a specific sequence and understanding depends on learning each prerequisite in order.

It should be pointed out that it may not be one teacher's responsibility to provide all of the prerequisites for a particular terminal goal. This means that for the learner to be successful, he must already possess certain basic concepts and skills, called *entry behaviors*. Entry behaviors differ from en route behaviors in that entry behaviors are prerequisite behaviors that might reasonably have been achieved in a previous year or semester, whereas en route behaviors are more immediate prerequisites. Of course, teachers do not always have the option to constitute their classes on the basis of students' entry behaviors, even though this may be desirable. They simply "accept students where they are and take them as far as they can go." This is one of the injustices of present administrative arrangements in the schools. There is a tendency with our graded system to give social promotions to children before they have the prerequisite entry skills for the next grade. Ordinarily students who are promoted on this basis have to face failure after failure because their deficiencies are compounded as they attempt to advance at the same rate as their peers. Careful attention to entry behaviors and proper sequencing for learning can do much to alleviate the suffering of these students.

Appropriate Practice

One of the important considerations which should be made when designing learning activities in science is that they should be appropriate to the goals sought. In other words, students should be provided with practice which will prepare them to demonstrate the behaviors called for in the objective. All too often science teachers organize learning activities which are ends in and of themselves. For example, a child may go on a field trip or do an experiment without having any discernible goals. All that can be said is that students had an experience. Its connection to some definable goal is at best hazy and many times nonexistent. Some learning experiences may be engaged in, where measurable ends may not be achieved. However, these experiences will usually be few and carefully defined in terms of expectancies.

Learning activities should involve appropriate practice.

Appropriate practice is usually divided into two components, *equivalent practice* and *analogous practice. Equivalent practice* is where learners are permitted to engage in practice involving the same behavior called for in the objective. The advantage of employing equivalent practice is self-evident and yet many teachers fail to employ it. For example, let us say that a teacher wished to have his students learn how to analyze speeches on air pollution control and identify inconsistencies and propaganda techniques. Many teachers in this situation confine the practice to a discussion, with the teacher providing all of the analysis and the students trying to memorize what she is saying and doing. A much better procedure is to allow students, at some point in the lesson, to make an analysis of actual statements about air pollution control and then provide them with teacher feedback.

In the following example, identify which activity is equivalent practice.

Objective: Students will be able to evaluate plans for energy conservation.

1. Teacher shows the student plans for energy conservation which he is expected to analyze.
2. A discussion is held regarding the techniques of evaluating energy conservation plans with the teacher demonstrating how evaluation is accomplished.
3. Students are given plans for energy conservation and must organize them into a hierarchy in order of their meeting given criteria and explain why they organized them in this way.
4. Students are taken to a factory and expected to evaluate the energy conservation efforts there.

Activity 3 is the correct answer. In activity 1, analysis is an important constituent of the terminal behavior but must be considered an en route behavior. In this activity no evaluation takes place; thus there is no equivalent practice. While it is important to precede actual practice in evaluation with conceptual development of what evaluation is, simply having a discussion about the subject is not equivalent to practicing actual evaluations. Consequently activity 2 is also preliminary to the equivalent practice of actually performing evaluation. In activity 4 evaluation does take place but the items to be evaluated are different from those called for in the objective.

A second type of practice which may be used in the classroom is *analogous practice.* In this case the student is given the opportunity to engage in activities which are simulations of the terminal behavior. A good example of analogous practice is in activity 2 above. In this case the student is involved in the process of evaluating energy conservation plans but the emphasis is upon how to evaluate with the teacher providing a demonstration rather than permitting students to evaluate the plans. In both cases the students go through the process of evaluation but in the case of analogous practice the student has the benefit of following the teacher rather than doing it on his own as provided for in the objective. It is imperative that equivalent practice be provided at some point in instruction. It should not be concluded from this, however, that analogous practice does not play an important role. For example, it is sometimes necessary to alter the mode of practice simply because the teacher will be unable to monitor practice in the mode expected in the terminal behavior. For example, the teacher wants students to be able to debate the issues in population control. It would be impossible for all class members to practice debating simultaneously in a classroom in a practice session. Students could, though, mentally prepare their arguments as analogous practice and later give their presentation, in pairs, in front of the class for their equivalent practice.

Chemistry and physics can provide us with additional examples of analogous practice. If we want students to be able to handle chemicals and use them in experiments, the teacher will likely need to give analogous practice by demonstrating how to use dangerous chemicals and then talking the students through the use of these substances in carefully sequenced steps. If the teacher wishes to involve students in the use of electricity, similar analogous practice will be required in advance of permitting students to work independently with electrical experiments.

We have now made distinctions between en route behaviors as well as two types of appropriate practice. Any activity which a student must master before he can learn about and practice terminal behavior is an en route behavior. The experiences and abilities of any given class of students help determine which en route behaviors are necessary in the attainment of the course goals. Analogous practice refers to those activities which are not equivalent to those called for in the terminal behavior but rather are simulations. When the practice is the same as the behaviors called for in the objective we call it equivalent. The following is an example of an objective along with appropriate en route behaviors and practice:

Objective:	Given from three to five articles on the American space program, students will be able to determine which article best explains the benefits of the space program and explain why.
En Route Behaviors:	1. Formulating criteria for judgment.
	2. Writing rationales.
	3. Learning the components of good writing.

Analogous Practice: Participate in a class discussion where articles on the American space program are compared and evaluated with regard to how much they benefit Americans.

Equivalent Practice: Evaluate articles in terms of how well they explain the benefits of the American space program and provide rationales for these evaluations.

Exercise 8–1   Appropriate Practice

Formulate your own objectives and determine the en route behaviors and appropriate practice.

Correspondence between Objectives and Strategy

As stated previously, strategy is a plan formulated by the teacher to insure that students do indeed achieve instructional goals. Thus far it has been pointed out that learning activities should be appropriately selected and sequenced and that the teacher should take into account the various learning problems of students in planning his/her strategy. The next step is to learn how to prepare strategies for helping students develop the specific mental skills referred to in the taxonomy of educational objectives (Bloom, 1956). It should be remembered that even though various methods may be suggested, the most important consideration is not the method used, but rather, the achievement of the objectives.

Concepts and Principles

The first two levels of the taxonomy will be discussed together. The knowledge level is composed of information recall, and comprehension refers to one's ability to understand. Even though much of the learning that takes place in science classes is at the knowledge level it is generally less desirable to teach with the exclusive intention that students simply remember science facts. It is much more desirable to teach concepts and principles along with the higher mental process and let facts be learned incidentally as they are needed or appear to be useful. For example, there are many facts associated with genetics, but students could learn them as they perform experiments which are designed to develop intellectual skills. Ordinarily when facts are taught separately and apart from concepts and principles, they have limited meaningfulness and their utility is not sufficiently explicit to the student. In addition, drill and recitation are often used in excess when teaching facts, and students consequently become bored and listless. Thus, this discussion will deal primarily with the strategies of learning concepts and principles.

A *concept* refers to any class of things which has a common characteristic. When the student understands a concept he should be able to identify things which are and which are not examples of a concept and identify the common characteristics or attributes of the class of objects which make up the concept. In addition, for some concepts, he must be able to formulate his own examples in order to demonstrate his understanding. If, for example, we wanted the students to demonstrate their understanding of the concept of simple machines we may ask them to determine whether specific objects were examples or nonexamples of simple machines. In addition we may ask the student to give his own examples of simple machines.

A *principle* is a statement which relates two or more concepts together. The following are examples of principles:

Gas expands when its temperature is increased.
The amount of energy gotten out of a machine does not exceed the energy put into it.
Balance in nature depends upon the orderly transfer of energy from one type of organism to another.
Changes in environment provide the basis for changes in living things over time.

For a student to demonstrate understanding of a principle it is necessary that he be able to restate the principle in his own words or to apply it in a situation or problem. Simply stating a principle as it has been explained does not necessarily show understanding, since to do this the student need only have memorized the appropriate word sequence.

There are two basic strategies for teaching principles and concepts, *expository strategy* and *discovery strategy*. With the expository model the teacher ordinarily first states the principle or concept with its accompanying characteristics or attributes. He next presents examples of the concept, or in the case of a principle, the situations or problems which illustrate the principle. Lastly, students are required to discriminate examples from nonexamples of the concept or to formulate their own examples. If it is a principle that is being taught the student is asked to apply it to some problem.

For example, if you wish to teach the concept "bird" you would provide students with the following characteristics of birds: body covered with feathers, two pairs of limbs with the anterior pair modified for flight, mouth a projecting beak or bill, no teeth, etc. Then examples would be presented of the concept in the form of pictures, models, or stuffed or live specimens. Finally, positive and negative examples would be given and students required to discriminate between them.

As an example of *expository strategy* for teaching a principle, consider the relationship between balance in nature and energy transfer and man's influence on various plant and animal communities. First the principle would be explained and then examples given. The effect on the deer population and resultant erosion as a consequence of killing of natural predators could be used to illustrate the principle. Students could then be asked to supply additional examples or to examine possible examples and determine if the principle held for those instances.

In using a *discovery strategy*, emphasis is placed upon the student's defining the concept or stating the principle. This process is what is commonly referred to as induction. In this process the teacher's role is to present examples and sufficient accompanying cues so that the student can determine the attributes characteristic of a concept, or to produce examples or situations from which appropriate principles can be derived (Emmer and Millett, 1970). Because students are in a sense discovering concepts and principles, the teacher will find it necessary to apply sufficient guidance in order to insure against unprofitable deviations and loss of time.

The discovery strategy requires that the student first be given several examples of a concept from which he can observe common attributes. The teacher may also include nonexamples and ask students to identify ways in which examples and nonexamples differ. Then he/she can proceed to label or name the concept represented by the common attributes or characteristics.

Suppose again that a teacher wishes to teach the principle of balance in nature and energy transfer using the discovery strategy. The example of killing deer predators and its consequences could be presented to the class and students asked to formulate the principle represented by the example. When this had been accomplished and the principle properly stated, additional examples may be sought for in order to check the validity of the principle.

Higher Intellectual Processes

Because higher intellectual processes depend on the student having mastered concepts and principles, it is essential that this mastery precede development in the areas of application, analysis, synthesis, and evaluation. These levels of mental activity form a hierarchy which can best be taught in a coordinated fashion. Each subject to be taught should be examined for the specific possibility of using it as a means of developing intellectual skills at each of the cognitive levels. Study of the subject matter should then be orchestrated so that concepts and principles are taught which later will be used in an applicatory sense. Later, these same concepts and applications can be used by students as a basis for analysis and so on through the skill of evaluation, with each mental operation building upon the previous ones. Some topics are better suited than others to be used in this way. However, maximum use should be made of all topics to aid in the intellectual development of students rather than having students simply perform routine memorizations.

One of the more common uses made of *application* and *analysis* skills in the classroom is problem solving. From the application viewpoint a student may be required to use principles which he has learned in an unfamiliar problem or situation. With analysis students may have to examine problems and situations, identify various subcomponents of the situation or problem, and determine which one of a number of principles or solution procedures best applies.

Problem-solving may also consist of divergent problems which may have more than one acceptable solution or of convergent problems which have only one correct answer. Most science teachers emphasize single solutions when in fact many situations should not be so limited. Certainly both kinds of problems should be included in the elementary school curriculum.

Usually the teacher formulates problems which the class has to deal with. She is more likely than the children to come up with viable problems which can be articulated with the rest of the curriculum. However, it is imperative that students also view the problem as viable to them. Therefore, the strategy for problem determination should include teacher guidance with input by the students.

Once a problem has been identified the teacher must decide whether to use an expository or discovery model for the solution. With the expository strategy, the teacher usually solves the problem herself and then asks students to repeat these behaviors for similar problems. Usually with the expository model the teacher also formulates the problem rather than encouraging contributions by students.

When the discovery approach to problem solving is used the student attempts to determine his own solution or solutions and apply them to the problem. In the discovery approach the teacher may provide guidance through such statements as "What would happen if . . . ?" "What if we considered . . . ?" "Suppose there were no environmental controls. . . ." "What do you believe would happen if we add hydrochloric acid?" The teacher may wish students to apply given concepts or principles to a solution or he may permit them to determine which they use. His questions need to be designed to bring about whichever purpose he intends.

In problem solving, where analysis skills are being focused upon, the teacher must emphasize logical development of solutions. His role is primarily to formulate questions which cause students to examine the subcomponents of situations or problems, determine consistencies or inconsistencies between these components and their relationships, and to identify any principles which may be applied in understanding and explaining the situations. His strategy is to be certain that students attend to the detail of what is being analyzed and that they make careful checks on subcomponents to determine how they fit together logically. If inconsistencies are discovered the students must be able to explain the nature of the inconsistency. The teacher's questions should be designed to achieve this end. For example, suppose the teacher wishes his class to analyze the following statement and determine the inconsistencies contained in it: "I am not going to support the demonstration for cleaning up city pollution because the leader of the demonstration has been convicted of several crimes and has served time in the state prison." After showing the class the statement the teacher may ask the students to identify any logical inconsistencies. Suppose a student responds by saying "It seems logical to me that we shouldn't support activities supervised by those who are proven criminals." The teacher could then respond by saying, "What can we assume regarding the honesty or integrity of persons who have spent time in prison?" The inconsistency which the teacher wants to expose through this strategy is the stereotype of all prison parolees being dishonest or lacking in integrity. A number of additional questions may be required to aid students in finding this inconsistency. In order to expose a second inconsistency the teacher could have asked, "What is the relationship between a person's prison record and their capabilities to successfully organize and lead a demonstration for cleaning up city pollution?" This inconsistency could then be elucidated through a series of questions designed to probe the responses of students.

Once students understand how to analyze the example statements the teaching strategy should be to provide them with additional statements to analyze without assistance from the teacher. It would be best if these statements could be checked by the teacher and feedback given each student regarding his analysis prior to the time of final evaluation. In the event this is too time consuming, the teacher may elect to spot check student responses and give feedback to the whole class regarding what he finds. The teacher needs to permit students the opportunity of trying out analytical skills rather than simply letting them observe while he performs the analysis. In the evaluation the students' capability to perform an analysis should be tested. In many classrooms students are required to remember teacher analysis only, even though the goal may have been to teach students how to analyze. Such consequences should obviously be avoided.

The strategy for helping students develop *synthesis* skills in science is considerably different from that of teaching analysis. This is so in part because synthesis involves putting elements together to form a consistent whole while analysis is just the opposite. In addition, synthesis requires creativity whereas analysis emphasizes a methodical step-by-step comparison of subcomponents. Because synthesis is based on creativity, one useful technique to produce a variety of ideas for consideration is brainstorming. Brainstorming is a good strategy for stimulating involvement and for getting original, though often poorly formulated, ideas into the open. During the brainstorming segment of synthesis, it is imperative that students be permitted to suggest any idea in spite of how ridiculous it may appear. Once an adequate list of ideas has been generated the next step is to examine each of the ideas carefully to determine how it fits into the total proposed scheme or product which is to be developed. This should be accomplished without criticism but with the use of good reasoning skills. The teacher's role at this stage is to draw the attention of the class to possible constraints, pertinent ideas which have not been considered, and faulty reasoning or construction in the formulation of the final product. For example, suppose that the teacher wishes students to be able to formulate a plan for equipping a spaceship with a life support system capable of maintaining the life of three astronauts during a space voyage from Earth to Mars. If students begin to make their plan to include such food materials as meat, bread, fruit, vegetables, etc., the teacher should attempt to direct their attention upon the limited food storage space in a spaceship. If dehydrated food is suggested, the teacher may question where sufficient water may be obtained to hydrate the food. In addition he may again focus attention upon the lack of space to store the necessary quantities of dehydrated food for such an extensive space flight. Hopefully, students would be led to conclude that some means must be found to grow food, which is not only nourishing but palatable, while in transit. Again, the teacher should not present his ideas but rather he should help students visualize legitimate constraints so that the final product has a logical consistency along with some recognizable value or utility. The elements which are synthesized must be articulated and formed into an organized whole. Simply generating creative ideas or forming loose unarticulated patterns should not be considered synthesis. The strategy of the teacher should be to insure through dialogue with students that a reasonable synthesis has taken place.

Once students have had sufficient practice and feedback in synthesis the teacher should attempt to evaluate their synthesis skill by requiring students to synthesize a similar but different product than that prepared by the entire class. Evaluation must not be limited to a judgment of the total class experience. Each student should be evaluated according to his individual capability. The synthesized product used for evaluation must be sufficiently different from the one used in practice so that synthesis skills are measured instead of simple recall. At the same time, the experience in evaluation should not be so dissimilar that it bears little relation to the practice one.

The highest level of mental operation in Bloom's taxonomy is *evaluation*. This skill incorporates the skills below it in the taxonomy, but adds a new dimension which must be developed by different strategies. In this case, students are taught how to judge the quality of things and explain the basis upon which the judgment is made. Judgment may be made either in a comparative sense by identifying which of the things being judged is the best or by determining which among the items being judged meets given criteria. Before valid judgments can be made students must first possess the requisite knowledge about the items which are to be evaluated, have formulated a defensible set of criteria with which to judge, and have skills in analysis so that item subcomponents may be examined and the appropriateness of their relationship compared.

Suppose we wish to train students to judge the quality of water pollution control plans. The evaluator may first obtain an understanding of the various types of possible water pollution control systems and the issues surrounding each control system. Next he should learn about the ecological concepts related to water pollution control. Following this, criteria should be developed by the evaluator for judging the adequacy of each skill and the evaluator given practice-feedback sessions where he attempts to apply his criteria for rating subskills. The evaluator should also be required to defend the criteria he chooses and the relative importance he attaches to each in making an overall evaluation. This, of course, must take place in classroom interaction. Once the evaluator is prepared with knowledge, analysis skill, and his criteria, he should be given an opportunity to use these in practice sessions where he can first evaluate water pollution control systems in a contrived or simulated situation (analogous practice) and finally allowed to judge a series of particular water pollution control systems (equivalent practice). Once the instructor believes the student evaluator is prepared, testing can take place.

Exercise 8–2 Strategies for Cognitive Level Objectives

Write an objective for each of the major levels of the cognitive domain and then prepare a written explanation of the strategy you would use to insure that students attain the goal. Include reference to en route behaviors, analogous practice, and equivalent practice.

Affective Goals

The basic sequential strategy for teaching values is inherent in the affective domain of the Taxonomy of Educational Objectives (Krathwohl, 1964). The levels of the taxonomy represent the stages of value development as they should proceed from initial value consideration to final characterization of a value system. This necessitates the articulation of value development goals at each succeeding taxonomic level. For example, if we wish our students to behave consistently in terms of a properly organized set of values with regard to energy production and environmental pollution control, then we must organize experiences for students which help them proceed in an orderly fashion from receiving instruction about energy production and environmental pollution control and acting out rudimentary behaviors consistent with these values to a well-articulated value system with its concomitant behavioral patterns. If we follow the outline of the taxonomy our first task is to insure that students receive the relevant information regarding the two values. Because this experience has affective components, an entirely different approach to instruction is required at this point. The first step in the strategy is to obtain an appropriate set. The setting experience must be emotive in nature rather than lingual-symbolic as ordinarily provided in cognitive goals (Searles, 1967). This means that feelings regarding the values must be aroused as related information is being attended to. The arousal of feelings may be generated through movies, field trips, pictures, verbal descriptions, or role playing. Whatever method is used it is imperative that genuine feelings be generated. For example, if role playing the energy-pollution controversy is selected as the means for arousal, students should be allowed to play a role not only in support of energy productions but also a role which favors extreme pollution control so that they come to feel the emotions that may evolve from the various parties. If a field trip is the method used, adequate planning will be required to insure that arousal goals are realized. If, for example, the teacher wishes to generate affect with regard to conservation, descriptions of what once was at a particular location will be inadequate. Students must be exposed to the waste and destruction of poor conservation efforts before arousal can be realized.

Once a proper set has been obtained and the students have become affectively involved with the subject the instructor may then expose his class to experiences which will enhance student knowledge about the values being considered. In the present example energy production and environmental pollution control are the values we wish students to incorporate. At this level (receiving) the objective is to get students to seriously consider the values for inclusion in their value systems. Evidence for achieving the objective is when students actively participate in experiences designed to have them reflect on and report their views regarding the value. Techniques such as role playing, field trips, and movies may be used with emphasis being placed on discussions about the content of these experiences. The important consideration at this stage is for students to have conceptualized each of the values separately and to have made some decision as to how they will act out the values behaviorally. The teacher should ensure that his class has the opportunity to achieve these ends through discussions and writing exercises.

The next stage is the *responding* stage. It is necessary at this point to have students involved in either contrived or real situations where they are permitted to act out the behaviors expected for one holding the values being considered. If energy production and environmental pollution control are the values we wish to develop, debates and editorial writing are logical situations in which these values may be developed and evaluated. One of the difficulties ordinarily experienced at this level is that of obtaining correspondence between the value and the behaviors which can be accepted as evidence of the value. Students may engage in certain behaviors for reasons other than those expected. They may, for example, attend a meeting on environmental cleanup which ordinarily would be accepted as evidence of environmental control appreciation, when in fact their attendance there is for other reasons (i.e., to accompany a friend, to please the teacher, or to get a good grade).

The next stage or level is *valuing*. At this level, evidence of commitment to values is desired. It is particularly difficult to incorporate valuing into the curriculum in the school. As an indication of valuing students may be observed supporting particular values by becoming active participants in organizations which embrace these values or by attempting to persuade others to accept the values. Ordinarily contrived situations do not permit display of commitment. We are thus left with the problem of organizing adequate real situations where commitment is possible. School clubs and community organizations are possible situations for development of commitment on a limited basis. Some values like not cheating, fair play, getting work in on time, and the like can be organized in the regular classroom. Other values may receive little attention because the school has little control over situations where commitment to them can be developed and measured.

Organization is the next level of value development. Here the student is expected to organize a value system that is consistent. There is, for example, some inconsistency between energy production and environmental pollution control. Energy production carried to its extreme would permit possible exploitation of the environment. Such exploitations are likely to create situations where the environment is damaged beyond repair. Because the organization level involves an interaction between the affective and cognitive domains, it is necessary to organize learning activities which require students to deal cognitively with values, especially where value conflicts exist. Again role playing is a useful procedure for helping students appreciate the inconsistencies which do exist and which must be resolved in the process of value system development. Role playing can only be used, however, to set the stage for discussions about the ramifications of certain behavior repertoires in terms of the values they appear to indicate. The teacher's role is one of helping students identify inconsistencies and formulating behaviors which represent the values they have determined for themselves. It is unwise for the teacher to moralize extensively or attempt to force students to organize their values along certain lines. Certain social, scientific, and democratic values may be encouraged, but these must be properly differentiated from the more personal ones which the teacher would be wise not to shape. It is imperative, however, that the student be encouraged and helped to formulate his value system to include general as well as personal values. Evaluation of this level can be made through a combination of written papers as well as observations. Written papers are useful as a means of determining how students have dealt with the various inconsistencies. The observations serve as a vindication of this organization.

The final level in value development is the *characterization* level and has limited application in the schools because it refers to an ongoing life style which is subject to periodic revision. Schools are unable to account for their influence over student behaviors subsequent to graduation and consequently are unable to state with any certainty what contributions may have been made to lifestyle development by the value education program. The same could also be said for lifestyle while the student is in school, but once the student has graduated, the school influence is an even more remote one. Strategy for this level consists of providing students with situations where they are free to exhibit whatever behaviors they wish and where they are confronted with situations which require them to reexamine the science values they hold in light of new experiences and information. If students have characterized their values, their behavior will consistently reflect adherence to these values.

Psychomotor Goals

Psychomotor skills consist of a sequence of subcomponent motor behaviors which are performed in a coordinated and integrated way.

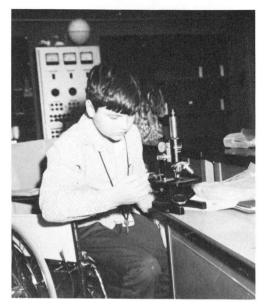

Using a microscope involves more than one psychomotor movement. Part strategy may therefore be required to help students master its use.

The common examples of psychomotor skills in science include constructing and manipulating science equipment, dissection, transferring bacteria from one medium to another, drawing and preparing models, and mock-ups.

Many times psychomotor skills are taught with a mistaken emphasis on only the motor aspect of the skill. This is a serious error because the development of the skill is not likely to exceed a rather low level if the cognitive and attitudinal components of the skill are not properly emphasized. For instance, using scientific equipment usually involves a complex of cognitive and affective behaviors in addition to the necessary psychomotor movements. Students need to know what movements to make and have a positive attitude regarding safety. If the associated cognitive and affective behaviors are ignored only rudimentary skill levels will be developed and proper safety precautions ignored.

There are basically two strategies in skill development, part strategy and whole strategy. Because skills are made up of component behaviors, part strategy is important in learning separate behaviors independently before practicing them in sequence. Each subcomponent of a skill usually has to be performed at a minimum level before it can reasonably be coordinated in a sequence with other components of the skill. In teaching students to properly use glassware in the laboratory, for example, the subcomponents of hand position on the glass tubing, how to position the tubing, and how hard to push when inserting it into a rubber stopper, all require specific instruction and practice.

Not only is part practice important in initial skill development, it is also essential where certain subcomponent skills require special corrective treatment subsequent to initial skill development or when one is trying to "sharpen" skills to a point of near perfection.

An essential constituent of part strategy is demonstrating the role played by each subcomponent skill in the total psychomotor movement. The purpose of this is primarily a motivational one. If students are unable to see the strategic necessity of part practice in the development of the final execution of the skill, they will be less likely to want to pursue the necessary practice on each subcomponent.

The sequence of part practice depends on the extent to which one subcomponent must be learned before another can be executed. In the case of inserting glass tubing into a rubber stopper, being able to properly position one's hand and the tubing necessarily precede the act of pushing the tubing into the stopper. Some skills do not require this kind of sequencing, however. For example, practicing the transfer of bacteria from a culture tube to a petri dish does not require that practice collecting bacteria on a wire loop from a culture tube precede streaking bacteria on the dish.

Whole strategy emphasizes the learning of the appropriate sequence of a series of component behaviors. In this case practice is directed toward the integrated performance of subcomponent behaviors rather than providing practice for each major component behavior.

Ordinarily, skill development will include both part as well as whole practice. The determination of which should be emphasized depends upon the nature of the skill itself. Skills which primarily involve well-coordinated sequencing, but whose component behaviors are easily performed will probably best be taught using the whole method primarily. Skills whose components involve new or unusual behaviors or which involve subskills which are prerequisite to whole skill performance lend themselves best to the part method (Emmer and Millet, 1970). The teacher will usually schedule both part and whole practice as needed to develop the terminal psychomotor skill by moving from one to the other as the skill development level of the student requires. When the teacher notices that students are experiencing difficulty with a particular subcomponent skill during whole practice he can schedule part practice to correct the deficiency.

The initial segment of the strategy for developing psychomotor skills ordinarily consists of modeling the behavior sequence as it should be executed. Then part and whole practice can be scheduled as needed. During these practice sessions the teacher should provide feedback to students so that appropriate corrections can be made until the behaviors exhibited correspond with what is expected. Feedback is a very important constituent of the strategy for developing psychomotor skills. Without it inappropriate behaviors are practiced and developed. Practice and feedback should always precede any attempt to evaluate the achievement of psychomotor goals.

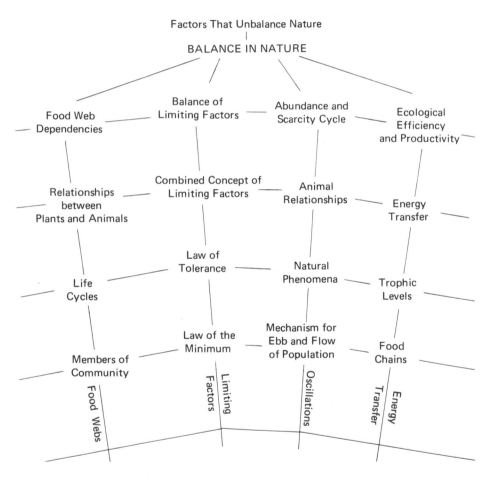

Figure 8–1

Using Cognitive Maps

Cognitive maps serve a useful purpose in the organization of teaching strategies for science. Taba (1967) indicates that there are two kinds of maps which can give teachers a perspective on direction in teaching. The first of these is a content map which indicates the content samples to be used, the main ideas to be developed, and the samples of specific descriptive facts which can be used in the development of the concepts and main ideas. The second type of map is based on process and outlines the structure and sequence of cognitive processes involved in the various learning tasks associated with the study of a particular topic. Content maps are very useful in helping the teacher to differentiate the relevant from the irrelevant content and to select specific descriptive facts which will be used by pupils as they learn the necessary information to achieve the instructional objectives.

Cognitive maps may take several forms. They can appear as notes regarding points to emphasize, as sequential steps within a teaching strategy, as diagrams of probable outcomes, or as end-products from a strategy. Figure 8–1 illustrates a cognitive map to be used in discussing the question: What are the relationships between living things in producing balance in nature? The vertical lines show divergent lines which may be used in answering this question. Awareness of these divergencies help the teacher avoid fixing her attention upon just one line of thought and suggests a fuller range of possibilities which students may initiate. The horizontal lines suggest the levels of thought which might be derived from the original direction which has been set. The cognitive map as a whole indicates some of the directions and levels of ideas which could be taken in a discussion in response to a question. The map helps the teacher anticipate the direction which the discussion may take by suggesting a number of divergent alternative answers to the question. This helps the teacher distinguish valid and promising leads from irrelevant, unfruitful, or illogical ones.

At least four possible directions are indicated in Figure 8–1 which may be taken from the question, "What are the relationships between living things in producing balance in nature?" The first of these is the idea that plants and animals depend upon one another because they are related in a complex way which can be diagrammed as a food web. If this line of discussion is taken, the flow of ideas begins first with the identification of plants and animals of particular communities which are living together. Next comes the examination of their individual life cycles and then how these life cycles bring them into relationship with one another. Finally there is a discussion of how these relationships constitute life dependencies and make up the balance of nature, and how disrupting these dependencies may result in the unbalancing of nature.

The second line of discussion centers around specific factors which limit the growth and development of plants and animals. The law of the minimum states that the essential material available in amounts most closely approaching the critical minimum needed for survival will tend to be the limiting one. In close association with the law of the minimum is the law of tolerance which states that the presence and success of an organism depends upon the completeness of a complex of environmental conditions. Absence or failure of an organism can be controlled by the qualitative or quantitative deficiency or excess with respect to any one of several factors which may approach the limits of tolerance for that organism. Any condition which approaches or exceeds the limits of tolerance for an organism is said to be a limiting condition or a limiting factor. If factors in the environment are altered so that a critical minimum is approached for an organism nature can become unbalanced. Introduction of polluting chemicals into the environment is a good example of this unbalancing.

A third line of discussion which may take place is that of the natural oscillations that exist in nature and the delicate balance that is often present in these ebbs and flows of nature. Understanding how populations of animals increase and decrease in response to one another indicates how closely related and interdependent they are. This illustrates how artificially influencing one population can have far-reaching repercussions throughout all of nature. In some situations the dependency is so complete that entire populations oscillate with one another with no other factors having any apparent effect.

There is also a fourth line of discussion which may be used. This one has to do with the production of energy from one trophic level to another. At the base of all food chains is the green plant which captures energy from the sun and transforms it into a form which can be used by animals. As energy is transferred from one trophic level to another some of it is always lost. There is never 100 percent efficiency in the conversion of energy. Total ecological efficiency and productivity depends upon the continuity of energy transfer chains. Broken links mean animals further up the line are deprived of their source of energy. This of course leads to an unbalancing of nature.

The sequence of concepts is a critical concern in developing strategies and organizing cognitive maps. The questions that should be asked about how to sequence concepts include: What should determine the order of succession of concepts and what should follow them and why, and what is the most advantageous time to acquire certain learning? There are at least four different ways to sequence ideas. The first is that which proceeds from the simple to the complex. Simple is defined as that which contains few elements or subordinate parts. Examples of this sequence are found frequently in the study of science. We proceed from one-celled animals to many-celled animals and from chemical elements to compounds. This method of sequencing is particularly useful in those instances where complex things are composed of similar organizational patterns as more simple but related things. One-celled animals, for example, carry on many of the same life functions as more complex animals. Studying one-celled animals first can serve as a means of helping children understand these processes in a simple form.

A second way to sequence learning is on the basis of prerequisites. This is particularly useful where there are many laws and principles involved and where one set of ideas or operations builds naturally upon preceding ones. In this case the child's ability to do one task may depend upon his ability to master a number of others. If elements of an area of study bear a logical relation to one another it is likely that they will be best learned in that relationship.

Another way to sequence learning is from whole to part. Sometimes understanding parts depends on the child's ability to conceptualize the whole. For example, understanding the niche of a particular animal depends upon understanding the plant and animal relationships in the larger community. Understanding the larger community depends upon knowledge about succeedingly greater geographic areas until the total world community is reached. All of these communities stand in relationship to one another and are influenced by one another. A good example of this is how understanding the air currents aids in understanding how weather is produced. Also, geographic features many miles away can have very marked effects on the weather in a particular locality.

The fourth kind of sequencing is chronological. In this case facts and ideas are arranged in a time sequence so that things are studied as they are related to one another in terms of time. The study of evolution is an example of one area that may be handled in this way. Another might be the development and evolution of plant and animal communities. Determining the probable course of development of a community depends upon its age and whether or not its composition is of organisms of a climax community. Climax communities are those where their action upon the habitat tends to make the area in which they live less favorable for their members and more favorable for other sets of organisms. In most communities there is a succession which is directional and future changes can be predicted. This is particularly useful to man because some of the organisms which man desires most to perpetuate are members of early serial rather than of late climax stages of development. Thus most of the game birds, many fresh-water game fish and many of the most valuable timber trees thrive best in what are actually temporary communities. Teaching children about communities in a time sequence helps them understand how things are related chronologically and how best to intervene to halt succession and keep the desired community permanently in existence. In other words the child will learn how best to use chronological relationships to enhance his own life and the lives of others.

Exercise 8–3   Preparing Cognitive Maps

Prepare a cognitive map for a set of science concepts you may want to teach to a group of elementary school children.

Questioning Strategies

The way in which teachers ask questions is usually quite loose and sometimes arbitrary. Many times questions do not follow one another logically. Often they do not follow in an appropriate sequence designed to raise the level of cognitive functioning. In summary, question asking is frequently a haphazard occurrence with little or no attention given to appropriate strategies. Greater care needs to be taken in organizing questioning strategies. Well-prepared strategies for questioning can increase clarity and understanding as well as help the teacher raise the mental activity level which students are required to engage in.

Before discussing the form questioning strategies may take, it is necessary to first consider the functions that questions provide when grouped within a particular scheme. Questions which are incorporated into strategies can have four possible functions: centering; expansion; distribution; and ordering (Hunkins, 1972). The *centering* function strives to converge students' thinking on some particular aspect of a topic. This is usually employed in the beginning stages of a lesson when the attempt is being made to get students to focus their attention. Centering may also be used to draw out of numerous possible considerations those that we desire to concern ourselves with. For example, a series of questions may be asked to determine which of a number of possible solutions to the problem of water pollution are worthy of further consideration. The goal is to decide which of many ideas or situations are most important or more significant.

Expansion is the second questioning strategy function. This function is designed to expand or extend student thinking. Question strategies which emphasize expansion stress divergent thinking. If students are thinking at the comprehension level the strategy most likely will lead them to extrapolate. At the application stage, the strategy may direct them to produce several conclusions or apply particular skills to an ever-increasing range of situations. The expansion function requires an increase in student participation and a greater precision in their responses. This is usually done at higher cognitive levels. Students are, for example, guided when they use analysis skill to not only identify elements and relationships, but to also apply information learned in one situation to other situations. Let's look at a specific example illustrating the expansion function. Suppose the lesson objective is to identify significant relationships in a forest community. Questions which you may ask include the following: "In addition to soil type and moisture what else influences the particular plant life in this community?" "How can we determine what else may serve as an influencing factor?" "Is there another way of looking at this community?" "Are there any contradictions with regard to the factors that have already been identified?" These questions seek first for divergence and then encourage analysis and comparison. Most importantly they ask the student to extend his thinking. Also, the student must consider information from varying positions and keep from prematurely deciding on any particular information. Students then make an analysis but at the same time keep themselves open for other possibilities. When student analysis has revealed some significant elements the questioning strategy can shift and work for an expansion to the analysis of relationships between the elements. You may ask, "Are there any relationships between the factors which influence the make-up of the forest community?" The next question may be, "What is the evidence of these relationships?" Finally, it may be asked, "Is there anything to show how these relationships influence possible alterations in the forest community?"

Now let us look at another example of the expansion function. Suppose that students are studying erosion prevention. You may perhaps begin by showing the class pictures of areas which are affected and pictures which are not affected. In addition experiments could be conducted using sand tables to help illustrate how various ground covers are related to water run-off. Books and other materials such as films may also be made available. Initial questioning may relate to one of the pictures which shows erosion. Referring to the picture you may say, "What is the condition of the land?" "What are some factors that might have caused this condition?" You may then desire to shift the stress of questions to the analysis of relationships by asking such questions as, "What are some relationships that might exist between some of the factors identified, such as climate, type of soil, depth of bedrock, or land contour?" "In what ways could such relationships influence the loss of top soil?" Here it should be stressed that there is a relationship between various factors and the condition of the top soil. Next, in order to raise the cognitive level to synthesis, questions like the following may be asked: "What are the potential uses for this information about the relationships between the various factors of an environment and erosion?" "From the study of materials and factors and from our field trip in the community, what are some generalizations that can be made about erosion?" "How are these generalizations applicable to other situations?" With the above sequence of questions students have been asked to raise the level of their responses to the synthesis level. Notice that there was a gradual building of a foundation of lower order questions before synthesis questions were used.

The third questioning function is that of *distribution*. The purpose of this function is to distribute questions among students in a way that they can be productively involved in the class. Questions should be distributed so that they motivate thinking and assess present levels of knowledge. This should be done without embarrassing students who do not know answers or who are caught daydreaming. The distributive function should be used to get as many students as possible participating in the class. Students need to become involved actively or they will mentally drop out and not benefit from the educational experience.

The last function of questioning is the *order* function. This function is used to provide a proper classroom atmosphere for discovery learning. Questions ordinarily refer to rules of classroom operation. For example, "What can we work with a teammate?" "What is the class policy about leaving your seat?" and "What should we observe to do when learning in our inquiry sessions?" Questions having the order function can also be used to provide emotional support to students who fail to get involved because of feelings of insecurity. These questions should encourage students to actively participate: "What are the reasons that keep you from participating in discussion?" "What are some situations where you would feel more comfortable joining in?" "How do you feel about what we are learning?"

Now that you have some idea regarding the function of questions let us turn our attention to the questioning strategies. Taba (1967) has stated that teachers rarely give serious thought to the questions they pose and the sequence in which they ask them. The sequencing of their questions is most often arbitrary. Taba ranked questions as "What?," "Why?," and "What does it mean?" Each of these questions is tied to three cognitive tasks: (a) concept formation; (b) interpretation of data; and (c) application of principles. Thus, at each of these task levels students would be asked questions starting with "What?" "Why?" and "What does it mean?" "What" questions can be equated in a loose way with the knowledge and comprehension levels in Bloom's Taxonomy of Educational Objectives (Bloom, 1956). "Why" level questions are roughly equivalent to Bloom's analysis level and "What does it mean" questions could be likened to synthesis and evaluation questions.

Generally, Taba advocated moving the whole class from one level of questioning to the next. Most of the class should be asked "What" questions, followed by "Why" questions and finally "What does it mean" questions should be asked. "What" questions would be used to help class members gain a basic understanding of the concepts under consideration. "Why" questions would be used to extend the level of thought and this would be followed by "What does it mean" questions to provide further expansion and lift thought to higher levels. Taba emphasizes that questions at each level should be adequate to involve even the slowest students. If this is not done, such students would likely become lost during the interaction process. In addition, students who have not had the opportunity to participate at one level will lack the requisite understandings and skills to effectively respond to higher level questions. Students who become lost in the early parts of the inquiry process, obviously will be unable to follow through as the process continues and thus become destined to fail and become a liability as far as discipline is concerned. As a teacher you should avoid the temptation to ask a higher level question based solely upon an especially powerful response from one student. It may provide a stimulus for that student to pursue higher level questioning based upon his earlier responses, but if you do it will be at the risk of losing the rest of the class. It is better to question a number of students at lower levels before extending or raising the level of questioning. This way there is greater assurance that the entire class has an understanding and will continue to be participants in the questioning.

Another questioning strategy has been outlined by Suchman (1958). In his strategy, the teacher assumes the role of guiding students and providing data. Students provide their own questions. Four types of questions are posed by students in this type of questioning: verification; experimentation; necessity; and synthesis. Verification questions are used to obtain specific information. They are designed to gather facts and provide an information base upon which further questioning can proceed. Experimentation questions are used by the student to verbally manipulate information gathered at the verification level and to determine the consequences of these manipulations. Necessity questions are used by the student to determine if particular data are essential for an event under investigation to exist. Finally, synthesis questions help the student ascertain if ideas, hunches, or conclusions being considered as the result of prior questioning are valid or warranted. This series of questions thus aids the student in using the scientific method in exploring various phenomena. At the highest level the student is directing his thinking toward formulating his own explanations of naturally occurring phenomena. The explanations or hunches which the child evolves can then be tested further to determine their significance.

The four types of questions can be asked about four different types of data: events; objects; conditions; and properties. Events refer to situations that happen or exist. They can vary from problems and experiments to local happenings. Objects are subcomponents or parts of events. In a science experiment, for example, an object may be a beaker full of some chemical which is part of the total experimental event.

Conditions refer to the alterable state of objects. In the experiment involving the chemical in the beaker referred to earlier, its temperature may be a condition. Temperature, obviously, is a condition that may vary. Properties are unalterable characteristics. Ether, for example, has the property of being volatile and mercury is a liquid at room temperature. The properties of an object may vary with conditions, but given a set of conditions the properties will remain the same.

In science, students will be experimenting with various events and their objects and will find it necessary to ask questions about events and objects as well as the conditions and properties associated with them. The teacher needs to help children learn not only what kind of questions to ask, but the topics about which these questions should be asked. With students properly oriented the teacher can then provide the function of guiding students and providing data while students formulate their own questions. The teacher's role is to encourage students to question productively, to provide a focus for inquiry and allow students sufficient time to inquire and then to furnish support through knowledge of results or redirection as necessary. It is important to remember not to make decisions or ask the questions for the student. The student should be encouraged to formulate his own questions and make his own decisions regarding how to answer them. The teacher can offer cues or assist the student in his thinking but should avoid formulating the inquiry questions for the student as well as prematurely giving the child too much structure in finding out the answers. This strategy can be used by individual students or groups of students. If individual students are using this questioning technique, you should be careful not to leave them floundering when they are unable to proceed further in the questioning process. If groups of students are using the method, one student should be allowed to continue questioning until he reaches a standstill. When this point is reached he should defer to another student. If a student is unable to determine when to defer, the teacher may have to encourage him to pass and ponder the situation further while other students become involved.

It can be seen from this description that Suchman's strategy varies significantly from that of Taba. Taba, it will be remembered, advocated that major student involvement should be reached before raising the level of thought. With Suchman's method, a student who is questioning can have the floor until he has reached a point where he can proceed no further. Both techniques have their strong and weak points. With Taba's method, some students may become bored while they wait for slower students to move along. With Suchman's method, some students may also become bored, but this time from being lost because of the rapid pace rather than a pace that is too slow. The method that is used will likely depend upon the composition of the class. If you have a lot of slow students, Taba's method may be more useful. If you have a perponderance of faster students you may find more success with Suchman's method.

Now let us examine Suchman's questioning strategy more carefully. Suppose you are teaching a lesson about factors which affect plant growth. The student would first begin by asking several verification questions. For example, he may ask, "What do we have to do to make seeds grow?" or "What factors effect plant growth?" These questions may lead the child to formulate necessity questions. Perhaps questions like the following would be asked: "What difference will varying amounts of water and fertilizer make?" and "How can I determine the extent to which various factors influence plant growth?" These questions would lead to the formation of experimentation questions. He might ask, "What if I varied the amount of water plants received as well as the amount of different minerals?" Once experimentation questions have been asked students should attempt to prepare synthesis questions. Such questions are preliminary hunches or predictions. In the above example the student may predict that the more water you give a plant the better it will grow. He may also predict that the more minerals that a plant has the better it will grow and develop. These "hypotheses" are tentative because they are simply first guesses. The student will want to alter his predictions as he obtains additional information. He may decide to conduct a series of experiments or do additional reading on the subject to find out if his hypotheses are valid.

If the Suchman questioning strategy is being used with a group of students, questioning may be shifted to another student as soon as the first student has reached the point of forming his hypotheses. This student as well as others may be asked to go through a similar set of questioning procedures and then compare their hypotheses. The teacher's role in all this consists essentially of helping the students formulate their questions. At the verification level he may ask the students what information he needs to provide himself a basis for inquiry. To help students to begin asking necessity questions the teacher may ask the student if he thinks he has sufficient and adequate information on the subject to make an inquiry. In order to help the students to ask experimentation questions he may ask them how they could test their ideas. To get them to ask synthesis questions the teacher simply needs to ask what the children believe their experimentation will show.

Not every student who formulates questions should ask all four types each time. Nor would he always proceed from verification or fact gathering to abstract levels of forming hypotheses or generalizations. This is particularly true of younger students. It should be remembered that younger students may find it impossible to think in terms of probability and be unable to hypothesize cause and effect relationships in situations where a number of factors are operating. In addition, inquiry questioning should not be used with a large number of children simultaneously. It is likely that as Taba has warned, that many children may become lost unless they can become adequately involved. Therefore, this method should be used with groups of from five to ten children.

Exercise 8–4   Questioning Strategy

Write down a series of questions that you would use in a questioning strategy. Include in your questions the various functions of questions and also evidence that your questions have been designed to raise the level of thinking beyond mere recall.

Strategy and Methods

As mentioned earlier, it is fairly common to base students' learning on various methods rather than upon strategies which incorporate appropriate methods. If methods become the focal point for instruction, there is a danger that the whole instructional process will consist of following through with a particular method without sufficient thought being given to whether or not the method is achieving desired objectives. Instruction which focuses upon methods, in fact, is likely to ignore objectives and thus the methods become the ends of instruction rather than the means. When strategy is used as the basis for instruction, various methods can be used as they are appropriate to achieving the objectives and altered any time they are not satisfying them. This is because strategy as a concept for teaching helps us focus our attention upon the ends of instruction and upon whatever means will lead to their achievement. With methods-oriented instruction, instructional goals can easily become obscure.

As already indicated, strategy involves the use of a variety of methods depending on what seems to be most useful in accomplishing specified instructional goals. In developing a strategy the teacher must select whatever methods she believes will be most helpful in achieving the objectives. This involves not only the selection of methods but also adapting methods to special circumstances as well as sequencing several methods when appropriate. In the preceding chapter you learned in considerable detail the procedures for implementing several different methods for teaching science. In this section you will learn the purposes for which various methods can be used.

Inquiry is a much talked about method in science education. It is most nearly like the scientific method itself and thus gives the children practice using the skills and thought processes most often used in science investigations. The purposes which can be served through the inquiry method include practice in critical thinking, learning how to gather and analyze data, developing the capability to draw conclusions, and learning to hypothesize. During at least part of their schooling children need to learn how to conduct an investigation and to do so with precision. The subject matter of science is an excellent area for developing this skill. Through the inquiry method children learn to consider the world around them more seriously and to more thoughtfully understand its meaning. With the use of this method children may for the first time learn how to measure and observe and to gather information and analyze it. As they get older and have more experience with inquiry techniques they will also learn how to formulate and test hypotheses.

In using the inquiry method, you will have to exercise certain cautions. It is not the kind of activity which children can engage in for the first time by themselves. In fact, a good deal of experience will be required before they can engage in inquiry successfully. Children's first experiences with inquiry will have to be more highly structured than later on when they have had some experience with the method. If they are left to themselves to inquire before they have had sufficient experience, this will likely lead to frustration and discouragement.

In deciding when and how to use the inquiry method, the following factors should be taken into consideration: (a) the intellectual development level of the children; (b) their former experiences; (c) the nature of the material being studied; (d) availability of materials; and (e) the purposes for which the method is being used. Usually the inquiry method is used to promote the development of the skills associated with it. It is assumed that much of the learning that we do in life could be improved through proper application of the skills which are part of the inquiry method. Because science lends itself well to use of the inquiry method, there are many instances in the study of science where these important skills can be emphasized. In doing this, however, it should be remembered that not all science experiences should be of the inquiry type. In addition to the fact that some science material can be learned more advantageously in other ways, you need to avoid overuse of any one method. Using a variety of methods helps keep children interested and involved.

Although closely associated with the inquiry method, *experimentation,* which we will discuss next, usually has different purposes. Experiments are usually more structured and used to illustrate certain principles in practical ways rather than leading children into creative thought. Experiments can be used for a number of purposes. They are an excellent way of arousing student interest and raising questions or problems. Because of their interest-arousing potential they can often be used successfully at the beginning of a lesson. Experiments are useful because they get children immediately involved with the tangible objects of science. Young children require concrete materials to manipulate while they think; consequently experiments using tangible objects are critical for their involvement and learning. Even older children will likely have patterns of thought based upon concrete referents and experiments provide them with the basis for abstract thought.

Experimentation can be a means not only of raising questions, but it can also provide a way to solve them. Experiments are ideal for problem solving. There are a variety of problems and questions that can be presented to children where experiments can be devised to find the answers. Such questions as the following can be used as a springboard to developing an experiment: Why do eyeglasses fog up in the winter when a person comes into a warm house from the outside cold? How do airplanes fly? Why do only certain kinds of plants grow in some kinds of soil? Why do you get a shock when you walk across a carpet and touch someone? These questions can, of course, be used in the inquiry method, but they can also lead to more structured experiments (Victor, 1970).

Experiments can also be used to apply what has been learned to new situations. If children are able to apply principles that they have learned in an experiment we can assume that they have understanding. Thus experiments can be used as a means of evaluating children's understanding. Experiments are also a good way to individualize instruction. Experiments can be designed for various levels and even for specific individuals. Students can work simultaneously on their own experiments with the teacher interacting with small groups or individuals as necessary. This way the slow learner can develop confidence in learning the basic processes of science at a level he is comfortable with while the fast learner can be challenged to a greater extent.

Sometimes it is not feasible for children to experiment. When such is the case *demonstration* may be a good method to use. Some experiments can be dangerous to small children. Others may be too expensive. In addition, many pieces of science equipment are far too complex or difficult to manipulate for elementary school children.

As well as providing a good substitute for experiments where limiting factors are present, demonstrations have some of their own inherent positive aspects. For example, demonstrations permit the teacher to capitalize on drama. With experiments, drama is ordinarily impossible. With demonstrations, however, the teacher is able to control and plan events in a strategic way that permits drama to be achieved. In this way the teacher is able to appeal to children's interest in well planned dramatic displays and to get them motivated and involved.

Strategically, demonstrations may also be used to model appropriate behavior. Young children often do not have a clear view of how to manipulate science equipment nor do they know how to conduct experiments. Demonstrations help them fix in their minds the basic movements and order of events in conducting experiments. Demonstrations can thus be strategically ordered to precede other laboratory experiences not only as a means of motivating students, but to also help them to conceptualize procedures that they will be expected to engage in by themselves. Clearly, demonstrations can best be used in conjunction with other methods. The temptation to use demonstrations simply to illustrate concepts should generally be avoided. Certainly there are instances where they may be used to illustrate concepts; however, the tendency is to overuse demonstrations for this purpose. Again, it may be that the students will be unable because of safety or expense to discover the concept experimentally for themselves and the teacher will have to use a demonstration to promote understanding. It is good to remember, though, that excessive illustration of science concepts through teacher demonstrations robs children of the benefits that may be obtained through learning by their own experiences.

Another purpose for which demonstrations can be used to advantage is to raise questions or problems while at the same time arousing student interest. To do this, it is necessary that the teacher avoid over-cuing students and answering the very questions that he wishes the demonstration to generate. By the same token, demonstrations may confuse students and fail to raise any questions at all if they are too vague and ambiguous. Much will depend upon the experience and age level of students when it comes to how demonstrations are done.

One important constraint regarding whether or not to use demonstrations is that of visibility. Far too often, some members of the class are unable to observe the entire sequence of a demonstration. When this happens misunderstandings may arise and disinterest develops. To avoid this the teacher should plan carefully not only how large the components of the demonstration should be but also the complete visibility of the various steps executed. She will also want to insure that seating arrangements are such that no one's view is obstructed. With these precautions being taken the chance for difficulties is greatly reduced.

Sometimes classroom demonstrations and experiments are too artificial to properly represent science phenomena. In such cases *field trips* can often be arranged which provide more realistic experiences. For example, the concept of the balance of nature can be more realistically portrayed in the natural environment than through pictures or mock-ups. If a child can see the destruction which is often produced by unbalancing nature he will certainly have a more viable learning experience, one which will serve as a bridge to memory as well as future learning.

Field trips should articulate well with the ongoing instructional program. Too often they are used simply as diversions. With the diversion type field trip, nothing is usually gained from the experience. However, when a field trip is planned as an integral part of the instructional program its benefits are much greater. As a teacher you will find it necessary to sequence field trips with other instructional procedures so that they enhance one another. On a field trip, for example, children should be prepared either to observe phenomena or to do something to phenomena. This may necessitate the development of certain skills and understandings prior to taking the field trip. Once the field trip is under way you will need to incorporate strategies which keep and maintain the interest and activity of students. When the field trip is over, certain follow-up activities will be necessary to insure proper conceptualization of the activities which have just been engaged in. Thus such methods as discussion, role playing, and demonstrations will need to be articulated with the field trip to insure that the purposes for which it is intended are realized.

A Strategy Example

The following is an example of a strategy which could be used to achieve the accompanying objective:

Objective
When presented with opinions concerning solutions to local environmental problems, the student will evaluate each opinion to determine which is best according to factual material identified in previous investigations of such community problems.

Strategy
1. Students are given a preassessment instrument to determine the specific knowledge they have regarding the components of the objective they are presently able to achieve, in addition to deficiencies they may have with regard to entry behaviors.
2. Students with insufficient mastery of entry behaviors will be given the environmental kit to give them the necessary preparation to begin this study.
3. In order to get the children involved and interested, a field trip will be taken to Sugar Creek to observe the effects of poor environmental control.
4. The objective of the lesson will then be explained to the class with special emphasis being given to making it completely clear. Students will be asked if they have any adjustments that they wish to make in the objective and to explain what value they think the objective will serve for them.
5. Students will be asked to read background material regarding environ-

mental action groups and to view films regarding the effects of community projects.

6. A discussion will be held regarding the information gleaned by students in their reading. As part of this discussion, students will be taught how to develop criteria for making judgments, and how to use these criteria in judging. Emphasis will be given to helping students develop a rationale for the judgments they make.

7. In those instances where there is apparent difficulty in learning how to make judgments, the self-instructional package on "How to Make Judgments" will be given. (More able students will be asked to help those experiencing difficulty.)

8. The teacher will model the process of making judgments between two possible environmental programs. Reference will be made regarding how this relates to the achievement of the objective.

9. Students will be asked to make judgments between some possible environmental programs The teacher will assist them by helping them learn to evaluate in a step-by-step fashion. Focus will be upon forming and using criteria to make proper judgments and developing rationales which explain the basis upon which the evaluation was performed.

10. Students will be given several examples of environmental programs and asked to rank them from best to worst and write an explanation justifying their rankings. The teacher will then show students how he would rank the programs and ask the students to compare their rankings with his. Differences in rankings between students and between students and teacher will be discussed and appropriate feedback given.

11. Students will be given a series of opinions concerning solutions to local environmental problems. They will be asked to evaluate the opinions and turn in their written evaluations to the teacher. Feedback will be given.

Notice in the strategy above, the application of principles outlined in this chapter. Step 1 makes reference to the preassessment necessary to determine if students have the appropriate skills necessary for a study of this kind. Entry behaviors are determined in step 1 and in step 2 remediation is provided. Perceived purpose is brought about in steps 3 and 4. First the children are involved and then asked to indicate what value achieving the objective may have for them. Revealing the objective takes place in step 4 and again in step 8. Feedback is given in steps 2, 6, 7, 9, 10, and 11. Individualizing instruction was evidenced in step 2 where remedial assistance was given to students without proper entry behaviors. The preassessment in step 1 was also evidence of individualization. In step 7 the self-instructional package that was given is further evidence of individualized instruction. Steps 5 and 6 are designed to serve as en route behavior activities. These steps provide the student with the knowledge about the terms and basic knowledge necessary to begin a study of evaluation. Steps 8, 9, and 10 constitute analogous practice. Notice how the teacher has planned to reduce the amount of his own input as students proceed through the steps. Finally, in step 11, students are given an opportunity for equivalent practice with feedback. After completion of this step students should be ready for evaluation.

Exercise 8–5   Preparing an Instructional Strategy

Write an objective and formulate a strategy for helping children achieve it which incorporates the elements that are illustrated in the example.

References

Bloom, Benjamin S. (ed.), *Taxonomy of Educational Objectives: The Classification of Educational Goals, Handbook I: Cognitive Domain.* New York: McKay, 1956.

Emmer, Edmund T., and Gregg B. Millett, *Improving Teaching Through Experimentation: A Laboratory Approach.* Englewood Cliffs, N.J.: Prentice-Hall, 1970.

Hunkins, Francis P., *Questioning Strategies and Techniques.* Boston: Allyn and Bacon, 1972.

Krathwohl, David R., *et al., Taxonomy of Educational Objectives: The Classification of Educational Goals, Handbook II: Affective Domain.* New York: McKay, 1964.

Popham, W. James, and Eva Baker, *Systematic Instruction.* Englewood Cliffs, N.J.: Prentice-Hall, 1970.

Searles, John E., *A System for Instruction.* Scranton, Pa.: International Textbook Company, 1967.

Suchman, J. Richard, *The Elementary School Training Program in Scientific Inquiry.* U.S. Department of Health, Education, and Welfare, Office of Education, Cooperative Research Project No. 216. Urbana: University of Illinois, 1958.

Taba, Hilda, *Teachers' Handbook for Elementary Social Studies,* Introd. Ed. Reading, Mass.: Addison-Wesley, 1967.

Victor, Edward, *Science for the Elementary School,* 2d ed. London: Macmillan/Collier-Macmillan Limited, 1970.

Wright, Theodore H., "Learning to Listen: A Teacher's or a Student's Problem?" *Phi Delta Kappan* 53 (June 1971): 625–28.

9
Planning Learning
Experiences in Science

In preceding chapters, we have shown many of the different components of the teaching/learning process, including the following:

1. Science includes concepts, attitudes, and processes.
2. Writing precise instructional objectives is the starting place for planning instruction.
3. It is wise to find out, by preassessment, where students are in relation to the stated objectives.
4. Organizing subject matter for conceptual development is more than displaying a collection of topics.
5. Students learn best when involved in their learning.
6. Strategies for learning science vary in accord with the purpose of the lesson.
7. Many different learning methods exist for providing a strategic learning process involving students.

Consider the situation in which you are assigned a group of students for the purpose of teaching them something in science. Your immediate concern would be something like "What shall I do with them?" Using the above brief list as a guide, thoughts such as the following should occur:

1. What I choose to teach in science should reflect the concepts, processes, and attitudes of science.
2. I should identify one or more end-points to the learning experience to specify the kinds of behaviors that would indicate that the student has accomplished the purpose of the lesson.
3. One of the first steps would be to find out what these students know and can do relative to the objectives specified.
4. Before planning the specific learning experiences I should decide on the concepts and skills to be developed and write the objectives in line with those concepts and skills.

5. The strategic plan for implementation of the learning experience should correspond with the type of behaviors specified in the objectives.
6. The learning experiences developed should involve the students to a great degree, with a high amount of the information to be learned coming from those experiences.

In this chapter we will discuss the techniques of planning for instruction in ways that will make maximum use of our knowledge of learning science. Planning for instruction is the process by which the broad goals of education for science are actualized in specific learning experiences. Planning occurs at the program level, the course level, the unit level, and the lesson level. Certain characteristics of planning are common to each level. These and other characteristics unique to a specific level will be discussed in this chapter.

OBJECTIVES

The reading materials and exercises of this chapter are designed to assist you in developing the ability to:

1. Develop a resource unit plan which includes a rationale, content, objectives, learning activities, materials, and evaluation activities.
2. Develop a teaching unit plan which includes a statement of content, objectives, learning activities, materials, and evaluation activities.
3. Develop consecutive lesson plans which contain as a minimum the objective, learning activities to achieve the objective, and evaluation activities to assess the accomplishment of the objective.

The Necessity for Planning

Making instructional plans is not a favorite topic of discussion among teachers or students planning to be teachers. What comes to mind when someone mentions "lesson plans" is usually a rather dreary image of a teacher laboriously writing lists of items in a plan book or in searching for materials to include in a resource unit. The textbook image of a lesson plan is usually very comprehensive. When a teacher of elementary school age children is faced with as many as eleven different subjects to be taught, it is not practical to think of constructing a one-page lesson plan for each subject, for each day of the week throughout the school year. That effort would result in approximately 2000 pages of lesson plans.

Nevertheless, the teacher will teach those 2000 lessons whether or not a separate, one-page lesson plan is made for each one. It goes without saying that the teacher, who obviously knows more about the subject area than the student, could create a very effective lesson for some topic without extensive prior planning. In addition, extemporaneous experiences in a classroom which result in learning are not uncommon. It also seems evident that most teachers can *not* operate an effective learning environment throughout the school year on an "off-the-cuff" basis. Where is the practical point between the extremes of no planning, on the one hand, and having one-page lesson plans for each subject, on the other?

Planning for instruction, in our opinion, is a necessity in order to provide an effective learning environment. It is also our opinion that planning instruction is an individual process. Some teachers will need to make more specific plans than others. For some teachers certain subject areas in which they are more comfortable will require less rigorous planning. The strategy to be used for instruction may suggest different degrees of planning for different individuals. The teacher with a good perception of the goals of the lesson, with the knowledge of the subject area, and with a knowledge of the students may be able to conduct an inquiry-oriented discussion armed only with one stated divergent question. On the other hand, lessons in which a directed discussion is needed may require a carefully developed plan even for the very experienced teacher.

Throughout the remainder of this chapter you should keep in mind that the primary goal of making good plans for instruction is for the improvement of the learning situation. If an instructional plan results in an effective learning experience, then it is a good plan. But, no matter how attractive or complete a plan is, it cannot be considered a good plan if it does not accentuate learning. In some schools all teachers file a weekly plan of their teaching with the principal prior to the beginning of the week. This practice allows the principal to keep in touch with what is going on in the classroom and also provides directions to a substitute teacher if one is required on the spur of the moment.

The Benefits of Planning

Instructional plans should assist the teacher in maintaining a close relationship between the goals of science education adopted by the school system, the units of study selected, and the daily experiences of students within those units. For example, you recall from our discussion about concept development that students require a great deal of experience, over a long period of time, to adequately develop a concept. Furthermore, the usefulness of a concept is in its application to the study of other phenomena. Without a coordinated program of study, the long-range development of concepts may never materialize. As another example, consider the situation in which students are taught the difference between observation skills and inference skills but then do not have the opportunity to develop the skills further in other units. The consequence of this is that, like any skill, the students will lose these abilities. Instructional planning serves to keep these kinds of long-range developments in mind.

Instructional plans should provide a means by which teachers can communicate about the teaching/learning situation. Teachers who share instructional responsibility for a group of students must devise means by which they can communicate about the intent of the learning situations. In some cases the point of articulation is in keeping all concerned with the situation informed of the experiences of the students. In some team-teaching situations, one teacher will do the planning for the entire team and then share the plans with other members of the team for their implementation. Team planning and teaching is gaining favor in many school systems. Benefits of group planning and providing for a range of expertise for the needs of special students is being recognized. The isolated teacher in the self-contained classroom is less of a fact today than it once was.

Instructional plans should provide a means by which the ability to forecast an effective learning environment can be improved. A plan of instruction is actually a prediction. You are predicting that "*If* I do such and such with the students, *then* they will gain in this way." It is not unusual for a new teacher or a teacher new to her students to make planning errors. However, if generalizations about effective teaching for these students can be obtained from the experience, then it is worthwhile. The desire to obtain feedback from students to improve instruction will be a strong motivation for keeping records of effective lessons. However, do not infer that we are proposing that you "perfect" a set of lesson plans and use them from year to year without deviation. Although groups of students will be different and some learning experiences will need to be changed, you will still profit from making use of plans used in previous learning situations if appropriate feedback has been made on those experiences and incorporated into revised plans.

Levels of Planning

Generally speaking, planning for instruction occurs at four levels. Program planning is the development of the scope and sequence of learning experiences which spread across several grade levels. Course or level planning is the development of more particular experiences for students of a narrow age or ability range, usually extending over a period of one or two semesters. Unit planning usually involves only a few weeks and will deal with a specific topic of concept or process. Lesson plans will be developed for short periods of thirty minutes to three hours and will usually deal only with one or two objectives.

Program Planning

School systems often have a science curriculum committee made up of teachers and administrators from all the grades in the building served by the committee. This committee's task is to make recommendations to the administration for the direction of the science program. This may include developing a scope and sequence for the program, writing program level objectives, identifying inservice needs, and developing a system for purchase and distribution of supplies and equipment. In many school systems a particular program is adopted. In this way the scope and sequence is identified, the necessary materials can be purchased in kit form, and, in some cases, the company will assist in implementing the program.

Course or Level Planning

School science programs are taught as courses or levels. In most schools science programs are organized by grade levels. However, in some schools, students are arranged in different kinds of groups, such as by ability levels, by broad-age groups, or by interest in the topics being studied. Whatever the type of student group, one or a few teachers will have charge of it for a few months. The science taught during this time will often be an assigned part of the commercial program. In this case the course or level planning will consist essentially of that which the program authors have built into the program. In instances where one or a small group of teachers design their own course, they must be sure to make it be a part of the total program, consistent with the program goals.

Unit Planning

A course or level of study is broken down into units, each lasting from one to a few weeks at the most. A unit will usually center around a topic of interest (insects, stars, motion) or around a process skill (observing properties, hypothesizing). Throughout a course of study the units of study may or may not have a relationship, depending upon the goals of the program. Generally there will be some sequential development from one unit to another. In many instances, a teacher will merely implement the unit of study as developed in the part of the program designated and purchased for use by his/her group.

Three types of units may be in use in a given school or by a given teacher. A commercial unit is a part of a purchased program for use in the school system. This unit will center around a textbook or laboratory experience and will be supplemented by various media, equipment, supplemental readings, and evaluation exercises. A resource unit is one constructed by a teacher for a topic of study. The resource unit contains a broad variety of possible learning experiences, materials, and evaluation activities. Teaching units are the actual plans made by a teacher for use with a specific group of students. The development of a teaching unit may begin with a commercial unit, a resource unit, or be developed specifically for this purpose. These three types of units will be explained more fully in subsequent sections of this chapter.

Lesson Plans

Lesson plans are those which are made to accomplish a specific objective(s). In some cases, these plans may be done daily. But in other instances, a single objective could be taught in as few as fifteen minutes or in several class sessions. The general make-up of a lesson plan will include an objective, the learning activities designed to help students achieve that objective, and the concepts or questions associated with achieving the objective. The lesson plan may also contain reference to how students will be evaluated. Lessons are derived from units of study. In this way the objectives will be consistent with those of the unit. It is not unusual for a teacher to plan lessons in isolation from a unit, and in some cases there may be justification for this. But in general, learning consists of a series of lessons which are part of a unit.

Although teachers seldom write out their plans for instruction in sufficient detail to be able to be used by someone else, there is usually a great deal of planning which takes place by teachers and school systems. In this exercise, you are given some suggestions for examining the amount and kind of planning which is used by elementary science faculty.

Exercise 9–1   Investigation of Practice of Planning for Instruction

Consider the points mentioned in the preceding questions and other questions you might have about planning instruction. Then visit a school system which does have a comprehensive elementary school science program. Ask questions such as the following:

1. Is there a school-wide plan for science education?
2. Who is responsible for coordinating the total science curriculum?
3. Is a commercial program(s) in use by the school?
4. Are there examples of units having been produced by local teachers?
5. Prepare a report summarizing the results of your visit. The report should be your interpretation of the amount of planning for science instruction in the school visited.

Unit Plans

Of the four types of plans described above, unit and lesson plans are of the most concern to teachers. In this section we want to explore in more detail the characteristics and use of the three types of units. Teachers will generally devise lesson plans based on units of study and our discussion later of lesson plans will be from this frame of reference.

Ultimately, the teacher must develop a teaching unit. The development of the teaching unit will most likely emanate from a resource unit constructed by the teacher or someone else or from a commercial unit purchased for use in the school. Our study of units will begin by exploring commercial units and resource units and then continue with a study of teaching units.

Commercial Units

Several years ago, a study of planning units would have included a category of "textbook units." At that time, almost all popular elementary school science programs included a student textbook. Teachers based their instructional program around a study of the units included in the textbook series. By contrast, many contemporary science programs do not include a textbook for each student. Due to this change in organizational patterns, a category of units termed "commercial units" is more appropriate.

The category of commercial units includes any type of science unit available for purchase. In most instances, commercial science programs are made up of a number of units on each grade or course level. All of the units in the K–6 or K–8 pattern form some type of unified whole. Chapter 12 of this textbook describes representative contemporary science programs available for use in schools.

In addition, teachers can sometimes locate special sources of commercial units. A steel company may produce a unit dealing with the process used in that industry or the benefits they provide society. A

Classroom instruction is often centered around a commercial science program.

group concerned with saving the environment may develop a unit for the purpose of teaching about some ecological problem. Reading professional journals' classified sections will often produce such unit sources.

The primary characteristic of the commercial unit is that someone has developed it in such a way that a "prescription" for teaching is built into the program. That is, the authors based the arrangement of the program on the development of concepts, processes, and attitudes they thought were most appropriate. Some of the recent curricular development literature has referred to these programs as "teacher proof." The implication is that if the teacher will merely follow the directions, then an effective learning environment for science will automatically follow. Few really condone this point of view, but in actuality, many teachers teach science exclusively by following the suggestions of the teacher's guide.

The benefits of following the scope and sequence of commercial units are appropriate to some situations. Using the units of a well-constructed commercial program will automatically build an articulated sequence of learning into the science program. In a situation where a less than acceptable science program exists the adoption of a single commercial program may provide the needed scope and sequence to the program.

Using a complete commercial program relieves the teachers of the burden of ordering and arranging the necessary equipment and supplies. This is especially true of the nontextbook programs which include a great deal of equipment. To have an adequate science program requires equipment; to have equipment requires time by the teacher unless it is purchased as a kit. Most teachers simply do not have the time.

Another reason for using commercial units is the quality of learning experiences included. Many contemporary science programs have been developed by a group of experts and thoroughly tested in the field. The input from many different people and practical experience of using these programs has resulted in well-developed programs which are rich in good science experiences for children.

One of the criticisms which may be made of commercial units is that they have been developed for use with a general population of students rather than the specific group of students in your community. They attempt to cater to the needs and interests of the mythical average population. However, your students may not conform to the average. Your community may have unique resources and needs. It is difficult to imagine any science program providing an optimum learning environment if only the basic commercial program is taught.

Even with these faults we believe that most teachers will find commercial units useful in their classrooms. We are quick to add, however, that in almost all situations it will be desirable to add to and take away from the unit to more specifically meet the needs of your students. We accept the point of view that a good commercial unit is a good starting point for planning science instruction. The following comments are directed at making effective use of commercial units for planning science instruction.

At the heart of most commercial programs of science is a teacher's guide. Two types of teacher guides are prevalent. The first type includes a copy of the printed student material as the core of most pages and places comments to the teacher around the margin. The second type, generally used with the nontextbook programs, is a separate publication intended for the teacher's use. In both cases you are likely to find the same parts provided for your assistance in planning lessons.

Although each commercial program is different, some characteristics are common to many of them. The paragraphs which follow illustrate some of these characteristics.

BACKGROUND AND RATIONALE

The commercial program authors' first purpose in helping you use the program is to convey to you the rationale explaining the intent of the unit. There is more than one approach to teaching students about batteries, bulbs, and circuits. This approach is reflected in the way in which the learning materials are written. To make effective use of the materials it is imperative that you understand the approach being used. In addition, it is necessary that you understand the content being covered by this unit and/or the process skills being developed. This is where you may wish to modify the program. If the rationale or the content is not in line with your interpretations of the task at hand, it is best to stop and identify another approach on your own or from another commercial program.

OBJECTIVES

In the margin of a student textbook page or some other more convenient place, it is now common to find some statement of objectives of the unit and lesson. These statements of objective range from being very precise in some programs to very ambiguous in others. In some instances, the statement of objective may be used to describe student activity rather than terminal performance ability. For example, consider the following statements:

1. Discuss life in a jungle.
2. Classify insects according to some obvious features.
3. Draw a graph of the temperature of water as it is cooled.
4. State an operational definition of a living object when provided with information about that living object.

The value of objectives is their assistance in providing for learning experiences for students. After reading the first statement, I am inclined to ask "Why?" or "What should be the point of the discussion?" This is more of an activity than the description of a terminal point to a lesson. The second statement describes a behavior which is a general class of behaviors, one which seems to have a purpose. By the same reasoning, the third statement is an activity, and the fourth statement an objective. Once again, the important point is to consider the value of the statement to you in planning the instruction and to the student in knowing the intent of the lesson.

Most teachers find it very difficult to adopt someone else's objectives as written. In most instances teachers will see the need for teaching a given unit, but will want to achieve different objectives. Before attempting to select learning and evaluation activities, a teacher should have a clear picture of the objectives he or she intends to pursue with the unit of instruction.

LEARNING ACTIVITIES

In some commercial programs, the student textbook is the center of the learning approach. In these programs, the teacher's guide will suggest moving from one unit to the next, in the sequence arranged in the text. Along the way exercises will be built into the text or in the student manual sometimes provided. Some of the exercises will be paper-and-pencil types with others being more experienced based and requiring the use of some type of laboratory equipment. In addition, films, film strips, and supplemental readings will be suggested. Most textbook programs will provide some suggestions for sequencing the daily routine of the classroom.

In the nontextbook science programs today, the focus of instruction is on the activities in which students are to be involved. The teacher's guide provides directions on how to conduct the activities with the students. Needed materials, films, filmstrips, or worksheets are recommended in the sequence as appropriate. Some programs offer a wide degree of flexibility in the sequencing of these activities while others are very specific.

In either type of program, the teacher still needs to plan the day-to-day routine of the learning experiences. The degree to which you follow the suggestions of the teacher's guide will depend upon the specificity of the guide, your familiarity with science, and with this program, and the needs of your own students as you perceive them. The point is this: In an activity-oriented study of science, it is very difficult to write a unit of instruction without specific knowledge of the teacher who will be using it and the students who will be learning from it. Almost all teachers will need to spend time with the commercial units in order to understand them sufficiently to make adequate lesson plans. If there is any one common error which teachers make in the use of commercial programs, it is that they blindly follow someone's written suggestions about how to teach the unit without taking into account the daily needs of their own students.

Commercial programs differ in the format used for teacher's guides. In some cases they are very explicit and in others very general. If the purpose of a teachers' guide is to provide assistance to the teacher in the use of the program, then an examination of various teachers' guides should determine the ease with which they can be used for planning instruction.

Exercise 9–2 Investigation of Teacher's Guides

Identify several programs for elementary school science. Obtain a teacher's guide from each program or a representative sampling of the teacher's guide. Consider the following points with one or more guides:

1. Examine the guide to see if it contains the parts listed in the reading portion of this section.
2. Examine the organization of the parts to see if they are arranged conveniently.

3. Use the guide to plan a lesson. Compare your plan to those of other students. Discuss the different plans made by others in order to compare the relative value of using the teacher's guide.

Resource Units

The most comprehensive of the units described here is known as the resource unit because of its purpose and use. The resource unit is made to be applicable to a variety of situations. It will consist of a wide variety of instructional components on some topic. It is common for college classes in teacher education to include the development of a resource unit. The college student is not likely to have a specific group of students in mind, perhaps not even a specific grade level. As a rule of thumb, the resource unit is never finished. New or updated materials are added on a continuing basis. Specific lessons can be derived from this "pool" of information at any time to suit the needs of students. The following paragraphs list and describe the components of a typical resource unit.

OVERVIEW AND RATIONALE

The development of a resource unit begins with the identification of a topic of study. The source of the topic may be a favorite area of study, a topic with which you are more knowledgeable, or one that is assigned to you because of the school system's overall plan for science instruction. Because of the extensive amount of time which goes into a resource unit, a team effort is often warranted. A group of teachers could decide on the topics to be developed and then each individual or small group of teachers identify the topic they will develop. The resource units could then be shared by all members of the planning team. Topics of resource units would be exemplified as follows:

Interest Areas
  The Moon
  Effects of Glaciers
  Worms, Snakes, and Other Crawling Creatures

Concepts
  Conservation of Energy
  An Ecosystem
  The Changing Universe
  All Things Interact

Processes
  Observations
  Observations and Inferences

Model Building
Constructing Hypothesis

Technology
Nuclear Reactors
Waste Treatments
Petroleum Refineries

After a topic for a resource unit has been selected, the teacher can begin to identify the concepts or subject matter to be covered in the unit and to organize these concepts into a knowledge structure. The structure of the knowledge to be covered in the resource unit is an important first step. Properly structuring knowledge will allow greater clarity and efficiency in writing objectives and selecting learning activities and materials. Most likely this section of the resource unit will consist of a list of concept statements depicting the knowledge structure with an included rationale for the unit.

OBJECTIVES

Certainly a great deal has been said in this text about the desirability of writing precise instructional objectives to describe the intended learning outcomes. We have also indicated that the use of objectives has been abused in some learning situations. For example, some teachers allow objectives to inhibit the flexibility of the learning situation by ignoring spontaneous ideas by students and strictly adhering to the original learning specifications. However, even though some flexibility may be lost by following a given set of objectives there is much to be gained by the increased continuity they provide in a well-organized resource unit. Once the unit is constructed and the objectives formed, a teacher may be as flexible as the situation requires. However, if he/she avoids organization for the sake of flexibility, chaos is likely to be the result. In preparing a resource unit the learning objectives should be written to correspond to the knowledge structure developed. It is useful to key the objective statement to the concept statement to which it relates. With this degree of correspondence between statements, the selection of learning materials and activities is greatly aided. In addition, the specification of objectives provides a convenient means of clarifying the intent of the knowledge structure to identify possible ommissions.

INITIATING ACTIVITIES

"You can lead a horse to water, but you can't make him drink." So it is with students. Simply because you choose to begin a study of the fossils in your region on October 18th at 10:00 A.M., there is no reason to expect that the students will also be inclined to pursue that topic at that time. The initial challenge of any unit of study is to bring the attention of the students to the topic being studied. In fact, initiating activities that could be termed "mind grabbers," "gee-wizz experiences," or "magic" effects could turn out to be the most significant part of the unit. Examples could be the color change when two liquids are mixed, the unexpected behavior of a bimetallic strip, or the unusual behavior of such plants as the Venus Fly Catcher. A teacher may not think of these events. However, elementary science "source books" or commercial programs usually provide ideas for initiating activities. More than one initiating activity may be needed for a unit of study in order to keep the students' attention on the task at hand.

LEARNING ACTIVITIES

From the Chapter 7 material on methods of learning science, it was pointed out that a great diversity of approaches might be taken to learn about science. In determining what approach should be taken two points should be kept in mind. The first is that in selecting learning activities you should make sure that they correlate with the stated objectives and offer practice in achieving these objectives. The second point is that a variety of activities should be included in order to maintain a high level of pupil participation. A steady diet of any one method will soon lose its edge for keeping students' attention to the lessons. The learning activities should be written separately on file cards so that the design and use of the actual teaching unit can be made more flexible. By doing this, the teacher can easily rearrange them to accommodate local constraints and pupil interests and needs. Note that in the resource unit, there is no need to confine the learning activities to those which would be appropriate to only one teaching strategy. Keep in mind that the purpose of the resource unit is to develop a "learning pool" for a specified topic of study from which the specific teaching unit can be developed.

MATERIALS

To conduct learning activities in science, you will obviously need some science equipment. Throughout the literature there are all sorts of "neat ideas" for building and/or using equipment. For example, most contemporary science programs contain some unique equipment which can, of course, be used in a number of different ways. The disadvantage of this unique equipment is its cost. On the other hand, is the fact that effective use can be made of very simple equipment, which can be purchased inexpensively or constructed with little cost or effort. For example, every student in the class can learn first hand about the equal arm balance by using a straw, a straight pin for support, and paper clips for weights. The advantage of maintaining resource units on your favorite science teaching topics is to accumulate the many good ideas you will encounter through the years. This is especially true of equipment ideas.

Material selection should be viewed in a broader perspective than just equipment used for experiments. Instructional media is the next most obvious category of learning materials. Films, filmstrips, transparencies, film loops, readings, audio recordings, and other such forms are appropriate. One limitation often experienced in using audio-visual materials is that they may be available to you but must be requested in advance. Care should be taken to indicate the source of the item so that it is available when you need it. In addition some items may be stored in various locations. You may also want to consider sources of science materials outside your own school system. Government agencies and industries often have available free and inexpensive materials for use by schools.

EVALUATION

Little will be said about evaluation at this time. The entire chapter which follows is devoted to this subject. However, something must be said regarding the relation of evaluation to the rest of the unit. The most obvious point is that the evaluation activities should correspond directly to the objectives specified by the unit. Another important point is that the resource unit can contain a variety of means to evaluate student performance and can be collected and made available as needed.

To develop a resource unit is a never-ending task. To be kept current you will change the contents as appropriate. To begin the development of a resource unit, follow the steps outlined below.

Exercise 9–3   Developing a Resource Unit

1. The initial step is to identify a topic for the unit. This topic is one which should be of a continuing interest to you. It may be on a concept, a process, or a technological aspect of science.
2. Through a study of the nature of the topic, begin a list of concepts, processes, and/or attitudes to further define the limits of the topic selected.
3. From the statements of concepts, processes, and attitudes, the next step is to write instructional objectives which could be used as descriptions of possible student learning.
4. Learning activities need to be identified which provide for the learning of the objectives. Source books, professional journals, and daily experiences provide a source of these activities.
5. Collect descriptions of equipment, supplies, and media which are possible materials to be used in the learning activities.

6. Develop a bibliography of readings for professional and student use.
7. Develop a pool of evaluation techniques for assessing the development of these objectives.

Steps 1 through 3 will probably need to occur first. Additional objectives and the rest of the items will occur as they are found, usually not in this systematic order.

Teaching Units

The teaching unit is the most specific in nature of the three categories of units used by teachers. Resource units are a pool of learning opportunities a teacher can select to design an instructional sequence. Commercial units are more specific than resource units because they are usually designed with a more narrow range of activities and in a suggested sequence. However, they, too, can be used, more or less, as a resource unit from which specific lessons can be drawn. In contrast, the teaching unit is defined as being the actual teaching/learning activities designed for use with a specific group of students. One might picture it as being made up of a sequence of lesson plans. Although this is essentially so, there is more to a teaching unit than putting together a series of lesson plans.

Teaching units are developed from a variety of sources. A majority of the teaching units developed by teachers probably emanate from the use of commercial programs. From these programs, the teacher develops the teaching unit to meet the specific needs of a given group of students. The specified content of the unit is accepted or modified. The objectives contained in the program will probably be altered somewhat. Suggested learning activities will be examined and others added as needed. Materials will be sought to support the learning activities. Depending upon the program and its quality, commercial programs may be the easiest source from which to construct teaching units. Two factors contribute to this. Many of the contemporary programs have been field tested on a population of students. In most cases materials for every student will have been purchased and will make it easy for you to plan and do the activities with your students.

The resource unit is another source of ideas for developing teaching units. The resource unit, as a pool of learning resources, provides a source of materials from which teachers can select and sequence a series of learning activities to meet the needs of students. The difficulties encountered in making use of resource units include the fact that the resource material you need may be unavailable as well as the difficulty you may experience in using them. Teachers will tend to develop resource units around favorite topics of study. Time and energy does not allow the development of them for all areas, especially for the beginning teacher. Furthermore, once they are constructed, some teachers will find them difficult to use due to the time needed to become familiar with the sources and develop them into a teaching unit. This accounts for the greater popularity of commercial units over resource units.

Sometimes the teacher may be confronted with the necessity of preparing a teaching unit on topics not covered in resource units and commercial programs. In this case, the teacher may simply develop a teaching unit without reference to predesigned sources of ideas. In the event of some new topic or one in which learning materials are not customarily developed for this age level, the teacher may be faced with the problem of teaching the unit without the benefit of other aids.

From whatever the source, a teaching unit will have the same characteristics. These characteristics are the sum total of the teacher's viewpoint on learning. If you have kept a running account of the major points expressed by the first eight chapters of this text, you have a list of the characteristics of a good teaching unit. Some of these points are listed in the introduction to this chapter.

The content of a teaching unit is probably obvious to you by this time. To provide for effective learning the teaching units should include the following:

1. Objectives: Precise statements of the behaviors to be expected of the students
2. Content: Description of the content to be taught by the unit (concepts, processes, and attitudes)
3. Learning Activities: The specific activities which will allow students to achieve the objectives
4. Learning Materials: Including reading material, worksheets, films and other media, and outside resources
5. Equipment and Supplies: All laboratory equipment
6. Evaluation Techniques: Descriptions of means by which the objectives will be assessed including test items.

Although the list of contents of a teaching unit is generally the same as those listed above, there is no one set format for organizing these elements into a teaching unit which is better than any other. Some teachers find that developing teaching units on file cards provides a highly convenient means by which to modify the unit as needs indicate. Another format used by teachers is a listing of the above categories in parallel columns. Development of the various parts can then be completed in a way which shows the parallel relationship of the parts. Whatever the format used, it is more essential to include all of the elements of planning than to conform to one specific form. The way in which the parts of the teaching unit are arranged should depend on the teacher's convenience. The inclusion of all of the parts in proper relationship should insure greater continuity and organization in the learning process and consequently be more beneficial to students.

Although teaching units vary greatly from one teacher to another, there are a few characteristics which are indicative of good teaching units. The first of these is continuity. It has been said that one way to visualize a teaching unit is as a collection of lesson plans. But to be a *unit* the lessons being taught must lead toward some predetermined concept, process, and attitude goals. It is difficult to predict what students will be doing on the thirteenth day of a unit because it will depend on the accomplishments of the students during the first twelve days. But it is possible to chart in a sequential order the direction of thought to be developed through the unit. This may be the primary purpose of making teaching units—to give purpose and direction to the day-to-day learning experiences of children.

Another characteristic of the learning activities in a teaching unit is variety. Maintaining student motivation for learning is a continuing concern of the effective teacher. A unit of instruction which incorporates a variety of approaches is likely to be more successful on this count than one in which the same learning style is used over and over again. By browsing through the chapter on learning methods, you can be reminded of the great variety of learning methods which could be used.

Students are living in a world full of scientific relationships. It is difficult to see why any unit of instruction should not have activities which relate the concepts being studied to the daily life of the children. Local industry, parks, and museums provide a rich connection with reality. Current events of a scientific nature are also valuable to the classroom teacher in making science instruction vital and relevant. Therefore, in preparing science units, the teacher should use materials which articulate science principles with their actual experiences.

To relate what has been said here concerning teaching unit plans to concepts presented in earlier chapters it may be useful to generalize on a pattern of logical development of a teaching unit. To describe "what" it is that is to be taught, one can develop a knowledge structure of the appropriate concepts (see Chapter 6). Doing this would identify a relationship between the concepts to be taught. A second step would be to develop the objectives to specifically delineate the intended learning outcomes. The next step would be to identify the strategy or strategies which could be employed to reach each of these objectives (see Chapter 8). The specification of the strategy then suggests the kinds of learning activities which would be needed (see Chapter 7), the time needed to develop the learning outcomes, and the materials which will be needed.

The most common activity of elementary school science teachers is adapting commercial units to local needs. The purpose of this exercise is to provide you with experience in going through that process.

Exercise 9–4 Developing a Teaching Unit from a Commercial Unit

1. Select a commercial unit appropriate to your interests.
2. Identify the concepts to be learned by developing a knowledge structure.
3. List the objectives to be developed as a result of this unit. Be sure to identify only the terminal performances you will expect of students.
4. Describe the strategy you will use during this unit.
5. List in order the learning activities to be used in this unit. Extensive detail to time, equipment, media are not needed at this time.

Developing Lesson Plans

Lesson plans are the instructional and evaluative activities designed for the accomplishment of one or a few related objectives. Some plans may result in learning after only a few minutes, and others may require several hours of instructional time. Teachers often refer to their plans as daily lesson plans, but this restrictive measure should not be placed upon a plan. With the abundance of opportunities for learning in science, there is no need to stretch a short lesson to a full forty-minute period. On the other hand, the development of a concept may be too rushed to try to accomplish in that amount of time.

The format of a lesson plan, like the teaching unit plan, is highly personal. Each teacher will discover the most manageable format for his use. In our discussions about lesson planning, we are more concerned here with the process of development than the exact format to be used. The student who is learning to develop plans should be more concerned with including the appropriate components than with the format suggested in this text or by an instructor.

The process of developing lesson plans is undoubtedly time consuming. However, with experience, you should be able to limit the time necessary to make good lesson plans. In learning how to develop lesson plans, you need to learn how to use resources, how to adapt ideas to fit the needs of specific students, and how to arrange these ideas on a page in a useful format. The time spent learning to plan correctly is well worth it if it pays off in increased learning for students. This is, of course, the reason that planning is such a necessary element of good classroom instruction.

Components of Lesson Plans

As with unit plans, the components of a good lesson plan for instruction of elementary school science have actually been explained in the first eight chapters of this text. A brief explanation follows as a summary reminder to you of the task of lesson planning. The order of presentation is not necessarily the order in which you will write the components as you construct your plans.

Learning activities should provide for appropriate practice by students in the behavior indicated in the objective.

OBJECTIVES

At the heart of every lesson is an instructional objective. In almost all cases it will be a precise instructional objective which describes the observable behavior, the conditions under which it is to be observed, and the criterion for assessing its achievement. There are times when a lesson centers around an "experience," without a definite, precise outcome specified. In these instances, of course, no precise measurement of student achievement is warranted.

CONTENT

Each lesson should specify the concepts, principles, or factual material to be taught in the lesson. This should be consistent with the broad concepts being developed in the unit. It should be written in the way that a teacher can make use of it during the lesson. For example, ideas should be in a list format. Key symbols, words, formulas, etc., should be noted. The way in which they are listed may be somewhat dependent upon the strategy being used as well as what seems convenient to the teacher using the plan.

LEARNING ACTIVITIES

Although the strategy of the unit or series of lessons within a unit is not listed within each lesson plan, it is reflected throughout in the way in which the activities are selected and sequenced. An expository approach to teaching will require a different series of learning activities from an inquiry approach.

Three types of activities are usually appropriate. The first of these is some type of initiating activity or set induction. Students need to have some type of activity which will draw their attention to the task at hand and relate the task to some previous learning. Learning cannot occur without having the students' full attention. It is too much to assume they are automatically attracted to whatever the teacher lays before them. In getting the students' attention, it is often appropriate to tie this lesson in with some previous experience or current level of understanding. Or you might attempt to capture their attention through a dramatic presentation or through a thought-provoking question.

The main body of the lesson provides for the appropriate practice of the behavior specified by the objective. This practice should definitely be consistent with that called for in the objective. The degree of practice as well as the number and kinds of learning activities depends upon the state of learning of the student. Students will differ extensively in terms of their readiness for learning. This information is available from the results of the preassessment. The activities provided should reflect the strategy being employed, a variety of methods as appropriate, and sufficient recognition of the specific needs of these students for learning.

In most cases, some culminating activity may be appropriate. This activity is usually in the form of equivalent practice for the objectives of this lesson. In many cases, it will be appropriate to use activities which relate a particular lesson to others before it, providing for the student some experience that allows him to generalize over this and other experiences.

Throughout all of the experiences, it is appropriate for the teacher to provide feedback to the students on their accomplishments. At no time should the students have an uncertainty as to their rate of accomplishment and how this relates to the objectives being sought. A student who is not aware that he is deficient in some aspect of the lesson is not in a very good position to correct that status. A student who actually knows the material but is unsure of it is needlessly wasting time and energy.

PREASSESSMENT

It is important that students be provided with an efficient learning environment. If the lesson is a duplication of previously learned material, it may be wasting the student's time. If the material is too difficult for the student, this also is wasting the student's time and providing unneeded frustration for both teacher and student. In some instances it is appropriate to assess the specific behavior being sought and in other instances it is appropriate to test for the prerequisite skills needed to learn the terminal skills. Refer to Chapter 4, on preassessment, for more elaboration of this point.

MATERIALS AND EQUIPMENT

Not having in hand, when needed, the appropriate media, supplemental readings, glassware, supplies, or other equipment is one of the most frustrating points in planning lessons. Unfortunately this factor prevents otherwise effective plans from becoming successful learning experiences. Some experience with the subject matter of the lesson and experience with student needs may be necessary before a teacher can adequately anticipate all of the materials and equipment needs prior to the beginning of the lesson. With regard to planning for and using equipment materials, real flexibility is required in order to be able to accommodate the students' needs and interests in the lesson. This factor alone may encourage teachers to use "packaged" science programs. Field testing of these programs has already provided knowledge about divergent needs in classroom situations and has been provided for in the kits of materials.

EVALUATION

The key idea in evaluation that you need to be concerned with is that the behavior identified be consistent with the objective. That is, the objective specifies the intent of the lesson, the learning activities practice that behavior, and now the evaluation activities should measure the extent to which the objective is achieved. More about the techniques of this component is given in the next chapter.

Sample Lesson Plans

Several lessons are provided here as samples of what a lesson plan could be. The purpose is not to show you the most appropriate kinds of learning experiences for the objectives stated in each plan. Rather it is to demonstrate the variety of organizational plans. The type of plans, the way in which you arrange the components, will depend upon your style of operating in the classroom, your familiarity with the content of the lesson, the degree of structure to the lesson, and the amount of time you have to devote to planning instruction.

The first lesson, designed from a student-centered contemporary program, consists primarily of descriptions of activities to be done with the student. As you read the descriptions, you will note that the information provided does not allow someone unfamiliar with the activities with enough information to do the activity. In this case, the teacher has read the teacher's guide from the program, is familiar with the scope of the unit being taught, and may have taught the lesson at a previous time. This would be enough to remind him/her of the steps to be taken during the lesson.

The second lesson is built around a simulation activity involving descriptions of living things. Certainly it would be more motivating and valuable to the student to work with the living things directly, but time and convenience may not permit this. This teacher has learned of this activity from another teacher or professional journal and is adapting it to meet the need of students to classify information.

Lesson Plan One

REFERENCE: *Subsystems and Variables*, Parts: Whirly Bird System, Rand McNally & Company, 1970.
OBJECTIVE: To determine the effect of changes in one variable of a simple mechanical system.
CONTENT: Experimentation relies on manipulating only one variable at a time and investigating the effect it has on other components of the system.
SEQUENCE: Follows "invention" of variable concept and skill of using histograms to display data.

LEARNING ACTIVITIES:

1. Set: Have students review the variables of the W-B system by listing them on the boards.
2. Relate objective to student.
3. a. Have each student build a system
   b. Record this system on Manual, p. 26, Box A.
   c. Have them change one variable—ask to tell it aloud—then try it and record in Box B.
   d. Continue for eight examples.
   e. Write section "What did you find out?"
4. Have some groups present results of experiment. Bring out the manipulation variable that leads to conclusion.

5. Have students attempt to build a system which will turn 15–20 times before stopping. Observe their behavior to see if they do only change one variable at a time. Have students draw their systems on the board. In discussion stress the importance of systematically changing one variable at a time.

MATERIALS: One complete whirly bird system for each group of two students.

EVALUATION:

1. Watch students during exercise to note process of changing only one variable at a time.
2. Note comments made during discussions which reflect this point.
3. If still unsure, have some or all students demonstrate another example experiment individually.

Lesson Plan Two

CONCEPT: Likenesses among living things are bases for classification.
OBJECTIVE: Classify a given set of descriptions of living things by their characteristics as listed.
SEQUENCE: Previous lesson devoted to describing living objects by their properties.

TEACHER ACTIVITY	LEARNER ACTIVITY	TIME
1. "How many different kinds of dogs can you list?" Relate to convenience to classify.	1. List dog names	5
2. State objective		
3. "Group these paper slips in two groups by one of the characteristics." Then ask why they did it that way. Establish difference between groups. (Expect need to demo for some.)	3. Groups of 3 work with paper slips to classify	10
4. "Go on to classify the rest."	4. More classifying	15
5. Demo chart for writing down classification scheme. Help them do the same.	5. Students write down chart for classification.	15
6. Discuss ways in which they are classified.		15

Teacher Activity	Learner Activity	Time
7. Give them each one more item to classify individually.	7. Each student classifies item.	5
8. Have each student work on scheme for items in Kit B. Review results in groups of 4.	8. Classify items and review with others.	15

MATERIALS: Kits A, B, and C of living things description.

EVALUATION: Give each student Kit C to develop a classification scheme.

Note that in neither one of the above lessons does the teacher write down something like, "Move about from student to student, offering assistance as needed." That is the usual pattern of operation for this teacher. It would be quite redundant to continually write such a phrase.

Exercise 9–5   Developing a Lesson Plan

Develop a lesson plan for a level which you are planning to teach. For the purpose of this exercise, include the following information.

1. Description of the students to be taught including grade level and any special characteristics you may wish to "invent."
2. Describe the unit of instruction from which this lesson is to be taken by indicating the broad concepts being taught and a brief rationale as to the role of this unit in the total curriculum.
3. Arrange the lesson plan to include the following: (a) objectives, (b) learning activities, (c) materials, (d) evaluation activities; and (e) source of lesson.

You may wish to review the elements of an effective strategy discussed in Chapter 8 of this book.

Characteristics of Lesson Plans

Maintaining pupil involvement is probably the one key idea to an effective lesson. Students must be involved in the preassessment to find out what they can do. Involvement in the initiating activities is often appropriate in order to obtain their interest. Involvement in the primary learning activities is necessary in order that students practice the behavior to be learned. Of course, evaluation activities require student involvement. Maintaining motivation is usually dependent upon some type of involvement.

A lesson plan should reflect a strategy which is consistent with the behavioral level of the objective, the learning style of the students, and the broad goals of the unit and the program. In the previous chapter a great deal of explanation was made of the need for appropriate strategies. Suffice it to say that the selection of an appropriate strategy is the critical point for the successful design and implementation of a lesson plan.

Lesson plans should be consistent within themselves. The behaviors described by the objective should be consistent with the behaviors of the learning activities and the behaviors of the evaluation activities. Lesson plans should reflect consistency between other lessons of the unit. For example, later lessons of the unit should build upon earlier lessons, providing a sequential growth pattern for students.

Students are individuals. The lesson plan should reflect the teacher's willingness to provide for the individual's learning rate and style. This can be reflected in the use of preassessment results, and in the provision of alternative learning routes as appropriate to the learning task.

Exercise 9–6   Developing Consecutive Lesson Plans

The purpose of this exercise is to allow you to demonstrate your skills for developing a sequence of lesson plans. These lesson plans should be leading toward a common goal of one or more concepts, processes, or attitudes. The series of lessons should demonstrate the use of the principles of learning, the methods of learning science, and the use of a specified strategy.

To demonstrate this skill, prepare a teaching unit based on a commercial unit of your choice. Include at least five lesson plans within the unit. Refer to the previous exercises and readings to recall specific characteristics of a complete unit plan.

References

DeVito, Alfred, and Gerald H. Krockover, *Creative Sciencing, Ideas and Activities for Teachers and Children.* Boston: Little, Brown, 1976.

George, Kenneth D., Maureen A. Dietz, Eugene C. Abraham, *Science Investigations for Elementary School Teachers.* Boston: D. C. Heath, 1974.

Nelson, Leslie W., and George C. Lorbeer, *Science Activities for Elementary Children.* Dubuque, Iowa: Wm. C. Brown, 1976.

Sund, Robert B., Bill W. Tillery, Leslie W. Trowbridge, *Investigate and Discover: Elementary Science Lessons.* Boston: Allyn and Bacon, 1975.

10
Evaluation

For a science program to be effective, it must have an adequate system of evaluation. Regardless of the form the evaluation might take, it must provide certain basic information for the students involved, for the teachers and administrators, and for others viewing the programs or even the process of evaluation.

From the student viewpoint, the evaluation must indicate whether he does or does not know the information required, whether he can or cannot perform certain precise skills, or whether he can apply these skills. Secondly, the evaluation must also provide the student with adequate feedback. Within a reasonable length of time, the evaluation results must provide the student with the knowledge of how well he has succeeded in terms of prespecified criteria, as well as his relative standing in the class. Hopefully, the evaluation results might also show the student where his specific learning problems lie. Should the student not succeed in the science program initially, he then has some solid basis for retracing his steps, finding the area(s) that needs more work, and then rebuilding his information system so that he can succeed at a later date. Should he succeed, he needs to know how well he did in relation to his peers or in relation to the criteria developed for success.

Most teachers have different needs for evaluation. One of the least substantive of these needs and yet a very "real" one in most educational systems is to provide grades at certain points during the school year. Secondly, many teachers need to know before instruction begins, what the student knows regarding specific subject areas. With adequate preassessment, students can be: (a) guided to areas of instruction most suitable for them; (b) bypass materials they already know and become involved with higher level applications of these materials; (c) be given adjusted learning modes for more efficient instruction; (d) be excluded from instruction in areas where they have attained a certain level of expertise; or (e) given new objectives that more precisely reflect their interests and capabilities.

Other teacher's needs for evaluation may include the assessment of a particular instructional program. Since teaching procedures are constantly changing and since new science materials are flooding the market, teachers need to know what types of techniques, materials, and so on result in a change in student learning from that gained via the previous techniques or materials. Only with sophisticated evaluation instruments and procedures can satisfactory results be obtained. When new science programs are introduced, their value must be assessed in relation to the previous programs that are being replaced.

While all of the previous reasons for evaluation are quite useful at specified times, the most general need for evaluation is to determine what a student knows, what he can do, or what his attitudes are when instruction has been completed. If a student successfully completes his final evaluation, few questions are asked by either the student or his instructor. If, however, a student fails in his final evaluation, many possible questions could be asked: Did the student work hard enough? Were the objectives clear? Did the student direct his learning to the specific objectives? Were the questions clear enough? Did the evaluation reflect the objectives? Did the preassessment direct the student to his weaknesses? Were the learning activities free of ambiguity or were they at a level the student could perceive? Was there some flaw in the evaluation instrument?

These same needs teachers have for evaluation are also felt by administrators as well as others (parents, curriculum experts, educators and lay people interested in a particular program, and evaluation experts) viewing the program from the outside. Admittedly, while the needs for evaluation by the above groups are similar to those of the teacher, their view of the evaluation process, of the evaluation results, and even of the particular evaluation items might be notably different.

OBJECTIVES

1. Students must be able to explain the differences between norm-based and criterion-based evaluation and their applications to test construction in the schools.
2. Students must be able to prepare a means for evaluating students in terms of the various levels of the cognitive and affective domains of knowledge and incorporate the various possible forms of testing in the process.

The evaluation process is obviously complex and involves a wide range of interested individuals. However, our main concern here is to prepare you to evaluate the specific goals of instruction that you have in your class. Once a teacher is confident that his/her class is prepared through appropriate practice to achieve the specific goals he has outlined, the next step is to allow each student to demonstrate his competency through a properly prepared evaluation experience. One of the most serious mistakes made in evaluation is to prepare tests which do not accurately measure the extent to which students achieve objectives. This is particularly true of objectives in the affective domain and at the higher levels in the cognitive domain. The reason for this is that evaluation items can be prepared at the lower cognitive levels with a great deal less time and effort and with greater validity and reliability. Validity refers to the tests' ability to measure what is intended and reliability refers to its ability to measure consistently from one testing situation to another. In tests where students are simply required to recall information it is an easy matter to say that a particular recall item is a valid measure for remembering facts contained in the item. However, when it comes to making the same judgment about items written to evaluate the development of higher cognitive skills it is more difficult to demonstrate this close correspondence between the skill and the test item. In addition, formulating test items which validly measure higher cognitive abilities is a complex and taxing experience. When a teacher attempts to prepare items for measuring attitudes and higher cognitive abilities it is not readily apparent how this can be accomplished. It is necessary that he/she invent the means to evaluate these goals. Such requirements obviously impede the work of preparing valid measures.

Ordinarily with specific goals there is an associated level of performance expected. This implies a defensible level of competency which students must meet in order to satisfy the requirements of the objective. Evaluation which has expected performance levels is referred to as *criterion-based evaluation* and differs significantly from *norm-based evaluation* which has been in vogue in testing for many years.

Most of the evaluation procedures in our schools today are norm-referenced. Norm-referenced evaluation usually answers the following questions: How do the students perform in relation to other students in the class? How do students perform in relation to all others in the school; in relation to others of his state or geographical area; in relation to others throughout the nation? In all of the above cases, students are evaluated in relation to others.

Criterion-referenced evaluation has an entirely different base. Rather than determining how well a student has done in relation to his peers, criterion-referenced evaluation is used to determine how well students perform in relation to a certain established level of competency.

Norm-Referenced Evaluation

Since all of the chapters of this book require a criterion-referenced evaluation, norm-referenced evaluation will receive less emphasis. Virtually every school system throughout the nation uses norm-referenced evaluation procedures at one time or another. In most school systems, norm-referenced evaluation is the standard for providing the grades that are eventually used to determine success or failure for students.

While the practice of not grading students exists and is perhaps becoming more popular, most schools still give grades. In some schools, traditional grading systems have been replaced by such hybrids as providing grades of *S* (satisfactory) and *U* (unsatisfactory). This compromise sometimes brings about other problems. Unless a written explanation accompanies the *S* or *U*, or a parent interview is used to explain in depth the meaning of these two grades, the parent (and perhaps the child as well) is unaware of what the student can or cannot do. One would wonder whether a particular student's *S* is as good as an *A* or as bad as a *D*. Or could an *S* mean working up to potential while a *U* means working below potential (work that was average but that should have been far above average)? Sometimes the *S* and *U* grading system is added to by providing students with *S+, S, S–, U+, U,* and *U–* working as the *A,B,C* system.

Norm-referenced evaluation, as stated previously, is an attempt to show a student's relationship to other members of his class. If everyone were to receive the same grade or nearly the same grade, the intent of showing plausible relationships would be defeated. Therefore, many teachers in building norm-referenced tests attempt to provide enough difficult items so that a spread in grades occurs. Thus, the goal in too many norm-referenced situations is not only to determine a student's mastery of a particular body of knowledge but also to spread the grades adequately so that later report card grades can be justified to students, parents, and administrators.

In some instances this attempt to provide difficult items leads to the use of questions that come from the minutia within a text, items that call for much memorization. Virtually every student can remember at least one course in which he was required to memorize or pay close attention to the footnotes in order to do well in the exam. In the few instances where the above has occurred, the main emphases of the course have been subverted by trivia.

A large percentage of the standardized tests now available are norm-referenced. They have been designed to show relationships among students having different levels of ability. They are particularly useful in comparing the ability of students from widely separated geo-

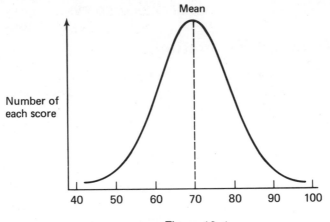

Figure 10–1

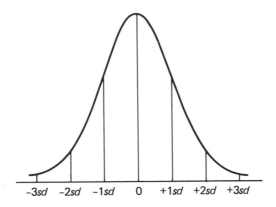

Figure 10–2

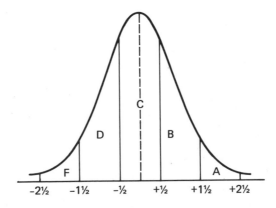

Figure 10–3

graphical areas. Should a standardized test be considered for a particular system, the faculty would want to look closely at the norm groups used for the tests under consideration. Other things being equal, one would logically select a test with norm groups that approximate the selecting school's population (Tyler, 1974).

In a typical norm-referenced situation where letter grades are given after a test or at the end of the grading period, the teacher would probably: (a) place all the grades (or averages of grades) on a continuum; (b) find the normal "breaking" points—shaded areas on the continuum where no grades occur, and (c) make these points the division points between grade groupings. An example follows with each X indicating a student score at that point:

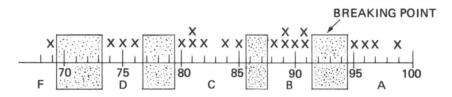

For the above class of twenty students, a teacher could easily rationalize grades of A, B, C, D, and F as noted above. More sophisticated methods can also be used where standard deviations and means are computed and grades correspondingly assigned. This procedure emphasizes norm-based evaluation to its greatest extent.

Norm-based evaluation in education is founded on the assumption that in most regular classrooms which are constituted randomly from the general population, test scores will follow a normal probability curve. Thus, as shown in Figure 10–1, there are more students who are at the mean (70), with fewer students scoring above or below it. In other words, the greatest preponderance of scores will be at the mean with greater and lesser scores decreasing in numbers proportionately as their distance from the mean increases. The process of assigning marks for student achievement based upon the normal curve is then a simple matter (see Figure 10–2). Using standard deviation as cut-off points between grades, average or C grades are given to students whose scores fall between +1 and –1 standard deviations on the normal curve. B grades are assigned to those whose scores fall between +1 and +2 standard deviations, Ds to scores between –1 and –2 standard deviations, As to scores above +2 standard deviations and Fs to students whose scores are below –2 standard deviations.

Sometimes a variation of the standard deviation is used to assign grades. Rather than C grades covering two full standard deviations and each of the other grades only one, the normal curve is divided into five parts, with each part being an equal distance along the base of the curve (see Figure 10–3). With this procedure C grades are given to students whose scores fall between +½ standard deviation and –½ standard deviation. B grades are given for scores between +½ standard deviation and +1½ standard deviation, etc. The standard deviation is obtained simply by dividing the range of scores by five.

When the assumption of normality is given to a school population the validity of tests becomes tied to this assumption. This necessitates the use of procedures for evaluating and revising tests which insure that student scores are indeed distributed normally. Such a procedure as item analysis is used to adjust the level of difficulty of a test and its ability to discriminate between low and high respondents. These methods are designed primarily to adjust the test so that it more closely meets the preconceived idea of how students should perform relative to one another. Simply stated, tests are prepared to insure production of a set of scores which satisfy the assumption of normality.

Since norm-referenced evaluation items are designed to spread grades, the person building the instrument must be sure that the items do indeed discriminate among those students who are good in the tested area and those who are not as good. Before building norms on a test, therefore, each item must be analyzed to be sure it discriminates. This can be done most easily after a test has been taken. Should an item not discriminate, many authorities advise not counting the item for that particular testing situation. For later tests the item would either be revised or omitted.

The table below is an example of how to arrange the data for test item discrimination:

ITEM	LOW-SCORING GROUP (LOWER 25%)		HIGH-SCORING GROUP (UPPER 25%)		DISCRIMINATION L–H	EVALUATION
	NUMBER OF ERRORS	PERCENTAGE OF ERRORS (I)	NUMBER OF ERRORS	PERCENTAGE OF ERRORS (H)		
1	7	35	3	15	20	Retain
2	16	80	7	35	45	Good
3	5	20	6	30	−10	Eliminate
4	9	45	8	40	5	Revise
5	4	20	4	20	0	Eliminate
6	12	60	9	45	15	Acceptable

The steps used to determine whether or not test items discriminate include the following:

1. Administer the test to eighty or more students, score the papers, and stack them in order of excellence—high scores on top. Remove the upper quarter: this is the high-scoring group (H). Similarly select the low-scoring quarter (L).
2. Tabulate the errors made on each item by the two groups.
3. Calculate the percentage of error on each item for the L-group; do the same for the H-group.
4. Find the difference (D) between the two percentages (L – H = D). This difference is a measure of the discriminating power of the item.

Criterion-Referenced Evaluation

In establishing how well a student has done in relation to a certain standard of competency, the instrument for criterion-referenced evaluation could in fact be quite similar to that used for norm-referenced evaluation. Both, for example, could be multiple-choice tests. Also, these types of instruments may be equally difficult. However, the level of difficulty in a criterion-referenced test should not lead the instructor to conclude that certain items should be eliminated. So long as the items can be demonstrated to be valid for the purposes the teacher has, they should be retained. Both types of tests may have other similarities. For example, both could test the same subject matter or the same process, whether cognitive, affective, or psychomotor.

The basic difference in the instrument lies in the purpose it serves. First, since the most important *question* is, "how well the student does in relation to an established level of competency," each item in the criterion-referenced instrument must relate specifically to this competency. Items that do not relate to the objective have no use in this type of evaluation. Second, since in criterion-referenced evaluation there is no attempt to provide a spread in grades, items from a norm-referenced instrument designed for spreading grades may be eliminated. Hence, the student no longer has to worry about memorizing little tidbits of information. Instead, he is able to focus on material that will lead him to the successful completion of the objective.

A third difference between norm-referenced and criterion-referenced evaluation lies in the degree of mastery required. In norm-referenced evaluation, a student's grade is related to that of his peers. If he scores higher than his peers, he generally receives a higher grade. If he scores lower than his peers, his grade generally reflects this as well. He is not *required* to achieve a passing average for each evaluation. He is only required to achieve a passing average for all evaluations. Failure to do so would result in his having to take the course over. In criterion-referenced instruction, the student is expected to pass the evaluation for each objective, at or above the level specified. Should he get a higher score than the specified level, he may receive a grade that represents his level of achievement. However, since grades are not often tied into criterion-level instruction, his reward for achieving above the criterion level is limited to an intrinsic recompence. Should he get a score lower than the specified level, he would be required to study or practice more and to repeat until he passes it at the appropriate criterion level.

With criterion-based evaluation there is no assumption of normality. Rather, minimum standards of achievement are set and students are expected to practice and study until they are able to successfully demonstrate the required level of competency. The emphasis in test construction then becomes one of formulating test items which validly measure the attitude or disposition called for in the objective. If the particular attitude or diposition is a defensible one, and the evaluation instrument is valid, the consideration of item difficulty and discrimination capability becomes irrelevant. These procedures serve a purpose in norm-referenced evaluation (Airasian & Madans, 1972).

There are at least two problems with regard to formulating criterion levels for instructional objectives and evaluating their achievement. The first of these is that of determining what the criterion level should be. For some tasks we experience little difficulty deciding upon the minimum acceptable performance level. For example, if we are training students to fold parachutes, or if we are teaching anatomy to surgeons, the expectation is near perfection. Low standards in sensitive areas like these could prove disastrous. In other fields, such high standards are not so easily defended. In teaching, for example, what should be the teacher's level of understanding of the various theories of learning and development? How well must the teacher be able to apply the various theories to curriculum development and classroom procedures? Obviously a high level of competency is desirable, but exactly what this level should be is difficult to determine. For children in science, the performance level may be even more questionable and arbitrarily applied by teachers. As a science teacher you will need to determine and defend the level of performance you expect your children to achieve.

The second problem is the difficulty of constructing test items which validly determine when criterion levels have been met. Here again the particular field of study for which tests are developed has a good deal to do with how valid test items can be. For example, if we are testing psychomotor skills or computational skills the problem of constructing valid test items is minimal. If we wish to measure the student's understanding of social theories and processes, test formulation is a much more complex and difficult task and our capability of constructing valid test items is much more limited. In developing tests in science both extremes are likely to be encountered. When test validity cannot be shown, the expected student performance levels cannot be adequately defended. This may necessitate the setting of criterion levels different from what might otherwise be expected. As the validity of test items is subsequently proven, performance levels can be adjusted accordingly. One procedure which is sometimes used to establish initial temporary criterion levels is to set an acceptable performance level and slide it either up or down to accommodate predetermined numbers of students who can ordinarily be expected to fall below criterion levels. This procedure is not devoid of pitfalls in the practical sense, however, because students will most likely view such actions as arbitrary and inconsistent. A superior procedure is to better establish the validity of a test in advance of the time students receive it. This can be accomplished through careful preparation, feedback from colleagues, and trial runs. With this procedure, a test will ordinarily have greater validity at the onset of its use and create fewer practical problems in its administration. Subsequent analyses of items should also be scheduled so that appropriate minor adjustments may be made.

Valid Levels of Expectation

As already mentioned, one of the basic problems in preparing test items for specific instructional goals is that of validly determining what the level of performance should be. For some types of goals, a well-defined high level of expectancy is imperative while for others the desired level of proficiency is not so clearly definable. In either case, it is necessary that criterion levels be justifiable. One basis upon which justification can be made is through task analysis. If it can be determined that a particular criterion level is the minimum acceptable behavior which can be tolerated because of dangers involved in performing certain tasks, it is relatively easy to support the standard as valid.

In some instances a clear and present danger cannot be demonstrated and yet performance levels can be established on the basis of functional requirements. Take, for example, the construction of precise instructional objectives. Teachers are expected to perform certain tasks at a minimum functional level. Assuming philosophical agreement with this approach, the teacher must be able to adequately formulate specific instructional goals in order to properly perform his/her role as a teacher. Inability to formulate goals leads to improperly devised learning procedures and ill-conceived tests. Goal formation in teaching is sufficiently critical to success that a high standard of achievement can be supported. Barring communication difficulties inherent in test items, a near perfect score should be expected on tests for preparing precise instructional goals. In teaching science to children there are also minimum functional standards. For example, a high level of understanding about applying the scientific method may be required because of its strategic importance to a large portion of the work they must do in science.

Justification for a particular level of competency can also be made on the basis of required entry behaviors for a particular task or job. In teaching it is generally considered essential for a first year teacher to at least be able to develop lesson plans and teach viable lessons using set induction. Set induction refers to the skill of motivating students both in terms of getting their attention as well as getting them involved in the lesson. In addition, properly prepared "sets" are directly related to the objectives and learning activities of a lesson. A first year teacher may legitimately be required to know how to prepare sets which adequately motivate and involve students and which properly relate to the lesson. Sets which are unlikely to motivate and involve students and which are tangent to lesson purposes should be considered substandard. The standard is that all three conditions be met at a minimum level of effectiveness. Entry behaviors for elementary children in science may include such things as being able to use some of the basic equipment of science. In most cases mastery level is arbitrarily set by the teacher or teachers, by using their best possible judgment. However good this method might be, teachers generally consider some of the following guidelines:

1. Some objectives require complete mastery or nearly complete mastery because of the nature of the objective (the surgical example).
2. Objectives that will be used later in the schooling process should have a higher level of mastery than those that will not be used again.
3. Mastery should be set at a higher level than that which could be achieved merely by guessing.
4. When only a few items have been prepared to measure an objective, the mastery level should be higher than when a large number of items have been developed (Clark, 1972).

Validity of Measurement

The second problem of criterion-referenced evaluation referred to earlier is the validity of measurement. The fundamental question which must be answered is, "does the test adequately determine the extent to which the objective has been met?" There are two considerations which must be dealt with in this regard. First, do all test items accurately measure some aspect of the objective, and second, does the test completely measure all expectations outlined in the objective? As indicated earlier, the "classic" criticism made of testing is that items are included which require recall of insignificant trivia. With norm-referenced testing such items are included many times to produce an adequate spread of scores. In criterion-referenced evaluation the test items are *constrained by the objectives* and it is required that they be consistent with one another.

One of the common failures of criterion measures is that they sometimes measure only a portion of the expected behaviors or that they measure tangential behaviors rather than those called for in the objective. This is likely a holdover from norm-based testing procedures where a sampling is used to infer understanding of a body of knowledge. Under these norm-based conditions, test items are prepared for only a portion of the content. However, sampling is not as critical for criterion-based testing. Instead, the focus should be upon how completely the test measures the whole behavioral outcome expected.

The nature of the testing procedure used is often responsible for obtaining nonvalid test results. A good example of this is the use of paper and pencil tests. Most skills are best demonstrated in the context in which they will be used in performance of a task. For example, the application of the skills of conducting an experiment is a significantly different experience than simulating actions on a pencil and paper test. Even where paper and pencil tests are not used, there is often a gross incongruence between expected behaviors and those which the student is asked to demonstrate. An example of this is the great difference that exists between having children conduct a science experiment on their own or having them follow through a cookbook approach. If the objective is to experiment in real situations, appropriate practice and valid evaluations should be applied. If the objective is to simply follow instructions then the cookbook approach would be more appropriate.

Specific test items may be considered invalid simply because they are poorly constructed, either in terms of language usage or the nature of the distractors used. Distractors are the incorrect choices in a multiple choice question. Ordinarily good test questions are composed of distractors which appear plausible to the student who is not adequately familiar with the knowledge or behaviors called for in the objective. Obviously, distractors which are "giveaways" should not be constructed. Test items without appropriate distractors do not require understanding in order to respond correctly.

In test construction one could well wonder at what point mastery of a particular situation is shown. The answer is not as clear-cut as educators would like it to be. First of all, remember that the evaluation of any objective only contains a sample of the questions or situations that represent the whole. To have selected the precise sample that will indicate whether mastery has or has not been obtained is always subject to question. In addition, it is difficult to set the level of mastery as well as verify that your test measures this mastery level.

Exercise 10–1   Norm-Based Versus Criterion-Based Evaluation

Explain the differences between norm-based and criterion-based evaluation in terms of their basic assumptions, the use of test item analysis, and the nature of the test items produced.

Test Items for the Cognitive Domain

A valid curriculum must include experiences which aid in the development of all mental skills. Thus it is necessary that evaluation materials be prepared which measure each of these skills adequately. In this section, example test items will be given for each of the major levels of the cognitive domain of knowledge.

Knowledge

1.   If the volume of a given mass of gas is kept the same, the temperature may be reduced by
    A. reducing the pressure.
    B. increasing the pressure.
    C. decreasing the density.
    D. increasing the density.
2.   The first step in the process of photosynthesis is
    A. giving off carbon dioxide.
    B. giving off oxygen.
    C. synthesizing sugar.
    D. absorbing sunlight.
    E. splitting off water.

The first item requires the student to remember a principle while in the second it is necessary to recall a process. Both are memory questions. The behavior which is ordinarily expected with regard to the principle measured in item one is that the student be able to apply the principle in solving problems where temperature, pressure, and volume may vary. The item thus measures an en route behavior rather than the terminal behavior ordinarily sought for.

Item two again is intended to measure the extent to which an en route behavior can be performed. The student is required to know the steps in a process. The terminal behavior itself may involve mental skills that exceed mere memorization.

Comprehension

1.   In a demonstration before the class, light two candles and allow enough wax to melt to cause them to stick to each other when they

are pushed together. Then have the class answer the following questions:
   A. Name the force that causes the molecules to stick together.
   B. Name the force that causes the molecules of the melted candle paraffin to stick when it is dripped on paper.
   C. Name the force that holds together the molecules of a candle.
   D. Name the force that was reduced when the candle wax melted.
2.   Pour 100 milliliters of water in a glass jar and mark the water level on the jar. Next drop a rock into the jar and compare the difference in the water levels. Then ask the children what is being investigated and have them mark their answer:
   A. Size of the rock.
   B. Weight of the rock.
   C. Area of the rock.
   D. Volume of the rock.

The first question requires the student to make a translation between concrete representations and verbal concepts. The goal in this case is not just to define concepts, but rather to be able to determine instances in life situations where the concept applies. We can have greater assurance that the child does indeed understand the concept if he is able to see it in contexts other than the one in which it was initially given, or in this case, in some form other than verbal. In addition he is asked to demonstrate an understanding of more than one force which is active in one situation and properly differentiate between them.

In the second question the student must be able to determine what measure of a rock can be supplied by a particular procedure. He must demonstrate that he does indeed understand the difference between volume, area, weight, and size and the means by which these can be measured.

Application

1.   James noticed that he was most likely to receive severe sunburn in the middle of the day. The reason for this is:
   A. We are closer to the sun at midday than in the morning or afternoon.
   B. Reflected sun rays are more plentiful at midday.
   C. Ultraviolet light from the sun is more readily produced at midday and is the primary cause of burn.
   D. When the sun's rays fall perpendicular to the earth's surface more heat energy is received than when the sun's rays fall at an angle to the surface.
   E. When the sun is directly overhead the sun's rays pass through less light absorbing atmosphere than when the sun is lower in the sky.

2. Using the principles of angle functions and angular and linear measuring devices, determine the height of the flagpole, the height of the First Security Bank building, and the distance across Miller Pond.

In question one, students must be able to recall principles of solar and planetary movement and apply them to each possible response to find the correct one. In question two it is necessary to recall principles regarding angular functions and apply their use to practical problem situations.

Analysis

1. Take a piece of tree branch and push the wood stem through a hole in a piece of cardboard. Put the stem in a glass of water and invert another glass jar over the tree branch, resting on top of the cardboard as depicted in the accompanying diagram. Prepare a control in the same way leaving out the tree branch. Let these set for a day and then ask the children to observe the inside of the top glass jars and note that in the one with the branch, moisture has formed, but that no moisture has formed in the other jar. Then ask the following: What does the experiment mean to you?

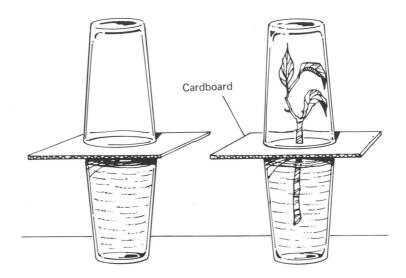

Cardboard

Mark each of the statements below in the following way:
Use (+) if the statement is true for the experiment.
Use (–) if the statement is false for the experiment.
Use (O) if the statement goes beyond the evidence obtained from the experiment.

A. The water droplets that formed inside the top glass jar evaporated through the cardboard from the water in the bottom jar.
B. A probable explanation is that the moisture in the top jar became saturated, was cooled by the glass, and condensed into droplets.
C. Another possible explanation is that the water from the lower glass was transported through the branch and leaves, then evaporated into the air enclosed by the upper glass jar, and finally condensed on the side of the glass.
D. A person can conclude that leaves are the only parts of plants that give off moisture.
E. An assumption can be stated that moisture given off by leaves was added to the moisture already in the air inside the top glass jar.
F. The experiment was limited to one kind of tree branch; the results may not be the same for other kinds of tree branches or other kinds of plants.
G. The results give sufficient evidence that leaves give off moisture.

All the items require students to make an analysis of the conclusions which can be reached from the data available through the experiment. This insures that the student actually makes an analysis on a broader base than he otherwise may. Questions which request a student to analyze something in a poorly described way usually permit simple observations to be made rather than careful analysis.

Synthesis

1. Design an experiment that will show what gas is given off by a plant while it grows.
2. Design an experiment to determine the concentrations of various compounds that are required for plant growth and those that prove toxic to plants.

Both exercises are designed to have students formulate an experiment in order to answer a question. In doing this the student will have to determine how to control his experiment and show that what he is able to conclude is not attributable to other causes. He must be able to visualize the kind of equipment and materials that he must use and how to use them appropriately. He must also be able to envision various possible causes and constraints and take these into account. Consequently these questions will probably exceed the capacity of younger students.

Evaluation
1. Rank order the five science fair projects from best to worst. Provide

> a reason for your choice and explain why you selected the criteria
> you did and how you applied them in making your judgments.
> 2.   Explain which of the two plans presented in class for maintaining the
> ecological balance is best and why. In your explanation be certain to
> test your criteria and describe how they helped you make your
> choice.

An important point to remember when testing students for evaluation skill is that a rationale (reasons why) should accompany their evaluative responses. In this way we can better guarantee that they are not simply stating their preferences. This requires the student to explain precisely how he used criteria to make a judgment. It is the only way we can determine exactly how he did use the criteria to make his evaluation. In both of the above questions this condition is met. This guarantees a greater correspondence between the evaluation item and the expected student performance.

Test Items for the Affective Domain

Validly measuring affective goals is an even more difficult task than evaluating cognitive goals. This is so primarily because less direct means have to be devised to determine the extent to which affective goals are achieved. With cognitive goals, questions can be asked or problems provided which can only be responded to by utilizing the appropriate mental skill. Affective goals, on the other hand, usually have to be measured by implication. A student's behavior has to be taken as evidence that a particular attitude or value is held.

Affect, of course, refers to emotions, interests, attitudes, feelings, values, or appreciations. There are special problems associated with writing test items in the affective domain. First, it is extremely difficult to determine whether the expressed affect is genuine or not. Second, it is hard to assess the level of intensity with which affect is being expressed. Our capability of validly measuring either the genuineness or the level of intensity of affect is extremely limited, and consequently we must optimize our chances of overcoming these problems through careful formulation of our objectives and proper execution of measurement activities.

As indicated in an earlier chapter, in writing behavioral objectives in the affective domain, it is necessary to first determine what value, appreciation, or attitude you want students to have. This must be incorporated within the objective. The next step is to indicate what behavior you will accept as evidence of that particular value, appreciation, or attitude. In evaluating the affective responses of children it is necessary

The genuineness and intensity of effect are difficult to measure. They have to be inferred from the behaviors of children.

that we insure that these behaviors are validly measured so that we may state with some certainty that the values, appreciations, and attitudes we sought are present.

Behaviors which are associated with affect may be either approach, avoidance, or neutral behaviors. Approach behaviors are activities the individual engages in which bring him into closer contact with a particular subject. Avoidance behaviors are those activities which take the individual away from the subject. A neutral condition is where the individual makes no effort to either come in contact with or avoid a particular subject. In the school situation, it is unlikely that you will desire to measure neutral attitudes. Likewise there will be little occasion to measure avoidance behaviors except on such subjects as drugs, tobacco, and alcohol. Approach behaviors are typically the indicators of affect that can legitimately be encouraged in the school and will constitute the emphasis in this section.

In determining what behaviors you will accept as evidence of a particular affective disposition, it is essential to identify those that have a good chance of occurring naturally. These are called high-probability behaviors. Some experience may be required before high-probability behaviors can be consistently identified and measured. One way to increase your experience is to make observations of individuals who definitely possess the attribute you are considering and compare them with behaviors engaged in by someone who does not have this attribute. Knowing the behaviors of students who possess and those who do not possess a particular attribute makes it easier to determine what situations will elicit genuine behavioral indicators of that attribute. In addition this will familiarize you with a fuller range of behaviors to look for in the measurement situation.

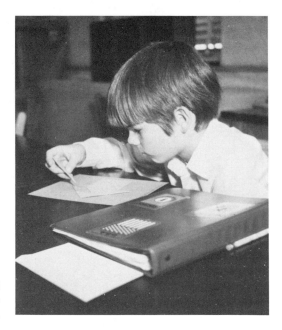

The study attitudes of children may be determined by observing them as they work in class.

In some instances, the teacher will find it necessary to rely on other individuals for observing student behavior. In addition, it may be necessary to measure behaviors through other indirect means. Direct observations are those instances where you personally observe the behavior. Indirect observations are those where the behavior is reported to you. You cannot always depend upon direct observation as the best means for obtaining information about a student's behavior. The teacher's presence will usually alter the student's responses if he believes that such behavior changes will favorably affect his grades or the teacher's attitude toward him. It may be that threat of grades or teacher's attitude have nothing to do with the student's behavior changes. Some students will be compelled to behave differently when any adult is present. The make-up of the peer group can also appreciably affect the behavior of individuals.

Once the affective attribute and its behavioral indicator have been carefully delineated, the next step is to determine conditions under which testing for the behavior will take place. With cognitive objectives, conditions usually refer to such things as not using notes or books or having to work alone. Affective objectives, however, require a much more complex set of considerations.

The first consideration with regard to formulating the conditions for measuring an affective objective is that of presenting the student with a set of alternatives. The purpose of this is to insure that students are given a free choice so that behavior is not restrained by the number of alternatives possible. Free choice is also enhanced when the teacher does as little as possible in the testing situation to influence which of the alternatives the student selects. Certainly the teacher should not coerce student behavior through threats of grades or disapproval and then expect to get a valid measure of attitudes. In addition, the student should not expect to get extra credit, special favors, or privileges for approach behaviors which are then taken to indicate the possession of some affective attribute.

Because students are likely to respond in the way they feel the teacher expects them to respond when they are being evaluated, a second important condition is to use methods of observation which minimize the visibility of the teacher. If direct observations are used it is important that students do not feel that their behavior will affect their grade or the teacher's attitude toward them. If indirect observations are used, students should not be aware that they are being observed. For example, if the teacher is trying to develop good study attitudes, he/she may obtain indirect data by engaging the help of other teachers to observe students in their respective areas of study.

Finally, the testing situation for affective objectives should be cue free. The students should have no indication of what is expected of them. Cues often come from the teacher, but may also be obtained from peers or other aspects of the situation. If you want to observe positive attitudes regarding ecology you may attempt to observe the class as they work together in a conservation project using indirect means. If the project takes place on the school grounds or adjacent property, it is possible that the students may anticipate that they will be watched just because they are near the school. It may also be that peers provide the cues for approach behavior when neutral behavior may be more representative of their attitudes. The target students may show positive responses just because their peers do or they may respond to the criticism or encouragement of peers.

In summary, then, in evaluating affective objectives, the following conditions should prevail:

1. Make sure that there is clarity regarding the situation in which the appropriate approach behaviors are to be observed. The situation should be one in which the behaviors can occur naturally.

2. Delineate the alternatives which the student may have in the situation.
3. Be certain the situation provides the student with free choice.
4. Avoid indicating that an attitude is being monitored if indirect observations are being made.
5. Be certain students feel free to express their true feelings if direct observations are being made.
6. Provide a cueless situation in which there is no indication of expected behavior.

Thus far we have discussed how to be more certain that behaviors truly indicate a particular value, appreciation, or attitude, as well as how to establish the proper conditions in the evaluation situation. The third part of the evaluation process is to determine whether the affective behaviors have reached the specified standard of performance. The purpose of this is to determine the level of intensity with which the value, appreciation, or attitude is held. It has already been pointed out that considerable difficulty may be experienced in making this determination. Therefore due caution should be exercised in the measurement process in order to avoid attributing greater or lesser affective intensity in a given situation than is demonstrated.

The criteria of performance is included in the objective in order to indicate how well, how often, or how much of an appropriate behavior must be demonstrated for the objective to be minimally achieved. Because affective objectives are not shared with students it is appropriate to include within them a statement regarding what percentage of the class you wish to demonstrate either a particular behavior or a certain number of instances of that behavior. The criterion can also consist of a statement of the performance level that should be achieved by *each* student. In the first instance, the concern is with how many students achieve the objective. In the second, attention is focused upon the number of behaviors which meet the minimum level of acceptability. For example, if we wish to focus on class minimum levels we may have a criterion statement in the objective like the following: "At least two thirds of the class will turn their homework in on time." If we wish to emphasize the number of instances of a particular behavior, the following kind of criterion would be appropriate: "Each student will turn in 80 percent of his/her homework on time."

It is not an easy matter to set criterion levels in the affective domain. It is difficult not to be very arbitrary in determining what the standard should be. In addition it is difficult not only to determine the correspondence between a behavior and its associated value, appreciation, or attitude, but also to measure the behaviors when they occur. This latter difficulty is encountered because of the special conditions which must be set up in order to more fully guarantee true behavioral indicators. To avoid part of the difficulty associated with the task of measuring affect, the following guidelines will be useful:

1. You must attempt to estimate how your students are likely to respond right now. Better still, you could record the responses of students in trial situations.
2. Attempt to determine honestly what student attitudes are regarding the subjects you wish to increase approach behavior for.
3. Estimate as closely as you can the criterion level which properly reflects what you could expect to achieve in an specified time period.
4. Try out the objective with the associated instruction and adjust the level as necessary.

With criterion levels expressed as quantities (i.e., 80 percent or four out of five times) it is necessary to express a note of caution. Obviously we are inferring from quantity of responses the extent to which a particular attribute is possessed by the student. However, the strength of a particular affective attribute may not necessarily be determined by the number of approach behaviors we are able to count in a test situation. Counting does remove the teacher from the responsibility of trying to make qualitative judgments with their inherent subjectivity. However, we should not lose sight of the fact that quantity and quality are not interchangeable entities.

Receiving

1. In the movie "Who's on the Side of Mother Nature" the value most clearly demonstrated by the farmer was
   A. Honesty.
   B. Keeping nature balanced.
   C. Soil conservation.
   D. Competitiveness.
   E. Pride in good work.

Evidence of receiving usually is demonstrated through student participation in instruction designed to bring information concerning values and attitudes to their attention. This may be accomplished through the student participating in a discussion regarding a particular value or listening attentively to a discussion or presentation about the values. Students may also indicate that they are considering information regarding values by responding to inventories designed to determine the extent to which they actually did receive the information. In addition, at this level students may be given examples of behavior sequences and asked to determine the attitudes and values held by the actors in the situation. The purpose in this case is not to measure skills in behavior analysis but rather to determine the students' awareness of behaviors which represent various attitudes and values.

Responding

1. Explain the degree of satisfaction you received from reading "Beaver Valley."
2. Explain what your attitude is regarding the safety rules which are used in the science work area.

The above two questions require a written response by the student and constitute an indirect and somewhat questionable procedure for obtaining information regarding affect. The procedure is legitimate if the results are tempered with a reasonable interpretation. Direct observation is an even more valid means for determining the values and attitudes which are indicated by student behaviors. These procedures, however, usually lack reliability, and are difficult to administer in the natural school setting. Some instances where direct observation may be useful include sportsmanship, honesty, and safety.

Valuing

1. Explain the support you would be willing to give to the science club.
2. What would you be willing to do in support of ecology and the conservation of energy?

The two exercises above permit the student to explain what his attitude is and the instructor can judge from the response whether or not the behavior is at the valuing level. Again this type of evalution item is subject to a variety of problems which limit validity. Greater validity could be obtained by direct observation during instances when there are limited biasing effects. Observing students at work or play when the teacher's presence and control are diminished provides a fairly good means of evaluation, but again such procedures have limited reliability and are difficult to operationalize.

Organization

1. Explain what you would do in the following situation: A friend whom you admire approaches you and asks you to support the ecology movement in spite of the fact that such support may contribute to a great reduction in the amount of available energy. How would you respond to this request?
2. A teacher who wishes to determine the extent to which students have properly organized the values of competiveness and fairness

into their value system, may rate his students by direct observation of their behavior in competitive classroom situations.

The response which the students give on the first question will help the teacher determine the extent to which the values of ecological balance and support of technological advance through increased energy productions have been properly organized into their system of values. The response given must not unnecessarily compromise one value in favor of the other. The teacher must judge the student's response to determine whether the behavior is indicative of a properly organized value conception.

In the second exercise direct observation is required. The values of competitiveness and fairness are related to one another and require a cognitive organization in order to avoid inconsistent behaviors. Competitiveness without fairness is not usually considered to be socially viable. The teacher must be able to observe student behaviors to determine whether an appropriate blend of the two values is manifest in natural classroom situations.

Characterization

Evaluating the extent to which values have been incorporated into an internally consistent value system and used as the foundation for behavior on a long-term, consistent basis is not an easy task. Evaluation at the characterization level, however, requires that long-term observations be made to determine whether behaviors are indeed consistent with organized values. We can get some indication of this level of value development from statements of philosophy, but making valid deductions from this data is especially precarious. Long term association between students and teachers or counselors is necessary to reach any valid conclusions with regard to characterization.

Exercise 10–2   Preparing Test Items for Various Levels of Objectives

Write an objective for each of the major levels of the cognitive and affective domains and prepare an evaluation item which will validly measure the extent to which the goals are achieved. Have a peer or instructor check your work.

Forms of Evaluation in Science

Tests in science may be divided into at least three categories: purely verbal tests, tests that involve pictures, diagrams, and graphs, and tests that make use of actual materials. Each of these types has its own strengths and weaknesses. Using actual materials has the advantage of being more realistic and can be used to evaluate learnings that verbal and picture tests cannot begin to measure. However, these tests are generally difficult to set up and administer. Verbal tests depend upon word interpretation. Students who lack verbal fluency are thus penalized by them to some extent. In some instances, however, verbal outcomes are considered important and these tests become important means of measuring. Tests which include pictures, diagrams, and graphs represent a sort of compromise between the other two. They are less difficult to arrange and administer and put less emphasis upon verbal skills. Each type of test may serve a useful purpose depending upon the purposes of the teacher. You should plan to administer the most valid test you can, given the ordinary constraints that you have, and avoid giving in to the temptation to provide only verbal tests, simply because they tend to be easier to score and administer.

Performance Tests

Performance tests are designed to measure the student's ability to use science materials and equipment to carry out certain operations. In this kind of test the needed materials and equipment are placed in front of the child, together with a statement of the operation to be done or problem to be solved, with the operations being left up to the child. The student may be expected either to demonstrate that he can perform each operation associated with arriving at the correct solution or to produce the correct answer to the problem. Both solutions and processes or just solutions may be used to arrive at a score.

Performance tests are particularly useful in measuring desired outcomes in science. Many of the defensible goals of science are process-oriented and performance tests are a valuable aid in measuring achievement of these goals. Unfortunately, the difficulties often experienced in contriving and administering this type of test have reduced its popularity. It is particularly difficult to administer to large groups. If equipment is involved, duplicate sets may be necessary, which can cause a lot of expense. If duplicate set-ups are not used, cumbersome rotation systems are required. On the other hand, this kind of test requires little or no verbalization and can be used to test understanding of concepts and principles which are hard to verbalize. In addition, the skills of pupils to manipulate science equipment and materials in the processes of science can be observed. The following is an example of this type of test experience: A child is given a miniature electric lamp, a dry cell, and a knife switch. A card which accompanies the materials reads, "Connect these so that the lamp lights up when the switch is closed."

Identification Tests

This type of test measures the child's ability to observe and identify. He is given a series of unknown specimens and materials, and equipment which he will need to test their properties and make his identification. With this type of test the child has the advantage of working with actual materials and demonstrating his ability to work with these materials and tools in using correct procedures for identification. In order to administer this type of test it is necessary that adequate materials and equipment be provided and that the students be provided with unfamiliar specimens so that no one is given unfair advantage. When materials that some students have already used in preparation for the test are used these students will obviously be better prepared to respond. The following is an example of an identification test: A pupil is given ten unfamiliar mineral specimens, together with equipment for determining such properties as hardness and streak. He is asked to give the names of the specimens.

Recognition Tests

Recognition tests differ from identification tests in that there are no procedures involved in determining the name of specimens. Students simply have to name the specimens by sight. The problem with this type of test is that it is frequently over-used as a measuring device. In fact it is often used when a higher level of response would be desirable. These tests have the same advantages and disadvantages associated with all tests using actual materials. There is the difficulty of supplying enough actual materials, as well as in having to cope with the noise and confusion which occurs during test administration. The following is an example of a recognition test: Ten mounted birds are held up one at a time and students are asked to write down the names of the birds in the order that they are presented.

Variations of the basic recognition pattern may be used. For example, students may be given a list of names of birds and asked to write the number of each specimen opposite the proper name. This form of recognition is easier to do and may also be used as an analogous practice experience prior to evaluation.

Another modification of the recognition test is to supply students with questions about the characteristics of the specimens. In this case, the student is asked to go beyond merely naming specimens. It is necessary also to know associated characteristics. One of the problems with this is that since one answer depends upon the other a pupil may fail to answer the whole question correctly because he does not know one of the answers. Many experts are critical of this type of testing. The following is an example of this type of modified recognition test: A microscope shows a single stomata in a bit of leaf epidermis. Beside the microscope is a card with the question, "Of what use is this structure to the plant?"

Picture Tests

In the testing situation, students may be given pictures and asked to answer accompanying questions. Pictures may be taken from magazines and books as well as other sources, but it should be remembered that each picture should adequately represent what is being tested and be sufficiently clear so that students are able to properly perceive it. If slides are used, these may be projected for the whole class to see. This greatly simplifies the process of pictorial display. Otherwise pictures may have to be stapled in file folders along with appropriate questions to be answered and passed from student to student. One of the major weaknesses of using pictures in testing situations is that pupils may experience difficulty interpreting two-dimensional images. High quality pictures can sometimes compensate for this weakness. In addition, with the use of pictures, the teacher is able to evaluate field trip experiences as well as store materials used in a test more efficiently. Actual specimens often spoil or are bulky and difficult to store. The following is an example of how pictures may be used: A clipping from a magazine shows a steep hillside and a valley with streams and lakes. Several features are identified by the teacher with letters written with colored ink so that they stand out. Question sheets contain blanks for the answers and such questions as the following: At which place will there be most rapid stream erosion? Where will most of the sediments be deposited? Where would you expect to find the clearest running water?

Diagram and Model Tests

Sometimes specimens and pictures are not available or they do not properly depict structures or other components which need to be tested. In these cases diagrams and models perform a useful function. Models may be displayed in front of the class for all to see or students may be rotated so they can make careful observations. Diagrams may be displayed as a chart on the chalkboard or on duplicated sheets. Letters or numbers can be used to identify various structures. Of course models and diagrams are often far removed from reality and may often generate an inaccurate conception of the specimen being studied. At the same time actual material may be too small or difficult to handle. The teacher must judge where the greatest advantages lie. When deciding whether to use models or diagrams it would be wise to remember that younger students have difficulty with abstraction. Diagrams require more ability to abstract ordinarily and thus can be less useful for the lower elementary grades.

Drawing Tests

In some instances, having students construct drawings may be the preferred form of evaluation. In addition to making the drawing they may be asked to label them and prepare appropriate explanations. The teacher will need to be cautious that judgments are not biased in terms of drawing ability for this type of evaluation. Most attention should be given to formulating a conceptual whole with the parts in proper relationship to one another. In order to reduce the dependence on drawing skill and still test a student's ability to visualize and construct a conceptual whole, you may prepare a test where students are required to complete drawings which are already partially drawn. For example, students may be asked to draw fins that are missing on a partially completed drawing of a fish. One problem with this type of test is that students may misinterpret the partially completed drawings if they are not very accurately drawn.

Essay Questions

Essay questions usually require a pupil to describe, in words which are organized into a paragraph, his knowledge on specific topics. The points he is to cover in his response may be outlined for him or may be quite open and require no specific directions. This type of evaluation allows the student to display how he understands a particular subject with no allowance for cues or guessing. It can give the teacher some indication regarding the orderliness of this thinking and his total grasp of the basic ideas being measured. Some students are said to be unduly penalized by essay examinations. This is a debatable point because it also assumes that students should have a sufficient command of language to express themselves clearly and concisely. Often the student's lack of understanding may be hidden behind apparent failure to communicate. The matter of scoring essay tests is another area of concern. Essay questions are usually easy to prepare but take a long time to score. In addition, reliability in scoring is difficult to achieve. The following is an example of an essay question that permits a rather open response: Explain how a submarine is made to rise or sink. The next example requires a more structured response: Describe the life cycle of the seventeen-year locust, indicating where each stage is spent and the seasons and times when important changes occur.

Short Explanation Questions

This type of question is a shortened version of the essay question. Usually the response sought for can be given in one sentence. The major advantage is that much greater economy of time is achieved both for the teacher as well as the student. This makes possible a greater sampling of material than the regular essay question. In this kind of response the ability of the student to organize his thoughts cannot be measured. The teacher needs to decide which of these outcomes is most important for each area of study. An example of a short explanation question is: What adaptions do desert plants have which enable them to survive with little water?

Completion Statements

Completion statements consist of statements which lack a word or phrase to complete their meaning. This type of test is intended to measure recall almost exclusively. It is relatively easy to administer and score and students are able to respond to the questions without elaborate directions. One problem with completion statements is that understanding is not measured, only the ability to recall. Also, it is not uncommon with completion statements to put in words which have a similar meaning to those being sought. In addition, it is very likely that the question may be misread and the wrong answer supplied simply through misunderstanding. An example completion statement follows: An explosive gas that is lighter than air is ———.

Multiple-Choice Tests

Multiple-choice tests are somewhat like completion tests except that the alternatives which may complete the statement are given. Thus the stress is upon recognition rather than recall. With multiple-choice items there is no danger, as there is with completion, that a student will supply an answer where judgment is required to determine its correctness. There is always one correct answer. One of the most critical problems comes in properly formulating multiple-choice test items. They should be prepared in such a way that the incorrect answers (distractors) appear plausible to the student who is unprepared. If four or five alternatives are provided in the question, and if appropriate distractors are used, there is little chance for guessing to have significant effect on test scores. Multiple-choice tests have the advantage of being easy to score as well as to administer. A wide range of subject matter can be tested in a very short time. The disadvantage is, of course, that usually only recognition is measured. The following is an example of a multiple-choice test item:

The portion of the sun's spectrum that causes sunburn is
a. infrared.   d. hertzian.
b. yellow.   e. orange.
c. ultraviolet.

Matching Tests

With matching tests there are ordinarily two parallel columns of words or phrases. Usually there are more items in one column than in the other. Students are asked to pair the words in the two columns and indicate their choice by writing the numbers or letters from one column which correspond with the other column. You should remember to keep such matching lists short so that students do not become confused. It is always possible that two or more associations will be made for any one item. Also, to avoid the problem of guessing, be certain to make one list with more items than the other. The following is an example of a short matching test: Choose from the list at the right the word that seems most closely related to each of the words in the left hand column and write the numbers of the words in the corresponding blanks.

refraction   1. mirror
light source   2. lens
absorption   3. incandescent wire
reflection   4. black cloth
light transmission   5. vacuum
                              6. night

Arrangement Tests

Sometimes the teacher wishes to test the student's knowledge of sequence and order. The student may be given a list of words or phrases which he must be able to arrange in a proper sequence. This may be useful any time that there are a series of steps in a process. For example there are a specific series of steps in staining and fixing bacteria on a microscope slide. One of the problems with this kind of test is that it is difficult to give partial credit where one or more steps in a process are out of order. The following is an example of an arrangement test: The following are the names of the planets. List them in order of their distance from the sun, beginning with the nearest:

Mars	Earth	Uranus
Pluto	Saturn	Jupiter
Mercury	Neptune	Venus

True-False Tests

This type of test consists of a number of statements which must be judged as accurate or inaccurate. With this kind of test, it is possible for the student to answer a lot of items in a short period and thus cover a very broad range of material. However, good true-false items are particularly difficult to write, because it is difficult to find items which are strictly true or false, without qualifying them in such a way that students can easily guess the correct answer. In addition, much of the material that lends itself to this type of testing is relatively unimportant in a science program. Teachers who write true-false items often attempt to cover up their inherent inadequacies by making their items long or complex or by introducing components outside the student's understanding and thus create confusion rather than providing some means of valid measurement. Although true-false items are one of the most popular kinds of test items because of the facility in scoring and administering them, they tend to be about the least effective means of valid measurement. The following is an example of a true-false test item:

> In the space at the left of each statement make a plus sign if you believe the statement to be true, make a minus sign if you believe it to be false. If you do not believe the statement can be called either true or false, make a zero in the blank and explain your reason below.
>
> _____ Ice must change to water before it can change to vapor.
> _____ Chlorine added to drinking water removes dissolved minerals.

Standardized Tests

In addition to their own tests, teachers may also wish to use standardized tests, a number of which are presently available. These tests have been prepared by test specialists primarily for nationwide use. Norms are usually available for each grade level so that teachers using the test can compare the achievement of their pupils with the achievement of other groups of children.

Generally, standarized tests have a high degree of reliability so that the scores are consistent from one administration to another. This means that the teacher can be confident that the test is performing reliably when he/she administers different forms of the test to the same class or when the test is administered to different classes. The tests also enable teachers to find out how their students compare with other children across the nation. In large school districts children can also be compared with one another across different areas of the district.

Standardized tests also have some serious limitations which you should be aware of if you plan to use them. First, many of the standardized tests are concerned primarily with the recall of facts rather than concepts and principles. Probably none of them properly determines the extent to which children can successfully demonstrate their ability to use the processes of science. If your main concern is how well students can apply science processes and understand concepts, standardized tests will not properly serve you.

A second problem with standardized tests is that they may not be valid, with respect to relevance of their contents, to the objectives of the teacher and the school system. Indeed it would be rare to find a teacher or school system whose objectives were the same as those that could be measured with a standardized test. If a standardized test were to be the means of evaluating children, teachers would undoubtedly react by trying to make their instruction conform to the test expectations. This is neither reasonable nor desirable. The teacher must have the freedom to decide on their appropriate use and avoid problems that would be created through the use of standardized tests. This does not mean, however, that standardized tests do not serve a useful purpose. They can be used to make comparisons on the variables which they measure, but their interpretations should be carefully made and in no case should they be used as a means of grading students and consequently constricting the curriculum.

A third possible abuse sometimes made of standardized tests is to use them to evaluate the teacher's effectiveness or the success of a particular program or unit of study. Again this may force the teacher to alter his/her program to conform to test expectations rather than carry out the program as it was intended. Students may learn things from a skilled teacher that are not measured in any way by standardized tests. If a standardized test is then administered it may appear as though nothing had been accomplished in the class when in fact it had been an outstanding experience for the children.

The best source of information regarding elementary science as well as other standardized tests can be found in *The Mental Measurements Yearbook* edited by Oscar K. Buros, which is published periodically by the Gryphon Press, Highland Park, New Jersey. This reference reports basic information about these tests, such as validity and reliability data. You will find this reference invaluable in determining which tests to use. The following are some of the more widely used standardized science tests:

American School Achievement Tests: Part 4, Social Studies and Science. Bobbs-Merrill Co. 4300 East 62nd St., Indianapolis, Ind.

California Tests in Social and Related Science: Elementary. California Test Bureau, Del Monte Research Park, Monterey, Calif.

Coordinated Scales of Attainment: Science Test. Educational Test Bureau, 720 Washington Ave., S.E., Minneapolis, Minn.

Every Pupil Test: Elementary Science and Health. Ohio Scholarship Tests, State Department of Education, 751 Northwest Boulevard, Columbus, Ohio.

Every Pupil Scholarship Test: Elementary Science. Bureau of Educational Measurements, Kansas State Teachers College, Emporia, Kansas.

Metropolitan Achievement Tests: Intermediate Science Test. Harcourt Brace Jovanovich, 757 Third Ave., New York, N.Y.

National Achievement Tests: Elementary Science, Forms A and B. Psychometric Affiliates, 1734 Monterey, Chicago, Ill.

Sequential Tests of Educational Progress: Science, Forms 4A and 4B. Educational Testing Service, Cooperative Test Division, 20 Nassau St., Princeton, N.J.

SRA Science Achievement Test: Elementary Science. Science Research Associates, 259 East Erie St., Chicago, Ill.

Stanford Achievement Test: Intermediate Science Test. Harcourt Brace Jovanovich, 757 Third Ave., New York, N.Y.

Oral Tests

As a teacher you may also wish to use oral or behavior observation methods of evaluation. Although objective tests are quite popular in the elementary school there is still a great need for oral methods of evaluation, especially in the lower elementary grades. In using this method you should remember that oral activities, such as discussions that are used for purposes of instruction, should not be used to evaluate student performance. It is alright to use such data to evaluate the quality of the learning activity, but these activities are designed to help students learn prior to evaluation. Given sufficient time a student will likely increase his performance well above the level demonstrated while he is developing a particular skill or mastering a particular area of knowledge during a learning activity. Therefore, it is usually best to withhold evaluation until the student is more fully prepared.

Even when oral evaluation methods are used they have some limitations. One serious drawback is that only a limited number of children can be reached with this method. The teacher either must listen to one child at a time, which is extremely slow, or to small groups with their inherent lack of reliability. Not only is testing small groups orally unreliable because of inadequate sampling, but also because the questions that are asked will usually vary in difficulty. Thus one child may end up having to answer questions with which he may not be familiar while another child gets questions only in areas that he knows. If the questions for the child in the unfamiliar area are also more difficult he is doubly disadvantaged.

Another problem with oral evaluation is that teachers may take a child's silence in a discussion to mean that he does not understand the concepts being measured. Many children learn very adequately by listening to the discussion of others while some children who talk a lot are inadequate in demonstrating understanding on a paper-and-pencil test or other kind of evaluation. Also the feasibility of making an adequate evaluation of student performance in a discussion situation is mind boggling. The teacher has enough to do to insure that the discussion takes a proper course without being encumbered with the necessity of also evaluating student achievement. The situation is just too complex and the efforts to obtain evaluation information may simply subvert the discussion. Discussions are better left for purposes of learning rather than evaluation unless one wishes to evaluate the discussion itself. In summary, evaluating student performance in discussion situations is certainly going to be unfair to students because of its inaccuracies.

Behavior Observation

Behavior observation may also provide a valuable means of evaluation. It is valuable, many times, because it can supply evidence that cannot usually be obtained by other evaluation methods. It may help the teacher get a more adequate and complete appraisal of a child. This is particularly so with younger children because their verbal skills may not be sufficiently developed so that verbal responses can be used as the only valid measure. Observations can play a vital role in obtaining information regarding childrens' ability to perform the key operations of science and to apply the principles that they are learning.

Behavior observation is often ignored by teachers who are either unaware of its potentialities or who are reluctant to accept it as a valid evaluative device. One concern that teachers have is that observations are so subjective. It is often concluded that subjective data cannot be either valid or reliable. It is true, of course, that this might be so but probably no more so than any other type of evaluation. At least this is true with regard to validity. Reliability is another matter, but the taking of certain precautions can greatly reduce the lack of reliability.

One way to reduce the detriment which subjectivity has upon the reliability and validity of educational measurement is to make sure that the objectives of your program are made explicitly clear and framed in specific behavioral terms. This will permit you to be looking for something specific in your observations. If you are looking for specific manifestations of behavior there will be less of a tendency to allow subjective considerations to have undue influence in your appraisals. In making observations you should arrange a schedule so that every child has equal opportunity to demonstrate the sought for behaviors.

Observations

One thing to keep in mind while making observations is that the quality of behavior will vary greatly among children at different grade levels and that standards should be adjusted accordingly. There are certain minimum levels which may ordinarily be expected which you need to keep in mind so that proper assistance can be given to children who fail to meet these expectations. On the other hand, it is a good practice to focus primarily upon the steady growth of students and avoid thinking in terms of absolute standards when it comes to observing students demonstrating basic science skills.

In making observations of behavior it is a good idea to develop some method of recording what you observe. Some of the more common techniques include descriptive records, checklists, and rating scales. Regardless of which technique is used it is imperative that it be as accurate as possible and reflect only that information that will be useful in evaluating the student's progress. These records may be consulted periodically to give you some indication of how well children are progressing and to help them focus attention upon the ways and means of helping them when they experience difficulty. At appropriate intervals you should have a conference with each child to make him/her aware of any problems that may be adversely influencing his rate of progress and to let him know of his current status.

Descriptive records may be made either in the form of anecdotal records or verbatim records. Anecdotal records consist of short statements which describe some action by a child that shows evidence of changing attitudes or skill development. Statements should be recorded as soon as possible after the observations to avoid descrepancies which often accompany delayed recording of data. Verbatim records are obviously better in most cases than anecdotal records because they tell precisely what the child said. Of course they can be used only for verbal responses unless expensive videotaping is used to capture nonverbal responses. One problem with verbatim records is that the teacher may not record other additional information that is often found on anecdotal records. For example, there may have been factors which contributed to a child's verbal responses that are significant, but which cannot be recorded. In addition, it is very difficult for a teacher to write down remarks of children verbatim while the class is going on, especially if there is a discussion. It is also time consuming whenever it is done. Tape recordings can be made of discussions periodically and used as a basis of compiling verbatim records. This will not, however, solve the problem of time consumption.

The behavior of children may also be recorded on either a checklist or rating scale. These devices can be used to evaluate either individual or group behavior. Recordings can be made of children conducting experiments, giving reports, solving problems and participating in other classroom activities. This information can be used to evaluate each child's progress over a period of time with very little trouble.

In using a checklist the teacher makes a list of desirable behaviors for each activity. Then, while observing the activity, he/she simply marks off whether or not the behaviors were manifested by the children. Code numbers can be assigned to each behavior and thus facilitate ease of recording. This way the teacher can still focus her complete attention on the activity in progress.

Rating scales are much like checklists, except that they introduce the factor of performance quality. With a rating scale, the teacher can record not only the observed behaviors, but also estimates of the quality of the responses. This provides the teacher with a good means of recording his immediate reactions to the student's performance unbiased by subsequent happenings in the classroom. You will need to decide the basis upon which these ratings are to be made. You may elect to rate students either on the basis of the progress he is making, on the basis of meeting prespecified standards, or by comparison to other students, if the school's grading system calls for such evaluations. In any case, ratings provide a comprehensive view of the work students are accomplishing in your class.

References

Airasian, Peter W., and George F. Madaus, "Criterion-Referenced Testing in the Classroom," *Measurement and Education* 3 (May 1972): 1–7.

Clark, D. Cecil, *Using Instructional Objectives in Teaching.* Glenview, Ill.: Scott, Foresman, 1972.

Lueck, William R., *et al.*, *Effective Secondary Education.* Minneapolis, Minn.: Burgess Publishing Company, 1966.

Tyler, Ralph W., "The Use of Tests in Measuring the Effectiveness of Educational Programs, Methods, and Instructional Materials," in Ralth W. Tyler & Richard M. Wolf (eds.) *Crucial Issues in Testing.* Berkeley, Calif.: McCutchan Publishing Corp., 1974.

11
Teaching Stimulation

The major concern of this chapter is to give you actual practice in teaching in a simulated situation. It is particularly useful to videotape your performance during these experiences so that appropriate feedback may be facilitated. Where videotaping equipment is unavailable, audio tape recorders are highly recommended. It is important to capture your performance so that it can be analyzed and evaluated. When this data is unavailable, analysis at best is superficial and limited in meaningfulness. Videotaping includes nonverbal information and thus

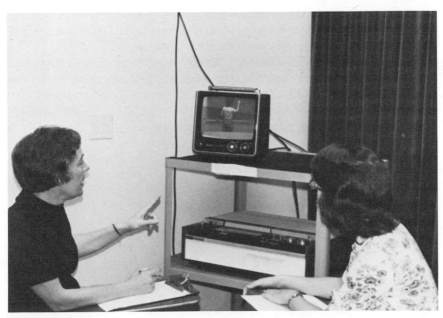

Being able to make a self analysis and change your teaching behavior accordingly is an important skill in teaching.

increases the data available. Its importance should not be underestimated. Analysis may be provided by supervisors during a videotaped replay of your lesson. However, the experience is also designed to provide the opportunity for self-analysis. Therefore there is some flexibility in completing the requirements in this chapter for teaching the concept lesson.

OBJECTIVES

1. *Lesson Plan:* Students will develop a lesson plan for teaching a science concept or principle. The lesson plan must contain the appropriate elements, objective, learning experiences, content, materials, and evaluation and be written in the appropriate form as illustrated in the examples given in this chapter.
2. *Simulated Teaching:* Students must be able to teach a fifteen-minute science concept lesson using the lesson plan developed for the objective above. The student must use the interaction style of teaching and adequately demonstrate the skills of set induction, stimulus variation, use of examples, repetition, and closure (Allen & Ryan, 1969). This lesson may be taught to a small group of peers or elementary school students and may be videotaped.
3. *Analysis:* Students must be able to make a written analysis of their teaching skill from viewing a videotape replay of their lesson. This analysis must be based on the categories of teaching behavior listed on the Critique for Simulated Teaching form. (NOTE: The student's lesson may also be analyzed by a Clinical Analyst.)
4. *Replan, Reteach, and Analysis:* Students must be able to replan and reteach their fifteen-minute lesson, eliminating the problem areas identified in their analysis of the first lesson. This second lesson may be analyzed from a videotaped replay using the Critique for Simulated Teaching form and a comparison made between the teach and the reteach cycles.

Introduction

The primary role of a teacher is to plan for and execute teaching behaviors designed to bring about purposeful student learning. In planning for instruction, the teacher must first identify and organize a defensible body of information, from which he/she can formulate viable instructional objectives which students must achieve in order to attain a desired level of mastery. The second task is to formulate the student learning activities and teacher behavior patterns which can reasonably be expected to result in student achievement of instructional goals, given the ordinary constraints operating in the classroom.

The teacher then must execute his plan with his class, readjusting his behavior and/or class activities as needed in order to meet his goals. Finally, the teacher must evaluate to determine the extent to which students are able to do those things specified in the objective. The experiences in this chapter are designed to provide practice in this single most important teacher role. In achieving the objectives of this chapter, you will learn to prepare appropriate lesson plans, execute specified teaching skills, and use specified methodologies to help students achieve objectives from various levels of the domains of knowledge. The methodology selected for you to use in teaching your concept lesson is the interaction method. The teaching skills which will be used include set induction, stimulus variation, use of examples, repetition, and closure. Specific definitions of the skills and methodology are referred to later.

The teaching skills and methods are to be demonstrated in simulated teaching episodes, which consist of short (about fifteen minutes) teaching experiences where you focus on a limited number of skills and try to increase your ability to use these skills appropriately. Simulated teaching should be differentiated from the popular method of microteaching, where single teaching skills are focused upon and analyzed. In the simulated teaching exercises, several skills are to be learned in conjunction with each other, thus increasing the meaning of the experience. In addition, you are encouraged to orient your lessons toward achieving specific science objectives. Ordinarily, the accomplishment of any objective requires you to use a number of skills in conjunction with one another. This is why you will be encouraged to master certain basic skills in teaching each of your simulated lessons. A small group of either public school students or peers may be used as pupils in the simulated teaching exercises.

The major advantages of simulated teaching for practice is that it lessens the complexities of a normal classroom situation and it provides for increased control of practice. It also provides a means of receiving feedback regarding teaching skill in a nonthreatening environment, thus providing you some basis for improving your performance prior to field testing your skills. The first teaching skill which will be considered is set induction. NOTE: It may be useful to add to the written descriptions of the various teaching skills protocols in the form of films or videotapes which display the actual behaviors which represent each skill concept.

Set Induction

It is patently true that most teachers do little in preparing their students for classroom activities. Most commonly the ineffectual, mind-stultifying phrase "today we are going to talk about" precedes nearly all class work. At best this phrase simply announces the fact that instruction is about to begin. At worst it may act as a signal for the student to "tune out" the instructor. In any case, such introductory statements contribute little to the process of stimulating student interest and enthusiasm for the learning they are about to engage in. For the lesson to be successful, the teacher must motivate the students by providing "setting" experiences.

A "set" is a predisposition to respond in some prescribed way toward a given set of learning experiences (Allen et al., 1969). In order to establish set the teacher provides motivating experiences which arouse interest and enthusiasm in the lesson. Student enthusiasm should be generated toward the specific learning task. He should be able to visualize the relationship between goals and learning experiences. Depending on the goals, set induction may take different forms. When the learning task is in the psychomotor domain, the mental set of the learner should take the sensate form. This means that his physical senses should be used to prepare him to physically act out his learning. When the learning task is cognitive, the mental set becomes symbolic and ordinarily the symbol is that of language. Consequently, the learning task and the resultant goals must be expressed in an arrangement of symbols. If the learning task is an affective one, the mental set is emotive. In this case learning must be primed by emotional sets and the result of learning must be expressed, at least in part, by emotional acts (Searles, 1967).

One way of establishing set is to focus the attention of the student upon some familiar person, object, event, condition, or idea. The teacher then uses this as a point of reference with which to link the familiar with new material. Also, seeing the familiar about a learning task is more likely to entice student interest.

Set may also be developed by the teacher asking thought-provoking questions which encourage students to become immediately involved in the lesson. Generally, these questions must call for the student to make an analysis, exercise a judgment, or create a divergent response. Low-level questions generally fail to create set.

A short description or story may also serve as a setting strategy as well as short dramatizations or role playing episodes. Many times goals which are explicitly and clearly taught to students also act as setting experiences.

Set generally is used to start a lesson but may be used any time you shift directions in a lesson or when student attention and enthusiasm are waning. Set may also be used at the conclusion of a lesson when students are to be encouraged to engage in some out-of-class activities or when specific preparations are needed for a subsequent lesson. Simply identifying what the learning task will be is not sufficient. Students should be made to see the task in its relationship to some visible science goal, and that goal should be presented in such a way that enthusiasm is generated.

One word of caution should be made with regard to providing setting experiences for students. First, it is essential that the set induction be directly connected to the learning task and that it leads naturally to the learning. Also, one needs to avoid setting experiences which may cause students to remember only the set and not the information that it was designed to lead to. One example of this kind of problem is a case where a teacher was attempting to prepare students for a discussion regarding the effects of discord on interpersonal relationships. She contrived an enactment of an argument between herself and one class member. All seemed to go well until a week later when the teacher was approached by a student who said he was still upset by the conduct of the teacher in the argument and could not understand how she could have done such a thing.

The following are examples of sets:

1. Lesson: Combustion.
   Set: Thrust a glowing splinter into a flask of oxygen and ask students to attempt to describe what is happening to cause the splinter to burst into flames.

2. Lesson: Interplanetary travel.
   Set: Say, "Imagine you had the responsibility of devising all life-support systems for a flight from earth to the moon and then on to other planets in our solar system. What factors must be taken into consideration and how would you deal with them?"

3. Lesson: Chemical reactions.
   Set: Pour water over a small pile of sawdust under which you have placed a chemical which reacts vigorously with water.

4. Lesson: The effects of gravity on projectiles.
   Set: Contrive an experiment where a steel ball is blown by an air gun at the same instant another steel ball is dropped from a magnet. Aim the trajectory of the air blown ball so that it intersects with the ball dropped from the magnet at a moment in time. Ask the class to explain why they collide.

Exercise 11-1   Set Induction

Attempt to formulate a set induction for a lesson you may teach. Remember that the set should be attention-getting and connected to the lesson in such a way that it naturally leads into the beginning of the lesson. When you have completed this task you are ready to consider the next teaching skill, stimulus variation.

Stimulus Variation

Most of us have experienced teaching behavior which has "put us to sleep." Most commonly it is a lengthy lecture where the teacher stands rigidly behind a podium with his/her only perceptible movement being the shifting of weight from one foot to another or the turning of the pages of notes. Most likely he spoke in a monotone and even if the topic was interesting, it was difficult to follow. Psychological experiments have shown that varying teacher behavior results in higher pupil attention levels (Allen, *et al.,* 1969). In order to maintain interest, it is therefore necessary to vary teaching behavior continuously.

There are a number of ways that stimulus variation can be achieved. One of the primary ways is through *movement.* This entails movement by the teacher to various parts of the room. Even though it may be acceptable to move to the back of the room or among students, the bulk of teacher movement should be in the front of the room where students can more readily observe him. Generally, movement causes the student to shift sensory channels from simply listening to watching. Movement can also be used to draw attention to an object in the room. Movement toward it will increase the likelihood that students' attention will focus on the object. Also, movement toward the class tends to create a sense of urgency or emphasis about what is being taught. In addition, it causes students to increase their efforts to follow what is being said. It is well known that movement into close proximity of misbehaving students generally causes them to refrain from their disruptive behavior and follow the lesson.

A second form of movement is *gestures* such as hand, head, and body movements. These movements help to convey meaning and emphasis in addition to providing variations in the stimulus. Many times oral communications do not convey the whole message. Gestures embellish and fill out the more exact meaning intended. It is important to remember that meaning is not conveyed simply by hand and head movements. It is essential that these movements correspond with the verbal message. If the same movements are used, no matter what the verbal message, students become bored or distracted. They begin to think about the ineptness of your movement and forget to concentrate on the intended meaning of what you are trying to communicate. It is also imperative that gestures are not overexaggerated. They should fit the message in terms of intensity as well as intent.

Focusing is another way to vary the stimulus. The teacher, through verbal statements and/or gestures, may attempt to direct students' attention to specified instructional components. The teacher may, for example, approach the board and point at a diagram while at the same time saying, "Now here's something which is very important." Focusing may also be directed by the voice level of the teacher. This may be accomplished by either lowering or raising the level beyond the normal range.

Altering interaction styles can also help in varying the stimulus and maintain the interest level of the class. For example, the teacher may begin by talking to the whole class, then speaking directly to one student. He may then redirect a student's response to another student for purposes of clarification or comment. The teacher may also ask a student to discover any fallacy in a remark made by another student or to give examples of what another student is saying. Shifting among these interaction styles helps to increase the interest of the lesson as well as increase attention.

Pauses may also be used to vary the stimulus. This is particularly important when expected responses require some thought. Quiet can be used as a natural way of breaking instruction up into absorbable units. It also has a tendency to force student attention. Most people are uncomfortable during silence in group situations. Yet, it is a very effective way of obtaining the attention of students when they are bored or distracted. Pauses also help provide the variety necessary to appropriate stimulus variations.

Shifting sensory channels is a final technique of stimulus variation. The teacher, in this case, shifts from one mode of communication to another. This causes the student to adjust his thinking patterns by changing his means of reception. For example, the teacher may shift from oral messages to diagrams on the blackboard or to tactile attention through handling actual objects. Such required adjustment of sensory channels induces a high level of attention.

The following is an example of how stimulus variation is used in a teaching situation:

Teacher: Have you ever wondered why plants always seem to grow with the roots down and the stem up? Today we are going to discuss why this is so. After our lesson you will be able to explain how certain factors affect the way plants grow. Now look at the plants you have been growing on the blotter between these two pieces of glass. (This type of stimulus variation is called aural-visual switching. This requires students to use their eyes as well as their ears to receive messages.) Remember we allowed the seeds to germinate and watched the root grow for a few days. Then we turned the glass over. Jim, can you tell us how the roots were affected by turning the glass over? (Here the teacher switches from herself to a student as a source of information to provide stimulus variation.)
Student: Well, the roots turned.
Teacher: Mark, can you tell us exactly how the roots turned? (In this case the teacher is using a different interaction style by redirecting one student's

response to another for comment or clarification. This is also a good way to vary the stimulus.)

Student: It looks to me like the root was growing toward the pan of water and when we turned the glass over, the root turned so it went toward the water again.

Teacher: That's an interesting observation, Mark. Let's look carefully at the germinating seeds to see if Mark may be right. (Teacher again switches from an auditory to a visual mode.) Audrey, look carefully at the seeds for a minute. Can you tell us about the environment they are in? (Here the teacher again focuses attention and redirects student's responses in an effort to vary the stimulus.)

Student: Well, they are laying against the blotter and it looks like they must be completely surrounded by water.

Teacher: Audrey has observed that the seeds are completely surrounded by water. Tim, how does this observation affect the idea expressed by Mark. (Another shift in the stimulus. This time the teacher again used redirection by asking one student, who now has the benefit of additional information, to reconsider a statement by another student.)

Student: I'd say that if the seeds are surrounded by water, that they couldn't possibly be growing toward water.

Teacher: If they are not growing toward water, then what is influencing their growth, Mary?

Student: I think they must be growing toward the earth because whenever the seeds were moved they started to point their roots toward the ground.

Teacher: (The teacher walks toward Mary and expresses a good deal of enthusiasm when she says the following:) That is exactly right: The roots do grow toward the earth. This is called geotropism. (The teacher writes the word "Geotropism" on the chalkboard and points to it. Change in stimulus variation from aural to visual in addition to focusing attention.) Now let's look at the plants we put in this milk carton. (A milk carton was cut in half and glass placed over it and seeds planted next to the glass. The plants were watered by putting water at the end of the carton away from the seeds.) Jane can you tell us about how the roots are growing. (Stimulus variation)

Student: They look like they started to grow down toward the earth but then began to grow toward the water.

Teacher: Very good. Plants' roots not only are affected by the earth but they are also influenced by water. This is called Hydrotropism. (The teacher writes "Hydrotropism" on the board and points to it. Then she walks toward the class and gestures in such a way to show the importance of her statements. Walking toward the class and executing appropriate gestures varies the stimulus and focuses the attention of the class on the important ideas produced in the discussion.)

Exercise 11–2 Stimulus Variation

As an exercise, attempt to write a student-teacher dialogue in which you portray each of the ways to vary the stimulus. When you have accomplished this you are ready to consider the use of examples as a teaching skill.

Use of Examples

One of the greatest determiners of teacher effectiveness is the ability to use appropriate examples. Even though it is an economy of time and effort to think in abstract terms, learning about a science concept or idea for the first time usually requires some kind of concrete representation of the abstraction before understanding can be brought about. If the teacher is unable to provide a concrete example, the students may not be able to comprehend the idea being presented. The teacher may also get feedback on student understanding of concepts by asking them to formulate examples.

There are two ways in which examples may be used to bring about the understanding of concepts. These are deduction and induction (Allen, *et al.*, 1969b). Deduction is accomplished by the teacher *first* identifying the concept he wishes students to understand. He *then* gives examples of the concept. This may be accomplished by oral presentation of a literal example, an analogy, or metaphor, or by presentation in the form of visuals, such as pictures, diagrams, and charts. Metaphors are words or phrases which are not literally applicable. For example, the phrase "the ship plows the sea" is meant to convey meaning about how a ship moves through the water. An analogy usually highlights similarities or differences between ideas which are understood and those which are not with the goal of bridging the gap between them. For example, an analogy may be made between a camera and the human eye. Caution must be exercised, however, not to use analogies which oversimplify or mislead the student.

The *third step* in the deductive approach is the process of relating the example back to the concept. The teacher must, in this instance, be careful to accurately compare the example with the abstraction. He or she may also at this point call for students to give examples and relate them to the concept as a means of determining the level of understanding of the class.

A second basic approach to the use of examples is induction. In this case the teacher begins instruction by giving examples of a science concept and encouraging students to identify the generalization or concept which the example illustrates. When the students perform the induction erroneously, the teacher either provides additional examples and/or identifies the fallacies in their inferences. The teacher should avoid telling students what the concept is, but rather permit them to discover it from examples.

One way of using examples is to provide negative as well as positive instances. In other words, in addition to providing examples which illustrate a concept, nonexamples should also be provided. This helps students more clearly discriminate between the concept you are teaching and others that may be related to it.

One problem that often develops in using examples is the tendency to expect students to relate the example to the concept by themselves. The teacher should not assume that the students will be able to perform this operation. The able instructor will show the way in which the example illustrates the idea and will check to see if it is understood.

For examples to be used effectively, they should reflect the interest and experiences of the learners. If the example is not in their experience field, it is unlikely that it will lead to understanding. In addition, if examples are used which are akin to student interest, the probability of understanding will increase.

The following are illustrations of the use of examples and analogies:

A camera is often used as an analogy for an eye.
A heart is often compared to a pump.
A brain is sometimes compared to a computer or a tape recorder.
The structure of an atom is often used as an analogy of the solar system and vice versa.

Exercise 11–3   Use of Examples

Complete the following exercise on the use of examples. Where examples are called for, devise them from the study of science.

1. What is an analogy?
2. Give an example of an analogy.
3. Give a positive and a negative example of a particular concept.
4. Identify a second concept and give two positive examples, two negative examples, and an analogy.
5. Identify several sources a teacher may use for examples.

Repetition

The major purpose of the use of repetition is to clarify and reinforce major ideas and concepts and to produce a state of overlearning. Research supports the fact that learning beyond initial mastery of a concept aids in the retention and understanding of the concept over longer periods of time.

Many times learners are unable to identify what the major points of a discussion are or are engaged in "mind-wandering" when important ideas are taught. Because of these two very natural occurrences, teachers should make a practice of repeating important ideas.

It is also a fact that limited "real" communication takes place in the classroom unless the teacher takes great pains to see that it occurs. Because of the differences in experiences and expectations of students, they develop divergent perceptual mechanisms. Repetition should be varied sufficiently to cater to these perceptual differences. In other words, repetition should not always occur in the same form as the initial instruction. This will bring about understanding for more students as well as add to the understanding of others.

Repetition may be simple, spaced, cumulative, or massed (Allen, et al., 1969b). *Simple repetition* occurs when concepts are repeated immediately following the initial presentation. This may be given, obviously, in the same or different form as the initial instructions.

Spaced repetition is where the teacher repeats a concept at various intervals during a lesson. This is a particularly useful technique because it increases understanding by relating all subsequent instruction to the initial concept being taught. Thus, the major idea can be viewed continually as the guiding principle during instruction.

Cumulative repetition is a procedure where all prior concepts in a sequence are reviewed before new points are presented. This technique is particularly useful when it reidentifies all concepts in order to conceptually organize new concepts which are being added. It is obviously useful to view the total context into which new ideas are being introduced. It should be remembered, however, that overuse of this technique may produce boredom. It should be used only when it is absolutely necessary to do so.

Massed repetition is where all major points are repeated together as they are sequenced or related. This generally is done at the conclusion of a lesson and serves to summarize and assist students in making a final conceptualization of the material.

Repetition, then, provides a means of permitting the student to come in contact with already learned materials in different contexts. The purpose of this is to help him overlearn the material or add to his understanding by relating previously learned material to new concepts being studied.

The forms that repetition may take are varied. The following is a list of possible forms: figures of speech, metaphors, verbal emphasis, analogies, focusing, visual highlighting, and gestures. It is desirable to use a number of these as well as providing the repetition in the same form as the initial instruction.

Exercise 11–4 Repetition

Complete the following exercise on repetition:
1. Define the following types of repetition:
    1. Simple.

    2. Spaced.
    3. Cumulative.
    4. Massed.

2.   Give a description of a specific instance of the use of each type of repetition. Use the actual content of teaching science.

Closure

Closure may be defined as the relative degree of logical organization or integration of learnings and understandings *as perceived by the learner.* Because closure takes place in the mind of the learner, it must be viewed as more than a quick summary of material given at the close of a lesson (Allen, *et al.,* 1969a). Closure entails the students pulling together the major points of the lesson and conceptually relating them to past knowledge and experience in such a way that a sense of achievement is reached. It must be possible for the student to see where he has been in terms of his development and where he is going. He must view this as a viable and orderly direction for him to proceed personally. In other words, he must know the purposes of the instruction and identify them and be able to visualize how each aspect of instruction articulates with these purposes. Closure is complementary, therefore, to the process of making the goals of instruction explicitly clear and of having logical rationales for these goals. If students do not agree that the instructional goals are viable for them, they will be reluctant to pursue them. If they are unable to visualize these purposes because they are not clearly defined, then they will make only nonpurposive responses in the learning situation and obviously obtain no closure.

Closure is also complementary to set induction. Set induction is made many times in a form which establishes a communicative link between a student's past experiences and knowledge and the materials to be presented. The teacher must then follow through and help the student obtain closure on these same terms. The teacher may, for example, thwart closure for his/her students by emphasizing subtopics which are of interest only to him, or a certain group of students may entice the discussion away from the proposed purposes, thus confusing and disillusioning their peers. The purposes of the lesson may also be interfered with by outside influences or discipline problems in the classroom. These problems may interrupt the flow of the lesson and successfully destroy any possibility for obtaining closure.

In addition to providing set induction, explicitly teaching objectives, and avoiding the problems identified above, the teacher can also engage in a number of other activities for the purpose of assisting students in gaining closure. First, she can carefully organize what is taught into a conceptual model, construct, or generalization. Doing this helps the student increase his understanding, which obviously assists in bringing closure. Second, she can provide the students with such organizational cues as "there are eight parts to the process" or "this discussion may be organized under three main headings, namely . . ." Third, she can use appropriate repetition procedures and allow sufficient time at the end of a lesson for a thorough review. Fourth, the teacher can emphasize closure periodically throughout the lesson, rather than attempting closure only at the end. Fifth, she should, as frequently as needed, connect previous learning to current lesson material. She may also attempt to relate previous and current learning to future learning as well. Finally, closure may be achieved by students demonstrating what they have learned and by the teacher providing feedback on their responses. The teacher also learns in this process the *extent* to which students are able to achieve the objectives. The teacher should not assume closure for a whole class when a few students are able to demonstrate understanding. At the same time, it should be remembered that evaluations cannot legitimately be made until the teacher is confident that the class is able to demonstrate their competency. It is, therefore, recommended that teachers provide all students an opportunity to try out their newly developed skills and obtain teacher feedback prior to evaluation.

Closure, then, is the process of helping students perceive logical organization in a lesson to the point where understanding is developed and a sense of achievement is reached. Most importantly, closure may be aided by the teacher, but it must take place in the mind of the student.

Exercise 11–5   Closure

Complete the following exercise on closure:

1. Explain the timing and purpose of closure.
2. Explain how a teacher may obtain closure; i.e., what procedures can be used to advantage in obtaining closure.
3. Give specific teacher strategies for obtaining closure in a specific lesson.

What Are Concepts and Principles?

A concept is a group of things that has common characteristics. In simple form, a concept may be things such as birds, baseball pitchers, and vegetables. Simple concepts may be delineated by simply naming their specific instances. More complex concepts include ideas like democracy, human rights, ecology, and evolution. To explain a complex concept, such as democracy, would require a rather lengthy and detailed treatise on the components and characteristics of a number of different examples of democracy.

Concepts usually have attributes which differentiate them from other related concepts. Thus, birds may have the attribute of flying or being flightless. The more complex concepts have a greater number of attributes and generally these attributes are more obscure (DeCecco, 1968). Often the teacher will want to reduce the complexity of some concepts by limiting the number of attributes discussed or by combining a large number of attributes into a smaller number of patterns. For example, in teaching about ecology, an instructor may wish to use only one particular ecosystem as an example, or talk about only a limited number of the most common characteristics of ecosystems.

Principles are statements of relationship between two or more concepts (Emmer and Millett, 1970). Other terms which are often used for principles are rules or generalizations. The following are examples of principles: (a) gas expands when its temperature is increased; (b) gas contracts under pressure; and (c) the numbers and distribution of plants in the environment depend upon having specific nutrients available at particular levels of concentration.

Ordinarily when making reference to teaching concepts in the classroom, teachers are really referring to teaching concepts as well as principles. It is important that a proper distinction be made between concepts and principles, but the concept lesson you teach may include concepts, principles, or both. A teacher should accept as evidence that students have learned a concept, the ability to render a definition of the concept, and the ability to identify things which are and things which are not examples of the concept. In giving a definition of concept, students should be able to state its characteristics or attributes.

An Interaction Model for Teaching Concepts and Principles

The following discussion is an explanation of an interaction method of teaching. This method is primarily oriented toward the teaching of complex concepts and principles and focuses on the procedures used by the teacher in helping students gain the view of a concept that he holds. This is the model which you should use in teaching your simulated concept lesson. You should be able to give a description of the model presented here and use the method in teaching a concept lesson.

The rationale for using this model in teaching can be illustrated by the following study: During World War II, the U.S. Navy had a station in a village in the interior of China which was beset by disease. So the sailors there embarked on an instructional campaign to rid the area of many of the flies which were carriers of disease. In the best pedagogical fashion they set out to show the locals why they should kill flies. They brought in a movie projector, and a screen, and projected a detailed drawing of the fly to show how germs were carried on the filth trapped on the legs. When the picture appeared, the audience walked out amidst uproarious laughter. Then the befuddled sailors found out the reason—no flies were that large. Magnification of a fly or any other object was outside the experience of the people involved and thus their perception of the image was impaired (Searles, 1967).

There are other things besides previous experiences that alter the way in which we perceive our environment. One of these factors is that of needs. We frequently perceive our environment in such a way that we exclude those things that are not directly related to the means for meeting our needs. One example of this is the case involving individuals confined in prisoner-of-war camps, who spend a high percentage of their time discussing the kind of food that they plan to eat when they get out. This illustrates that the need for food tended to dominate their focus of attention. There are also examples of people perceiving items of food where they did not exist when they were subjected to conditions of great hunger.

A third item which alters the way in which we perceive is that of expectations. This is simply a matter of seeing or hearing those things that we expect to see or hear. If a child goes looking for something in a forest, for example, he may ignore a multitude of factors which a more open perception may permit. Indeed the unperceived factors may be more important than those he has set his attention upon. You need to be aware of this perceptual problem so that you can understand why students often misperceive.

These problems with perception illustrate the point that communication is often difficult because of the different experiences, needs, and expectations that we have. In the classroom situation, the teacher may be expected to have to deal with students who have had a wide variety of experiences, and who have divergent needs and expectations. This obviously makes the problem of communicating with children a more complex one. An example of this is a child who has spent his total life in a city environment and has never had an opportunity to see mountains; consequently, ideas related to the concept of mountains are difficult to teach. The problem for the teacher then becomes one of portraying concepts in such a way that students are able to comprehend them in terms of their present set of experiences. But how does one

Teaching skills can be practiced in a short lesson by selecting a convenient concept and teaching that concept to a small group of children available at a time when the regular class is not in session.

portray concepts when students come to the learning situation with such a wide variety of experiences and variable readiness? This whole problem of misperception and miscommunication implies the need for some kind of feedback system in the communication process in the classroom.

A learning model that illustrates a feedback system is depicted in Chapter 5 (See Figure 5–11). You may recall that events and objects in the environment are perceived through sensory intake by the various sense organs of the body. These perceptions are then registered in the central nervous system and related to the present stock of concepts contained there. They are then used by the individual to alter his concepts or to change his values regarding the concepts. The concepts are then used in a decision-making process. The person decides how the new concepts will be acted out in terms of behavior. This process obviously requires the incorporation of value judgments. The person proceeds to act out his changed conceptions by making a trial response while the teacher provides feedback. If the trial according to the teacher's judgment shows that the individual has a misconception, the teacher is able to assist the student in correcting this misconception by providing additional experiences or altering the objects or events in the environment. The student is then asked to make another decision and try out the concept in some behavioral way. One of the significant problems in education is that a portion of this learning cycle is frequently omitted in the process of teaching and learning in the classroom. It is not unusual to find the student engaged in sensory intake and retrieval with little or no time given to decision making, trial, and feedback. The student more often than not is evaluated on his performance with no opportunity to receive feedback beforehand. Thus, the teacher has little information concerning whether or not the student is prepared for final evaluation until after the evaluation is given. If a student's poor score results from a misconception, the teacher is unaware of this. He is forced to conclude only that the student made a poor test response. Ideally, through the teacher's assistance in a feedback situation, the student could polish his skills and be reasonably confident of his ability in a testing situation. Perhaps the necessity of distributing grades has forced many teachers to limit the time and effort needed to provide adequate feedback to students prior to evaluation. If most students were able to meet the objectives, the teacher would find it difficult to distribute grades based on the normal curve.

In teaching a concept to students there are logical steps which the teacher may follow to increase the likelihood that students will under stand what is being taught. First, the teacher must provide some kind of motivation, or establish set. The primary purpose of this procedure is to influence the student to become engaged in the educational task. The next step the teacher should take is to carefully and specifically outline the objective, so that students know what they are expected to be able to do after instruction. When the teacher is confident that all the students understand the objectives of the lesson, he is ready to make some kind of presentation of the learning task. In accomplishing this he must help the student understand the science concept. The teacher has to ask himself how to evoke an accurate and understandable image of the concept. One way to do this is by vicarious experience. Movies and filmstrips are frequently used for this purpose. One might also dramatize experience through role playing or group dynamics, or through modeling the concept by using graphs, charts, maps, or diagrams. Actual experiences may be used when feasible. The teacher must portray the concept so that it is understood by as many students as possible. This reduces the amount of subsequent clarification necessary. It requires thought about the readiness of the class to perceive the materials. Once this initial presentation has been made, the next step is to induce the students to make a trial response. The nature of this trial response depends, of course, on the nature of the objective for that particular lesson. The students may be expected to give an explanation of the concept in unusual conditions. Then the students' trial behaviors must be monitored and feedback given them concerning the correctness of their responses. A series of trial feedback experiences may be necessary before the teacher is satisfied that the students are able to perform the particular task. When student response is satisfactory, the concept must be fixed in their minds. This is accomplished by drill or practice. Hopefully, this procedure will assist students in recalling the concept from memory when necessary. At this point evaluation of whether or not the objective of the lesson has been achieved should take place.

In teaching a concept lesson, one of the skills that must be demonstrated is that of breaking down the component parts of a concept in a logical way and organizing them appropriately for student understanding. The teacher then teaches the concept in an orderly, sequenced pattern so that the image perceived by the student is the same one the teacher intends to portray. The teacher may accomplish this in at least one of two ways, by induction or deduction. During the inductive process, information is ordered so that the student moves from the specific to the general. He is given examples and is expected to discover the concept they represent. Deduction requires the student to move from the general to the specific. In this case the teacher indicates the concept and then gives examples of it.

One important aspect of the interaction model is that of the action of minds on ideas (Searles, 1967). Central to this consideration is the perceptual screen. Because individuals have a variety of experiences, needs, and expectations, their perceptions of portrayed materials will vary. Ideas presented will likely reflect the concerns that the student has at that particular time. Student responses during dialogue will also reflect these personalized aspects. Student contributions have to be interpreted by the teacher and used as constituents of the lesson. If the lesson is to have a consistent direction, a good deal of skill must be developed in handling student responses which, because of the action of minds on ideas, digress from the direction intended by the teacher. It is imperative that despite distortion of the concept by student input, the teacher help the class see the direction of the lesson and make statements which encourage students to pursue that direction. Otherwise, confusion will result. A common example with young children is for a lesson to precipitate a comment concerning last night's TV programs. The comments may have nothing at all to do with the lesson. It may appear that the possibility of having a lesson fail because of misdirection is not worth the risk. However, even though student-to-teacher interaction is a difficult form of teaching, more stands to be gained than where the teacher simply transmits information. Foremost among the possible benefits is the increased likelihood that students understand what is being taught. Secondly, the teacher is able to determine through the feedback process the extent of student understanding and gear his teaching appropriately.

The interaction model for instruction involves a number of related activities. Fundamental to the model is the problem we have in making accurate perceptions and communicating with one another. Because of this difficulty, feedback must occur for communication to be effective.

This is critical in education because of the great amount of communication that takes place. Not only must the student accurately perceive the concept portrayed by the teacher, but the teacher must be able to determine when communication has been understood by the student. If he does not get feedback from the student, he will not know when the student is prepared for evaluation. As part of the total model, the teacher has to focus upon the strategy that will bring about the understanding of the concept. He also has to know how to properly organize and sequence knowledge for instruction. In the use of the dialogue, the teacher must be aware of the problems of encouraging student input in the learning situation and be able to receive these inputs and use them in a directed consideration of the concept.

Exercise 11–6 Concepts and Principles

Complete the following questions.

1. What is a concept?
2. What is a principle?
3. Write two examples of a concept and two examples of a principle in science.
4. Write a science concept and give one example and one nonexample of the concept.
5. Why is an interaction method for teaching a concept or principle recommended?

Writing a Lesson Plan

As you read the following examples of lesson plans, begin thinking of a topic from your major field which you could use in a simulated lesson. Then organize a concept lesson which facilitates engaging students in interaction. Plan your lesson so that you will be able to demonstrate the skills of set induction, stimulus variation, use of examples, repetition, and closure. Make certain that your lesson follows the format outlined in the examples presented here.

SAMPLE LESSON PLAN

Class: Upper Grades
Title: Energy Transfer in Biological Systems
Preassessment: Have students define the following terms: energy, potential energy, and food chain.
Objective: Students will be able to satisfactorily explain the transfer of energy in a food chain, pointing out the influence on energy transfer of the following items:

      1. The length of the food chain and available energy.
      2. Energy loss.

Content: Basic Concepts

      1. Energy may be transformed from one type to another but is never created or destroyed.
      2. Because some energy is always dispersed into unavailable heat energy, no spontaneous transformation of energy (light, for example) into potential energy (protoplasm, for example) is 100 percent efficient.
      3. In each transfer in a food chain, a large proportion of the potential energy is lost as heat.
      4. The number of links in a food chain is usually limited to four or five.
      5. The shorter the food chain, the greater the available energy that can be converted into biomass. (*Biomass* is living weight, including stored food.)

Learning Experiences:

      1. Use the overhead projector to portray the energy-flow diagram and discuss it.
      2. Discuss the concepts outlined in the content of the lesson and explain how they are related to the concept of energy transfer. Get written responses from every student and provide feedback.
      3. Direct students to appropriate laboratory experiments regarding energy transfer.
      4. Take a field trip to Lackley Pond to observe food-chain relationships.

Materials:

    Overhead projector, laboratory equipment, biological material, and bus arrangements.

Evaluation: Sample Questions

      1. Explain how energy transfer occurs in a typical food chain. In your answer explain how the length of the food chain is related to energy transfer.
      2. Identify the various points of energy loss in a food chain including herbs, deer, and mountain lion.

    Read the following two sections carefully. These will explain the format which should be used in making an analysis of your simulated teaching. Read and study them thoughtfully so that you can make a similar analysis of your teaching. Also examine the "Concept Lesson Analysis Guide," which will help you make an analysis of your video-taped lesson. Write your analysis as you view a videotaped replay of your lesson and keep it for use when you prepare the written analysis of your lesson.

How to Analyze a Simulated Lesson

The "Critique For Simulated Teaching" form should be used as a basis for analyzing your lesson. Each of the teaching skills should be described in terms of the specific way in which you performed during the first lesson and how you could have improved or did improve your performance in the second lesson on that particular skill. For example, if your set induction was not sufficiently motivating, identify the reason for this and describe exactly what you could have done or said to improve it, and how you were able to accomplish this in your second lesson. You should avoid analyzing your lesson by making general statements regarding your behavior—how you appeared or how you felt. Such statements as "I was really nervous" or "I didn't know what to do with my hands" contribute little to an analysis.

It is important that you understand what behavior is represented by each of the skills, or you will be unable to make an appropriate analysis. If, for example, you believe closure to be synonymous with a review, your analysis will disclose your misunderstanding of this term.

When analyzing your objective, it is essential that you make a judgment not in terms of how you stated your objective, but rather on the extent to which your students knew what was expected of them subsequent to instruction. They should clearly understand how they must respond and how you will judge their performance. The purpose of the lesson and how students are expected to respond in terms of the lesson objective should ordinarily be taught at the beginning of the lesson but reference should be made regarding the objective at other strategic places in the lesson. It is generally good practice to begin a lesson with set induction and follow this immediately with a statement of the expected student outputs; then, during the lesson, students' attention can be focused on how specific learning activities will help achieve objectives.

The learning experiences in which you engage students should contribute to achieving the objectives you have identified for them. You should check your lesson carefully to see if there is a close correspondence between the objectives and the learning activities in which students participated. In your lesson it is expected that students enter into a dialogue with the teacher and that the teacher give feedback on the students' trial responses. This type of learning activity is important because it is usually necessary for the teacher to correct student responses a number of times before they are adequately exhibited. In your analysis, attempt to make a judgment regarding the clarity with which this dialogue proceeds. Are you supportive of student responses? Are you empathetic? Do you ask students to clarify ambiguous statements they make? Do you give good examples in addition to asking students to formulate their own examples? These questions will help in making an analysis of your lesson.

SIMULATED LESSON ANALYSIS: AN EXAMPLE

The following is an example of the written analysis you should make of your lesson. Study its contents carefully so that you can use it as a format for your own lesson analysis.

Set Induction. My second lesson was a significant improvement over my first one. Set induction was particularly weak in my first lesson. I simply stated that "Today we are going to learn about stomates." This statement stood for both the set induction and the objective. For my set induction I could have begun with the statement "A single corn plant may transpire four quarts of water a day. An acre of corn may give off 300,000 gallons of water in a single growing season. How do you think such a large water loss is possible?" I could then have shown the class a magnified picture of a leaf, showing stomates, and explained that water is lost through these minute openings at varying rates depending on the size of the opening and the number of openings per unit of area on the leaf surface. I could then have asked if they would expect desert plants to have more or fewer stomates than tropical plants. I did this in my second lesson. I had their immediate attention.

Objective. I would then teach the lesson objective to the students in the following manner: "We are going to study stomates and their functioning. When we have completed this lesson, you should be able to explain the mechanism by which the stomate opens and what factors influence this opening."

Stimulus Variation. In my first lesson, stimulus variation was good. I think I did an adequate job of using student-to-student and student-to-teacher interaction. I also think that my movements about the room and gestures were natural and expressive. The one improvement that I wanted to make in my second lesson was to include variations in terms of aural and visual stimuli. In order to accomplish this I used the chalkboard to diagram what I was talking about. I believe that student attention as well as understanding was enhanced by this change.

Use of Examples. In my first lesson students found it difficult to understand how the two stomate guard cells could expand and contract in such a way as to cause an opening and closing of the stomate. For my second presentation I constructed a mock-up of a stomate using a bicycle innertube with additional thicknesses of tubing glued to its inner surfaces. As air is forced into the innertube, it opens in a way similar to stomates. This example clarified the process very well. One thing that I failed to do in both lessons was to ask for examples from the students. I could have asked if anyone knew examples of osmotic pressure and how it operated.

Repetition. In my first lesson I failed to have any repetition at all. I thought I was being understood. Only at the end of the lesson did I realize that students were unable to understand how new information related to previously covered material. In my second lesson I carefully reviewed the concepts of turgor and osmotic pressure before illustrating how the guard cells expanded. This procedure greatly increased the understanding of the students.

Closure. In my first lesson I did not achieve closure at all. I reviewed at the end of the lesson but each of the parts of the lesson was not understood by students in terms of its relationships, and thus a review was pointless. I decided that misconception of the process of osmosis was the basic problem area and the major reason why students were unable to obtain closure. In the second lesson I set up a demonstration of osmotic pressure using a semipermeable membrane to show students that water actually flowed into areas of higher concentration of dissolved substances. I then made a diagram on the board like the one illustrated:

3 percent Sugar	5 percent Sugar		7 percent Sugar	5 percent Sugar

Students were able to obtain closure on stomate opening with a proper conception of osmosis as I explained the diagram.

Interaction and Feedback. One of the major problems in my first lesson was the small amount of student-to-teacher interaction during the time the most complex part of the lesson was presented. I didn't permit students to try out what they were learning and, of course, I couldn't then provide them with feedback on their responses. In my second lesson I improved somewhat, but I still have a tendency to lecture and not engage the student in interaction.

Mannerisms. In my first lesson I noticed that I played with the chalk and used the expression "Okay" excessively. In my second lesson I did not play with the chalk, but I did not successfully reduce the number of times I said "Okay."

Use of A-V Aids. In my second lesson the use of mock-up and the chalkboard as aids greatly improved the understanding of the concepts I was teaching. However, I should have checked the pump I planned to use to blow up the innertube on the mock-up. It didn't work at first and acted as a deterrent to maintaining the attention of the class.

Achievement of the Objective. In my first lesson I'm not sure if I achieved my objective or not. I seriously doubt it. In the first place I didn't check by asking students questions about the concept. Also, I believe that many of my statements were unclear. In addition, I appeared to expect students to be able to see inside my mind for understanding because I didn't connect the subcomponent parts of the concept I was teaching. I acted as though I expected them to make all of the connections themselves. I didn't realize this until I was watching the playback. In my second lesson I did a better job of connecting the various concepts together. It was still very evident that my communication skill is limited. For one thing, I tend not to complete statements. I just trail off in the end expecting the class to fill in what I don't complete.

It is expected that individuals using this form for purposes of evaluation give written explanations and criticisms which correspond to the questions above as well as check an overall rating in each category. It is particularly useful for raters to include suggested improvements for the lessons they view.

CRITIQUE FOR SIMULATED TEACHING

Concept Lesson

Teacher _____ Date _____

Evaluator _____

	Unable to Observe	Not Achieved	Below Average	Average	Strong	Superior
	0	1	2	3	4	5
1. *Set Induction.* Was the set induction motivating and properly related to the learning task? How could it have been improved?						
2. *Stimulus Variation.* Did the teacher change the mode of the stimulus so that there was adequate variation? How could improvements be made?						
3. *Use of Examples.* Did the teacher use clear and appropriate examples? Did he request examples from students? Where would examples have been appropriate when they were not used?						
4. *Repetition.* Did the teacher provide repetition in appropriate places as a means of enhancing the learning of his students? How could it have been improved?						
5. *Closure.* Did the teacher make appropriate use of closure? How should this skill have been employed?						
6. *Objectives.* Were the objectives of the lesson clearly understood by the students? How could they have been improved?						
7. *Empathy.* Was the teacher empathetic in his corrections of students' misconceptions and did he display skill in interpreting the intent of student questions? Give instances where empathy was shown or where there was lack of empathy.						
8. *Interaction Skill.* Did the teacher demonstrate skill in engaging students in interaction?						

9. Enthusiasm?

10. Appearance and Mannerisms?

11. Communication Skills?

12. *Skillful Use of A-V Aids.* Did the visual aids add to the lesson or detract from it?

13. *Learning Activities.* Were learning activities appropriate in terms of the objectives? Describe the ways in which they were or were not.

14. *Objectives Achieved.* Were the objectives of the lesson achieved?

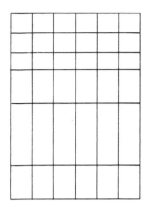

Concept Lesson Analysis Guide

1. Cite two instances of giving examples of the science concept you were attempting to teach.
2. Cite one example where you asked a student to provide an example of the concept.
3. Cite one nonexample which you used to clarify the concept. If no nonexamples were given, formulate one and identify where it could have been used to advantage in the lesson.
4. What evidence do you have that learners understood and achieved your objective? Cite at least two instances of student behavior which indicate the objective was achieved.
5. Cite at least two instances which give evidence that students were interested in your lesson. How could you have gained more interest in your lesson?
6. Cite two specific instances of how you varied the stimulus in your presentation. What was the student reaction to your maneuver? How could you have improved your stimulus variation?
7. Cite at least two instances where your questions were unclear. How did learners respond to these questions? How could you have rephrased your questions to reflect the appropriate clarity?
8. Identify two specific instances where you tried to obtain closure. Give evidence, in terms of student responses, that you did achieve closure or identify the reason that you were unable to achieve closure.

Replanning a Lesson

One of the skills which should be developed in teaching is that of making appropriate analysis of teaching and formulating alternative approaches which will diminish the weaknesses pointed out in the analysis. Since you will be replanning and reteaching a number of lessons, you should carefully consider the points outlined below.

The perfect lesson has probably never been taught in the schools. Even with a well taught lesson, careful analysis invariably reveals weaknesses, which when corrected, improve subsequent presentations. The tendency for the beginning teacher is to say that he did alright in asking higher order questions or in cuing or in demonstrating any of the other teaching skills when they are, in reality, demonstrating a very minimum level of acceptability. In teaching, minimum acceptable levels can and should be improved upon. This requires that a careful analysis be performed regarding the planning and teaching of a lesson and that subsequent planning and teaching reflect revisions designed to overcome the problems which are evident. It is desirable that you begin developing sophistication in analyzing teaching and planning so that you do not come to consider mediocre teaching as acceptable or believe you are doing alright when you could do better.

As part of this simulated teaching exercise you are required to make an analysis of the presentation of your simulated lesson. Using this analysis as a basis, you must formulate a new lesson plan which will help in overcoming the problems identified in the first lesson. It is essential that in rethinking your lesson you develop alternative approaches. For example, if in your first lesson you failed to bring about closure for part of the class as a result of questioning only a few students during the discussion, you may alter this procedure by requiring all students to make a trial response during the lesson. This change would be reflected in the "learning experiences" section of your lesson plan.

You should examine each part of your lesson plan and lesson presentation with the intention of altering each of these components appropriately. Some components may not need much change, but each should be carefully considered.

Simulated Teaching and Analysis

Teach a concept lesson to a group of pupils using an interaction model and incorporating the skills of set induction, stimulus variation, use of examples, repetition, and closure. (Pupil participants should be asked to provide the teacher with an evaluation of his lesson.) If possible, videotape your lesson as you teach it. While viewing the videotape replay, make a self-analysis of your lesson using the procedure explained in the previous sections of this chapter. Also use the "Concept Lesson Analysis Guide" in making your analysis.

Replanning, Reteaching, and Analysis

Using the information from the pupil evaluations as well as your own analysis, reorganize your concept lesson and reteach it. Pay particular attention to overcoming the problems identified in your first attempt at the lesson. Identify how you could improve in the use of the following skills: set induction, stimulus variation, use of examples, repetition, and closure. Check to see if your objective was carefully taught to and understood by the class. Identify any annoying mannerisms or poor communication skills. Determine whether or not you could reasonably expect your students to be able to achieve the objectives. It is imperative that the reorganization of your lesson reflect a careful restructuring of your strategy based on the analysis of your first lesson. You should be able to produce a significantly different approach to the lesson. Videotape the retaught lesson. Get evaluations from your pupils. Make a self-analysis of your lesson while viewing the videotaped replay. Use the format outlined in the previous sections of this chapter. NOTE: Supervisory personnel may also provide feedback and evaluation during the simulated teaching experiences.

Teaching the Inquiry Lesson

OBJECTIVES

1. *Lesson Plan.* The student will develop a lesson plan for teaching an inquiry lesson. The lesson plan must follow the format outlined in the "Sample Analysis Lesson Plan" in this chapter.
2. *Simulated Teaching.* The student will teach a fifteen-minute lesson which he has developed, having an instructional objective which requires pupils to use the inquiry method. He must appropriately demonstrate the skills of set induction, cuing, reinforcement, higher order questions, and closure. This lesson will be taught to elementary school students or peers and may be videotaped.
3. *Analysis.* After viewing the videotape of his lesson, the student will make an analysis of his teaching. He must be able to evaluate his teaching skill in the use of set induction, cuing, reinforcement, higher order questions, and closure. He must also be able to determine the extent to which his students learned how to perform analysis skills and how skillfully he used the guided discussion method.
4. *Replan, Reteach, and Analysis.* The student must be able to replan and reteach his fifteen-minute lesson, eliminating the problem areas identified in his analysis of the first lesson. The student must make a written analysis from the videotaped replay of his lesson, using the "Critique for Simulated Teaching" form and including a comparison between the teach and reteach cycles.

Review the descriptions for the skills of set induction and closure found in the description of a concept lesson. Then read the following descriptions of the skills of cuing, reinforcement, and asking higher order questions and complete the exercises which accompany these descriptions.

Cuing

Justification for cuing can readily be made from the fact that wrong as well as right answers strengthen themselves as soon as they occur. Consequently, merely correcting responses will not reduce their tendency to occur. In other words, making inappropriate responses will reduce one's ability to make the appropriate ones subsequently. Cues help to guide the student in making the correct responses. Usually cues are diminished gradually as the student demonstrates his ability to make appropriate responses.

The teacher must make a decision regarding the timing and nature of cuing. If it appears that a good deal of preparation for an adequate response is necessary, the teacher may have to provide the appropriate cues a day or so in advance. The teacher must also decide whether or not the cuing should be public or private. Private cuing a day in advance may be the best way to get an overly shy person to participate in class (Allen, *et al.*, 1969c).

Occasionally a particular cue is not sufficient to prepare students to respond appropriately. A series of successive approximations is recommended as a strategy for gradually helping the student to make the desired response. This means that students are cued in stepwise fashion, gradually building until they are able to make the appropriate terminal response. Several cues may be presented before a student responds. Additional cuing may be engaged in subsequent to the student's response if the teacher desires to clarify the student's thinking. The teacher thus shapes the student's responses until they are appropriately given.

One should use appropriate timing when cuing students. Each cue should be followed by a sufficiently long period of silence to permit students to formulate their response. Over-cuing in rapid succession exceeds the thinking capabilities of most students and results in the teacher rather than the students giving the desired responses. The length of time the teacher should wait between cues is directly proportional to the difficulty level of the question and the proximity of the cue to the appropriate response. This requires the exercise of judgment. A good deal of experience is usually required to adequately master this skill. The following are some examples of how cuing may proceed:

1. Teacher: If you were going on a trip to Mars, what
                  special systems would have to be developed

		in order to support life on such a voyage?
Class:	Silence.
Teacher:	What would you do about food? (This cue helps the student limit the field from which to formulate his response.)
Student:	You would have to carry a lot of dehydrated foods and high energy foods I suppose.
Teacher:	If you couldn't carry enough food with you, how could you obtain it? (This cue is designed to help the student focus attention away from a less plausible response to one that is more reasonable.)
Student:	I suppose you could grow it.
Teacher:	What kind of food could be grown in a space ship that would meet requirements for such a long voyage? (This cue helps to focus the students' attention upon the problem of what kind of food could be grown in limited confines of a space craft.)

2. Teacher: From the diagrams can you determine whether sodium or nickel would be more reactive?

Class: Silence.

Teacher: How many electrons are there in the outer shell of each element? (This cue helps the student determine what he needs to consider in making an appropriate response.)

Student: Sodium would be more reactive because it has only one electron in the outer shell.

Exercise 11–7 Cuing

Complete the following exercise on cuing:

1. Describe different instances where cuing is appropriate.
2. Write a difficult or complex question and identify the cues you would use in clarifying the intent of the question so that students are able to answer it. (Include questions and instructions that are necessary.)

Reinforcement

One of the most fundamental functions of the classroom teacher is providing appropriate reinforcement to students in his class. The research on the use of reinforcement in the classroom has been extensive and generally conclusive. Reinforcing a response or set of responses increases the likelihood that that particular behavior will reoccur (Allen, *et al.,* 1969c). In addition, it increases the response frequency. It is important to review the difference between reinforcement and punishment because of the widespread misunderstanding regarding these terms. Reinforcement refers to an *increase* in the number of responses as a consequence of presenting or removing some kind of stimulus. Punishment is characterized by a *decrease* in the number of responses as a consequence of presenting or removing a stimulus. Usually the teacher defines these procedures in terms of what he does rather than the effect his actions have on the number of student responses. This should not be done. For example, a teacher who scolds a disruptive student usually believes that he is punishing the child and that the consequence will be a reduction in disruptiveness. However, it is common for such teacher behavior to increase the disruptive behavior output of some students. In other words, the scolding is reinforcing the student's deviant responses. It is absolutely essential that the teacher understand which responses he is reinforcing and which ones he is punishing.

A good model to follow in dealing with students in the classroom is to generally ignore inappropriate student responses and reinforce appropriate ones. The more appropriate the behavior which is encouraged the less time students have available to be disruptive. There is a tendency for beginning teachers to focus attention on disruptive behaviors rather than ignoring them. It will undoubtedly require considerable thought and practice to avoid focusing attention on disruptive behaviors and reinforcing desirable ones.

One of the principles which has consistently shown up in studies of reinforcement is that the closer reinforcement follows the desired behavior the more influence it has on the behavior. Thus, the longer reinforcement is delayed the less impact it will have. Of course, it is not always possible to immediately follow a particular response with the appropriate reinforcement. This has led some teachers to provide the student with some indication (in the form of a token which can be exchanged for a desired reinforcer) that they will receive the reinforcement later, thus bridging the time gap.

Another principle the teacher would be wise to utilize in terms of reinforcement is that of paying attention to students' deprivation states. ("Deprivation state" is a condition in which an individual has a strong need or desire for a particular thing at a particular time.) The effect of reinforcement is directly related to the degree of deprivation which that particular reinforcer would satisfy. For example, if it can be determined that a student has an intense need to be recognized, the teacher can arrange for the student to be recognized when he behaves appropriately. There is usually a good deal of difference in terms of potency between verbal reinforcers, tangibles, and special privileges. Tangibles are such things as candy, money, trinkets, stars, etc. Special privileges are such things as going to the lunchroom early, being the teacher's assistant, and running the projector. Some students can be strongly influenced by any of these but may respond poorly to verbal reinforcement. One way to get around this difficulty is to pair verbal reinforcement with tangibles or special privileges. Later when the behavior has been brought under control, you can gradually diminish tangibles and special privileges while continuing to maintain an adequate amount of social reinforcement.

A good deal of reinforcement may be necessary to encourage appropriate behavior by students initially. It is hoped that this level of required reinforcement can be reduced when the students become more interested in the subject matter itself as a consequence of their involvement with it. Thus, the subject matter itself can provide a reinforcing function and reduce the frequency of teacher reinforcement needed to a manageable level.

It should be pointed out that some educators have developed arguments against the exclusive use of external reinforcers for managing the behaviors of students and encouraging appropriate academic responses. In this brief discussion it can only be noted that these individuals believe differently about human nature and the nature of motivation. They believe that man has purposive motivations built in rather than motivation based on drive reduction or satisfaction which comes from external reinforcement. Rather than organizing the environment to influence behavior in specified directions, they believe that one should be expected, as a result of natural consequences, to develop responsible behavior. This behavior repertoire should help the individual engage in meaningful interpersonal relations which satisfy his needs of relatedness and respect (Glasser, 1965). The management procedures which are used involve helping the individual identify unacceptable behavior and its consequence and formulating acceptable alternatives which can be adhered to and which logically will help achieve relatedness and respect in the real world.

In delivering verbal reinforcement, the teacher should be careful to temper his/her response to correspond to the responses made by the students. Matter-of-fact reinforcers that usually appear in normal conversation such as "Right," "Un-huh," and "Good" provide low-key feedback to the student. If a student response is particularly outstanding, the teacher may make such exclamations as "Excellent," "Very Good," or may even provide such verbalizations as "Fantastic!" and "Tremendous!" Each of the above verbalizations can be given different connotations by simply varying the tone, expressing differing nonverbal feedback such as smiling, nodding the head, or gesturing with the arms and hands. The important point to remember is that the reinforcement should correspond to the response so that it does not appear either "bland or gushy."

One very useful kind of reinforcement which the teacher can employ is to use the ideas presented by students to enhance a discussion. He can also explain how important a particular student response is in understanding a particular topic. For example, if the class were discussing the topic of evolution and a student volunteered the fact that without genetic mutation evolution would be impossible, the teacher may provide reinforcement by saying, "Jim has provided us with one of the most important considerations in evolution. If there was no mechanism for altering the genetic material there would be no chance for new biological types to be tried out in the environment." In this statement the teacher has identified just how important Jim's contribution was and has gone on to elaborate the concept Jim has identified.

The teacher may also draw attention to the importance of student responses by referring the class to earlier statements made by class members and showing how these responses relate to or clarify the present discussion. For example, the teacher may say, "Do you remember a very important statement made by Bill at the beginning of the class which helps to clarify how the strength of an electromagnet can be determined?" The teacher could also say, "Bill stated at the beginning of the class that he thought he had observed different strengths depending on the number of coils. How do you think Bill's ideas contributed to our present understanding of electromagnets?"

Reinforcement may also be given to students by getting them involved in classroom activities. Participation is self-reinforcing. A good way to encourage participation is to give adequate verbal and nonverbal reinforcement, use student ideas by incorporating them into the discussion, and to deal with student emotional responses in a positive way. The teacher should also reduce the frequency of controlling and criticizing responses.

Success is another strong reinforcer. Too frequently, schools provide success experience for only a select few. This group is usually composed of highly intellectual, convergent thinkers who are able to conform to classroom routine with a minimum amount of dissatisfaction. Their behavior is reinforced by their success in getting good grades. This norm-based model does not take into account the need for all students to gain a feeling of success in their school work. Students simply will not pursue those activities which they do not succeed in. The wise teacher will encourage student involvement by formulating strategies which insure success for every student in science activities.

Exercise 11–8   Reinforcement

Complete the following exercise on reinforcement:

1. What are the modes of expression of reinforcement?
2. Give an example of how you would reinforce a student response in each of the following ways: (a) extending a student idea; (b) having a student extend his own idea; and (3) having the student's peers extend his idea.

Higher Order Questions

The great majority of questions in the average science classroom call for the student to simply recall information. This is done in spite of the fact that most teachers maintain that their purpose is to get students to think. A number of reasons may be postulated for the emphasis on remembering facts, but none of them seems justifiable. For example, some support the teaching of facts on the basis that it is too difficult to validly measure the higher mental processes in science. Others say that a knowledge of many facts is necessary for every properly functioning individual in our complex society. It should be noted that it is not the learning of facts which is to be condemned but rather learning them exclusively. Some facts are necessary, but even many of these should be learned in conjunction with the development of higher mental processes rather than by rote.

Higher order questions are those questions for which students obtain answers by engaging in the processes of analysis, synthesis, and evaluation. The student has to go beyond factual or descriptive information and learn to compare and contrast concepts and principles, determine meaningful patterns in a body of information, discover principles, make inferences, perceive cause and effect relationships, generalize, formulate consistent wholes, and evaluate products and possible problem solutions and courses of action (Allen, *et al.*, 1969d). Higher order questions require the student to discover and use science concepts and principles. Rather than the teacher figuring out the answers and requiring the student to remember them, higher order questions lead the student to inquire and figure out the answers himself. One of the key words used in higher level questioning is "Why?" The why question forces the student to go beyond the facts to justify, classify, infer, relate, and organize.

The teacher must know how to formulate questions which cause students to engage in specific kinds of mental activities. He/she must also be able to determine whether a student response is derived from a specified kind of mental activity. There are three factors which determine the kind of thinking which is brought about in the mind of the student by a particular question. First, one may consider the nature of the question in terms of its classification in the Taxonomy of Educational Objectives (Bloom, 1956). This factor will be the primary consideration of this discussion. Secondly, one must be aware of the knowledge about the subject which each student brings to the classroom. Each student has a different frame of reference based on the sum of his knowledge as well as his experiences and values. Consequently, a question which causes one student to engage in higher mental activities may only require another to recall information. For example, if the teacher asks students to differentiate between pro-ecology and pro-energy statements, one student may be required to engage in an analysis activity while another may simply have to recall having read the statement as it was made by a well-known spokesman whose position on the issues can be readily fixed.

The third factor which determines the kind of thinking a student has to do in response to a particular question is the instruction which precedes the asking of the question. If the answer to the question has already been dealt with in class, no opportunity exists to do anything more than simply recall information.

Questions may be formulated by the teacher which require the student to engage in specifiable mental operations. The Taxonomy of Educational Objectives is one convenient system for helping the teacher identify the kinds of questions which may be asked. It calls the teacher's attention to a number of possible kinds of thinking in which he may help students engage in the inquiry process. Without such a classification system, teachers are less likely to provide opportunities for students to develop these skills.

The first level which will be considered in this discussion is analysis. The following are examples of analysis questions. (It should be pointed out that some authorities may consider some of the low-level analysis questions listed here to be in the comprehension level of the taxonomy. Also, some questions may elicit either an analysis response or comprehension response. The examples shown are not limited to formal logical processes. It is assumed that analysis is indeed involved in responding to appropriately formulated questions where formal rules of logic are not necessarily used.)

Analysis is the examination of subcomponent parts of a communication or object designed to determine their relationships, inconsistencies, and principles. The following instructions and questions require the student to engage in *analysis* skills.

1. Compare the results of Jim's experiment with those of Ann's.

2. Which of the two arguments has the best support from the results of the experiment?
3. What principle applies in each of the four situations?
4. What is the relationship between the plants of this particular area and the temperature, rainfall, and soil constituents.

Synthesis questions are designed to cause students to formulate original communications or products from a number of subcomponent parts. These communications and products must reflect careful organization and integration of ideas. The following questions require the student to engage in *synthesis* skills.

1. If you were to embark on a journey to Mars, what would you take with you? Why?
2. What hypothesis can you suggest about the changes in the material on the aquarium bottom?
3. What kind of procedure can we use to determine how many different kinds of plants and animals inhabit the area around the school?
4. What kind of experiment could we devise to determine what different seeds need in order to germinate?

Evaluation questions are designed to cause students to determine the quality of communications or products. The following questions require students to engage in *evaluation* skills.

1. Which science fair project do you think is best? Why?
2. Which of the two experiments best controls extraneous variables?
3. Which transfer of bacteria was most expertly executed?

Success in teaching depends in large measure on the extent to which the teacher is able to use appropriate questioning skills. In order to effectively accomplish this, you must view yourself, not as a dispenser of information, but rather as one who can engage students in purposeful thinking processes. Beginning teachers find difficulty keeping this perspective. It is, therefore, recommended that you expend the necessary time and energy to bring about competency in this area.

Exercise 11–9   Higher Order Questions

Complete the following exercise on higher order questions:

1. What is a higher order question?
2. Identify the levels of higher order questioning; i.e., what kinds of higher order questions are there?
3. Write a question at each of the higher order levels.

Conducting a Guided Discussion

You will be expected to use the guided discussion in helping students learn the inquiry process. You will therefore need to read the following section carefully.

Discussion is commonly engaged in by people in all walks of life. The employee who has to clearly understand the explicit wishes of his employer resorts to a discussion of the issues. Examination of political issues, possible solutions to social problems, and many other topics are best handled after discussion sessions. Because of the wide use of discussion techniques, it seems advisable to differentiate between guided classroom discussions and other forms of discussion.

First, guided discussion is not an undisciplined "bull session." A "bull session" is the type of discussion which usually takes place in unstructured situations but which is occasionally resorted to by the classroom teacher. Generally, this form of discussion lacks purpose and moves aimlessly among a variety of topics. Any and all inputs are acceptable, and conclusions are rarely reached. It is not uncommon in these sessions for irrational ideas to dominate simply because they are sponsored by a more enthusiastic and forceful person. Ideas tend not to be weighed and considered in relation to one another, but rather to simply be asserted and supported. This kind of experience serves a useful function in generating new ideas but has limited utility in developing inquiry skills.

The open-ended discussion is a second type of discussion which should be differentiated from the guided discussion. Unlike the "bull session" this type of discussion does have a purpose, but it has very little direction. Usually, the purpose is to formulate an original set of ideas for developing a product, accomplishing an action, or understanding a phenomenon. The emphasis is upon the uniqueness of what is produced and thus little direction is given by the instructor. This type of discussion may be useful once children have developed inquiry skills, but is too open to permit initial development of these skills.

The guided class discussion has as its purpose the orderly investigation of a problem or issue with the intent of exploring all constituent parts and their relationships. Many times group agreement is sought, although this is not always necessary or even desirable. The important point is that all issues are examined rationally and logically and that possible points of disagreement or divergence be identified and explicated. Essentially, the task of the teacher is to lead the group to bring appropriate evidence to bear on the crucial issues of a problem. He must attempt to clarify student ideas which may be vague and ambiguous. In addition, he must monitor student contributions and relate each new bit of information to the whole problem while at the same time helping the class members to discard those ideas which are irrelevant or inaccurate. The teacher must exercise a high degree of support for students when their ideas are incongruent and help them formulate more appropriate responses. If the teacher fails to be supportive and helpful when inaccurate or inappropriate ideas are offered by students, he will alienate them and reduce or eliminate future participation.

The teacher must also aid the group to focus on ideas which are related to the problem under consideration but which no one has thought to consider. For example, if a group is discussing the topic of how to determine what a plant needs in order to grow, students may fail to realize that there may be nutrients of various kinds in the soil and not attempt to control for this variable in setting up their experiments. The teacher may say, "You have indicated what you think a plant needs to grow. Do you think the kind of soil you plant in will make a difference?"

The teacher should through appropriate questioning skills guide the class to identify inconsistencies in the arguments of one another. Rather than always pointing out these inconsistencies, a good practice is for the teacher to refer the matter to other students. The teacher may say, after listening to the response of a student, "What do you think, Ned, about Lynn's idea that we should put our plants in sandy soil so we can control the nutrients they receive."

There are a number of conditions which ordinarily must be satisfied if a guided discussion is to function smoothly. First, there must be a problem to solve through which the group can maintain some interest. Second, the group must have the requisite skills to deal with the problem and produce viable solutions. Third, the related facts must be at the disposal of the group and become part of the preparation of the group prior to discussion. Fourth, individual values and ideas must find their way into the discussion for possible consideration.

Certain steps should be followed in planning for and teaching a guided discussion. The first is that of identifying the problem or issue to be considered. It is essential that the selected topic be one that students have an interest in. If the topic is not directly related to student interests, the discussion should be developed so as to bear upon student interests. Topics which cannot be so developed are of little value for discussion because little participation will be generated. Controversial issues such as whether or not we should support population control lead naturally to discussion. However, with this type of topic the teacher should not be overly concerned with arriving at a consensus. Because there are a number of views on controversial topics, there is an increased likelihood that the various positions will be identified and compared. In addition, issues which are controversial frequently have two or more very plausible viewpoints. Attempting to identify differences and make comparisons among supportable but conflicting positions naturally engages students in discussion and aids in the development of inquiry skills in the process.

Once the problem for discussion has been identified, the teacher must begin planning goals and strategy and formulating his lesson plan. It is obviously apparent that the teacher must familiarize himself thoroughly with the topic. This entails knowing the basic arguments and questions which might be considered on all sides of the problem. He must also direct his students to sources of information which will adequately prepare them to engage in meaningful discussion. Lack of preparation by students is a viable deterrent to a successful discussion. Once the teacher has familiarized himself with the basic issues and questions involved with a problem, he should next construct an outline of these in the form of questions for inquiry. They should be organized so that the discussion generated by the questions flows smoothly and sequentially. The teacher's role then is to pose the questions, clarify questions and comments, direct resolution of different viewpoints, interpose intermittent summaries as needed, steer the discussion into new areas as the occasion demands, and finally to formulate and help execute student research. One tendency which the teacher should guard against is the practice of occuping too central a role in the discussion in terms of premature exposure of his personal values on the subject or performing too much of the inquiry himself. He would be better advised to refer questions to students rather than answering them himself. His purpose is to formulate questions and probe the responses of students, redirecting their comments as necessary, not verifying his authority by giving the "final word" on each issue. This display of authority encourages students to wait for the teacher's judgment and analysis rather than offering their own.

The third step has to do with how the analysis of the problem should proceed. The first consideration in making the analysis is to define the terms and limits of the problem. Then the teacher and the class members are to begin to identify each of the issues connected with the problem. Discussion should elucidate each of these issues. It is imperative that the basic assumptions which are associated with each consideration be identified and their validity checked. For example, if we wish to insure that our experiment on growing plants is properly controlled we may wish to check carefully the assumption that sandy soil can be used because it lacks the nutritive value of other soil types.

Because it is sometimes desirable at the close of the inquiry process to reach consensus, it is necessary that criteria for making judgments be evolved in the discussion process before conclusions are reached. This involves the skill of synthesis while the application of these criteria to the process of making a judgment requires evaluative skills. Frequently, a decision cannot be reached by the group because advantages and disadvantages weigh evenly against one another. In order to avoid this difficulty, it is recommended that when criteria for making judgments are identified, effort be made to order them in terms of priority. Then the solution which best satisfies prior criteria can be selected with little difficulty. The solution which is reached should be initially held as tentative. The purpose of this is to allow students an opportunity to gather additional information or to test out the solution as one would test a hypothesis using the experimental method. The guided class discussion can thus be used as a vehicle for teaching inquiry skills and for initiating library research and/or conducting experiments. Discussions which lead to consensus tend to be dead-end experiences while those which indentify unresolved issues lead to further inquiry and involvement on the part of the student. Both orientations serve their purposes, and most all classrooms should probably engage in both types of discussions.

INQUIRY LESSON PLAN

Examine the following "Sample Inquiry Lesson Plan." Then organize an inquiry lesson which can be taught in a fifteen-minute period which facilitates the use of a directed discussion. Plan your lesson so that you will be able to demonstrate the skills of set induction, cuing, reinforcement, higher order questions, and closure. Make certain that your lesson plan follows the format outlined in the "Sample Analysis Lesson Plan."

SAMPLE INQUIRY LESSON

Class: Fifth Grade

Title: The Movement Behavior of Ants

Objective: Students will be able to propose a means of inquiry into the movement behavior of ants which includes a description of the following: materials and equipment needed, observation and recording techniques, and procedures.

Content:

1. Ants move in a direction that will maintain a constant angle between their line of motion and the sun.
2. Ants use the sun as a means of orientation.
3. To locate their nest, ants depend on chemical substances they deposit on the trails.

Learning Activities:

1. Discuss with the children what they would have to do to determine what influences the movements of ants.
2. Ask them to suggest some means to determine were ants move and what may influence that movement.

3. Ask them what observational scheme they might use.
4. Ask them how they would determine how ants reacted to formic acid, food, and heavy objects placed in their path.

Evaluation:

Students will be evaluated upon their abilities to prepare a plan to investigate the movement of ants and to devise ways to plan and implement a plan or experiment.

Simulated Teaching and Analysis

Teach a fifteen-minute analysis lesson using the lesson plan which you have prepared. Have the lesson videotaped. Your lesson should be taught to either peers or elementary school pupils with each learner preparing an analysis of the lesson. While viewing the videotaped replay, make a self-analysis of your lesson using the procedure explained in "How to Analyze the Simulated Lesson" and "Simulation Lesson Analysis: An Example." Fill out the "Inquiry Lesson Analysis Guide" as you view your videotaped replay. In making your analysis you must be able to correctly identify your problems and formulate viable corrective measures.

Replanning, Reteaching, and Analysis

Using the analysis information from your lesson, reorganize and reteach your inquiry lesson. Pay particular attention to overcoming the problems identified in the first attempt at the lesson. Determine how you could have improved in terms of each of the following skills: set induction, cuing, reinforcement, higher order questions, and closure. Check to see if your objective was carefully taught to and understood by the class. Indentify any annoying mannerisms or poor communications skills. It is imperative that the reorganization of your lesson reflect a careful restructuring of your strategy based on the analysis of your first lesson. You must be able to produce a significantly different approach to the lesson. Videotape the retaught lesson and have the learners evaluate your presentation. A clinical analyst may also evaluate your lesson and provide feedback. Make a self-analysis of your lesson while viewing the videotaped replay. Again, the "Inquiry Lesson Analysis Guide" will be helpful in gathering data from which to make your analysis.

Inquiry Lesson Analysis Guide

1. What evidence do you have that students actually engaged in inquiry skills? Cite at least two instances. If there was no evidence, what would

you have done differently in the lesson in order to engage students in inquiry?

2. Cite at least two instances where you helped students differentiate between subcomponent parts of the subject under inquiry.
3. What evidence do you have that learners understood and achieved your objective? Cite at least two specific instances of student behavior which indicate that you achieved your objective.
4. Cite at least four higher order questions which you used in your lesson. Explain, in terms of the student responses to your questions, the extent

CRITIQUE FOR SIMULATED TEACHING

Inquiry Lesson

Teacher _____ Date _____

Evaluator _____

	Unable to Observe	Not Achieved	Below Average	Average	Strong	Superior
	0	1	2	3	4	5
1. *Higher Order Questions.* Did the questions asked require students to use higher order cognitive skills? What additional higher order questions could have been asked?						
2. *Reinforcement.* Did the teacher adequately reinforce the responses of students? Was it genuine and frequent enough?						
3. *Cuing.* Did the teacher demonstrate skill in cuing students? In what way could this skill have been improved?						
4. *Objective Taught.* Was the objective clearly understood by the students? How could this have been improved?						
5. *Objective Achieved.* Was the lesson objective achieved?						
6. Did the teacher engage students in meaningful discussion? Describe.						
7. *Learning Activities.* Were learning activities appropriate in terms of the objective? Describe the way in which they were or were not.						
8. Enthusiasm?						
9. Communication Skills?						
10. Appearance and Mannerisms? (Identify specific mannerisms which may create problems for the individual as a teacher.)						
11. Skillful Use of A-V Aids?						

to which your questions were clear or unclear. How would you rephrase your questions?

5. Identify four specific statements which could be considered reinforcing. How could you have increased the reinforcement value of these statements?

6. Cite at least two instances which give evidence that students were interested in your lesson. How could you have gained more interest in your lesson?

7. Identify two specific instances where you tried to obtain closure. Give evidence, in terms of student responses, that you did achieve closure or identify the reason you were unable to achieve closure.

8. Cite two specific instances of cuing. Explain why the cues were given and the effect they had on learners. How could you have rephrased your cue to improve it?

Individuals using the form for purposes of evaluation should give written explanations and criticisms which correspond to the questions above as well as check an overall rating in each category. It is particularly useful for raters to include suggested improvements for the lessons they view.

Teaching an Affective Lesson

OBJECTIVES

1. *Lesson Plan.* The student will develop a lesson plan for teaching an affective lesson. The lesson plan will follow the format of the lesson plan for teaching a concept.

2. *Simulated Teaching.* The student will teach an affective lesson in which he/she exhibits skill in set induction, probing questions, divergent questions, appropriate use of silence, nonverbal cues, and closure.

3. *Written Analysis.* The student will make a written analysis of his/her teaching based upon his own observations as well as those of his peers. In this written analysis the student must evaluate his skill in demonstrating each of the following skills: set induction, probing questions, divergent questions, silence, nonverbal cues, and closure.

4. *Replan, Reteach, and Analysis.* The student will replan and reteach his/her affective lesson, eliminating the problem areas identified in his analysis of his first affective lesson.

When a teacher incorporates any material in his/her teaching, he must be aware that there are two distinct and important aspects of that material to the learner. These are, first, the content, concept, or skill itself and, second, the meaningfulness, value, or importance of the content to the learner. In recent years, teachers have spent much of their time focusing on the first aspect of the relationship of content to their students. That is, they have been intent upon the transmission of a given body of content to their students to the exclusion of affect. In teaching science there is a place for both types of teaching. Objectives in the affective domain focus on the meaningfulness of that particular concept to the learner or they may involve teaching scientific values. As such, the affective domain represents the identification, clarification, and exploration of beliefs, values, appreciations, emotions, and attitudes. It may also validly represent the teacher's attempt to inculcate within the learner specific values or attitudes.

Thus, we may view the effective domain as the emotional set with which each person interacts with content. It is comprised of his values, attitudes, interests, appreciations, feelings (both positive and negative), for or toward a given body of content or segment of content. It determines the uses to which the student will put cognitive material. Whereas in the cognitive domain the student can perform certain manipulations with content, the affective domain contains the means of governing how he will use those capabilities of cognitive manipulation. For example, science may contain many ideas which are potentially destructive and must be controlled through proper values.

The affective domain deserves careful attention, exploration, and evaluation. Unfortunately, far less has been done in the affective domain than in the cognitive. And there are valid reasons for this being so. First, there is a common belief that what a person holds as his value system is a personal area and that the teacher should not attempt to teach values, or force his own value system upon students. Even if it is granted that the person does remain the determiner of his own value system, the question still remains, "Why give a person massive amounts of information and then not give him any direction or directions by which to utilize that information?" For example, to give students information regarding the ecological systems of the earth and the relationships between those systems without instilling in them a value for the ecological system and how its balance is critical, may encourage the destruction of our earth itself by misuse of natural resources. The school does have a place in attempting to teach values to the student in order to direct the use of information gained by the student.

It must be pointed out that the teaching of values in the public schools is more controversial than the teaching of content and skills. One major reason for this is that objectives in the affective domain are much harder to write and even more difficult to evaluate. Another reason is that society determines to a great extent the values that would be acceptable as valid educational concerns. Thus, some values such as democracy, conservation, truthfulness, honesty, etc., are acceptable values to be taught in American schools. But some values are controversial and their encouragement may be subject to question.

In teaching your affective lesson you will be adding four new teaching skills. They include probing questions, divergent questions, silence, and nonverbal cues. These are to be used in addition to the techniques previously mastered in teaching the concept lesson and the inquiry lesson. However, emphasis should be given to developing these new skills.

Probing Questions

The purpose of probing questions is to extend the student's thinking. They are questions that clarify or elaborate upon the statement that has been made. They help the student find additional implications in previous statements. They seek to make points more explicit or complete (Allen, *et al.*, 1969d). Probing questions forestall superficial answers by forcing the student to go beyond his first response. Thus, the cue to probing questions is the student's response. Without the response, there can be no probe. The particular form of the probing question used is determined by the student's response. The teacher can never know beforehand exactly what questions to ask in probing a student's response.

Three ways a teacher may use probing questions are: clarifying responses, justifying responses, and relating responses to another area. If a teacher seeks clarification, he may use a probing question such as "Would you explain exactly what you mean?" "Could you rephrase that statement?" "Would you elaborate on that point?" "Will you define the term you are using?" If the teacher seeks to increase the student's critical awareness or justify his response, he might use some of the following: "What facts or conditions are you assuming?" "What is your rationale for your response?" "Are there other component parts that you have not covered?" "Assume the opposing position to this point. How would you respond?" If the teacher wishes to have the student relate his response to another issue, he might use some of the following: "How is this related to plant growth?" "How would you analyze your answer?" "If we assume that this is true, what are the implications for your experiment?"

In the following dialogue, classify each of the probing questions as to its function (clarifying, justifying, or relating).

Teacher's Opening Question: Why do you think that Ray's experiment will answer the question about whether plants convert sugar to starch in darkness? *Student Response:* Because the presence of starch is measured before and after placing the plant in the dark.

1. *Probing Question:* Why would this answer the question? *Student Response:* Because his experiment uses plants without starch and then lets them produce starch.
2. *Probing Question:* Does this tell us anything about sugar? *Student Response:* Well we already know that sugar is produced in plants.
3. *Probing Question:* Does this tell us, though, that plants change sugar to starch in darkness? *Student Response:* I guess it doesn't.
4. *Probing Question:* How could the experiment be redesigned so that this could be determined?

You should have classified probing question 1 as justification. In asking why, you are asking the student to justify or give his rationale for his response. Probing question 2 seeks clarification of what the student thinks. Probing question 3 also calls for clarification. Probing question 4 has as its goal relating the response to redesigning the experiment.

Exercise 11–10 Probing Questions

Construct a dialogue in which you give at least three student responses. One of your probing questions should ask for clarification, one for justification, and one should seek the relationship of the response to another area.

Divergent Questions

Divergent questions are another technique that a teacher can use to help a student explore affect. This kind of question is probably the least often asked in the classroom. If a teacher wants his students to develop their ability to deal with affect, he must vary his questions. Divergent questions, in particular, help to develop the student's and the teacher's creative dimension. In his research, Gallagher (1963) found that slight increases in the percentage of teacher divergent thinking questions yield a large increase in the divergent production of students.

Divergent questions have no right or wrong answers (Allen, *et al.*, 1969d). They are open-ended and require students to use both concrete and abstract thinking in order to arrive at an appropriate response. The student is free to explore the problem in whatever direction he chooses, think creatively, leave the comfortable boundaries of the known and reach out into the unknown. Frequently this is an uncomfortable situation for the teacher. It can easily be seen that a teacher who is authoritarian and "knows" the "right answers" would find it difficult to engage his class in divergent thinking. In using divergent questions, you should not sit as a judge, handing down sentences of correct or incorrect. You merely serve to help students think creatively, placing knowledge in a juxtaposition and seeing if they can come up with new knowledge. You may point out fallacies in the student's logic, offer suggestions by other questions, or reinforce, but you must be careful to refrain from making judgmental statements or the value of the divergent thinking is lost. Students respond in like kind to their teacher's behavior.

Some examples of divergent questions might be: "What will happen to the results of the experiment if you increase the concentration of salt?" "What would happen if the knowledge uncovered by scientists was permitted to be followed by anyone who wanted to?"

Exercise 11–11 Divergent Questions

In the area of science state a topic you would use to teach an affective lesson.

List five divergent questions you might use in teaching this topic.

Silence

The third technique that a teacher may use in order to teach an affective lesson is that of silence. Silence is a rarity in many classrooms. Some teachers find silence in the classroom intolerable. Students may use silence to control the teacher's behavior. The teacher asks a question of a student, but the student says nothing. In a few moments the teacher is uncomfortable and probably breaks the silence himself. He may reword the question, give more information, or ask another student. By silence the student has forced the teacher to behave differently than he planned to. Silence may also be used to advantage by the teacher. He may use it to encourage student participation, to create drama, or simply to allow students to collect their thoughts. Teachers can use silence to *direct thinking and facilitate learning.* Silence allows the student time to cogitate thoughts, try out things in his head. It allows reflection. It allows him time to restructure his thinking to include or exclude new facts presented to him. Silence is necessary in using probing and divergent questions. Since the student is being asked to extend himself or to propose to the class an answer to a divergent question, he must have time to reflect on his answer, to try one response out in his mind, discard it, and try another and another.

Nonverbal Cues

Since teaching affective lessons often involves responses through class discussion, three main kinds of nonverbal cues may be used by the teacher to encourage student response (Allen, *et al.*, 19693).

Facial cues are the easiest for the students to detect, and are therefore likely to be the most powerful. Sometimes these cues are regarded by the student as the most valid indication of what the teacher really means and may be accepted while inconsistent verbal responses are ignored. A smile encourages and tells a student to continue. A frown indicates displeasure, causing the response to take one of two forms. The student may halt his response, or he may feel that he must justify his response by further clarification. Other facial expressions that cue the student are: (a) looking thoughtful as the student responds, thus indicating that the teacher is considering the response; (b) smiling while the student is responding and thus encouraging him to continue; and (c) looking quizzically as though the student's answer was not clear, which generally stimulates the student to reword his answer or clarify it.

Head movement is another type of nonverbal cue. A smile or nod of the head on the part of the teacher can encourage a student. Nodding indicates that the student is on the right track. Likewise, a teacher by merely shaking his head indicates to a student that his response is unacceptable and the student may change his response. To indicate to a student that he is listening to the response, the teacher merely needs to tilt his head and ear toward the student and assume a thoughtful look.

The third kind of nonverbal cue is that of *body movement.* Simply by moving a bit closer to the student responding, the teacher indicates that he is interested in what the student is saying. By assuming a thoughtful pose (fist under chin, etc.), the teacher indicates to the class that he is considering the student's response. In using these nonverbal cues, teachers try to encourage student participation.

Exercise 11–12   Nonverbal Cues

1. What are the three major types of nonverbal cues?
2. What facial cues could a teacher use to encourage a student to respond?
3. What facial cue could a teacher use to curtail a student's response?
4. What head movement could a teacher use to encourage a student to respond?
5. What head movement could a teacher use to curtail a student's response?

CRITIQUE FOR SIMULATED TEACHING

Affective Lesson

Teacher _____ Date _____

Evaluator _____

	Superior	Very Good	Average	Below Average	Very Poor	Not Applicable
	5	4	3	2	1	

1. Rate the teacher on each of the following skills:
   a. Set Induction
   b. Factual Recall Questions
   c. Higher Order Questions
   d. Probing Questions
   e. Silence and Nonverbal Cues
   f. Reinforcement
   g. Closure
2. *Strategy.* Was the strategy appropriate for the lesson taught?
3. *Objective.* Was the objective understood by the students?

6. What body movement could a teacher use to encourage a student to respond?
7. How do nonverbal cues help the teacher in interpreting students' feelings?

Teaching the Evaluation Lesson

OBJECTIVES

1. *Lesson Plan.* The student must be able to develop a lesson plan which will aid them in engaging students in evaluation skills. The lesson plan must contain the appropriate elements as illustrated in the "Sample Evaluation Lesson Plan" in this chapter.
2. *Simulated Teaching.* The student will teach a fifteen-minute lesson in which he/she exhibits the following teaching skills: set induction, use of examples, higher order questions, probing questions, divergent questions, and closure. Learners may be peers or elementary school pupils and must be engaged in the development of evaluation skills.

3. *Lesson Analysis.* Students must be able to make an appropriate analysis of their fifteen-minute simulated lesson while viewing it on a videotaped replay. The analysis must follow the format outlined in "How to Analyze the Simulated Lesson" and "Simulated Lesson Analysis: An Example."

Evaluation Skill

Evaluation skill is one of the most necessary and yet neglected competencies which the schools purport to develop. Usually little or no effort is made to help students master this high-level cognitive process because so much time is taken up in the memorization of science facts. There are, however, some instances where students are called upon to state their preferences, but this cannot be passed off as evaluation because more often than not well-formulated rationales supporting preferences are neither required nor encouraged. Evaluation is the highest level of cognition according to Bloom's Taxonomy of Education Objectives (Bloom, 1956). Because the taxonomy is arranged in a hierarchical fashion, each mental skill below evaluation in the arrangement has to be engaged in as part of the evaluative process. Therefore, it is imperative that learning activities which are aimed at increasing skill in evaluation include as prerequisite tasks the development of analysis, synthesis, and comprehension skills. Even though this skill may be beyond the grasp of younger children, its rudiments may be encouraged even in the primary grades. The teacher must adjust his expectations according to the appropriate age level.

Evaluation consists of appraisals or judgments about things, people, events, products, or ideas. The judgments which are rendered must be based upon well-defined criteria. The criteria may be adopted from some authoritative, established source or they may be generated by the student himself. If the student generates the criteria, it is particularly important that he be able to logically support them. If defensible criteria are not insisted upon, judgments tend to be made from preferences which have no reasonable basis. Judgments so rendered are an exclusive part of the affective domain and require little or no cognition. However, it should not be concluded from this that evaluation is completely value free. The evaluative process consists of an appropriate blend of the affective and the cognitive with the affective components being supported by rational considerations.

Essentially, what is expected in evaluation is for the student to make judgments regarding the quality of some object or performance, either in terms of its absolute merit or as it relates to similar objects or performance. For example, a student may be asked to evaluate science fair projects or pollution control plans. The student may be expected to determine if something is good or bad, right or wrong, ugly or beautiful, acceptable or unacceptable; or he may have to compare things and decide which is the best, the most beautiful, or the most acceptable. As already mentioned, these judgments have to be made on the basis of defensible criteria.

One procedure for determining whether or not judgments have been made from supportable criteria is to require the students to explain why they made a particular judgmental response. This necessitates the exposure of the criteria which he used and requires a rational reason for their inclusion.

Judgments are sometimes complicated by the necessity of choosing between alternatives which meet criteria equally well. If more than one criterion is used in making the judgment, it may be necessary to determine which criterion is the most important. The object or performance which satisfies the most important criterion to the greatest extent can then be judged as best. The above process entails not only making judgments in using criteria, but also in making judgments about the criteria themselves. Both procedures require rational input.

Evaluation Goals

The formulation of objectives at the evaluation level is an essential part of the teacher's responsibility. These goals have to be formulated in such a way that they clearly convey the instructional intent and specify what evaluative skills the student must exhibit subsequent to instruction. There is a tendency for some teachers to exclaim that a particular subject area does not lend itself to the development of evaluation skills. However, nearly every subject deals with content or skills from which viable evaluation objectives may be derived. It is because most teachers have not viewed the various subject areas as anything more than a body of facts to be remembered or psychomotor skills to be mastered that the development of higher order cognitive skills has not been fostered. A more thoughtful appraisal is necessary to determine how the content of science may be used as a means of developing higher order mental operations. To do otherwise is an abrogation of your responsibility as a teacher.

Exercise 11–13   Evaluation Level Objectives

Write three objectives from the evaluation level in a particular subject area. Underline the behavior, put a double line under the conditions, and place a wavy line under those parts of the objective which represent the standard of performance expected.

Learning Activities in Evaluation

The most essential principle which must be adhered to when selecting learning activities is to be certain that they provide appropriate practice for achieving the lesson objectives. In the case of evaluation objectives, the student should spend at least a portion of his time practicing the actual skill that is called for in the objective. The student's time need not be limited to equivalent practice, but it should consume as much of the available time as necessary to insure mastery of the terminal behavior. In an evaluation lesson, it is likely that students will need to first receive some descriptive information about how to use evaluation skills. The teacher may then show examples of evaluation procedures and call attention to the principles involved. This would be followed by the teacher coaching the class as a whole through an evaluation experience. This procedure necessitates the involvement of students in trying out their skills with the teacher offering feedback on their trial responses. The teacher thus guides the class through the steps involved in evaluating. In doing this he/she must formulate questions which direct students to produce defensible criteria and apply them in making judgments. The teacher's responsibility is not to tell the students what the criteria should be, but rather to question students about the logic of their selection and to help them identify inconsistencies which need further consideration. The teacher's role, then, is to call attention to items which the students may overlook and to redirect student responses so that they benefit from the input of their peers in clarifying their thinking. The teacher should withhold judgment at this point and permit students to develop their own reasoning powers during the interaction process. The same kind of role should be used by the teacher in applying criteria to the evaluation process. In this evaluation process it is necessary that he direct the discussion so that inconsistencies are eliminated and valid judgments are applied. Many of these inconsistencies can be ferreted out in the discussion by calling attention to overlooked areas of consideration, asking probing questions, and redirecting student responses. The important point for the teacher to remember is that students need to try out evaluation skills and receive feedback on them rather than simply listen to the teacher's descriptions about how to evaluate or by observing a demonstration of the evaluation process. Descriptions and examples represent important preliminary instruction, but the major teaching process should be actual practice and feedback sessions with the students. In the fifteen-minute simulated teaching experience, this in-class trial and feedback session is generally the extent of the lesson. In an actual teaching situation, where more time is available, the teacher should provide students the opportunity to try their evaluation skills independent of the influence of the teacher and peers. Students should then be provided feedback on this experience prior to the time judgments are made on their competency in evaluation processes.

The rating of the student's evaluative skill should be made with materials other than those practiced within the classroom. Otherwise, the student has only to recall information generated in the class discussion rather than exhibiting his own evaluation skills. It should be remembered that the science facts and concepts dealt with in teaching evaluation skills are incidental to the more important consideration of developing evaluation processes. The teacher's objectives, learning activities, and evaluation should all be oriented toward the mental process of evaluation rather than the acquisition of knowledge.

Exercise 11–14 Learning Activities Based on Evaluation Objectives

List the learning activities which would help students achieve the three objectives described earlier.

Sample Evaluation Lesson Plan

Examine the "Sample Evaluation Lesson Plan" which follows and then construct a lesson plan for teaching evaluation skills using the same format.

SAMPLE EVALUATION LESSON PLAN

CLASS: Sixth Grade
TOPIC: Evaluating Science Fair Projects
Instructional Objective:

Students will formulate a set of at least three criteria for judging the quality of science fair projects along with a written justification for each criterion. The student must then apply his criteria for making a valid judgment about which of six science fair projects is best.

Content:

The following are some examples of possible criteria for judging the quality of science fair projects.

1. The uniqueness of the project.
2. How well the project is organized.
3. How clearly the project portrays its central message.

Learning Activities:

1. The teacher will give a description of the evaluation process.
2. The teacher will explain how the evaluation processes are used in an example situation. The example which will be used is evaluating a specific science fair project.

3. The teacher will lead a directed discussion where students are to formulate and defend a set of criteria for judging the quality of science fair projects and then apply these criteria in judging the relative worth of three projects.

Evaluation:

1. Students will be asked to prepare: (a) at least three criteria for judging the quality of science fair projects; and (b) a rationale for their list of criteria.
2. Students will apply their criteria in making judgments about which of six science fair projects best meets their criteria and explain why.

Review the principles of analysis discussed in "How to Analyze the Simulated Lesson" and "Simulated Lesson Analysis: An Example." In the analysis of your evaluation lesson remember that you will be examining the skills of set induction, use of examples, closure, higher order questions, divergent questions, and probing questions. You may wish to review each of these skills. Also examine the "Evaluation Lesson Analysis Guide" which follows. You will write your responses in this guide as you evaluate your lesson.

In making the analysis of your lesson, you should also focus your attention upon how well you were able to get the students to exhibit evaluation skills. Determine if your questions were formed so that students had to demonstrate higher order mental operations in order to respond. Ask yourself the question, "If I was to require the learners to display evaluation skills in a different but related area, would they be able to do so?"

One of the most important skills which you should develop in teaching your simulated lessons is that of making an accurate and detailed analysis of pupil-teacher and teacher-pupil interactions. As a teacher, you cannot rely upon supervisors and administrators to provide you with a basis for improving your teaching performance. Their presence in the classroom is too sporadic to be sufficiently effective. If you are to become a better teacher, you must assume the responsibility for accomplishing this task. It is therefore recommended that you make certain that you understand the concepts and skills you must exhibit in simulated teaching and that you are able to recognize the behaviors which they represent in a lesson. In addition, it is necessary that you be able to determine the relative effectiveness of these behaviors and how to formulate alternative behaviors for increased effectiveness.

As you make your analysis, identify the specific areas of your presentation which are unsatisfactory in any way and then attempt to formulate alternative ways to achieve better results. You should proceed both microscopically and macroscopically with your analysis by examining both the larger problems and inconsistencies as well as the minute difficulties. The Evaluation Lesson Analysis Guide which follows will help in making an analysis of your lesson.

Evaluation Lesson Analysis Guide

1. What evidence do you have that the students actually engaged in evaluation skills? (e.g., made judgments based on established criteria). Cite at least two instances. If there was no evidence, what would you have done differently in the lesson in order to engage students in evaluation?
2. If possible, cite two instances in which you helped the students differentiate between what was based on fact and what was based on opinions or values. If there were none, why was it not necessary to help in this differentiation?
3. When you compare your objective stated on the lesson plan to that which the pupils listed on the critique forms, state how they are similar or different. What evidence do you have that the pupils understood or did not understand the objective of the lesson? Cite at least two instances.
4. Cite at least two questions you asked which were of a recall type and two probing questions.
5. Cite at least two higher level questions you asked.
6. Based on questions 4 and 5, how could you have improved the phrasing of your questions in order to encourage *pupil* participation or to have communicated more effectively? State at least two ways.
7. What evidence do you have that the pupils were interested or disinterested in the lesson? Cite at least two instances. How could you have made it more interesting right from the beginning (set induction)? Cite at least two other specific ways you could have made it interesting.
8. In terms of the basic skills (set induction, use of examples, probing, recall, higher order, or divergent questions, and closure), state at least three ways you would improve this lesson (or consider other alternatives) if you were to reteach it.

Simulated Teaching: Teach a fifteen-minute evaluation lesson based on the lesson plan you have prepared, in which you demonstrate skill in set induction, use of examples, higher order questions, probing questions, divergent questions, and closure. You must also engage your pupils in evaluation processes. Obtain feedback from learners by having them fill out the "Critique for Simulated Teaching: Evaluation Lesson" form. A clinical analyst may also evaluate your lesson.

Lesson Analysis: Using the "Evaluation Lesson Analysis Guide" and following the format for analysis explained in "How to Analyze the Simulated Lesson" and "Simulated Lesson Analysis: An Example," make a written analysis of the videotaped replay of your lesson.

CRITIQUE FOR SIMULATED TEACHING

Evaluation Lesson

Teacher _____ Date _____

Advisor _____

	Unable to Observe	Not Achieved	Below Average	Average	Strong	Superior
	0	1	2	3	4	5

1. Which of the following skills were used effectively? Comment about each skill in terms of possible improvements or alternatives:

   a. Set Induction

   b. Use of Examples

   c. Higher Order Questions

   d. Probing Questions

   e. Divergent Questions

2. What was the objective of this lesson? (State it behaviorally as you recall it.)

3. Were the strategies, content, and learning activities consistent with the objective as you understood it? Why or why not?

4. Did the teacher allow the students to discuss the issue? Cite instances which illustrate that the teacher wanted pupils to participate or did not want them to participate.

5. Were you asked to give your opinion on something without relating it to some standard or criteria? Give an instance which explains your answer.

6. To what degree were you interested in this lesson? How could it have been more interesting to you?

7. How could the teacher have improved this lesson? State at least two specific ways which suggest improvement or other alternatives that the teacher could have used.

Cumulative Simulated Teaching Experience

For your final simulated teaching experience you will be asked to draw upon all of the teaching skills that you have learned in the previous lessons, in addition to learning a new way of evaluating your teaching. The skills that you should incorporate in teaching your lesson include: Set Induction, Stimulus Variation, Use of Examples, Repetition,

Closure, Cuing, Reinforcement, Higher Order Questions, Probing Questions, Silence, and Nonverbal Cues. Each of these skills should be used in the process of teaching your lesson. Therefore, you will need to plan a lesson which permits you to demonstrate your ability to use these skills in teaching. Again you will be asked to make a self-analysis of your lesson.

In addition to focusing on the teaching skills, you will be asked to make an analysis of your lesson in terms of how much your students learned. This will require you to prepare and administer a teacher performance test to your students and then use the results of this test to make an analysis of your lesson.

OBJECTIVES

1. Students will be able to teach a lesson wherein they demonstrate the appropriate use of the skills of Set Induction, Stimulus Variation, Use of Examples, Repetition, Closure, Cuing, Reinforcement, Higher Order Questions, Probing Questions, Silence, and Nonverbal Cues. These skills must be used to achieve a specified lesson objective.
2. Students must be able to construct and administer a teacher performance test and in making an analysis of their lesson, show specific instances where their behavior is related to the results of the test.

Preparing a Teaching Performance Test

The problem of how to validly determine the quality of a teacher's instructional skill is indeed a perplexing one. If it was readily discernible, practicing teachers could be told how to improve and teacher trainees could be helped more readily to develop these skills. The fact of the matter is that evaluating the quality of teacher performance is a complex and taxing process, fraught with inconsistencies and contradictions. There are various opinions regarding what good teaching is and few means of measuring the existence of these qualities.

Typically teachers are rated by supervisors after observing them teach one or more lessons. Ratings ordinarily contain rather general kinds of observations by the rater such as classroom control, presentation techniques, and ability to maintain student interest. Ratings of this sort yield very little information with which the teacher or prospective teacher can alter and adjust his behavior. In addition raters may be entirely wrong regarding what they report in their evaluations. Usually raters have had classroom experiences of their own and have a preconceived idea of what good teaching is. More often than not the bias is in favor of their own teaching style. Getting valid estimates of teacher performance is extremely difficult with this type of system.

Recently, more precise instruments have been developed to rate teaching that focus upon more specific and definable aspects of the teaching act. The micro-teaching skills, such as set induction and stimulus variation, are examples of this (Allen and Ryan, 1969). There are also observation scales which emphasize pupil-teacher interactions and attempt to show relationships between student behaviors in the classroom as they are related to those of the teacher. One of the more popular of these is the Flanders Interaction Analysis System (Flanders, 1970). With this system, teacher as well as student behaviors are categorized, analyzed and quantified in terms of how they related. The kind of data that is generated is the percent of teacher talk and the percent of student talk. Also the instances of student-initiated responses are compared with different types of teacher behaviors. The basic idea is to determine whether the teacher is sufficiently indirect in his approach to teaching and whether this indirectness is directly related to self-initiated responses by students. It is assumed that student-initiated responses are superior to those initiated by the teacher. You may find it useful to learn the Flanders Interaction Analysis System and use it in the analysis of your final simulated teaching experience.

Teaching performance tests have been suggested as a viable alternative to the various systems of teacher evaluation. In fact, advocates of the teaching performance test tend to be critical of other forms of teacher evaluation. According to Popham, "Use of the teaching performance test is predicated on a central assumption that the chief reason for a teacher's existence is to make beneficial changes in learners, that is, modifications in the learner's knowledge, attitudes, and skills." This being the case, then the basis upon which teaching skills should be evaluated is not teaching behaviors per se, but rather the behaviors which pupils are able to exhibit as a consequence of the instructional process (Popham, 1973).

A teaching performance test, then, must assess a teacher's ability to accomplish prespecified changes in learners, using whatever instructional procedures he/she wishes. If the objectives of instruction are kept constant, and teachers are allowed to use whatever instructional tactics they think best to achieve those objectives, we are able to compare teachers with respect to their ability to promote the pupil's attainment of prespecified instructional objectives.

For your cumulative simulated teaching experience you will need to prepare a teaching performance test. To do this you will need to plan a lesson based upon a clearly stated objective which has as one of its components a stated, measurable learner performance. Plan to select a lesson that requires a higher level of student performance than simple recall. Problem-solving lessons are ideal for this type of experience. Once you have determined what your objective is to be, you can construct a series of test items (ten or fifteen) which validly measure student performance. You should prepare items which can be scored objectively.

In teaching your cumulative simulated lesson use the following steps to guide you:

1. Formulate an objective along with a valid teaching performance test.
2. Prepare a lesson which you believe will result in your students achieving the objective you have developed. Make certain that it will facilitate the demonstration of the skills of Set Induction, Stimulus Variation, Use of Examples, Repetition, Closure, Cuing, Reinforcement, Higher Order Questions, Probing Questions, Silence, and Nonverbal Cues.
3. Conduct your lesson and if possible have it videotaped.
4. Administer your teaching performance test to learners.
5. Score your teaching performance test and use the results to analyze your videotaped lesson. Attempt to determine what specific problem in your lesson may have led to the performance you observe in the learners. At the same time analyze the teaching skills to determine if they are in any way related to the performance of your learners.
6. Prepare a written analysis of your findings.

References

Allen, Dwight W., *et al., Creating Student Involvement: Teacher's Manual.* Morristown, N.J.: General Learning Corporation, 1969a.

Allen, Dwight W., *et al., Presentation Skills: Teacher's Manual.* Morristown, N.J.: General Learning Corporation, 1969b.

Allen, Dwight W., *et al., Increasing Student Participation: Teacher's Manual.* Morristown, N.J.: General Learning Corporation, 1969c.

Allen, Dwight W., *et al., Questioning Skills: Teacher's Manual.* Morristown, N.J.: General Learning Corporation, 1969d.

Allen, Dwight W., *et al., Response Repertoire: Teacher's Manual.* Morristown, N.J.: General Learning Corporation, 1969e.

Allen, Dwight and Kevin Rayn, *Microteaching.* Reading, Mass.: Addison-Wesley, 1969.

Bloom, Benjamin, *et al., Taxonomy of Educational Objectives: Cognitive Domain.* New York: McKay, 1956.

DeCecco, John P., *The Psychology of Learning and Instruction: Educational Psychology.* Englewood Cliffs, N.J.: Prentice-Hall, 1968.

Emmer, Edmund T., and Gregg B. Millett, *Improving Teaching Through Experimentation: A Laboratory Approach.* Englewood Cliffs, N.J.: Prentice-Hall, 1970.

Flanders, Ned A., *Analyzing Teaching Behavior.* Reading, Mass.: Addison-Wesley, 1970.

Gallagher, James J., and Mary Jane Aschner, "A Preliminary Report on Classroom Interaction," *Merill-Palmer Quarterly of Behavior and Development* 9 (July 1963): 183–94.

Popham, W. James, *Evaluating Instruction.* Englewood Cliffs, N.J.: Prentice-Hall, 1973.

Searles, John E., *A System for Instruction.* Scranton, Pa.: International Textbook Company, 1967.

12
Contemporary Programs for Science

The science program for an elementary school is subject to many forces. Among these forces are the nature of science, the way in which students learn, and the needs of modern man and society. But these forces and others are specific to each school system. Such local variances include the type of industry and geography familiar to the student, the background of the teachers, the degree of local school commitment to provide for science education, and the relationship of science to other areas of the curriculum. Ideally speaking, the most effective science program for a given school cannot be purchased as a ready-made product. Rather it is one which is designed for and by the teachers of the local school system for their own students.

Most school systems lack the resources, and perhaps the commitment to science, to customize a science education program to their needs. It is, therefore, pertinent to examine in some detail the kinds of elementary school science programs available for purchase. It is likely that the school system in which you will teach will have a "science series," a single commercial program for all students throughout the school. In some schools, the first few grades will use one series and the later grades a second, and possibly a third series.

The purpose of this chapter is to provide reference to a variety of programs available for teaching elementary school science. No attempt will be made to cover all programs. Rather, programs have been selected to show the diversity of choice now available to schools, teachers, and students. We urge you to consider these pages merely as an introduction to the programs described here. You are encouraged to obtain copies of current editions of the various programs and examine them first hand.

Prior to the explanation of the programs, we will survey the recent developments in elementary school science and discuss some of the general trends in the teaching of science.

Two Decades of Science Curriculum Development

During the late 1950s a number of prominent science education experts increased their efforts to improve the teaching of science. This effort was spurred on by the popular notion that our youth may be receiving an inferior education in the sciences and by the increased availability of money to support new curriculum development. Reform in the sciences began with the area most important to the college science educators who were at the center of the movement to improve science education. Early efforts were in new programs for high school physics, chemistry, biology, and engineering. Focus then shifted to the elementary and junior high school years.

Most of the contemporary science curriculum trends are of a common focus. In general, each attempts to make the student the center of the program. A visitor to a classroom using a more traditional program finds the teacher at the center of the learning situation. In the more contemporary programs, the student is frequently at the center, with the teacher in a more consultative role. As you investigate the programs which follow, several characteristics will be evident.

Trends in Current Science Programs

Although there are a great variety of programs available to teach elementary school science, there are several trends in program development which can be identified. The trends identified in the following paragraphs are not common to all programs. They represent characteristics common to many programs and characteristics which are more prevalent in the programs developed in recent years.

MULTIPLICITY OF AUTHORS

The traditional science program was written by a small group of authors, often college science professors. In recent years, the general trend is for elementary school science curricula to be developed by a group of authors, representing a diversity of expertise. Typically the initial effort still comes from the college science educator. With the support of outside funds, the curriculum development projects have sought the assistance of psychologists to help design effective learning approaches. Materials developed have been used in test centers with actual classroom teachers and students. The assistance of these trial teachers has often proved to be the prime factor in a successful program. Others involved include equipment design specialists, media specialists, and consultants for special purposes.

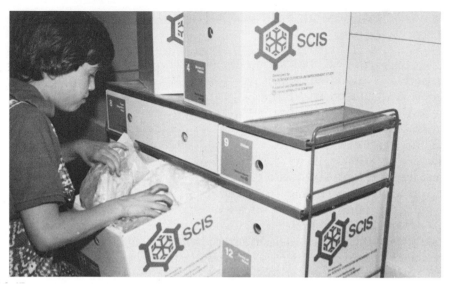

Contemporary science programs often provide equipment in sufficient quantity and package for use by individual or small groups of children.

EXTENSIVE FEDERAL FUNDING

A commercial publishing company, with the usual narrow margin of profit, is not going to be able to fund the extensive writing team and field test described above. The usual source of funding for curriculum development projects has been through the U. S. Office of Education and the National Science Foundation. Many private agencies, universities, school systems, and commercial companies have also provided some support.

TEACHER, NOT STUDENT, READING MATERIAL

The traditional science program organization includes a student text, a teacher's guide, and a kit of program materials. The newer science programs do not provide very much, if any, reading material for the student. The student material consists of worksheets or manuals to be completed. The emphasis is placed on the teacher's guide where numerous descriptions are giving regarding activities to be done with the student. The record of these activities or investigations is then kept in the student recordbook provided.

EQUIPMENT FOR EVERYONE.

Whereas the typical science "kit" provided some laboratory equipment for the student and teacher, the newer programs provide equipment sufficient in quantity to be used by all students for each project. The teacher of a few years ago would be called upon to do many demonstrations. With the use of contemporary programs, the students can now do the experiment for themselves. This equipment used by students in their investigations is usually conveniently packaged for easy distribution by the teacher.

FIRST-HAND DATA

Traditional science tests usually consisted of a display of the facts, principles, and concepts of science for the student. Laboratory investigations were then used to verify these ideas. By contrast the newer programs have students find the information from their own experiences. This factor heavily influences the content chosen for the course. Experience with these new programs indicates that a great deal of learning can take place in this fashion.

FROM MEMORY TO UNDERSTANDING

Too much science instruction of the past sought to have students develop the ability to recall a vast amount of information. Definitions, formulas, constants, and principles were memorized and then recalled to answer questions on the examinations. Newer programs seek to develop inquiry skills for the investigation of scientific phenomena and help students understand the broad concepts of the discipline. Students will have many experiences on the same concept or skill to insure a solid understanding of it. This understanding is reinforced by subsequent use in later units of the program.

MANY TOPICS TO A FEW

The traditional program in science for grades K–8 has been a "general science" approach. Very often this meant that each year of science consisted of many topics studied for just a few weeks. Newer science programs are more likely to have just a few topics studied at each grade level. Due to the fewer number of topics, each topic can then be pursued in greater depth for a longer period of time. At the same time these topics are usually organized sequentially so that they lead toward a broader understanding of the topics.

FROM TEACHER-CENTERED TO STUDENT-CENTERED

Whereas in science lessons of the past the teacher could be found in front of a group of students, the newer science programs place the teacher among the students. The daily routine of the teacher of yesterday would probably be conducting a group reading session, telling the class about some phenomena, or demonstrating a point brought out by the text. Today the teacher is more likely to be involved right along with the students in the investigation of some phenomena. The emphasis is upon the student developing the inquiry skills and concepts outlined by the program developers.

Contemporary Science Programs

As you read the following sections describing some contemporary science programs, keep in mind the general characteristics listed and described on the preceding pages. Each program is unique, but all have some common points. The descriptions are not intended to be comprehensive. Enough information has been provided to allow some understanding of the nature of the program materials only.

Science—A Process Approach

"Science is best taught as a procedure of inquiry" (AAAS 1970). So begins the description of a science program for the elementary school years which is most concerned with the development of process skills for inquiry. This program, *Science—A Process Approach* (SAPA), began in 1963 by the Commission on Science Education of the Association for the Advancement of Science (AAAS) with support from the National Science Foundation. In the years since then program materials have been developed for seven levels, typically used in grades K–6. The program has undergone recent revision and is now known as *Science —A Process Approach II* (SAPA—II).

A primary concern of the developers of the SAPA program was the need to teach students the "processes" of science, the nature of inquiry. The goal of teaching the processes was considered far more important than the goal of teaching selected science concepts. This can be seen when one examines the organization of the learning materials.

The difficulty in developing a program based on the processes of science was to identify those processes. As described more fully in Chapter 2, no one scientific method can be identified. But the developers did identify thirteen parts, eight basic processes and five integrated processes. The eight basic process are: observation; using space/time relationships; classifying; using numbers; measuring; communicating; predicting; and inferring. The five integrated processes are: controlling variables; interpreting data; formulating hypotheses; defining operationally; and experimenting. Explanations of these process skills are provided in Chapter 2. The eight basic processes were found to be less complex and therefore appropriate for the primary years. The integrated processes are more complex and consequently more suitable for the intermediate grades.

A second departure from tradition was to develop a highly structured hierarchy of objectives as the organizational scheme of the program. The psychological theory which forms the basis of this program comes from Gagne. Gagne believes that learning is more probable if all prerequisite behaviors have been previously learned. If these prerequisite behaviors have not been learned then the terminal behavior is not likely to be learned. The organizational pattern of the SAPA program is a hierarchical arrangement of the process skills to be learned (Gagne, 1970).

To develop the hierarchy of process skills it was necessary to specify the process behaviors to be learned. That is, it was necessary to identify the student behaviors which would prove that the process skills were attained. The developers were very specific about the way in which the objectives were stated. To accomplish this feat, they identified a series of nine terms (identify, name, order, describe, distinguish, construct, demonstrate, state a rule, and apply a rule) which were used throughout the program to describe student behaviors. Note that each describes a student behavior which can be observed. The SAPA developers were able to describe all objectives of the program and all of the process skills to be attained through the use of these nine student behaviors.

To develop the hierarchy of objectives of the program, the developers began with the complex, terminal behaviors to be attained by the program. Prerequisite behaviors were then identified. During subsequent field testing these prerequisite-terminal dependencies were validated. If students could do the terminal behavior without mastery of one or more of the prerequisite behaviors, then the dependency was revised. If mastery of prerequisite behaviors did not provide for learning of the terminal behavior, then additional prerequisite behaviors were sought. Subsequent field testing continued until a high percentage of students were able to succeed with the learning hierarchy. A small segment of this hierarchy can be examined in the model lesson which follows this description of the program (AAAS, 1968).

The primary characteristics of the program center around the emphasis on process skills, the highly specific nature of the objectives, and the highly structured hierarchy of learning objectives. The other characteristics of the program focus on the nature of the learning materials themselves. No student textbook was created for use in this program. The teacher's materials consist of approximately twenty pamphlets for each grade level. Each pamphlet describes the objectives, equipment needs, learning activities, and evaluation activities for a unit of study. In the new edition of the program, there are sixty teacher packets, or modules, for the primary grades K–3. These modules form a continuum of science, but are packaged in a way which provides for purchase in small groups of topics rather than as an entire grade-level unit.

The evaluation activities form another distinctive departure from the traditional program. Because each module or unit of study has a highly specific set of objectives, it is possible to be very specific about the nature of the evaluation activity. If the objective asks the student to "identify" some aspect of a given phenomenon, then it is obvious that this is what the student will do in the evaluation. Two types of evaluation are available; the first is a group appraisal for all students in the class, the second is an individual measure for use in instances where the teacher needs to be more precise about the competencies of one individual. The evaluation measures are provided at the end of each module.

The equipment for students' investigations are packaged in plastic drawers. Each drawer provides equipment for one or more units of study. Some consumables need to be supplied from local sources. But, in general, the kits can be purchased with almost all of the materials needed for each unit conveniently available for teachers to use. The equipment itself is largely made up of simple materials with only some use of specially designed apparatus.

Teaching lessons with an emphasis on process rather than content is the primary goal of this curriculum. Because of the unique focus on learning, the developers of the program have produced a *Commentary for Teachers.* This publication provides an overview of the program with an orientation to each of the process skills. A lesson is provided for each skill which the teacher can use to learn about the process in the same fashion that the students will be learning about the processes later on (AAAS, 1970).

Science Curriculum Improvement Study

Robert Karplus, a college physics teacher, is credited with the initiation and direction of the Science Curriculum Improvement Study. Along the way since its inception in 1958, many other scientists, psychologists, and classroom teachers have contributed to its development. Although not grade-level specific, the program is now in widespread use in grades K–6. This program is distinguished by its emphasis on conceptual organization, as well as process skill development through the direct experiences of students.

As with other recently developed programs, SCIS began with extensive field testing of pilot materials. Classroom teachers provided feedback on the nature of the instructional materials. Student evaluations provided evidence of the amount of learning which took place. Later trial editions were tested at field centers throughout the country. These extensive developmental activities yielded a final, commercial edition that is now being published.

In the *SCIS Teacher's Handbook,* the developers of the program state that "A primary concern of SCIS is that children's science experiences be consistent with the experimental nature and conceptual structure of science" (SCIS, 1974). To accomplish this end, they constructed a hierarchy of concepts for the physical sciences and one for the life sciences. These two strands run parallel throughout the program as students, through direct experiences, develop an understanding of simple to more complex concepts.

The SCIS program centers on the development of one "big idea," the concept of interaction. Interaction is defined as " . . . the relation among objects or organisms that do something to one another, thereby bringing about a change" (SCIS, 1974). This thought is brought out in both the life and physical science strands of the program. The four major scientific concepts used to develop this theme are matter, energy, organism, and ecosystem. In addition to these, four process-oriented concepts are also used; these are property, reference frame, system, and model. To gain a better idea of the use of these concepts, study the chart in Table 12–1. In this chart, the unit titles for both the life science and physical science units are listed for each grade level. The particular concepts developed by that unit of study are listed below each title.

In the program the study of the life sciences begins with observations to develop the concept of organism. The students are then led through extensive experiences to make first-hand observations of the behavior of organisms as they interact. From this information the concepts of habitat, growth, population, environment, and community develop along with other concepts. Eventually, students study the interrelationships of systems of organisms in order to develop the concepts of ecosystems. The study of the development of scientific concepts is from the simple to complex. Along the way process skills are also developed. These include the simple types of observations as well as the more complex experimental situations.

Learning psychology has had a significant effect on the work of Karplus and the others from the very beginning of the project. Although the resulting program reflects a composite view of the theories of learning, the most influential theory is that of Piaget. He has identified several stages through which children pass as they mature (see Chapter 8 for more information on this learning theory). Out of their study of the theories of learning, the SCIS developers identified a three-part learning cycle as the basis of their learning activities. The first stage

TABLE 12-1   SCIS FINAL EDITION PROGRAM

BEGINNINGS

color	odor	quantity
shape	sound	position
texture	size	organisms

ORGANISMS

organism	habitat
birth	food web
death	detritus

LIFE CYCLES

growth	biotic potential
development	generation
life cycle	plant and animal
genetic identity	metamorphosis

POPULATIONS

population	food web
food chain	community
plant eater	predator-prey
animal eater	

ENVIRONMENTS

environment	range
environmental	optimum range
factor	

COMMUNITIES

photosynthesis	producers
community	consumers
food transfer	decomposers
	raw materials

ECOSYSTEMS

ecosystem	oxygen-carbon
water cycle	dioxide cycle
food-mineral	pollutant
cycle	

MATERIAL OBJECTS

object	serial ordering
property	change
material	evidence

INTERACTION AND SYSTEMS

interaction	system
evidence of	interaction-at-a-
interaction	distance

SUBSYSTEMS AND VARIABLES

subsystem	solution
evaporation	variable
histogram	

RELATIVE POSITION AND MOTION

reference object	polar coordinates
relative position	rectangular
relative motion	coordinates

ENERGY SOURCES

| energy transfer | energy source |
| energy chain | energy receiver |

MODELS: ELECTRIC AND MAGNETIC INTERACTIONS

| scientific model | electricity |
| magnetic field | |

Reprinted with permission from SCIS Newsletter, No.29, published by The Science Improvement Study. Copyright © March 1976 by The Regents of the University of California.

is the *exploration* stage, wherein the student is provided with an opportunity for wide experiences in self-directed, unstructured investigations. These experiences are chosen to provide the background for the students to develop the anticipated concepts. Following this experience, the "invention" of the concept is made. In this stage a new concept is defined as a way of generalizing the experiences of the exploration stage. With this new tool for learning, the discovery stage is entered, where the student seeks the opportunity to apply this new generalization to additional experiences. In this way the student's conceptual understandings are reinforced and extended. Process skills can be used throughout. The actual experiences can often be modified to fit the interests and needs of the students.

To illustrate this learning cycle, we will use a portion of one of the units. In this case we will make use of Unit Two of the *Interactions and Systems* unit, the physical science unit from level two of the SCIS program. During one or two class periods, the student "explores" the effect of individual items on one another from a set given him. The students as a group identify the effect one object appears to have on another. In the following lesson the teacher "invents" the term interaction and defines it for the student as the term to be used to describe what happens whenever one object does something to another. Several demonstrations are done with the class to illustrate other types of reactions in addition to the ones already experienced by the students. In the discovery phase, the students are provided additional experiences with chemical and physical phenomena to observe the evidence of an interaction. This unit on interaction serves as the background for the development of the next concept, system.

As indicated in Table 12–1, the SCIS program consists of thirteen units. There is one unit for Kindergarten, and two units for each of the other grades, 1–6. No student text was developed for the program. Instead, each unit has a teacher's guide of approximately 100 pages. Each grade-level teacher has a teacher's guide for a physical science unit and a separate guide for a life science unit. A student recordbook is included for use by students to help in recording data and conducting group discussions. Each unit also comes neatly boxed, with sufficient quantities of equipment to teach that unit to thirty students. Although materials can be purchased separately, the program materials kit provides a convenient way to order, store, and retrieve the materials needed for the unit.

To assist the teachers in implementing the program, several items have been published. The *SCIS Teacher's Handbook* provides background rationale, an overview of the program, an outline of the equipment in each kit, instructions on caring for the live animals, and a glossary of concepts being developed. The *SCIS Omnibus* is a collection of readings dating back to 1962 by individuals who have been associated with the project during that time. These articles provide the teacher with a more extensive look at the basic ideas which went into the development of the program, as well as some evidence regarding its successes. The *Handbook* also includes a listing of the 16mm films produced by the project which depict classrooms in which the program is used. Several of these films depict single units in depth while others overview several units of the program.

Evaluation activities have been prepared for each of the units with the exclusion of kindergarten. Each *Evaluation Supplement* contains suggestions for three types of evaluation: attitudes in science, perceptions of classroom environment, and concept/process skills. Attitudes in science include four areas: (a) curiosity or interest; (b) inventiveness or creativity; (c) critical thinking; and (d) persistence. Example student behaviors are provided for each of these attitude areas. For perception of the classroom environment, the students are asked, through a variety of means, for their perceptions regarding what kinds of activities took place during the lesson. The students may have perceived a very open, responsive environment even though the teacher's perceptions of the students' behavior indicated they felt constrained by the activities. The concept/process skills assessment procedures correlate with the objectives for the sections in that unit of study. For example, if the objective was for students to be able to "identify interacting objects in demonstrations and photographs" (SCIS, 1970) then the evaluation activities would provide demonstrations and photographs unfamiliar to the students to see if they could identify the interactions being depicted. Each evaluation supplement consists of instruction cards for each evaluation activity, a ditto master for the student handouts required, and a single page roster on which to record all evaluation activities.

For each unit of study a teacher's guide is provided. In each unit, the teacher's guide is divided into several parts. The unit of study, approximately a semester in length, usually begins with a review of pertinent concepts developed in previous years. New students can be helped by identifying deficiencies and providing remedial assistance. Each unit then provides learning activities to take students through the three-part learning cycle in developing an understanding of the basic concepts. The teacher's guide provides sufficient directions for implementation of the learning cycle but leaves the teacher with some choice of activities and their sequence. Supplementary activities are also provided.

Elementary Science Study

Every elementary school science curriculum has been developed to accomplish some purpose. For example, the authors' interpretation of the needs of elementary school children and the nature of science give direction to the development and utilization of the program. Choosing an elementary school science curriculum should be consistent with the purpose of the authors of the program or else the local school should anticipate the need to revise the program accordingly. Elementary Science Study (ESS) is one elementary school science program that

Figure 12–1 Suggested Grade Levels for ESS Units

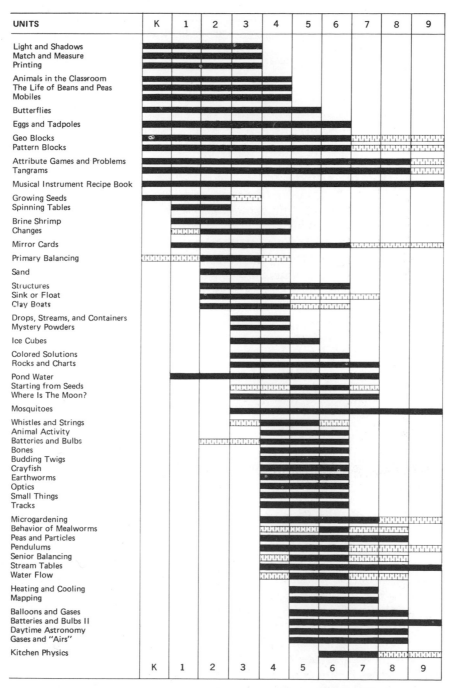

UNITS	K	1	2	3	4	5	6	7	8	9
Light and Shadows	▦	▦	▦	▦						
Match and Measure	▦	▦	▦	▦						
Printing	▦	▦	▦	▦						
Animals in the Classroom	▦	▦	▦	▦	▦					
The Life of Beans and Peas	▦	▦	▦	▦	▦					
Mobiles	▦	▦	▦	▦	▦					
Butterflies	▦	▦	▦	▦	▦	▦				
Eggs and Tadpoles	▦	▦	▦	▦	▦	▦	▦			
Geo Blocks	▦	▦	▦	▦	▦	▦	▦	▧	▧	▧
Pattern Blocks	▦	▦	▦	▦	▦	▦	▦	▧	▧	▧
Attribute Games and Problems	▦	▦	▦	▦	▦	▦	▦	▦	▧	▧
Tangrams	▦	▦	▦	▦	▦	▦	▦	▦	▧	▧
Musical Instrument Recipe Book	▦	▦	▦	▦	▦	▦	▦	▦	▦	▦
Growing Seeds	▦	▦	▦	▧						
Spinning Tables	▦	▦	▦							
Brine Shrimp		▦	▦	▦						
Changes		▧	▦	▦						
Mirror Cards		▦	▦	▦	▦			▧	▧	▧
Primary Balancing	▧	▧			▧					
Sand			▦	▦						
Structures			▦	▦	▦					
Sink or Float			▦	▦	▦	▧	▧	▧		
Clay Boats			▦	▦	▦	▧	▧			
Drops, Streams, and Containers				▦	▦					
Mystery Powders				▦	▦					
Ice Cubes				▦	▦					
Colored Solutions				▦	▦	▦				
Rocks and Charts				▦	▦	▦	▦			
Pond Water		▦	▦	▦	▦	▦	▦	▦		
Starting from Seeds				▧	▧	▦	▦	▧		
Where Is The Moon?				▧	▧	▦	▦	▧		
Mosquitoes				▦	▦	▦	▦	▦	▦	▦
Whistles and Strings				▧	▦	▦	▦	▧		
Animal Activity				▦	▦	▦	▦			
Batteries and Bulbs			▧	▧	▦	▦	▦			
Bones					▦	▦	▦			
Budding Twigs					▦	▦	▦			
Crayfish					▦	▦	▦			
Earthworms				▦	▦	▦	▦			
Optics					▦	▦	▦			
Small Things					▦	▦	▦			
Tracks				▦	▦	▦	▦			
Microgardening					▦	▦	▦	▧	▧	▧
Behavior of Mealworms				▧	▧	▦	▦	▧	▧	
Peas and Particles					▦	▦	▦			
Pendulums					▦	▦	▦	▧	▧	▧
Senior Balancing				▧	▦	▦	▦	▧	▧	
Stream Tables					▦	▦	▦	▧	▧	
Water Flow				▧	▦	▦	▦	▧	▧	
Heating and Cooling						▦	▦	▦		
Mapping						▦	▦	▦		
Balloons and Gases						▦	▦	▦	▦	
Batteries and Bulbs II						▦	▦	▦	▦	
Daytime Astronomy						▦	▦	▦	▦	
Gases and "Airs"						▦	▦	▦	▦	
Kitchen Physics						▦	▦	▦	▧	▧
	K	1	2	3	4	5	6	7	8	9

has been designed to allow each individual teacher and student a high degree of flexibility to arrange the program to suit their purpose.

The developers of the Elementary Science Study designed over fifty units of instruction which have been found to be of use in grades K–9. Two criteria were utilized in the development of the units. First of all, topics were chosen on the basis of their appeal to children. It was assumed that children are basically curious about the world around them and that this curiosity can be channeled into profitable science instruction and learning experiences. The second criteria for curriculum inclusion was the scientific significance of the materials being studied. The titles of the units listed in Figure 12–1 provide some indication of the diversity of topics consistent with these criteria. Among the titles are "Butterflies," "Earthworms," "Balloons and Gases," "Whistles and Strings" and "Where Is the Moon?"

In contrast to other elementary school programs, the program developers did not seek to develop specific concepts or process skills in each unit. To develop a unit a topic was chosen that would interest students. The final product which emerged for commercial sale was the result of the authors' experiences working with students in the field test schools. The field testing consisted of several rewritings based on its use in the test class. In fact, no overall curriculum scheme, hierarchy of process skills, or scope/sequence chart was developed. The program now consists of over fifty units of study, of varying sizes, styles, and time of study. Figure 12–1 provides a list of titles and indicates the grade range over which each unit of study has been found to be useful with students.

The diversity of subject matter is evident from reading the titles. Grouped by subject area, there are nineteen in the biological sciences, twenty-five in the physical sciences, five in the earth sciences, and seven in the study of mathematical skills. Although some of the topics are broad enough to include study of more than one discipline, the above break down of titles does provide a representation of the breadth of subject matter involved.

The lack of structure to the ESS program allows the local school system to design their own elementary science program around these, and possibly other program materials. The number of units provided in this program far exceeds what most any school will need to offer a complete program. The initial question is not "How shall we arrange these units?" but rather "Which of the units shall we use?" The use of the program might begin with only one teacher making use of one unit of study for several class periods. On the other extreme, all fifty-six units may be in use in one or more classrooms in a larger school system. Units can be shared among teachers as needed.

The same degree of flexibility exists within units of study. The teacher's guides for each unit suggest many activities which can be done, often in a highly flexible arrangement. The teacher's guides provide an overview of the subject being studied, a list of possible activities, a suggested schedule of activities, and helpful information regarding operation or construction of equipment. In most units more than one sequence of activities is suggested. In all cases the approach is student centered with a great deal of "messing around." The material to be learned is from the direct experience of the students.

Equipment for use in each unit of study also varies in its complexity and amount. Units such as "Budding Twigs," "Butterflies," "Starting from Seeds," and "Structures" do not have kits of materials which can be purchased. In these units the materials are easily obtainable from local sources. In some units such as "Brine Shrimp" and "Clay Boats" the kit is simple and will cost about one dollar per student. In other instances the equipment is more sophisticated and will cost more. Throughout the program the user is likely to find very simple equipment which can be assembled into kits from local sources. If time does not permit the accumulation of the materials for each unit, the kits can usually be purchased from the publisher.

Although no sequence of units is recommended, nor are objectives specified for most units, each local school can develop the degree of structure desired for the scope and sequence of the units. Each teacher or group of teachers can decide just what each unit can accomplish for them. The concepts and process skills being developed in each unit can then be sequenced into a total program pattern. A group of teachers in California worked with the publishers of the program and developed specific objectives for each one of the units. This compliation of objectives can be purchased from McGraw-Hill Book Company under the title *Evaluation Program for ESS.*

Because no formal means of evaluation is offered with the program, evaluation of the student's accomplishments depend upon local option. The developers of the program do suggest, however, that the high degree of involvement by each student provides a ready means for the teacher to see the students performing. From these daily performances, the teacher can form judgments as to the concepts and skills being developed.

In total, the program should be viewed as a pool of resources from which to draw upon to build an elementary school science program. In addition to the teacher's guides and equipment kits provided, several film loops have also been developed. Topics of film loops include "Brine Shrimp," "Bones," "Butterflies," "Gases and Airs," "Seeds," and "Water." Some student handouts suggested in the teacher guides are actually printed and available for purchase. Used in the manner anticipated by the authors, the program materials have been shown to be valuable as supplements to another program or as the basis for a basic program. The ability to choose is the key concept to utilization of this program.

Conceptually Oriented Program in Elementary Science

In a 1966 issue of *The Science Teacher,* Morris Shamos wrote the following as part of a section titled "Defining Science:"

> The essence of science lies not so much in seeking out the detailed workings of nature as in trying to understand it. Science is a very special way of looking at ordinary things. It is a continued search for "first principles," broad, inclusive statements or schemes in terms of which we seek to account for the familiar facts of nature.
> These conceptual schemes, models, or theories—call them what you will; call them educated guesses if you like—are the creation of man, not of nature. They represent the pinnacle of explanation in science . . . Such unifying theories are the main goal of science and should be at the focal point of a science curriculum.

In seeking to implement this point of view in a science curriculum, Professor Shamos has directed a curriculum development effort known as *Conceptually Oriented Program in Elementary Science* (COPES).

The primary focus of the COPES curriculum is to have the students experience common phenomena to conceptualize the fundamental and pervasive schemes of modern science. The development of the program began with a pilot study designed to build a sequence of learning activities for the elementary school grades which would all lead to the development of the conceptual scheme of conservation of energy. Figure 12–2 depicts the scope and sequence of concepts developed in these materials. The first three units, used in grades K–2, provide a common basis for later learning in science. The beginning of the conservation scheme is in grade three with the study of both mechanical energy and heat energy. With the subsequent development of such concepts as force, temperature, work, kinetic energy, and potential energy the students are able to build toward a conceptual scheme of conservation of energy.

One difficulty with the development of the original COPES unit is that concepts are intertwined with other conceptual schemes. It is difficult to instruct in one scheme without developing some other schemes. The COPES curriculum has become a spiral development

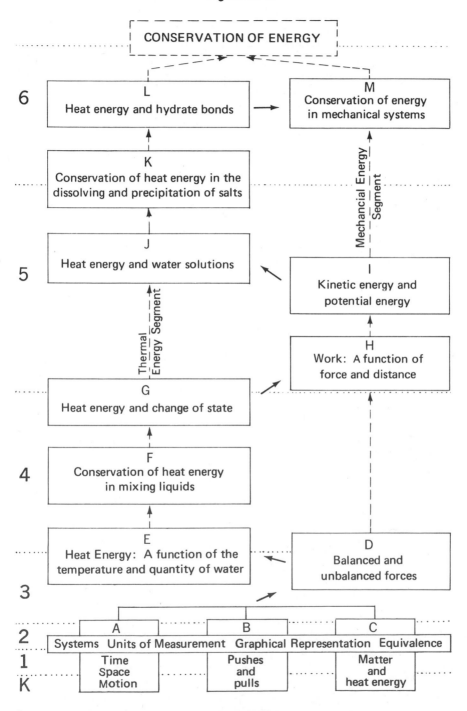

Figure 12- 2

CONSERVATION OF ENERGY

6

L
Heat energy and hydrate bonds

M
Conservation of energy
in mechanical systems

K
Conservation of heat energy in the
dissolving and precipitation of salts

Mechancial Energy
Segment

J
Heat energy and water solutions

I
Kinetic energy and
potential energy

5

Thermal
Energy Segment

H
Work: A function of
force and distance

G
Heat energy and change of state

F
Conservation of heat energy
in mixing liquids

4

E
Heat Energy: A function of the
temperature and quantity of water

D
Balanced and
unbalanced forces

3

A	B	C
Systems Units of Measurement	Graphical Representation	Equivalence

2

1

K

| Time Space Motion | Pushes and pulls | Matter and heat energy |

Source: From Overview of Concepts of COPES, COPES Project, New York University.

around five conceptual schemes. Learning the schemes begins in grade three and continues through grade six. The difficulty in building the curriculum lay in the identification of the conceptual schemes which would yield the most fruitful learning experiences for students. Once those conceptual schemes were identified, the concepts which were most relevant to the development of these themes for elementary science were identified. The development of these concepts was then sequenced and the learning activities designed.

The COPES project has identified five conceptual schemes. These schemes and a brief explanation of them follow:

1. *The Structural Units of the Universe.* The composite universe is made up of units of matter such as atoms, molecules, crystals, cells, organisms, plants, animals, planets, stars, etc. Identification of structural units allows man to study nature.
2. *Interaction and Change.* Units of matter interact. The evidence of these interactions is change. Chemical reactions, nuclear reactions, erosion, automobiles colliding, and growing organisms are examples of changes resulting from the interaction of units of matter.
3. *The Conservation of Energy.* Even though changes take place, the energy of a system remains constant. A car rolling to a stop has lost energy of motion, but the heat created by the friction in the brakes can be identified and measured to establish the conservation of energy.
4. *The Degradation of Energy.* Although energy is conserved, the study of a given situation indicates that the direction of energy flow within the system has a natural direction. This natural direction is exemplified by the tendency of all objects in a system to come to the same temperature. The natural direction of energy flow is toward the state in which it will do no useful work.
5. *The Statistical View of Nature.* The behavior of nature can be predicted only on the basis of the probability that a given event will occur. One can predict genetic events or the movement of atoms only within the degree of accuracy of change. A classroom of all boys is very unlikely, but a classroom of nearly equal numbers of boys and girls is highly likely. (Adapted from COPES, 1972)

Instruction in the K–2 grades provides basic experiences for all of the conceptual schemes. Units of study include systems, units of measurement, graphical representation, and equivalence. In grade three units of study are sequenced such that all of the five conceptual schemes are developed. The learning activities provide experiences with common phenomena for the development of the concepts. No student textbooks are provided. Instead a comprehensive teacher's guide is provided for each grade level. The developers of the program recommend that the COPES materials be used for about 80 percent of the science program and that reading materials be used to enrich the program.

The Assessment materials were designed to support the primary goal of COPES, the development of concepts. Assessment of specific details or factual materials and the development of skills are not emphasized. The assessment materials consist of two types of evaluation activities. The first type is a group assessment activity to determine which students have mastered the concepts. The second type is an individual evaluation device designed to find out why those students who have not mastered the materials are having difficulty. Through a series of questions the teacher is able to determine which concepts the student has understood and which still need further work.

Intermediate Science Curriculum Study

One of the most unique science programs available today is the Intermediate Science Curriculum Study (ISCS). Developed at Florida State University with the primary support of the National Science Foundation, this program seeks to develop science concepts and process skills through an individualized instruction format. ISCS is a three-level program for the middle grades, typically used in grades seven, eight, and nine. The program is designed for the general education student.

The ISCS program begins with the construction of a storage cell.

The development of the ISCS program began with the desire to build a program which would bridge the gap between the secondary science programs developed earlier and the more recent elementary school science programs. The specialty courses at the high school level have been standard and easily accommodated by the newer program. On the other end of the continuum, science programs have begun with grade one, or kindergarten, and progressed up through the sixth grade. The so-called middle school or junior high school years have long been ignored by the developers of science curricula. Schools have a great variety of organizations with the greatest variety existing in the middle grades. There is also a great variety of science programs offered in schools in these years. Some schools regard the seventh and eighth grade as the "oldest" of the elementary school years. For these schools, a science series which includes a seventh- and eighth-grade book is typical. In other schools, the seventh- and eighth-grade students are the "youngest" of the high school. For these students, the school is likely to choose a course in one of the separate disciplines such as life science or earth science.

At the beginning of the developments of the ISCS program, one of the few constants in the science field was that almost all students did take a full-year course in biology. It seemed logical that the middle-school program to be developed should prepare students for this type of course. For this reason and others, the Level I ISCS course begins with topics from physics (force and motion) and ends with the inclusion of some chemistry. The primary goal of this level is the development of the theme of conservation of energy. Level II begins primarily with chemistry and later involves some biological science concepts. The third level of the program includes a wide diversity of topics including weather, ecology, space science, and geology.

Like most science courses for grades K–8, the ISCS program is aimed at the general education student. Also, like most other science courses today, students seek information through a laboratory approach. Unique to this program is the individualized and self-pacing feature of the program. The design of the program materials provides for the student's movement through the program at a pace determined by the interest and ability of the student and other restrictions imposed by the teacher or the situation. In addition to the rate of accomplishment, the students are provided with alternative routes through the program. All students work their way through a basic core of material. At various points in the program students are referred to the "Excursions" section of the program for one of three types of material: remediation, enrichment, or review.

The materials developed by the ISCS group at first resemble those of other, more typical, science programs. There is a student textbook, a teacher's guide, a student workbook, kits of materials, and an evalu-

In an individualized program a means of handling materials and equipment needs to be used which allows some student freedom and easy maintenance by the teacher.

ation program. However, it is the way in which these materials are organized to provide for individualization that sets this program apart.

Apparatus designed for use in the program is not complex. The apparatus can be used by the student with only the instructions provided in the reading material. This characteristic is a necessity since students will be arriving at the various points in the program at different times and would otherwise require teacher assistance in a highly repetitive manner in order to make use of the equipment.

In terms of actual classroom implementation, the structure of the student reading material provides the key. The Level I program begins with very structured learning experiences in which students build a storage battery. This device can then be charged and used to do various forms of work. All students begin at this point in the program. As the activities progress, students begin to accelerate into the program at different rates according to interest and ability. Before long there is a wide diversity in the activities of the students. During this period of time the learning activities become less structured. More emphasis is placed on the student's ability to direct his own learning activities.

The question may be asked "Can the student direct his own learning activities to some extent?" The answer is yes. This program, like most contemporary programs, began in a field test situation. Trial centers were developed around the country and the early sections of the materials were tested as they were developed. Evidence of classroom use substantiated that students can succeed in self-directed learning in science. They can comprehend the physics and chemistry provided in the early parts of the program. They can learn to work at their own rate of accomplishment with the right kind of teacher assistance.

Based on the concepts, process skills, and study skills developed in Levels I and II of the ISCS program, the third level provides for a great deal of student self-direction. The program consists of nine separate units of study on a variety of topics. Experience suggests that students can typically complete about four of these units. With the variety of topics available, several program organizational formats are possible. A teacher or school system may select about four topics for study by all students. Several topics might be made available to students for their selection based on their interest. In larger schools, all topics could be made available for study in the third year and in later science courses. Some teachers have chosen one or two of these units for use in supplementing other programs. The design of learning experiences in these units is the most open-ended of the program, relying on a great deal of student self-direction for completion of the material presented.

Compared to teaching other junior high school science programs, the teacher of ISCS will find his/her role significantly different. Whereas in the usual programs the teacher will spend more time leading, telling, directing, and making assignments, the ISCS teacher will be advising, asking, helping, and checking students' individual progress. Due to the high structure of the program and the emphasis on having students make choices, the teacher will spend very little time making lesson plans. More time will be spent in finding ways to help students over rough spots in the program or working with individual students in helping them make choices. Because of this changed role, teachers will require assistance in the form of inservice training to make use of the program properly.

The primary philosophy of the ISCS program is summarized in the following statement taken from the teacher education publication produced by the ISCS developers:

> ISCS believes that a student best gains a real understanding of science and its methods by facing reasonably significant questions and working out ways to attack them. The project is equally committed, however, to the concept that students should acquire a repertoire of ideas and intellectual skills before engaging in free inquiry of this sort (ISCS, 1970).

The organization of the program is consistent with this point of view regarding curriculum development. Along with the development of skills of inquiry the student is allowed to develop a broad and significant reserve of scientific concepts. These topics can be seen on the chart in Figure 12–3.

Exploring Your Environment

A second program which seeks to teach science to middle grade students through an individualized mode is entitled Exploring Your Environment (EYE). This relatively new program is in contrast to most traditional science programs and is in some contrast to the ISCS program. The EYE program is a three-year program which has been utilized in grades six, seven, eight, and nine with all types of students in each grade. The program has no sequence of units of instruction for the three years. In this way it can be utilized in an extremely flexible manner with a good deal of variability both in sequencing units as well as activities within units.

The program of EYE consists of six units of study, entitled: *Experimenting with Living Plants; Investigating Life Processes; Measuring Forces and Reactions; Examining the Earth's Crust; Discovering Changes in Matter;* and *Observing the Invisible World.* The units can be used in any order because the basic material of each unit has approximately the same level of difficulty. Each unit consists of both teacher and student materials. The student materials include a Laboratory Manual for each of five problem areas with each unit and a card bank. The card bank is a box of cards divided into skill cards, experiment cards, research cards, and information cards. Teacher materials include a teacher's guide, quizzes, and an answer key.

Each unit is organized into five problem areas. Each problem area is then subdivided into several experiments or subproblem areas. The problem areas and experiment titles for the unit *Observing the Invisible World* are provided in Table 12–2. Each student is provided with a recordbook in which there is primarily blank paper. With this the student literally constructs his own science book. The information put into the book describes his own experiences in science. Each student manual contains a "Work Flow Chart For Exploring Your Environment" as reproduced in Figure 12–4. This provides a general diagram by which the student proceeds through a unit of study.

Three processes of science are stressed throughout the program. The processes are observing (gaining information through the senses), inferring (explaining one's observations), and hypothesizing (generalizing one's experiences). Throughout the Laboratory Manuals are "Inference Reports" in which the students complete responses to the following two statements:

Based on observation made in this experiment I can make the following inference:

The most important observations I used to make this inference were:

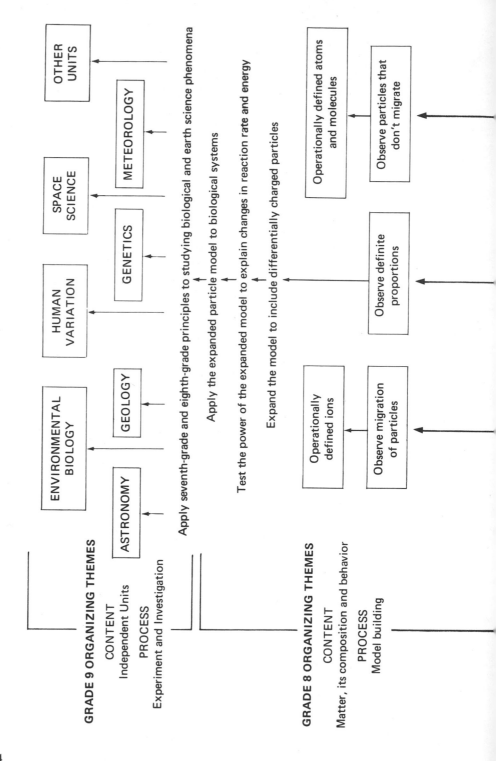

Figure 12–3   Diagram of ISCS Content Flow: Probing the Natural World Grades 7 through 9

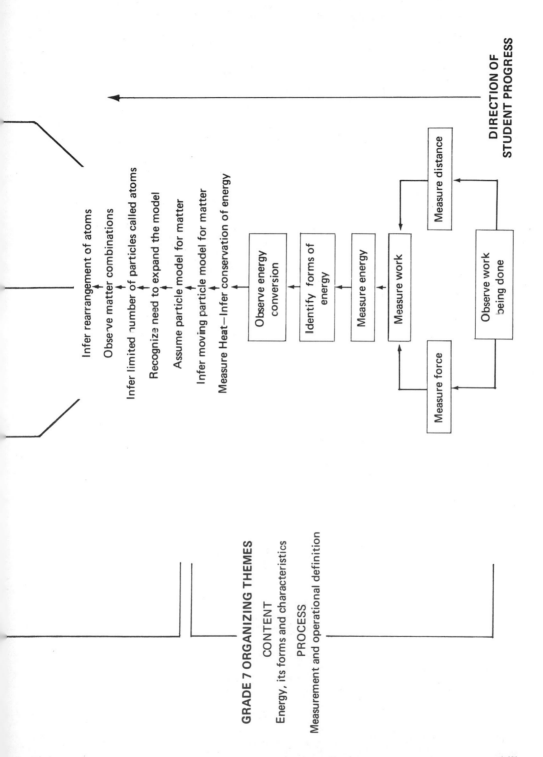

GRADE 7 ORGANIZING THEMES
CONTENT
Energy, its forms and characteristics
PROCESS
Measurement and operational definition

Infer rearrangement of atoms
Observe matter combinations
Infer limited number of particles called atoms
Recognize need to expand the model
Assume particle model for matter
Infer moving particle model for matter
Measure Heat—Infer conservation of energy

Observe energy conversion
Identify forms of energy
Measure energy
Measure work
Measure distance
Measure force
Observe work being done

DIRECTION OF STUDENT PROGRESS

Figure 12-4   Work Flow Chart for Exploring Your Environment

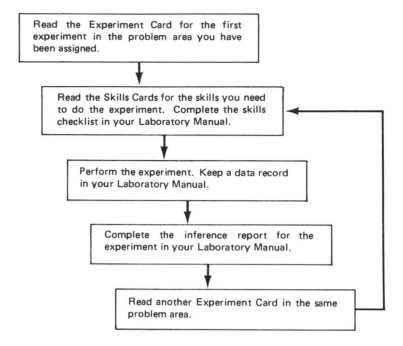

Read the Experiment Card for the first experiment in the problem area you have been assigned.

Read the Skills Cards for the skills you need to do the experiment. Complete the skills checklist in your Laboratory Manual.

Perform the experiment. Keep a data record in your Laboratory Manual.

Complete the inference report for the experiment in your Laboratory Manual.

Read another Experiment Card in the same problem area.

After you have completed all the experiments in the problem area . . .

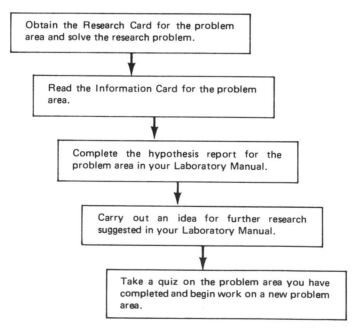

Obtain the Research Card for the problem area and solve the research problem.

Read the Information Card for the problem area.

Complete the hypothesis report for the problem area in your Laboratory Manual.

Carry out an idea for further research suggested in your Laboratory Manual.

Take a quiz on the problem area you have completed and begin work on a new problem area.

From Keeline, *Observing the Invisible World,* Litton Educational Publishing, Inc.

TABLE 12-2   OBSERVING THE INVISIBLE WORLD

PROBLEM AREA "A"—"How Do Micro-organisms React to Changes in Their Environment?"

Experiments:

A-1   How Do Brine Shrimp Respond to Different Amounts of Light?
A-2   How Do Brine Shrimp Respond to Gravity?
A-3   How Do Brine Shrimp Respond to Changes in Temperature?
A-4   What Effect Does Ultraviolet Light Have on Yeast Cells?

PROBLEM AREA "B"—"How Do Micro-organisms Affect Their Environment?"

Experiments:

B-1   What Changes Occur in Milk Exposed to Air at Room Temperature?
B-2   How Do Micro-organisms Affect Red Cabbage Juice?
B-3   How Does Yeast Affect a Sugar Solution?
B-4   What Changes Do Micro-organisms Produce in Fruit Juices?

PROBLEM AREA "C"—"Where Are Micro-organisms Found?"

Experiments:

C-1   Where Are Micro-organisms Found in Your Environment?
C-2   What Are Some Micro-organisms on Your Fingers?
C-3   What Are Some Micro-organisms Living in Pond Water?
C-4   What Are Some Micro-organisms Living in Soil?

PROBLEM AREA "D"—"How Do Micro-organisms Grow and Reproduce?"

Experiments:

D-1   How Do Yeast Cells Grow and Reproduce?
D-2   What Do Yeast Cells Need to Grow and Reproduce?
D-3   What Is the Structure of Bread Mold?
D-4   What Effect Does Light Have on Growth of Bread Mold?

PROBLEM AREA "E"—"How Do Environmental Conditions Affect the Growth of Micro-organisms?"

Experiments:

E-1   How Does Temperature Affect the Growth of Micro-organisms?
E-2   How Do Antiseptics Affect the Growth of Micro-organisms?
E-3   How Do Salt and Sugar Solutions Affect the Growth of Micro-organisms?
E-4   How Do Antibiotics Affect the Growth of Micro-organisms?

Later in the Manual there is a "Hypothesis Report" in which the students complete the following two statements:

Based on my observations and inferences for each of the experiments in this problem area, as well as other information available to me, I can make the following hypothesis:

The most important observations that support my hypothesis are:

The Laboratory Manual concludes with a self-quiz to help the student ascertain his accomplishments in the unit.

The focus of the EYE program is keeping the student involved in order to maintain interest, develop basic processes of scientific investigation, and develop scientific knowledge and attitudes. Very little reading material is provided. Student choice, insofar as allowed by the teacher, is available for the student. The ability to make choices and to learn from those choices in a basic program constituent. The evaluation activities provided with the program can then be utilized to assess the student's learning in this area. In addition the teacher has the opportunity to observe students' behaviors to such an extent that further assessment along this line may be unnecessary.

Selecting a Science Program

As stated earlier in this chapter, the ideal program for elementary school science is one which is designed locally to meet the needs of your students. Typically, a school's science program consists of one, or possibly two, commercial programs. Teachers need not use all of the program as intended by the developers. Modifications in the original program will occur primarily because of differences in teacher interests, equipment availability, and the existence of local science-related interests of the community. All of these factors make it difficult to derive a set of criteria for selecting the right program for a school.

Actually, the most crucial factor in the development of a sound elementary school science program is likely to be the involvement of all science teachers, or a representative committee, in the organization and maintenance of the program. For example, unless the original scope and sequence of the commercial program is followed without variation, some local efforts will probably need to be made to coordinate the scope and sequence. Some teachers may have chosen to avoid science entirely and this will need to be dealt with for the benefit of the students.

The factors influencing the elementary school science program selection listed below are written in general terms. Each local school, in a continuous, year-to-year effort, will need to examine each characteristic for its relevancy to the local school science program.

Organization of the Program

K–12 SCOPE/SEQUENCE

The selection of an elementary school science program should include consideration of the scope and sequence of the entire science program of the school system. This is not to say that the only goal of the elementary school science program is preparation for taking junior high school science, or for junior high school science to prepare for high school science. However, there should be coordination of the content to be studied and the concepts being developed. To teach students a process skill in one grade level without using it in subsequent grade levels is not the most efficient use of instructional time.

CORRELATION WITH OTHER AREAS

In a self-contained classroom, the teacher has the convenience of being knowledgeable of the other areas of study besides science. In this way science can be coordinated with mathematics, social studies, health, and others. This same coordination should exist throughout the school system. A science program with an investigative nature is going to make use of mathematics and this use should be considered when selecting and modifying science programs. The study of the natural world in science finds many applications to the study of history and other social sciences.

FLEXIBILITY

As has been noted in the review of some of the contemporary programs, there is a wide range of flexibility built into them. This is especially so in the "packaged" programs. A school system needs to decide the degree of flexibility desirable in the local science program. Some feel a structured program is necessary because of the need to have a single science program throughout the district. Others may desire the same type of program but for different reasons. For example, teacher insecurity or background deficiency may be a limiting factor.

RELATIONSHIP TO EVERYDAY LIFE

Elementary school science programs of the past have often had a heavy emphasis on the technology of the world and its relationship to science. Contemporary programs do not usually emphasize technology. But they do concern themselves with science appropriate to everyday living. For example, most children will find the study of small animals very relevant. The experiences are taken from topics which students might encounter. The prospective science programs should be examined to see if the content included in the program and the manner in which it is arranged is consistent with the everyday needs of the children in this school.

INDIVIDUALIZING INSTRUCTION

Can this program be utilized in a manner that will allow the teacher to individualize instruction as appropriate? Much of the professional education literature today refers to the need for providing instruction in which the individual student can learn at a rate commensurate with his interest and/or ability. It may be said that any program could be "individualized" if sufficient modifications were to be made. It is usually not within the realm of practicality to think that most teachers will have the desire and time to make such modifications. The selection of a science program should carefully consider the role of individualizing instruction as a selection criterion.

Implementation of the Program

In reality, there seems to be an assumption that any certified teacher can effectively use any available instructional program. The generalization which seems more justified would seem to be that any certified teacher can be trained to effectively make use of most instructional programs. When the "new" elementary school science programs were becoming popular, many administrators purchased the programs for their faculty without providing training in their use. This same phenomenon may be observed in other subject areas and at other levels of education.

If indeed the teacher is the key to classroom instruction, and there is a growing amount of evidence that this is so, then it appears to be sound policy to spend the money, time, and effort on training faculty to use the program. In actuality, it may be more appropriate for a school system to train teachers to make better use of the existing program than to purchase a new program without providing training.

The training is not usually needed in the content area so much as in the methods of teaching the materials. Much of the content presented in the new programs is explained sufficiently in the teacher guides that a teacher can learn quickly the "right answers" to the questions. What is often more difficult is to learn how to teach the units so that students learn to find their own answers rather than having them provided by the teacher. Most contemporary programs require that the teacher learn the process skills to a greater depth than the content. New program adoptions must describe the needed teacher training features and how these experiences can be provided.

COINCIDENCE OF PURPOSE

Each contemporary science program differs slightly in terms of the purpose it is trying to fulfill in the elementary school science program. It is imperative that this purpose be clear to the teacher who will be teaching the program and the administration responsible for the program. The relative emphasis between concepts and processes is a prime example. A second is the role of "hands on" experiences to be provided to the student and the subsequent need for easy access to utilities and the allowance for messy rooms. It is generally agreed that we do not know all of the factors that constitute a "best" science program. Indeed, there may not be one best approach. But if the purpose of the school system are coincidental to the purposes of the program, then implementation is going to be more effective and the resulting instruction for students will be improved.

Other Influences on Program Selection

Several special interest groups are attempting to influence the elementary school curriculum. Among these are those concerned with metric education, drug education, sex education, environmental or outdoor education, consumer education, and career education. These areas are not unique to science, but involve other areas of the curriculum, such as social science and mathematics. Although these subjects may be treated in separate courses, very often the present course offerings are expected to integrate these topics into the curriculum. The relative emphasis of these topics to the local school should be examined prior to selection of a science program.

METRIC EDUCATION

The history of concern for metric system use in the United States dates back to 1866 when the Congress permitted the use of the metric system in the U.S., or 1790 when the Congress first discussed the new system then adopted by the French Academy (Suydam, 1975). But in recent years the effort has been intensified to the point that metric education is now mandated. It seems that science curriculum is one place where the student can develop the skills of measuring using the new units. Although many science programs do not emphasize the use of the system, most programs provide the means by which use of the system of metric units can be included.

ENVIRONMENTAL AND OUTDOOR EDUCATION

These terms are not synonymous. They are used together here because of the proximity of their actual classroom implementation. Common concerns of pollution, conservation practices, and overpopulation allow these concerns to overlap in the classroom. Both overlapping areas of study seek to remove man's ignorance of the problems, sensitize him to his environment, and orient him toward positive action (Sale and Lee, 1972). The specific way in which each community attacks this concern will vary depending on local factors. After a study of these factors, the science program most suited for proper emphasis of these factors should be sought. In most cases, teachers should expect that the basic program will need to be supplemented with locally available materials and experiences.

HEALTH EDUCATION

Under the broad title of health education, one can categorize several contemporary concerns of man including drug and sex education. Although the intensity of interest rises and falls, the basic issues have been there for some time. How much should the elementary school do in these controversial areas. Many schools choose to do nothing. Here, as in the other areas, the local school is in the position to determine how far they will go in implementing these factors into the curriculum. If the issues are going to be dealt with, then a local committee of the teachers, administrators, and community members should carefully define the scope and sequence of the concepts to be covered. Many of the topics can be dealt with as a part of the science curriculum. These decisions will affect the choice of a curriculum.

CAREER EDUCATION

As explained in more detail in Chapter 2, career education is said to begin in the elementary school years with an awareness program to show students the great diversity of occupations in the field of science. Career education continues in the junior high school years with career exploration, which involves a more intense investigation of the occupations of most interest to the student. Training for a career can begin in the high school years. Most contemporary science programs do very little with this aspect of education. The school seeking to do something with career education will need to adopt a program which can be modified to fit the local goals.

CONSUMER EDUCATION

One way of motivating students to study science is to relate it to everyday events. By using scientific information and process skills to study the relative merits of products available for sale, the student may be able to achieve this level of motivation. Students can conduct experiments to determine the comparative characteristics of two or more brands of some product they use, such as pencils, paper, or food. The alert teacher can use these situations as an indication of the attitude students have toward use of the process skill of science to everyday situations.

Adoption and Adaptation

The purpose of this chapter was to provide a fund of information to assist you in beginning your study of science programs. It is not assumed that a reading of this chapter will have made you sufficiently aware of the programs so that you could defend your choice of a program. It is hoped you will have access to the program materials themselves and will be able to explore select programs to a greater degree before you make a decision.

There are very few schools where the authors of a science program would find it being used just as they had intended it to be used. That is, it is unlikely that a school, with the usual variety of teachers and students, could *adopt* someone else's program. It is more likely that the school system and each individual teacher will adapt a program to suit local demands. This does not mean that the commercial program should not be used, at least in part. The purchase of the basic program provides the teachers with a solid place from which to begin.

Adapting packaged programs is to be expected. Teachers add content with which they are more familiar. They include information and experiences centered around local industry. They interrupt the regular routine to accommodate students' interests. Although this kind of program modification is to be expected, it may need to be coordinated. Someone in the building may need to be designated as the coordinator of the program and have the responsibility of keeping track of science education in that building.

References

American Association for the Advancement of Science, Commission on Science Education, *An Evaluation Model and Its Application.* Washington, D.C.; The Association, 1968.

American Association for the Advancement of Science, Commission on Science Education, *Commentary for Teachers.* Washington, D.C.; The Association, 1970.

Blough, Glenn O., *et al.* "Teaching and Evaluating Science in the Elementary School," *Rethinking Science Education,* Ch. 8. Washington, D.C.: NSSE, 1960.

Gagne, Robert M., *The Conditions of Learning.* New York: Holt, Rinehart, and Winston, 1970.

Hurd, Paul D., *New Curriculum Perspectives for Junior High School Science.* Belmont, Calif.: Wadsworth, 1970.

Lee, Eugene C., *New Developments in Science Teaching,* Belmont, Calif.: Wadsworth, 1967.

National Science Teachers Association, *Keys to Careers in Science and Technology.* Washington, D.C.: The Association, 1970.

Sale, Larry L., and Ernest W. Lee, *Environmental Education in the Elementary School.* New York: Holt, Rinehart and Winston, 1972.

Shamos, Morris, "The Role of Major Conceptual Schemes in Science Education," *The Science Teacher,* 1966, pp. 27–30.

Science Curriculum Improvement Study, *Interactions and Systems.* Berkeley: University of California, 1974.

Science Curriculum Improvement Study, *Omnibus.* Berkeley: University of California, 1973.

Science Curriculum Improvement Study, *SCIS Teachers Handbook.* Berkeley: University of California, 1974.

Suydam, Marilyn, "Historical Steps Toward Metrication," *A Metric Handbook for Teachers,* pp. 26–27. National Council of Teachers of Mathematics.

Index